Meaning and Context

Meaning and Context

Quentin Skinner and
his Critics

EDITED AND INTRODUCED BY

James Tully

Princeton University Press
Princeton, New Jersey

Published by Princeton University Press, 41 William Street,
Princeton, New Jersey 08540

Library of Congress Cataloging-in-Publication Data
Meaning and context.

   Bibliography: p.
   Includes index.
   1. Skinner, Quentin—Contributions in political
science.   I. Tully, James, 1946–
JC257.S54M43   1989   320.5   88–23816
ISBN 0–691–07796–7
ISBN 0–691–02301–8 (pbk.)

Printed in Great Britain

Words are deeds

Ludwig Wittgenstein
Culture and Value

Contents

Acknowledgements

The authors and the editor are grateful to the following publishers for permission to reprint the articles presented as chapters in this collection.

1 James Tully, 'The pen is a mighty sword: Quentin Skinner's analysis of politics', revised, *British Journal of Political Science*, 13 (winter, 1983), pp. 489–509
2 Quentin Skinner, 'Meaning and understanding in the history of ideas', *History and Theory*, 8 (1969), pp. 3–53
3 Quentin Skinner, 'Motives, intentions and the interpretation of texts', in *On Literary Intention*, ed. D. Newton de Molina (Edinburgh, Edinburgh University Press, 1976), pp. 210–21
4 Quentin Skinner, '"Social meaning" and the explanation of social action', in *The Philosophy of History*, ed. P. Gardiner (Oxford, Oxford University Press), pp. 106–27
5 Quentin Skinner, 'Some problems in the analysis of political thought and action', *Political Theory*, 23 (1974), pp. 277–303
6 Quentin Skinner, 'Language and social change', revised, in *The State of the Language*, ed. L. Michaels and C. Ricks (Berkeley, University of California Press, 1980), pp. 562–78
7 Martin Hollis, 'Say it with flowers', *Supplementary Proceedings of the Aristotelian Society*, 52 (1978), pp. 43–57
8 Keith Graham, 'How do illocutionary descriptions explain?', *Ratio*, 22 (2) (1981), pp. 124–35
9 Joseph V. Femia, 'An historicist critique of "revisionist" methods for studying the history of ideas', *History and Theory*, 20 (1981), pp. 112–34, copyright © 1981 Wesleyan University
10 Kenneth Minogue, 'Method in intellectual history: Quentin Skinner's *Foundations*', *Philosophy*, 56 (1981), pp. 533–52

11 Nathan Tarcov, 'Quentin Skinner's method and Machiavelli's *Prince*', abridged, *Ethics*, 92 (4) (July, 1982), pp. 692–710

NOTE ON ABBREVIATIONS

All references to and quotations from the articles by Quentin Skinner which are included in the volume, and the cross-references made by Quentin Skinner in his reply to his critics (part IV of this book) to other chapters in this collection, are followed by the chapter number and page number in brackets. For example, a reference to 'Language and social change' is followed by (6: 119), the page number referring to the appropriate page number in this present volume. This enables the reader to move back and forth from criticism to original source and to Skinner's concluding remarks, and so to treat the text as a dialogue.

All the information needed about articles by Quentin Skinner which are not reproduced in the volume will be found in the note section to each chapter at the end of this book, and full details of all his principal publications can be found in the bibliography.

List of contributors

Joseph Femia is a Senior Lecturer in the Department of Political Theory and Institutions of the University of Liverpool. He is the author of *Gramsci's Political Thought* (Oxford, Clarendon Press, 1981), and is working on a book entitled *Democracy and Marxism*, to be published by Oxford University Press.

Keith Graham is Lecturer in Philosophy at the University of Bristol. He is author of *The Battle of Democracy* (Sussex and New York, Wheatsheaf, 1986), and is currently working on a book on Marx.

Martin Hollis is Professor of Philosophy, University of East Anglia. He is the author of *Models of Man* (Cambridge, Cambridge University Press, 1977), and *The Cunning of Reason* (Cambridge, Cambridge University Press, 1987).

John Keane is Professor of Politics and a Fellow at the Centre for Communication and Information Studies at the Polytechnic of Central London. In 1987 he was a Fellow at the Zentrum für interdisziplinare Forschung, Universität Bielefeld, the Federal Republic of Germany. His most recent books are *Democracy and Civil Society* and *Civil Society and the State: New European Perspectives* (both London, Verso 1988). He is currently working on the contemporary relevance of the early modern ideal of the liberty of the press.

Kenneth Minogue is Professor of Political Science at the London School of Economics and Political Science. His most recent book is *Alien Powers: The Pure Theory of Ideology* (London and New York, St. Martin's Press, 1984).

Quentin Skinner is Professor of Political Science at the University of Cambridge.

Nathan Tarcov is Associate Professor of Political Science and in the College at the University of Chicago. He is author of *Locke's Education for Liberty* (Chicago, University of Chicago Press, 1985), and is working on a book on revolutionary principles and American foreign policy.

Charles Taylor is Professor of Political Science and Philosophy at McGill University. His most recent book is a two-volume collection of his philosophical papers, *Human Agency and Language* and *Philosophy and the Human Sciences* (Cambridge, Cambridge University Press, 1985).

James Tully is Associate Professor of Political Science and Philosophy at McGill University. His most recent publication is 'Governing Conduct', in *Conscience and Casuistry in Early Modern Europe* (Cambridge, Cambridge University Press, 1988), ed. E. Leites.

PART I

Introduction

Overview

In 1978, at the age of 37, Quentin Skinner was elected to the position of Professor of Political Science at the University of Cambridge. The appointment to this prestigious chair served to give recognition to his extensive scholarly contribution to two broad and inter-related fields of study: the methodology of history, social science and literary criticism, and the application of his original methods to both contemporary political philosophy and the history of political thought and action. His work in these areas is supported by a number of studies in the philosophy of meaning. *The Foundations of Modern Political Thought*, published in 1978, is his two-volume survey of political thought during the Renaissance and Reformation. Since 1978 he has continued to make contributions in all these areas, including writing a book on Machiavelli in the Oxford Past Masters series and co-editing and contributing to a collection of articles on the relation of philosophy to its history, *Philosophy in History* (1984). This collection inaugurated a continuing series of monographs in intellectual history under his editorship, entitled *Ideas in Context*. Many other publications have followed. The range and depth of his scholarship can be seen by consulting the bibliography of principal publications at the end of this book.

The thought of Quentin Skinner has been received with high praise and sharp criticism by a large number of scholars in numerous disciplines. The critical responses to his work generally are of a very high quality and, given the range and importance of Skinner's writings, they address many of the leading issues in philosophy of social science, political philosophy and the history of political theory. Consequently, it was thought to be worthwhile, for both scholars and students, to try to bring together a representative sample of Skinner's articles, a collection of the most critical, penetrating and wide-ranging responses to his work, and a reply by Skinner in which he would respond to his critics, perhaps modify his earlier views and sketch out the lines of his present research. *Meaning and Context* is the result.

The most difficult task was selecting the critical articles. There are so many good ones it was difficult to trim the collection down to a reasonable size. I have tried to pick critiques that present the sharpest challenges to Skinner's projects and collectively represent a broad range of political and philosophical perspectives. Unlike most collections of essays in the human sciences, this reader is not the collective enterprise of one school. Rather, it is a clash, a contest, a set of 'essays' or 'trials' of the major schools and, it seems to me, so much the better for it. It forces Skinner to reflect very hard on his own thought in his concluding article, and, I hope, it helps the reader to think for herself or himself about these important issues.

The first article, 'The pen is a mighty sword', is an introductory survey of Skinner's approach and an attempt to draw three substantive themes about the nature of modern political thought from his major work, *The Foundations of Modern Political Thought*. Five articles on method by Skinner follow in the second section. 'Meaning and understanding in the history of ideas' is his first systematic discussion of the shortcomings of alternative approaches to interpretation and understanding. It is, first, one of the most searching and destructive criticisms of the discipline of the history of ideas in recent times. Second, Skinner begins to advance his own approach, that to understand a text it is necessary to understand it as a complex of linguistic actions and thus to recover what the author was doing in writing it – the text's 'point' or 'force' – by placing it in its convention-governed linguistic context. Third, he goes on to argue that the point of this type of study is self-knowledge. The four following articles refine, expand and modify this initial declaration. These articles, in turn, are supported by and draw upon a number of more specialized articles listed in the bibliography. To appreciate fully the range, utility and value of Skinner's approach, one should, in addition, turn to its application in *The Foundations of Modern Political Thought*.

I turn now to a very brief and incomplete description of some of the issues raised in the critical articles. Each article is of course more complex than this outline suggests. Our first critic, Martin Hollis, questions whether Skinner can avoid explanation of motives or if his approach does not presuppose a certain motivation on the part of the author. Furthermore, he asks if Skinner does not have to assess more explicitly the rationality of the beliefs he studies and to reflect on his own beliefs and assumptions (a question raised by Charles Taylor as well). In his closely argued article, 'How do illocutionary descriptions explain?', Keith Graham questions whether illocutionary force is equivalent to an intention in acting and, secondly, if the redescription of an act in terms of its illocutionary force constitutes in itself, as Skinner claims, a form of social explanation. Concentrating primarily, but not exclusively, on Skinner's article 'Meaning and understanding', Joseph Femia argues that explanation in terms of authors' intentions, far from being an historical form of explanation, is an impediment to learning anything of value for us from the past and is incompatible with the tradition of historicism, especially as exemplified in the works of Gramsci. And, he goes on to argue, the approaches which Skinner criticizes are those approaches we ought to employ in order to use the past to think about politics in the present.

Kenneth Minogue turns to *The Foundations of Modern Political Thought* to ascertain how successful Skinner's methodology is in practice. He questions whether it has been very useful and argues that historians of political thought are better off without the constraints of speech-act theory. Indeed, he finds Skinner's method 'pernicious'. His major point is to uphold a distinction, which Skinner's work calls into question, between the tasks of political philosophers and historians of political thought. This is based on a distinction between the independent and universal dimensions of ideas, which political philosophers analyse and evaluate, and the historical and contextual dimensions of ideas, which historians study. Thus, complementary to Femia but from a different perspective, he argues that Skinner's method forecloses a legitimate manner of studying the classics of political philosophy. The following article by Nathan Tarcov continues the assessment of Skinner's method in the light of *The Foundations of Modern Political Thought*. He argues that the shortcomings of Skinner's approach can be seen most clearly by a close examination of the ways in which Skinner allegedly misinterprets Machiavelli in the central chapters of volume one of *The Foundations of Modern Political Thought*.

Three main criticisms are addressed to Skinner by John Keane in the penultimate article. The first is that Skinner mistakenly *identifies* understanding a text with understanding an author's intentions in writing it, thus ignoring the 'productivity' of the language in which the text is written. The second criticism is that the constitutive idea of Skinner's approach, that of a non-prescriptive and descriptive 'survey' (which, it should be noted, he shares with Wittgenstein and Foucault), is said to be based upon the old positivist or reproductive fallacy of the unvarnished recovery of meaning. Keane argues that the idea of a survey must be replaced by the idea, originally developed in Biblical hermeneutics, of a dialogue of negotiation and fusion of horizons between interpreter and author. Third, Keane argues that Skinner's method is uncritical and so tends to reinforce relations of power and interest. Keane's remedy for this, adapting the work of Jean-François Lyotard, is a plurality of perspectival narratives of the past. The article written by Charles Taylor for this volume, 'The hermeneutics of conflict', discusses Skinner's work by way of the first published version of my introductory article 'The pen is a mighty sword'. (The first chapter in this volume is a revised edition of this article, rewritten in the light of Taylor's helpful comments.) His major question is whether Skinner can avoid taking a stand on, and becoming *engaged* with, the truth and validity of the political theories he studies; or, in a more questioning manner, whether Skinner means his survey to be disengaged in this sense. Here again, and in Chapter 1, the merits of the survey approach of Skinner, Wittgenstein and Foucault, are weighed against the dialogue approach of Gadamer and Taylor. In the second part of his article, Taylor questions one thesis I draw from *The Foundations of Modern Political Thought*: that political conflict and war are major factors in explaining why political ideologies gain or retain dominance in the early modern period.

The final section comprises Skinner's reply to this formidable contestation of his approach and its application. As he answers the questions raised by his critics, clarifies misunderstandings, explains, defends and makes modifications, he also carefully situates his replies in two contexts: the discussion in this book and the broader discussion throughout the human sciences on the explanation and interpretation of meaning and context. He shows us where he follows the customs and conventions of these complex discussions and where he departs from convention and presents original arguments. He thereby enables us to understand this late twentieth-century debate and what he is doing in writing within it and contributing to it. And, in replying in precisely this reflexive manner – using his approach to explain the meaning and context of his approach – he both illustrates and vindicates his way of studying the meaning and context of thought and action.

I would like to thank all the contributors for their generous assistance. Charles Taylor deserves a special note of thanks, as do Tony Giddens at Polity Press and Cathy Duggan at McGill. Above all, my gratitude and admiration go to Quentin Skinner, whose brilliant work has been an inspiration and model of scholarship for me, and whose kind support has made this volume possible. I would like to thank the Humanities Grant Committee of McGill University for their financial support.

1

The pen is a mighty sword: Quentin Skinner's analysis of politics

James Tully

My aim in this introduction is to review Skinner's methodological writings and his study of early modern European politics, and to show the inter-relation between the two. In the first section, accordingly, I lay out and explain the five major components of his approach, using illustrations from his historical work. In the second section I assess his major historical work in the light of the first section, and this in order to lay out three original theses on the foundations of modern political thought which I believe follow from his work. By giving these theses on modern political thought the place of prominence in this chapter I hope to show that Skinner is not solely concerned with history and method, but also with using both to throw light on the present.

Almost since its inception, his work has revolved around a tripartite axis: interpretation of historical texts; surveyance of ideological formation and change; and analysis of the relation of ideology to the political action it represents.[1] His initial interest in methodology developed out of a dissatisfaction with the dominant liberal and Marxist forms of analysis for addressing these issues, especially with reference to early modern politics. In a marvellously iconoclastic article in 1969 he argued that the available textualist and contextualist procedures were wholly inadequate and that a new contextual and historically more sensitive practice was required (2). From 1969 to the present he has fashioned and assembled a collection of interpretive and analytical tools to meet this requirement; a collection applicable across a broad range of the social sciences and humanities.

The five steps that comprise his procedure can best be seen as ways of answering the following five questions: (a) What is or was an author

doing in writing a text in relation to other available texts which make up
the ideological context? (b) What is or was an author doing in writing a
text in relation to available and problematic political action which makes
up the practical context? (c) How are ideologies to be identified and
their formation, criticism and change surveyed and explained? (d) What
is the relation between political ideology and political action which best
explains the diffusion of certain ideologies and what effect does this have
on political behaviour? (e) What forms of political thought and action
are involved in disseminating and conventionalizing ideological change?

SKINNER'S APPROACH

The first step

Starting within the historical or *Verstehen* school, best represented by
Collingwood in England in the first half of this century, Skinner has been
able to draw on the renewed philosophical interest in interpretation in the
1960s and 1970s to overcome the inadequacies he sees in orthodox
procedures for studying the history of politics. He has also been able to
benefit from the mutual support of two scholars working in the same
general intellectual milieu; the historian John Pocock and the political
theorist, John Dunn. The horizon and general orientation of his work is
furnished by the following approach put forward by Wittgenstein in the
Philosophical Investigations and *On Certainty*. Language is an intersubjectively shared multiplicity of tools for various purposes, yet one in which
only some elements are open to subjective criticism, modification, and
change at any time. This is so because language is woven so deeply into
human action that the whole – language and ways of acting – itself provides
the grounds in the light of which criticism and change take place. However,
it was the specific speech act theory developed by Austin, Searle and Grice
from within the general framework of Wittgenstein's linguistic pragmatics
that initially provided Skinner with conceptual resources he could turn to
his own purposes.[2]

Austin, Searle and Grice argued that if speaking and writing are viewed
pragmatically, as linguistic activities performed by speakers and writers,
then they can be seen to comprise at least two kinds of action. First, the
author is saying or writing something: putting forward words, sentences,
arguments, theories and so on with a certain 'locutionary' or 'propositional'
meaning (with, that is, sense and reference). Second, and of more importance
for Skinner, the author will be *doing something in* speaking or writing the
words, sentences, arguments and so on: he or she will be doing so with a
point or an intended force. Austin named this the 'illocutionary force' of the
linguistic action, co-ordinate with the locutionary meaning, and suggested

that a necessary condition of understanding a speaker or writer is to 'secure uptake' of the illocutionary force of his or her utterance. This theory, which has been pressed into service by Habermas in his quest for a universal pragmatics, was adapted earlier by Skinner, in the light of his historical research, to provide the basis for the first two steps in his project (a project which is an oblique challenge to Habermas' enterprise, as we see in the second section, 'An assessment', below).[3] Thus, to understand fully the 'historical meaning' of a text, or parts of it, written in the past and considered as linguistic action performed by its author, it is not sufficient to understand its locutionary meaning. It is also necessary to understand what the author was doing in writing it; the 'point' or 'force' of the author's argument (4:83).

Let me present one of Skinner's examples and then use it to illuminate the first two steps. In chapter 16 of *The Prince* Machiavelli advises that 'Princes must learn when not to be virtuous' (2:61–3; 4:86).[4] One part of recovering the historical meaning of his piece of advice is to understand its locutionary meaning: the sense and reference of the terms included. This can be a demanding exercise in itself; determining precisely what sense of 'virtuous' is under attack here and what range of virtues Machiavelli is recommending that the prince lay aside.[5] Second, and more importantly, what is Machiavelli's point in advancing this advice; not only what is written but why was it written?

The route to the first answer to this question, step one, is to situate the text in its linguistic or ideological context: the collection of texts written or used in the same period, addressed to the same or similar issues and sharing a number of conventions. An ideology is a language of politics defined by its conventions and employed by a number of writers. Thus, scholasticism, humanism, Lutherism and Calvinism are ideologies and both scholasticism and humanism comprise the general ideological context of the Italian city-states during the Renaissance. In the case of Machiavelli's *Prince* the specific ideological context is comprised of all the literature giving 'advice to princes' and the conventions which govern this writing constitute the relevant segment of the humanist ideology. The term that does all the work here is 'convention' and Skinner uses it heuristically to refer to relevant linguistic commonplaces uniting a number of texts: shared vocabulary, principles, assumptions, criteria for testing knowledge-claims, problems, conceptual distinctions and so on.[6] The justification for placing the text in its conventional context is that linguistic action, like other forms of social action, is conventional and thus its meaning can be understoood only by attending to the '*conventions* surrounding the performance of the given type of social action in the given social situation' (4:94).

In the example of Machiavelli one of the conventions of the 'advice to princes' literature is always to advise the prince to act virtuously. By reading Machiavelli's advice in the light of this convention we can understand that what he is doing in advancing it is 'to challenge and repudiate an accepted moral commonplace' (4:86). In general terms, therefore, this technique enables the historian or social scientist to understand 'how far' authors 'were accepting and endorsing, or questioning and repudiating, or perhaps even polemically ignoring, the prevailing assumptions and conventions of political debate'.[7] Skinner calls this activity the manipulation of the conventions of the available ideology.

He has made a number of claims about this form of explanation, the first of which is, as we have seen, that it is an element of the historical meaning of the text: what the author 'meant' by writing it. This in turn, following Searle and Grice, is equivalent to one of the authors' intentions in writing the text (4:84). Second, this form of explanation is non-causal because it is a redescription of characterization of the linguistic action in the terms of its ideological point, not in the terms of an independently specifiable condition. The *explicans* is an intention in performing the linguistic action, not a preceding intention to perform it (4:87). Third, this step enables the student to ascertain precisely the originality – in the sense of non-conventionality – of the text under study (5:106). It is also obvious that this kind of understanding of a text is unavailable to those who practise a solely textualist approach or to contextualists who ignore the linguistic context.

I would like to introduce a distinction between the ideological point or points of a text relative to the available conventions and the author's ideological point or points in writing it. The former is not necessarily the same as the latter and a range of historical evidence is usually required to close the gap. Skinner is explicitly aware of this distinction although he sometimes writes as if they were equivalent (2:52–3; 5:106–7).

The second step

The second question is, to rephrase it in the terms of the first step, what is an author doing in manipulating the available ideological conventions? That is, in our example, what was Machiavelli's point in challenging and repudiating a long-standing piece of political advice? The first question asks about the character of text as an ideological manoeuvre; the second question asks about the character of the ideological manoeuvre as a political manoeuvre. The path to the second step is, accordingly, to place the text in its practical context: that is the problematic political activity or 'relevant characteristics' of the society the author addresses and to which the text is a response. Skinner believes that in advancing answers to questions of ideological debate the political theorist is responding to the political problems of the age. As he refreshingly puts it: 'I take it that political life itself sets the main problems for the political theorist, causing a certain range of issues to appear problematic, and a corresponding range of questions to become the leading subjects of debate.'[8] Political theory, then, is, as Aristotle and Marx would say, a part of politics, and the questions it treats are the effects of political action.

To return to our example, the practical context is the collapse of the Florentine Republic in 1512, the disunity of the Northern Italian city-states, the presence of relatively large French and Spanish armies, yet, fortuitously, a strong Medici prince in Florence and an equally strong Medici pope in Rome. Thus, according to Machiavelli, there was the possibility of the Medici family uniting Northern Italy, throwing out the French and Spanish barbarians and, perhaps, laying the foundations for a renaissance of the Roman Republic. However, the kind of activity Machiavelli believed necessary for success – parsimonious violence, lying and deceit – was 'vicious' and so unjustifiable and illegitimate in the face of the widely held belief that a prince ought always to act virtuously. Therefore, if Machiavelli was to convince the prince and the humanist elite that this activity was not only necessary but justifiable, he had to redescribe it in morally neutral or even commendatory terms. The obstacle to this was the convention condemning all vicious princely activity and so it was necessary for him to challenge and repudiate it to make his political point, which was to excuse and encourage a range of vicious activity on the part of the prince. What he was doing politically in manipulating the ideological conventions was attempting to justify, and so render legitimate, a range of untoward political activity.[9]

This rough sketch is sufficient to illustrate the methodological point. Since a political ideology represents political action (institutions, practices, etc.), to change some of the conventions of the ideology is to change the way in which some of that political action is represented. The manipulated conventions redescribe and so recharacterize the political action. The second step, then, is to compare how the relevant political action is rendered by the conventions of the ideology with how it is redescribed by the manipulation of these conventions in the given text. This new characterization will be the key to the political point of the text.

Let me present one other example to clarify the first and second steps. First, Bartolus, the early fourteenth-century legal theorist, is well known in legal and political history for questioning the major convention of the glossatorial school of Roman law, that the facts must always be adjusted to conform to the law, because the law, Roman law, is an unchanging standard. In the 1320s Bartolus reversed this and argued that when law and facts conflict, the law must be altered to accommodate the new facts – thus laying the methodological foundation for post-glossatorial legal study. Second, the facts in question turn out to be the *de facto* independence of the Northern Italian communes from the Holy Roman Empire and the law in question is the Roman law in virtue of which the present Emperor can be said to exercise *imperium* over Northern Italy. Thus, in reversing the glossatorial convention, Bartolus is delegitimating imperial claims and legitimating the communes' wars for *de jure* independence from the emperor, just as his opponents' arguments serve to legitimate imperial claims. Bartolus, as Skinner concludes, 'clearly set out with the intention of reinterpreting the Roman civil code in such a way as to supply the Lombard and Tuscan communes with a legal ... defence of their liberty against the Empire'.[10] Just as it would be impossible to understand what Bartolus was doing ideologically unless his texts were placed in the linguistic context of the legal writing of the thirteenth and early fourteenth centuries, so it would be impossible to understand what he was doing politically without placing this ideological move in the practical context of the communes' anti-imperial wars of independence.

With respect to the second step the same distinction as in the first step reappears. It does not necessarily follow from a text serving to make a political point in its practical context that this was what the author was doing in writing it. Again the inference would have to be supported with a range of historical evidence of various kinds. For example, even though *The Prince* serves to legitimate a vicious prince, it does not necessarily follow that this was Machiavelli's political point in writing it. Therefore I want to distinguish between the political point a text serves in its political context and the author's political point in writing it. Skinner has always kept these separate.

The third step

Once the concept of an ideology comprised of conventions was introduced as a tool for understanding the point of a constituent text, Skinner then turned his attention to the study of ideologies themselves. Minor texts of a period are carefully dusted off and surveyed to identify the constitutive and regulative conventions of the reigning ideologies and their inter-relations before they are employed as benchmarks to judge the conventional and unconventional aspects, and so the ideological moves, of the major texts. Thus, viewing the first and second steps from the perspective of the intersubjective ideology it is possible to demarcate the precise point in history ideological change (or reinforcement) is attempted, and perhaps achieved, and why, politically, the change was essayed.

The Foundations of Modern Political Thought is not only a map of the great political ideologies of early modern Europe, it is also a guide to the location and the ideological and political explanation of the incremental manipulations and grand transformations of them. This third step is the exact opposite practice of those who, following Hegel, take the classics to be the expression of the consciousness or assumptions of an age. What Skinner's surveying continually demonstrates is that the great texts are almost invariably the worst guide to conventional wisdom: they are often classics because they challenge the commonplaces of the period. In any case it is possible to discover which is true only by engaging in this kind of patient weighing of minor and often forgotten linguistic facts surrounding the classics.

The fourth step

Just as the second step is designed to illuminate one relation between political thought and action in the case of an individual text, so the fourth step is set up to do this in the case of an ideology. The ground here is the claim that any political vocabulary will contain a number of terms that are intersubjectively normative: words that not only describe, but, in describing, also evaluate. This evaluative dimension is called the word's speech-act potential and may be positive or negative, serving to commend or condemn, approve or disapprove (5, 6). They are 'intersubjective' in the sense that not only the criteria for their application (sense) and their reference, but also their appraisive dimension is a property of the words in their standard use; not something bestowed on them by the conventional, individual user. The class of such descriptive/evaluative terms in any society's vocabulary of self-characterization or ideologies is extremely large – as a moment's reflection on the role of 'democracy', 'objective', 'efficient', 'rational', 'tolerant', or 'dictatorship', 'subjective', 'inefficient', 'irrational', 'dogmatic', in our liberal-technocratic societies shows. It follows that political vocabulary in standard use describes and evaluates political action or, in Skinner's words, 'helps to constitute the character of . . . practices' (6:132). By 'constitute the character', he means describe and evaluate or 'characterize' practices. And this is just to conclude that one role of political ideologies is that of 'helping to legitimate social action', or that one relation between ideology and action is that of legitimation (6:132).

'It is', Skinner says, drawing out the Gramscian thesis, 'essentially by manipulating this set of terms that any society succeeds in establishing and altering its moral identity' (5:112). Using these terms in the conventional way serves to legitimate customary practices. Manipulating the conventions of a prevailing ideology, however, involves changing the conventions governing the sense, reference or speech-act potential of some of these normative terms. Viewed from his nominalist perspective, political theories can be analysed as justifications of the alteration or reinforcement of use-governing conventions. The alteration of the sense, reference or evaluative force of terms of an ideology will then serve to recharacterize, or re-evaluate, the political situation it represents; legitimizing a new range of activity or beliefs, delegitimizing or reinforcing the *status quo*, and so on. Political theories are about contemporaneous legitimation crises caused by shifting political relations, therefore, not by any choice or intention of the theorists but because the language in which they are written serves to characterize political relations. Due to this way in which ideological conventions attach to political relations, it is thus appropriate to analyse political theories as contributions to ideological controversies and as weapons of vindication or subversion in the strategies of local political forces whether or not the author intends or recognizes it.[11]

The second aspect of the fourth step is to calibrate the two kinds of effect an ideology, as a causal factor itself, has on the conduct it serves to legitimate: repressive and productive. First, the use-conventions governing the prevailing normative vocabulary cannot be manipulated indefinitely and so cannot be employed to legitimate any unusual practice. Thus, the extent to which ideological manipulation can be justified will set the limit to, and so be a causal constraint on, legitimate unorthodox campaigns (5:131 – 2).[12] As Skinner summarizes:

> Thus the problem facing an agent who wishes to legitimate what he is doing at the same time as gaining what he wants cannot simply be the instrumental problem of tailoring his normative language in order to fit his projects. It must in part be the problem of tailoring his projects in order to fit the available normative language.[13]

The constraint here has two aspects: ideological and political. An attempt to 'stretch' ideological conventions requires a justification and this standardly takes the form of grounding the change in the terms of what is already accepted and taken for granted. An ideologist changes one part of an ideology by holding another part fast; by appealing to and so reinforcing convention. For example, Bartolus' main justification for bringing the law in line with the facts was the conventional argument that long use or practice standardly constitutes a basis for a claim of legal right. Machiavelli justified his advice, that a prince need not always act virtuously, by arguing that this would enable a prince to achieve what everyone assumed a prince should achieve: i.e., act with virtue in laying down good arms and good laws and so achieve honour, praise and glory. Since Machiavelli is standardly taken to be one of the most radical of theorists, Skinner's analysis shows very graphically the conventional limits to ideological innovation.

The second constraint is the extent to which the ideology confines the political conduct it serves to legitimate. One of his many examples will clarify this. The German princes used Luther's doctrines that the church is an institution with no jurisdictional powers and no title to extensive worldly goods to legitimate their resistance to the power and wealth of the papacy. Even if they did not believe in their Lutheran principles but only in the utility of espousing them (the worst case for testing his hypothesis), they were none the less restrained to promulgate and to act in conformity with the Lutheran ideology in order to appear legitimate: 'Whatever their motives, the outcome was . . . the same: the spread of the Lutheran heresy proved to be the price of their breach with Rome'.[14] He captures both these aspects of repression in his pithy conclusion: 'Every revolutionary is to this extent obliged to march backward into battle' (5:112).

The second way in which the diffusion of an ideology acts as a material factor is not as a repressive instrument but, rather, as a productive one; causing changes in consciousness. Skinner's work here is still quite tentative, yet he has presented three hypotheses. A successful manipulation of the criteria for the application of a term – that is, a manipulation which becomes conventional – causes a change in 'social beliefs and theories'. The conventionalization of an alteration of reference causes a change in 'social perceptions and awareness'; and, finally, the successful modification of the evaluative force of a term brings about change in 'social values and attitudes' (6:123 – 30). He is working on a study of the extent to which capitalist behaviour was constrained and produced by the Protestant vocabulary that initially legitimated it. Thus, although the practical context is primary, as we have seen, the ideological context is not wholly superstructural. It, in turn, affects the base in at least these two ways, and this as a result, ironically, of its superstructural role of legitimation.

The fifth step

Finally, the fifth step is the capstone of his whole approach: the explanation of how ideological change comes to be woven into ways of acting; how it comes to be conventional. This is a historical question for which his approach and studies provide two types of guideline: ideological and practical. On the ideological side the spread of conceptual innovation is partly a function of how well it fits in with other available schools of thought. As he shows in the case of the spread of Lutheranism,[15] Luther could draw ideological recruits from Ockhamism, humanism and other intellectual and populist movements because his criticisms aligned closely with critical elements in these traditions. The second ideological factor is the ability of the ideologues to control the instruments of dissemination, such as university, church and, by the sixteenth century, printing press. These factors are sufficient to transmit ideological change, and to have some effect on, say, university students through the generations, but insufficient in themselves to bring about the corresponding change in practice. The primary agency of large-scale change in both thought and action is the unstable configuration of power relations that makes up the practical context, and which the ideological controversy represents. Ideological change becomes orthodox and authoritative in so far as the clash of political forces involves or succeeds in either defending or establishing practices that the ideological manipulation is utilized to characterize and legitimate. As Skinner's studies show, it is not necessarily or normally the immediate political struggle, but rather the circulation and adaptation of an ideology in the strategems of a wide range of similar struggles that accounts for ideological entrenchment and hegemony. Bartolus' innovation spread not only because it was utile in the communes' wars of independence but also because it served the same purpose for the French monarchy and German feudal lords. Lutheranism's success was dependent not only on the German princes and peasantry as a power base but also on its circulation in similar struggles throughout sixteenth-century Europe, and so it helped to forge the ideological and practical alliances which make up the Protestant Reformation. The explanation of change and persistence in European political thought and action is partly the force of argument but primarily the clash of political forces – the force of arms.

AN ASSESSMENT

The first thesis

I would like to turn now to an assessment in terms of three theses on modern political thought drawn from his work. To set the stage for this I want to underline the point that Skinner's work in the philosophy of social science or method has always been informed by his historical research and vice versa. Like the late Michel Foucault, in the comparable position at the Collège de France, Skinner has made major contributions in both social theory and history, and the achievement in each field is the result of research in both. Both authors' wilful disregard of the academic division of labour between philosophers, methodologists and theorists on one side and historians and social scientists on the other, accounts, I believe, for the originality of their work in both fields.

Accordingly, the three theses cut across these academic divisions and so each is both theoretical and historical. The first, which I will call the history of the present, to highlight its similarity to Foucault's genealogy, is the elucidation of Skinner's claim that his approach provides a 'genuine historical' account of the political thought and action to which it is applied.[16] The claim comprises two elements, the first of which is, as has been partially recognized in the secondary literature, the treatment of author, text, ideology and practice in the manner laid out in the section 'Skinner's approach', above. The second element is of paramount importance yet has passed almost without remark – perhaps without recognition – in many of the commentaries.[17]

The key to this second dimension is the title itself: the foundations of modern political thought. What Skinner is concerned to discover in Medieval, Renaissance and Reformation political thought and action is how the motley of conventions that later (from Grotius to Marx) became foundational for modern political thought were constructed in this earlier period. He is not *primarily* concerned with the foundations of the political thought he surveys, which are of course either classical or theological, but, rather, with a range of vocabulary that is erected on these foundations in this period and which becomes foundational for us (moderns) once the classical and theological foundations are chipped away in the seventeenth, eighteenth and nineteenth centuries.

His orientation to the present is stated in the preface. He says, 'I hope to indicate something of the process by which the modern concept of the State came to be formed' and adds that this ambition set the chronological boundaries of the study. It was in this period 'that the main elements of a recognizably modern concept of the State were gradually acquired', and this, he announces, is what 'I shall seek to show'.[18] He notes that the relations between the elements were not clearly delineated and, in the conclusion, remarks that no one had yet written a recognizably modern theory of the state, but the vocabulary that eventually became foundational was complete. The concept of the state – 'its nature, its power, its right to command obedience' – became the focus of political analysis by the seventeenth century. 'One of the main aims of this book', he repeats, 'has been to suggest how this development came about'.[19] 'Genuinely historical', thus, means both a survey of the political thought and action of the period and a survey of the 'gradual emergence of the vocabulary of modern political thought'.[20]

Skinner has always maintained that the history of political theory is and ought to be guided by the judgements and concerns of the practitioner. As he put it in 1974: 'the decisions we have to make about what to study must be our own decisions, arrived at by applying our own criteria for judging what is rational and significant' (5:100 – 1). The question I want to ask now is whether his seemingly anachronistic concern to provide a genealogy of the emergence of modern political vocabulary is compatible with his aim to provide an historically sensitive survey of the political thought and action out of which our modern political language emerged. To answer this I turn to what he takes the foundational vocabulary of modern political thought to be.

The foundations of modern political thought which have been the focus of Skinner's research so far are one dominant ideology and one subordinate counter-ideology.[21] (The subordinate ideology, to which I return below, is republican humanism, best represented by Machiavelli's *Discourses*.) The dominant ideology, which I will call the juridical to underline again the similarity with Foucault, contains the following elements.[22] The state is represented as an independent, territorial monopoly of political power. Political power is the right to kill in order to enforce universal rule of either objective right or subjective rights, such as rights, natural law, common good, tradition, majority will, modernization, or the constitution. Political power is exercised either directly by some sovereign body (monarch, community as a whole, elite) or indirectly by some representative body (parliament, estates, councils) to whom power is either delegated or alienated by a sovereign body (the people, either individually or collectively). Also, political power is exercised through the law over a legally undifferentiated population and is limited by the standard of right. If political power is delegated then it devolves back to the sovereign people when power is exercised beyond the rule of right and they exercise it to overthrow government and establish a new one.

The main question which *The Foundations of Modern Political Thought* answers is: how did the heterogeneous elements that comprise this great juridical edifice, which dominates conservative, liberal and Marxist social theory from Bodin and Buchanan to Rawls and Habermas, and is woven into modern political and legal institutions and practices from absolute monarchies to direct democracies, come to be set in place?[23] Although it is summarized in the conclusion, the full answer is given in the course of the two-volume study itself. This is so because, first, the juridical ideology is made up of components from all the ideologies surveyed. A typical illustration of this is the popular sovereignty variant of juridicalism, presented in a recognizably modern form by Mariana in *The Kingdom and the Education of the King* in the 1590s. As Skinner comments, 'The Jesuit Mariana may thus be said to link hands with the Protestant Buchanan in stating a theory of popular sovereignty which, while scholastic in its origins and Calvinist in its later development, was in essence independent of either religious creed'.[24]

How, secondly, do these elements come together to form the modern juridical ideology? Skinner's answer is that the foundations of modern political thought are the unintended and mostly unrecognized product of 400 years of political thought and action. Each tactical manipulation of a convention within local ideological controversies, and each use of this as an artifice in parochial political struggles are shown, from the perspective of the present, to add in effect an element in the construction of the juridical form of political representation.[25] An illustration of this is one of the steps by which the proposition that the rule of right, which both justifies and limits the exercise of political power, is and ought to be secular, came to be circulated and conventionalized.[26]

One group to advance this claim that political power has secular ends was the Huguenots in the course of the French religious wars in the late sixteenth century. Unlike Calvinists in Scotland, they were a small minority in French society and thus only a justification of their resistance to persecution by the Catholic ruler which would appeal to some segment of the Catholic majority, and so broaden their power base, had a chance of success. In fact, what they did in the classic Huguenot resistance theories was to justify resistance in the terms of the monarch's abuse of his power relative to purely secular, constitutional ends, without appealing to any specific religious duties on the part of rulers or subjects, as Protestants had standardly done, which could have alienated Catholic support. The point here is, first, that this form of argument was available to them from the Ockhamist tradition, where it had been employed in quite different ideological and political struggles (to subordinate secular authority to the Catholic Church). Second, the introduction of a non-sectarian standard for the exercise of political power can be completely explained in the terms of the local context. None the less, this move, in conjunction with others, unintentionally provided a standard which could be used by both absolutists and constitutionalists to legitimate the civil wars of the next 200 years, and, as a result, came to characterize the legal and political institutions of the modern secular state.

In the course of hundreds of local ideological manoeuvres and counter-manoeuvres like this, political thinkers incrementally and accidentally constructed the components of the juridical ideology. In the course of their use as legitimating elements in diverse local stratagems, these components came to be set in place and so to constitute the foundations of modern political rationality. Thus, far from being problematic, Skinner's two aims — to provide a historically sensitive survey of early modern political thought and action, and to trace the lineages of juridicalism — are complementary: the former *discloses* the latter.

The book in this respect is a vindication of his claim in 1969 that there is a way of studying the history of politics that will illuminate 'what is necessary and what is the product of our contingent arrangements' in the present, yet will not presuppose any transhistorical rationality or subjectivity (2:67). Like Nietzsche he has now shown that what we take to be necessary and foundational politically is the unplanned product of contingent controversies and struggles. This is analysed in meticulous detail, without evoking a hidden hand, the cunning of reason or the will to power, in the terms of the consequences of local politics gradually giving rise to the juridical ideology, which, constituting the *character* of modern political and legal institutions, now governs our political thought and action in its sovereign splendour. He promised in the same article that this form of analysis would provide 'the key to self-awareness itself.' The key is that we as modern political selves, as political subjects with individual rights, are the subjects of this modern sovereign.

The second thesis

The second thesis I will call historical pragmatics in order to underscore its dissimilarity to Habermas' universal pragmatics; that is, his theory of the universally valid conditions under which claims to know what is right and true could be advanced and rationally adjudicated. Skinner does not treat political theories solely as rational arguments, the truth and rightness claims of which are to be assessed. The primary question with which he approaches his study is not 'what is politically true and right?' It is rather, as we have seen, 'what counts as politically true and right, or as grounds for testing political knowledge claims, in different ideologies and contexts?' and 'how do we explain their uses, conventionalization and change?' That is, an historical rather than a universal pragmatics. I believe I have already illustrated this orientation *en passant*, but I would like to show briefly that his research provides a justification for it.

In his analysis of the minute steps that led to the constitution of humanism, he singles out as the threshold the gradual conventionalization in the fourteenth and fifteenth centuries of the wholly conventional belief that the classical past is significantly different from the present. Petrarch immediately drew the primary conclusion that was in effect to legitimate the humanist project for six hundred years: if there is a difference then it takes a special art, interpretation, and a special education, the humanities, to understand the past.[27] The causal effect of the gradual ·acceptance of belief in significant difference, from its heterodox enunciation with Petrarch to its orthodox status by the 1450s within the humanist intellectual and political elite, was the formation of historical consciousness.

How did these elements become conventional? His answer is, again, in the course of ideological controversies in the universities and political struggles in the city-states. The humanists used their convention of significant historical difference, in conjunction with other claims, to justify charges of anachronism against the universalist claims of the scholastic students of Roman law and to legitimate the establishment of the humanities and legal humanism. These arguments in turn were utilized to undercut imperial claims to dominion over the city-states and so to legitimate armed resistance. The weapon of anachronism was then used by Valla to prove that the Donation of Constantine was a forgery, thus undermining papal claims to sovereignty over secular rulers and sanctioning wars of resistance against papal forces. In turn, their claim that history is cyclical served to sanction the education and advising of politicians in the humanities, thus fulfilling the prophecy of a renaissance of classical republicanism.[28]

The first point the example serves to illustrate is that criteria for testing knowledge-claims are normally ideology-dependent. Valla's claim that the Donation of Constantine is a forgery may be tested once the concept of anachronism has been acquired, and this in turn presupposes the primary humanist convention of significant historical difference between classical past and the present. But if a person does not have this convention, they will appeal to other criteria; criteria in the light of which Valla's claim appears groundless. For example, that the document should be read in the light of what popes, councils and traditional authorities have said on the matter and on the assumption that history, from the death of Christ to the second coming is significantly the same. In the case of Roman law, the scholastic will read it in the light of what the great commentators have said and on the assumption that it is the proximate embodiment of universal legal standards. What the humanist is doing is not just advancing an argument, but a new rule for settling arguments, namely an historically sensitive interpretation by someone with an education in the humanities and in the light of the convention and consciousness of significant historical difference. Once the main beliefs of an ideology have been acquired, the changes this acquisition effects in 'social perceptions', 'attitudes', 'values', behaviour and in characterizing motives will help to reconfirm the beliefs in the light of everyday experience (6).

This is not to say that Skinner's concept of an ideology is that of a closed set of conventions, since he shows precisely how it was rational to move from one ideology to another, as, for example, when some Ockhamists and humanists became Lutherans. The hypothesis that his research tends to confirm is, rather, that rational assessment takes place within convention-governed contexts, which are themselves always contested and modified in the course of rational assessment, both in the way illustrated above and in the piecemeal way outlined in his account of ideological innovation earlier. Critical reason thus circulates within the conventions in which a knowledge-claim had its home, or within some other, imputed conventions – as, for example, when political philosophers today, working within the juridical framework, scrutinize these early texts in the light of their own conventions (2:36 – 8, 64 –6).

Historical pragmatics, in sum, is an approach dictated by the nature of political knowledge in the west. The foundations of modern political thought, whether juridical or humanist, lack rational foundations, and this because we lack a language, each convention of which has been independently grounded, in the terms of which we could assess all the conventions of all our ideologies.

This thesis seems to me to differ in one important respect from the universal version of anti-foundationalism put forward by Richard Rorty in *Philosophy and the Mirror of Nature*. He argues that all knowledge is opinion plus a reasonable justification; a reasonable justification is showing that a knowledge-claim conforms to the intersubjective beliefs the audience have no reason to doubt at that time; these intersubjective beliefs cannot all be tested because this would presuppose another cluster of background beliefs and so on; and these background beliefs change in time and vary historically, cross-culturally and intra-culturally. This general thesis about knowledge is dependent on the fourth proposition above about the variability of criterial beliefs, but this proposition seems reasonable because we accept, *inter alia*, the humanist convention of significant historical difference. (The rule-of-faith controversy, the revival of scepticism and the struggle for toleration in the sixteenth century are other important factors).

Anti-foundationalism seems reasonable as a result of the contingent historical fact that the humanities and their conventions became institutionalized in European universities by the late sixteenth century and that humanists educated and advised European ruling classes for three hundred years, including Rorty and some of his audience. It does not seem very reasonable to those who have been educated in departments that continue the universal traditions of scholasticism: logic, mathematics, pure philosophy. It also seems counter-intuitive to those trained in the social sciences, since these disciplines utilized the universalist conventions of the natural sciences to legitimate the move from their base in state administrative units, prisons, armies, factories and bureaucracies into a position of hegemony in the university – universalist conventions that the natural sciences had previously taken over from scholastic natural law in the seventeenth century to sanction their studies in the face of church opposition. Nor, finally, does it stand to reason to those educated or working within juridicalism, which includes most of us in our legal and political activity and those in moral, political and legal philosophy and social theory as it is standardly taught. Juridical thought has tended to retain strong, universalist conventions. People trained in these fields say, quite reasonably, that the varying criteria are not significantly different, and if they are, then they are probably wrong, just as their scholastic predecessors replied to the first humanists. (We have another modern ideology, Hegelianism, which is a concatenation of juridicalism, scientism, scholasticism and humanism, but is just another ideology for all that.) The ideological controversies in the philosophy of social science today, not surprisingly, have a familiar ring to them for anyone who has read the earlier humanist–scholastic debate and they no doubt serve in effect, but not necessarily in intent, the same purpose of legitimating control of the curriculum.

Therefore, Rorty's thesis of anti-foundationalism is not universal but, rather, another ideological manoeuvre to extend the intellectual empire of humanism. Its foundations are as contingent and rationally ungrounded as he claims all others are. From the point of view of Skinner's history of humanism, the anti-foundational perspective is made available by the emergence and persistence of humanism and that alone underwrites historical pragmatics. If modern political thought lacks rational foundations what kind of foundations does it possess? I now turn to this final thesis.

The third thesis

The third thesis, which I call the primacy of practical conflict, is both a theme of the book and a justification of his approach. Most practitioners of interpretative humanism from Valla to Geertz are concerned with reconstructing or reproducing diverse language games, traditions, paradigms or ideologies, showing one's way about within them, mapping their transformations and, perhaps, going on to compare, contrast and evaluate them in the light of our horizons. This has never been the sole concern for Skinner because his further objective has always been to disclose the relation or relations between political thought and political action.

Wittgenstein left us with a sublimely general description of this relation: a way of acting, a form of life, lies at the bottom of a language-game. By this he meant that although language-games lack rational foundations they do have practical foundations; they are grounded by being woven into human activity and practices.[29] How is this to be specified? One answer is that the language-game itself is the best guide to and description of the activities that hold it in place; that the activity conforms to or is 'internally' related to the language. This has been put forward by those, such as Gadamer and Taylor, working within a framework of historicized Kantian idealism in the form of the thesis that language 'constitutes' human practices, social reality.[30] Although this over-emphasis on the constitutive role of language has been refuted by Habermas and Rorty,[31] it continues to encourage and underwrite the view that the language must be the best, and often the only, guide to the activity it describes. Skinner is only in agreement with this hermeneutical convention in its negative form, as the rejection of the view that the practitioners' language of description has no influence on the practice. As we have seen, he concludes, in the course of citing Taylor, that a language constitutes the 'character' of its practices, not the practices themselves, in describing and evaluating them. It follows that an ideology is only a very rough guide to the forms of life it characterizes: the limits of the stretchability of the available ideologies sets the limits to legitimate action. Second, the study of ideologies or traditions themselves is the worst guide to what is actually going on in any significant detail precisely because components of the ideologies are continually adjusted to mask and disguise as customary forms of action that would otherwise be considered unreasonable, immoral or illegal.

By concentrating on the relation of legitimation between ideology and action Skinner has been able to set aside the interpretists' methodological injunction to stay within or tied to the practitioners' language-game and so to study what practical forms of activity set and hold ideologies in place. The answer his study provides is that the shifting power relations in early modern society explain, in general terms, ideological persistence and change and the alterations in ideological conventions in response to, and in legitimation of, these shifts explain in detail the character the configurations of power relations take on. In turn, the predominant form of practical activity that destabilizes, realigns and codifies shifting political relations in this period is warfare. There are moments when arms are set aside, but then the struggle is carried on by political means in the councils, royal courts, universities and churches, thus investing political life with the relations of war and conflict. Effectual changes in European political thought and action in this period are the consequences of wars and practical struggles and, secondarily, the outcome of the ideological response to the legitimation crises engendered by the shifting power relations that give way to battle. I cannot think of one counter-example in the two volumes, from the eventual triumph of Thomism over Ockhamism at the Council of Trent, from the emergence of humanism to its marginalization as a political force by the 1520s, from the incremental changes in Lutheranism and Calvinism to the emergence of the juridical foundations of modern political thought. The eventual hegemony of the juridical ideology is basically the result of its role in legitimating both the wars that have centralized the modern state and the constitutional revolutionary wars that have formed in integral counterstroke to its absolutist character.[32] Thus it is practical conflict and war that lie at the foundations of modern political thought: not a war of all against all nor of economic classes, but of shifting yet analysable alliances.

The primacy of practical conflict may therefore explain why Skinner conceptualizes political theory and argument in the language of war – tactics, strategies, opponents, battles, controversies and so on – as well as in the language of rational debate. It is not that political theorists necessarily conceptualize their activity this way but because political writing in European society, as a result of its legitimating function, is unavoidably caught up with and etched into more fundamental political relations, which are themselves partly shaped by relations of confrontation and armed struggle. We might provisionally reverse Clausewitz's question: 'Is not war merely another kind of writing and language for political thoughts?'[33] War is, after all, an obvious fact about European society, but Marxist, rationalist and interpretative approaches have for a long time now averted our gaze from its relation to political thought and action. Skinner's work thus seems to me to put forward a hypothesis for further study and research similar to one advanced by Foucault: 'Here I believe one's point of reference should not be to the great model of language (*langue*) and signs, but to that of war and battle. The history which bears and determines us has the form of a war rather than that of a language: relations of power, not relations of meaning.'[34] Although this quotation serves to highlight the common turn away from hermeneutics and towards practical conflict, it is misleading. Foucault went on to modify and refine his view by distinguishing between relations of power and relations of war.[35] I have adapted this distinction in formulating the third thesis. This is not to say that Skinner would formulate his findings in exactly this way, only that his work suggests this line of enquiry. If his work encouraged studies along these lines it would be an important and enlightening advance. It is difficult today to find an approach in political philosophy which even recognizes that (alas) warfare – along with language, labour and politics – is a fundamental human activity, let alone one which tries to analyse the complex relations between warfare and political thought and action.[36]

The five methodological steps, and the three hypotheses, in both their methodological and practical aspects, require, and no doubt will receive, much more refinement, extension and application. This is especially true with respect to analysis of the power relations that make up the practical context. Also, his analytical techniques should be applied to our contemporary world, where the relations between the pen and the sword are at least as complicated and dangerous as in earlier times.[37] It seems to me that it is one of the most original and promising forms of political analysis available. However crudely and inadequately I have presented Skinner's approach I hope I have managed to convey something of the richness and erudition of that promise.

PART II

Quentin Skinner on interpretation

2

Meaning and understanding in the history of ideas

My aim is to consider what I take to be the basic question which necessarily arises whenever an historian of ideas[1] confronts a work which he hopes to understand. Such an historian may have focused his attention on a work of literature – a poem, a play, a novel – or on a work of philosophy – some exercise in ethical, political, religious, or other such mode of thought. But the basic question will in all such cases remain the same: what are the appropriate procedures to adopt in the attempt to arrive at an understanding of the work? There are of course two currently orthodox (though conflicting) answers to this question, both of which seem to command a wide acceptance. The first (which is perhaps being increasingly adopted by historians of ideas) insists that it is the *context* 'of religious, political, and economic factors' which determines the meaning of any given text, and so must provide 'the ultimate framework' for any attempt to understand it. The other orthodoxy, however (still perhaps the most generally accepted), insists on the autonomy of the *text* itself as the sole necessary key to its own meaning, and so dismisses any attempt to reconstitute the 'total context' as 'gratuitous, and worse'.[2]

My concern in what follows will be to consider these two orthodoxies in turn, and to argue that both in effect share the same basic inadequacy: neither approach seems a sufficient or even appropriate means of achieving a proper understanding of any given literary or philosophical work. Both methodologies, it can be shown, commit philosophical mistakes in the assumptions they make about the conditions necessary for the understanding of utterances. It follows that the result of accepting either orthodoxy has been to fill the current literature in the history of ideas with a series of conceptual muddles and mistaken empirical claims.

The attempt to substantiate this assertion must necessarily be somewhat critical and negative. I undertake it here, however, in the belief that it can be shown to yield much more positive and programmatic conclusions; for the nature of the current confusions in the history of ideas points not merely to the need for an alternative approach, but also indicates what type of approach must necessarily be adopted if such confusions are to be avoided. I believe that this alternative approach would be more satisfactory as history, and moreover that it would serve to invest the history of ideas with its own philosophical point.

I

I turn first to consider the methodology dictated by the claim that the *text* itself should form the self-sufficient object of inquiry and understanding. For it is this assumption which continues to govern the largest number of studies, to raise the widest philosophical issues, and to give rise to the largest number of confusions. This approach itself is logically tied, in the history of ideas no less than in more strictly literary studies, to a particular form of justification for conducting the study itself. The whole point, it is characteristically said, of studying past works of philosophy (or literature) must be that they contain (in a favoured phrase) 'timeless elements',[3] in the form of 'universal ideas',[4] even a 'dateless wisdom'[5] with 'universal application'.[6]

Now the historian who adopts such a view has already committed himself, in effect, on the question of how best to gain an understanding of such 'classic texts'.[7] For if the whole point of such a study is conceived in terms of recovering the 'timeless questions and answers' posed in the 'great books', and so of demonstrating their continuing 'relevance',[8] it must be not merely possible, but essential, for the historian to concentrate simply on what each of the classic writers has *said*[9] about each of these 'fundamental concepts' and 'abiding questions'.[10] The aim, in short, must be to provide 'a re-appraisal of the classic writings, quite apart from the context of historical development, as perennially important attempts to set down universal propositions about political reality'.[11] For to suggest instead that a knowledge of the social context is a necessary condition for an understanding of the classic texts is equivalent to denying that they do contain any elements of timeless and perennial interest, and is thus equivalent to removing the whole point of studying what they said.

It is this essential belief that each of the classic writers may be expected to consider and explicate some determinate set of 'fundamental concepts' of 'perennial interest' which seems to be the basic source of the confusions engendered by this approach to studying the history of either literary or philosophical ideas. The sense in which the belief is misleading, however, appears to be somewhat elusive. It is easy to castigate the assumption as 'a fatal mistake',[12] but it is equally easy to insist that it must in some sense be a necessary truth. For there can be no question that the histories of different intellectual pursuits are marked by the employment of some 'fairly stable vocabulary'[13] of characteristic concepts. Even if we hold to the fashionably loose-textured theory that it is only in virtue of certain 'family resemblances' that we are able to define and delineate such different activities, we are still committed to accepting *some* criteria and rules of usage such that certain performances can be correctly instanced, and others excluded, as examples of a given activity. Otherwise we should eventually have no means – let alone justification – for delineating and speaking, say, of the histories of ethical or political thinking as being histories of recognizable activities at all. It is in fact the truth, and not the absurdity, of the claim that all such activities must have some characteristic concepts which seems to provide the main source of confusion. For if there must be at least some family resemblance connecting all the instances of a given activity, which we need first of all to apprehend in order to recognize the activity itself, it becomes impossible for any observer to consider any such activity, or any instance of it, without having some preconceptions about what he expects to find.

The relevance of this dilemma to the history of ideas – and especially to the claim that the historian should concentrate simply on the text in itself – is of course that it will never in fact be possible simply to study what any given classic writer has *said* (especially in an alien culture) without bringing to bear some of one's own expectations about what he must have been saying. This is simply the dilemma, familiar to psychologists as the (apparently inescapable)[14] determining factor of the observer's mental *set*. By our past experience 'we are set to perceive details in a certain way'. And when this frame of reference has been established, 'the process is one of being *prepared* to perceive or react in a certain way'.[15] The resulting dilemma may be stated, for my present purposes, in the formally crucial but empirically very elusive proposition that these models and preconceptions in terms of which we unavoidably organize and adjust our perceptions and thoughts will themselves tend to act as determinants of what we think or perceive. We must classify in order to understand, and we can only classify the unfamiliar in terms of the familiar.[16] The perpetual danger, in our attempts to enlarge our historical understanding, is thus that our expectations about what someone must be saying or doing will themselves determine that we understand the agent to be doing something which he would not – or even could not – himself have accepted as an account of what he *was* doing.

This notion of the priority of paradigms has already been very fruitfully explored in the history of art,[17] where it has caused an essentially historicist story which traced the development of illusionism to yield place to a story which is content to trace changing intentions and conventions. More recently an analogous exploration has been made with some plausibility in the history of science.[18] Here I shall attempt to apply a similar set of concepts to the history of ideas. My procedure will be to uncover the extent to which the current historical study of ethical, political, religious, and other such ideas is contaminated by the unconscious application of paradigms the familiarity of which, to the historian, disguises an essential inapplicability to the past. I do not, of course, seek to deny that the methodology which I am concerned to criticize has occasionally yielded distinguished results. I do wish, however, both to insist on the various ways in which to study simply what each classic writer *says* is unavoidably to run the perpetual danger of lapsing into various kinds of historical absurdity, and also to anatomize the various ways in which the results may in consequence be classified not as histories at all, but more appropriately as *mythologies*.

The most persistent mythology is generated when the historian is *set* by the expectation that each classic writer (in the history, say, of ethical or political ideas) will be found to enunciate some doctrine on each of the topics regarded as constitutive of his subject. It is a dangerously short step from being under the influence (however unconsciously) of such a paradigm to 'finding' a given author's doctrines on all the mandatory themes. The (very frequent) result is a type of discussion which might be labelled the mythology of doctrines.

This mythology takes several forms. First, there is the danger of converting some scattered or quite incidental remarks by a classic theorist into his 'doctrine' on one of the mandatory themes. This in turn can be shown to generate two particular types of historical absurdity, one more characteristic of intellectual biographies and the more synoptic histories of thought, in which the focus is on the individual thinkers (or the procession of them), and the other more characteristic of actual 'histories of ideas', in which the focus is on the development of some given 'idea' itself.

The particular danger with intellectual biography is that of sheer anachronism. A given writer may be 'discovered' to have held a view, on the strength of some chance similarity of terminology, on some subject to which he cannot in principle have meant to contribute. Marsilius of Padua, for example, at one point in his *Defender of the Peace* offers some typically Aristotelian remarks on the executive role of a ruler, compared with the legislative role of a sovereign people.[19] The modern commentator who comes upon this passage will of course be familiar with the doctrine, important in constitutional theory and practice since the American Revolution, that one of the conditions of political freedom is the separation of executive from legislative power. The historical origins of the doctrine itself can be traced[20] to the historiographical suggestion (first canvassed some two centuries after Marsilius's death) that the development of the Roman Republic into an Empire demonstrated the danger to the liberty of subjects inherent in entrusting any single authority with centralized political power. Marsilius, of course, knew nothing of this historiography, nor of the lessons that were to be drawn from it. (His own discussion in fact derives from Book IV of Aristotle's *Politics*, and is not even concerned with the issue of political freedom.) None of this, however, has been sufficient to prevent a brisk and wholly meaningless debate on the question of whether Marsilius should be said to have had a 'doctrine' of the separation of powers, and if so whether he should be 'acclaimed the founder of the doctrine'.[21] And even those experts who have denied that Marsilius should be credited with this doctrine have based their conclusions on his text,[22] and not at all by pointing to the impropriety of supposing that he *could* have meant to contribute to a debate the terms of which were unavailable to him, and the point of which would have been lost on him. The same anachronism marks the discussion which has centred around the famous *dictum* offered by Sir Edward Coke on Bonham's case, to the effect that the common law of England may sometimes override statute. The modern (especially American) commentator brings to this remark all the much later resonances of the doctrine of judicial review. Coke himself – like everyone in the seventeenth century – knew nothing of such a doctrine. (The context of his own suggestion is very much that of a party politician assuring James I that the defining characteristic of law is custom, and not, as James was already claiming, the will of the sovereign.)[23] None of these historical considerations, however, has been enough to prevent the reiteration of the wholly meaningless question of 'whether Coke actually intended to advocate judicial review',[24] or the insistence that Coke must have *meant* to articulate this 'new doctrine' and so to make this 'remarkable contribution to political science'.[25] Again, moreover, those experts who have denied that Coke should be credited with such clairvoyance have based their conclusion on the historico-legal reinterpretation of Coke's text,[26] rather than attacking the prior logical oddity of the implied account of Coke's intentions.

Besides this crude possibility of crediting a writer with a meaning he could not have intended to convey, since that meaning was not available to him, there is also the (perhaps more insidious) danger of too readily 'reading in' a doctrine which a given writer might in principle have meant to state, but in fact had no intention to convey. Consider for example the remarks which Richard Hooker makes in *The Laws of Ecclesiastical Polity* (book I, chap.X, section 4) about the natural sociability of man. We might well feel that Hooker's intention (what he meant to do) was merely – as with so many scholastic lawyers at the time who mentioned the point – to discriminate the godly origins of the Church from the more mundane origins of the state. The modern commentator, however, who inescapably sees Hooker at the top of a 'line of descent' running 'from Hooker to Locke and from Locke to the *Philosophes*' has little difficulty in converting Hooker's remarks into nothing less than his 'theory of the social contract'.[27] Similarly, consider the scattered remarks on trusteeship which John Locke offers at one or two points (paras 149, 155) in the *Second Treatise*. We might well feel that Locke merely intended to appeal to one of the most familiar legal analogies in the political writing of the time. Again, however, the modern commentator who sees Locke standing at the head of tradition of 'government by consent' has little difficulty in piecing together the 'passages scattered through' the work on this topic, and emerging with nothing less than Locke's 'doctrine' of 'the political trust'.[28] And similarly, consider the remarks James Harrington makes in *Oceana* about the place of lawyers in political life. The historian who is looking (perhaps, in this case, quite properly) for the views of the Harringtonian Republicans on the separation of powers may be momentarily disconcerted to find that Harrington ('curiously') is not even talking about public officers at this point. But if he 'knows' to expect the doctrine among this group, he will have little difficulty in insisting that 'this does seem to be a vague statement of the doctrine'.[29] In all such cases, where a given writer may appear to intimate some 'doctrine' in something that he says, we are left confronting the same essential and essentially begged question: if all the writers are claimed to have *meant* to articulate the doctrine with which they are being credited, why is it that they so signally failed to do so, so that the historian is left reconstructing their implied intentions from guesses and vague hints? The only plausible answer is of course fatal to the claim itself: that the author did not (or even could not) have meant after all to enunciate such a doctrine.

This same tendency for the paradigms applied to the history of ideas to cause its subject matter to mutate into a mythology of doctrines can also be illustrated, in a rather different way, from those 'histories of ideas' in which the aim (in the words of Professor Lovejoy, a pioneer of the approach) is to trace the morphology of some given doctrine 'through all the provinces of history in which it appears'.[30] The characteristic point of departure in such histories is to set out an ideal type of the given doctrine – whether it is the doctrine of equality, progress, Machiavellism, the social contract, the great chain of being, the separation of powers, and so on. The particular danger with this approach is that the doctrine to be investigated so readily becomes hypostatized into an entity. As the historian duly sets out in quest of the idea he has characterized, he is very readily led to speak as if the fully developed form of the doctrine was always in some sense immanent in history, even if various thinkers failed to 'hit upon' it,[31] even if it 'dropped from sight' at various times,[32] even if an entire era failed (note the implication that they *tried*) to 'rise to a consciousness' of it.[33] Similarly, the story of the development of such a doctrine very readily takes on the kind of language appropriate to the description of a growing organism. The fact that ideas presuppose agents is very readily discounted, as the ideas get up and do battle on their own behalf. Thus we may be told that the 'birth' of the idea of progress was quite easy, for it had 'transcended' the 'obstacles to its appearance' by the sixteenth century,[34] and so 'gained ground' through the next hundred years.[35] But the idea of the separation of powers had a harder time, for though it nearly managed to 'emerge' during the English civil war, it 'never quite managed fully to materialize', so that it took another century 'from the English civil war until the mid-eighteenth century for a three-fold division to emerge fully and take over'.[36]

The reification of doctrines in this way gives rise in turn to two kinds of historical absurdity, both of which are not merely prevalent in this type of history, but seem more or less inescapable when its methodology is employed. First, the tendency to search for approximations to the ideal type yields a form of non-history which is almost entirely given over to pointing out earlier 'anticipations' of later doctrines, and to crediting each writer in terms of this clairvoyance. So Marsilius is notable for his 'remarkable anticipation' of Machiavelli;[37] Machiavelli is notable because he 'lays the foundation for Marx';[38] Locke's theory of signs is notable 'as an anticipation of Berkeley's metaphysics';[39] Glanvill's theory of causation is notable for 'the extent to which he has anticipated Hume';[40] Shaftesbury's treatment of the theodicy problem is notable because it 'in a certain sense anticipated Kant'.[41] Sometimes even the pretence that this is history is laid aside, and the writers of the past are simply praised or blamed according to how far they may seem to have aspired to the condition of being ourselves. Montesquieu 'anticipates the ideas of full employment and the welfare state': this shows his 'luminous, incisive' mind.[42] Machiavelli thought about politics essentially as we do: this is his 'lasting significance'. But his contemporaries did not: this makes their political views 'completely unreal'.[43] Shakespeare ('an eminently political author') was sceptical about 'the possibility of an interracial, interfaith society'; this is one of the signs of his value as 'a text in moral and political education'.[44] And so on.

The second historical absurdity generated by the methodology of the history of ideas is the endless debate – almost wholly semantic, though posing as empirical – about whether a given idea may be said to have 'really emerged' at a given time, and whether it is 'really there' in the work of some given writer. Consider again the histories of the doctrine of the separation of powers. Is the doctrine, they ask, perhaps already 'there' in the works of George Buchanan? No, for he 'did not fully articulate' it, although 'none came closer'.[45] But is it perhaps 'there' by the time of the Royalists' *Defence* of 1648? No, for it is still 'not the pure doctrine'.[46] Or consider the histories of the doctrine of the social contract. Is the doctrine perhaps already 'there' in the pamphlets of the Huguenots? No, for their ideas are 'incompletely developed' (note again the unargued assumption that they are *trying* to develop the doctrine). But is it perhaps 'there' in the works of their Catholic rivals? No, for their statements are still 'incomplete', although they are 'decidedly more advanced'.[47]

The first form, then, of the mythology of doctrines may be said to consist, in these various ways, of mistaking some scattered or incidental remarks by one of the classic theorists for his 'doctrine' on one of the themes which the historian is *set* to expect. The second form of the mythology, to which I now turn, may be said to be the converse of this mistake. Here a classic theorist who fairly clearly *does* fail to come up with a recognizable doctrine on one of the mandatory themes is then criticized for his failure to do so.

The historical study of ethical and political ideas is dogged currently by a demonological (but highly influential) version of this mistake. Ethical and political theory, it is said, is or ought to be concerned with eternal or a least traditional 'true standards'.[48] It is thus thought appropriate to treat the history of these subjects in terms of the 'decided lowering of tone' said to be characteristic of modern reflection 'on life and its goals', and to take as the focus of this history the assessment of blame for this collapse.[49] Hobbes, or sometimes Machiavelli, is then made to stand condemned for man's first disobedience.[50] Their contemporaries are then suitably praised or blamed essentially according to whether they acknowledged or subverted the same 'truth'.[51] The chief proponent of this approach, confronted with Machiavelli's political works, thus 'does not hesitate to assert' that Machiavelli's teaching is to be denounced as 'immoral and irreligious'.[52] He also does not hesitate to assume that such a tone of denunciation is perfectly appropriate to the stated aim of trying to 'understand' Machiavelli's works.[53] Here the paradigm accepted for the nature of ethical and political thought determines the direction of the whole historical investigation. The history can only be reinterpreted if the paradigm itself is abandoned. Quite apart from the question of whether the paradigm is a suitable one to apply to the past, this is in itself an astonishing impasse for any historical investigation to have reached.

The main version, however, of this form of the mythology of doctrines consists of supplying the classic theorists with doctrines which are agreed to be proper to their subject, but which they have unaccountably failed to discuss. Sometimes this takes the form of extrapolating from what these great men said to some speculation about a topic they did not mention. Aquinas may not have pronounced on the subject of 'foolish "civil disobedience"', but surely 'he would not have approved'.[54] Similarly, Marsilius would surely approve of democracy, since 'the sovereignty he espoused pertained to the people'.[55] But Hooker 'would not be entirely happy' with democracy, since 'his own noble religious and spacious conception of law has been desiccated into the mere fiat of popular will'.[56] Such exercises may seem merely quaint, but they could always have a more sinister undertone, as these examples may seem to suggest: a means to fix one's own prejudices on to the most charismatic names, under the guise of innocuous historical speculation. History then indeed becomes a pack of tricks we play on the dead. The most usual strategy, however, is to seize on some doctrine which the given theorist, it is in effect claimed, ought to have mentioned, although he failed to do so, and then to criticize him for this so-called omission. Perhaps the most remarkable evidence of the hold of this most essentialist approach is that it was never questioned, as a method of discussing the history of political ideas, even by the most anti-essentialist of all contemporary political theorists, T. D. Weldon. The first part of his book on *States and Morals* sets out the various 'definitions of the State' which political theorists all 'either formulate or take for granted'. It is thus established that 'all theories of the State fall ... into two main groups. Some define it as a kind of organism, others as a kind of machine'. Armed with this discovery, Weldon then turns 'to examine the leading theories about the state which have been put forward'. But here we find that even 'those writers who are generally regarded as the leading theorists in the subject' let us down rather badly, for very few of them manage to expound either of the two theories without 'inconsistencies or even contradictions'. Hegel, indeed, turns out to be the sole theorist 'completely faithful' to one of the two stipulated models which, we are reminded, it is the 'primary purpose' of each theorist to expound. A less confident writer might well have wondered at this point whether his initial characterization of what all these theorists ought to be doing can possibly have been correct. But Weldon's only comment is that it seems 'rather odd that, after more than two thousand years of concentrated thought' they are still in such complete confusion.[57] The exegetical literature is filled, moreover, with this type of more or less unselfconscious critical application of the mythology of doctrines. Consider, for example, the place in political thought of questions about the process of voting and decision-making, and public opinion generally – questions of some importance in recent democratic political theory, though of very little interest to theorists writing before the establishment of modern representative democracies. The historical caveat might scarcely seem worth adding, but it has not in fact been enough to prevent commentators from criticizing Plato's *Republic* for 'omitting' the 'influence of public opinion';[58] or from criticizing Locke's *Second Treatise* for omitting 'all references to family and race', and for failing to make it 'wholly clear' where he stands on the question of universal suffrage;[59] or from regarding it as remarkable that not one of 'the great writers on politics and law' devoted any space to the discussion of decision-making.[60] Consider, similarly, the question of the social basis of political power – a question of great importance, again, in current democratic theory, though of little relevance to the theorists of pre-industrial society. Again the historical caveat is obvious, but again it has not been sufficient to prevent commentators from offering it as a criticism of Machiavelli,[61] of Hobbes,[62] and of Locke,[63] that none of them offers any 'genuine insights'[64] into this almost wholly twentieth-century discussion.

A scarcely less futile and even more prevalent form of this mythology consists in effect of criticizing the classic writers according to the – wholly *a priori* – assumption that they must have intended whatever writings they produced to constitute the most systematic contributions to their subject which they were capable of executing. If it is first assumed, for example, that one of the doctrines which Hooker (that most implausible runner in the classic race) must have been trying to enunciate in the *Laws* was an account of 'the basis of political obligation', then it is doubtless a 'defect in Hooker's political views' that he fails to devote any attention to refuting claims to absolute power.[65] Similarly, if it is first assumed that one of Machiavelli's basic concerns in the *Prince* is 'the characteristics of men in politics', then it is not hard for a modern political scientist to go on to point out that as such, Machiavelli's poor effort is 'extremely one-sided and unsystematic'.[66] Again, if it is first assumed that Locke's *Two Treatises* include all the doctrines he might have wished to enunciate on 'natural law and political society', then doubtless 'it might well be asked' why Locke failed to 'advocate a world state'.[67] And again, if it is first assumed that one of Montesquieu's aims in *L'Esprit des lois* must have been to enunciate a sociology of knowledge, then doubtless 'it is a weakness' that he fails to explain its chief determinants, and doubtless 'we must also accuse him' of failing to apply his own theory.[68] But with all such alleged 'failures', as with the converse form of this mythology, we are still – remembering that failing presupposes trying – left confronting the same essential and essentially begged question: the question of whether any of these writers ever intended, or even could have intended, to do what they are thus castigated for not having done.

I now turn to the second type of mythology which tends to be generated by the fact that the historian will be unavoidably *set* in approaching the ideas of the past. It may be (and indeed it very often happens) that a given classic writer is not altogether consistent, or even that he fails altogether to give any systematic account of his beliefs. If the basic paradigm for the conduct of the historical investigation has been conceived as the elaboration of each classic writer's doctrines on each of the themes most characteristic of the subject, it will become dangerously easy for the historian to conceive it as his task to supply or find in each of these texts the coherence which they may appear to lack. Such a danger is exacerbated, of course, by the notorious difficulty of preserving the proper emphasis and tone of a work in paraphrasing it, and by the consequent temptation to find a 'message' which can be abstracted from it and more readily communicated. To write a textbook in the history of ideas, of course, is simply to fall prey systematically to this temptation – which, incidentally, is why textbooks in the subject are not merely poor things, but are actively misleading, and why this difficulty is not to be circumvented even by providing textbooks in which the 'message' is given in the author's own words. The inevitable result – which can be illustrated from far more respectable sources than the synoptic and pedagogic histories – will still be a form of writing which might be labelled the mythology of coherence. The writing of the history of ethical and political philosophy is pervaded by this mythology.[69] Thus if 'current scholarly opinion' can see no coherence in Hooker's *Laws*, the moral is to look harder, for 'coherence' is surely 'present'.[70] If there is doubt about the 'most central themes' of Hobbes' political philosophy, it becomes the duty of the exegete to discover the 'inner coherence of his doctrine' by reading the *Leviathan* a number of times, until – in a perhaps excessively revealing phrase – he finds that its argument has 'assumed some coherence'.[71] If there is no coherent system 'readily accessible' to the student of Hume's political works, the exegete's duty is 'to rummage through one work after another' until the 'high degree of consistency in the whole corpus' is duly displayed (again in a rather revealing phrase) 'at all costs'.[72] If Herder's political ideas are 'rarely worked out systematically', and are to be found 'scattered throughout his writings, sometimes within the most unexpected contexts', the duty of the exegete again becomes that of trying 'to present these ideas in some coherent form'.[73] The most revealing fact about such reiterations of the scholar's task is that the metaphors habitually used are those of effort and quest; the ambition is always to 'arrive' at 'a unified interpretation', to 'gain' a 'coherent view of an author's system'.[74]

This procedure gives the thoughts of various classic writers a coherence, and an air generally of a closed system, which they may never have attained or even been meant to attain. If it is first assumed, for example, that the business of interpreting Rousseau's thought must centre on the discovery of his most 'fundamental thought', it will readily cease to seem a matter of importance that he contributed over several decades to several quite different fields of enquiry.[75] Again, if it is first assumed that every aspect of Hobbes' thought was designed as a contribution to the whole of his 'Christian' system, it will cease to seem at all peculiar to suggest that we may turn to his autobiography to elucidate so crucial a point as the relations between ethics and political life.[76] Again, if it is first assumed that even Burke never essentially contradicted himself or changed his mind, but that a 'coherent moral philosophy' underlies everything he wrote, then it will cease to seem at all unrealistic to treat 'the corpus of his published writings' as 'a single body of thought'.[77] Some measure of the lengths to which such procedures of abstracting the variety of a man's thoughts to the level at which they can be said (all passion spent) to 'attain' some coherence is provided by a recent study of Marx's social and political thought. Here it has seemed necessary, to justify the exclusion of Engels' thoughts, to point out that Marx and Engels were after all 'two distinct human beings'.[78] It does sometimes happen, of course, that the aims and successes of a given writer may remain so various as to defy even the efforts of such exegetes to find a coherent system in their scattered thoughts. Frequently, however, this merely generates the converse form of this historical absurdity: for such lack of system is then made a matter for reproach. It is thought, for example, to be a point of some ideological urgency as well as exegetical convenience that Marx's various pronouncements should be available under some systematic headings. Despite the efforts of his critics, however, such a system remains hard to find. We might ascribe this to his concern at different times with a wide range of different social and economic issues. But it has instead become a standard criticism in the textbooks that Marx never managed to work out what is supposed to be 'his' basic theory in anything but a 'fragmentary manner'.[79] Such criticisms occur even more readily when the given writer is first classified according to a model to which he is then in effect expected to aspire. If it is first assumed that all conservative thinkers must hold some 'organic' conception of the state, then doubtless Bolingbroke 'should have had' such a conception, and doubtless it is odd that he did not organize his thoughts in this approved way.[80] Again, if it is first assumed that each philosopher who writes about justice may be expected to 'contribute' to one of three 'basic' views on the subject, then doubtless the fact that neither Plato nor Hegel did so can be taken to show that they 'seem to resist taking a definite position' on the subject itself.[81] In all such cases, the coherence or lack of it which is thus discovered very readily ceases to be an historical account of any thoughts which were ever actually thought. The history thus written becomes a history not of ideas at all, but of abstractions: a history of thoughts which no one ever actually succeeded in thinking, at a level of coherence which no one ever actually attained.

The objection is a very obvious one, but it has not in practice proved sufficient to forestall the development of this mythology of coherence in two directions which can only, in the most pejorative sense, be called metaphysical. First there is the astonishing, but not unusual, assumption that it may be quite proper, in the interests of extracting a message of higher coherence from an author's work, to discount the statements of intention which the author himself may have made about what he was doing, or even to discount whole works which would impair the coherence of the author's system. The current literature on both Hobbes and Locke may be used to illustrate both these tendencies. In the case of Locke, it is now known that he was concerned, in his earliest works of ethical and political thinking, to set out and to defend a markedly authoritarian position.[82] Yet it is still apparently possible in the face of this knowledge to treat Locke's politics as a body of views which can simply be labelled the work of a 'liberal' political theorist, without further consideration of the fact that these were at best the views which Locke held in his fifties, and which he would himself have repudiated in his thirties.[83] Locke at thirty is evidently not yet 'Locke' – a degree of patriarchalism to which even Filmer did not aspire. As for Hobbes, it is known from his own explicit statements what character he intended his political thought to bear. *Leviathan*, as he put it in the review and Conclusion, was written 'without other design' than to show first that the 'civil right of sovereigns and both the duty and liberty of subjects' could be grounded 'upon the known natural inclinations of mankind', and second, that a theory so grounded would centre on 'the mutual relation of protection and obedience': a politics of rational calculation is thus predicated on something like an assimilation of politics to psychology.[84] Yet it has still seemed possible to insist that this 'scientific part' of Hobbes's thought is nothing more than a rather ineptly detached aspect of a transcendent 'religious whole'. The fact, moreover, that Hobbes himself appeared unaware of this high order of coherence provokes not retraction but counter-assertion. Hobbes merely 'fails to make clear' that his discussion of human nature 'in fact' subserves a religious purpose. It 'would have been clearer' if Hobbes had 'written in terms of moral and civil obligations' and thus brought out the 'real unity' and basically religious character of his whole 'system'.[85]

The other metaphysical belief to which the mythology of coherence gives rise is that a writer may be expected not merely to exhibit some 'inner coherence' which it becomes the duty of his interpreter to reveal, but also that any apparent barriers to this revelation, constituted by any apparent contradictions which the given writer's work does seem to contain, cannot be real barriers, because they cannot really be contradictions. The assumption, that is, is that the correct question to ask in such a doubtful situation is not whether the given writer was inconsistent, but rather 'How are his contradictions (or apparent contradictions) to be accounted for?'[86] The explanation dictated by the principle of Ockham's razor (that an apparent contradiction may simply *be* a contradiction) seems not to be considered. Such apparent incompatibilities, it is often said instead, should not simply be left in this unresolved state, but should be made to serve instead in helping towards 'a fuller understanding of the whole theory'[87] – of which the contradictions, presumably, form only an unsublimated part. The very suggestion, indeed, that the 'contradictions and divergences' of a given writer may be 'supposed to prove that his thought had changed' has been dismissed by a very influential authority as just another delusion of nineteenth-century scholarship.[88] So it comes about that much current practice in the history of ideas deliberately endorses one of the more fantastic doctrines of the scholastics themselves: the belief that one must 'resolve antinomies'. The aim, for example, in studying the politics of Machiavelli need not therefore be restricted to anything so straightforward as an attempt to indicate the nature of the developments and divergences from *The Prince* to the later *Discourses*. It can be – and has been – insisted instead that the appropriate task must be to construct for Machiavelli a scheme of beliefs sufficiently generalized for the doctrines of *The Prince* to be capable of being *aufgehoben* into the *Discourses* with all the apparent contradictions resolved.[89] The recent historiography of Marx's social and political thought reveals a similar trend. Marx is not allowed simply to have developed and changed his views from the humanistic strains of the *Economic–Philosophical Manuscripts* to the apparently very different, far more mechanistic, system outlined over twenty years later in *Capital*. Either it is assumed that the appropriate task must be to construct 'a structural analysis of the whole of Marx's thought' so that the apparent divergences can be viewed as part of 'one corpus',[90] or else it is assumed that the very existence of the earlier material can be used as a basis for claiming that 'the element of myth' must still somehow be present in the later works, that this shows Marx to have been 'obsessed with a moral vision of reality' all the time, and that all of this can be used to discredit Marx's scientific pretensions, since he 'appears not as the scientist of society that he claimed to be, but rather as a moralist or religious kind of thinker'.[91]

It is true that this belief in the desirability of trying to resolve contradictions has recently received an explicit and interesting defence. The clue, it is suggested, to understanding any apparent 'blunders' committed by any 'master of the art of writing' lies in recognizing the effects of persecution on the art of writing. During any 'era of persecution' it becomes necessary to hide one's less orthodox views 'between the lines' of one's published work. ('The expression', one learns with relief, 'is clearly metaphoric.') It follows that if 'an able writer' in such a situation appears to contradict himself in setting out his ostensible views, then 'we may reasonably suspect' that the apparent contradiction has been deliberately planted as a signal to his 'trustworthy and intelligent' readers that he is really opposed to the orthodox views he may appear to hold.[92] The basic difficulty with this defence of the practice of resolving antinomies is that it depends on two *a priori* assumptions which, although they are extremely implausible, are not merely left unargued, but are treated as if they are 'facts'. First, the inquiry gains its whole direction from the unargued assumption that to be original *is* to be subversive. For this is the means by which we know when to look for writing between the lines. And second, any given interpretation based on reading between the lines is virtually insulated from criticism by the alleged 'fact' that 'thoughtless men are careless readers'.[93] For this amounts to the (purely semantic) claim that to fail to 'see' the message between the lines *is* to be thoughtless, while to 'see' it *is* to be a trustworthy and intelligent reader. But if we now insist on some more genuinely empirical criteria for knowing when we are or are not dealing with one of the relevant 'eras of persecution', and for knowing when in consequence we should or should not try to read between the lines, all that we find are two circular arguments. When should we *stop* trying to read between the lines? The only criterion given is 'when it would be less exact than not doing so'.[94] And what *constitutes* an era of persecution, such that we should expect to have to read between the lines? We are told on the one hand 'that the book in question must have been composed during a period of persecution' if there is to be any expectation that it does contain secret writing. And we are told on the other hand that a period of persecution is to be defined as one in which a heterodox writer will need to develop this 'peculiar technique of writing' between the lines.[95] Despite this explicit defence, therefore, of the scholasticism of resolving antinomies, it remains hard to see how the whole enterprise of looking for the 'inner coherence' of a given writer's doctrines can yield anything except a mythology of coherence – a mythology, again, in the sense that the history written according to this methodology can scarcely contain any genuinely historical reports about thoughts that were actually thought in the past.

II

Both the two mythologies I have discussed derive from the fact that an historian of ideas will unavoidably be *set*, in approaching any given writer, by some sense of the defining characteristics of the discipline to which the given writer may be said to have contributed. It may well seem, however, that even if such mythologies proliferate at this level of abstraction, they will scarcely arise, or will at least be very much easier to recognize and to discount, when the historian comes to operate on the level simply of describing the internal economy and argument of some individual work. It is indeed usual to insist that there can be nothing very problematic, at this more particular level, about the business merely of anatomizing the contents and arguments of some classic text. It is thus all the more necessary to insist that even at this level we are still confronted with further dilemmas generated by the priority of paradigms, and still confronted in consequence with a further set of ways in which historical exegesis can lapse into mythology.

In the first place, it is rather easy, in considering what significance the argument of some classic text might be said to have for us, to describe the work and its alleged significance in such a way that no place is left for the analysis of what the author himself meant to say, although the commentator may still believe himself to be engaged in such an analysis. The characteristic result of this confusion is a type of discussion which might be labelled the mythology of prolepsis. Such confusions arise most readily, of course, when the historian is more interested – as he may legitimately be – in the retrospective significance of a given historical work or action than in its meaning for the agent himself. A convenient example of the problem which then arises is given in an important recent discussion of such tensed situations. We might wish to say that with Petrarch's ascent of Mount Ventoux the age of the Renaissance began. Now this might, in a romantic sort of way, be said to give a true account both of the significance of Petrarch's action, and so of its interest for us. The point is, however, that no account under this description could ever be a true account of any action Petrarch intended, or hence of the meaning of his actual action. There could be no intention 'to open the Renaissance', for 'to give such a description requires concepts which were only available at a later time'.[96] The characteristic, in short, of the mythology of prolepsis is the conflation of the necessary asymmetry between the significance an observer may justifiably claim to find in a given statement or other action, and the meaning of that action itself. One such prolepsis which has constantly been exposed, and yet has constantly recurred, has been the attempt to consider Plato's political views in *The Republic* as those of a 'totalitarian party politician'.[97] Another very similar case has been the attempt to insist that Rousseau's political views not only 'provided the philosophical justification for the totalitarian as well as the democratic national state',[98] but that the force of this 'provision' is such that Rousseau should in effect be credited with just this *intention*, and should thus be 'given special *responsibility* for the emergence of totalitarianism'.[99] In both cases an account which might be true of the historical significance of the works becomes conflated with an account of what they were doing which could not in principle be true.

Such crude versions of this mythology, of course, are (and have been) very readily exposed. But this does noent seem to have been sufficient to prevent the same type of prolepsis from continuing to recur, in a less noticeable fashion, in discussions of other admittedly influential political theorists, such as Machiavelli and Locke. Machiavelli, we are very often told, 'was the founder of the modern political orientation'.[100] With Machiavelli 'we stand at the gateway of the modern world'.[101] Now this may well provide a true account of Machiavelli's historical significance (though it seems to presuppose a somewhat naive view of historical causation). But this is also frequently used to preface discussions of the characteristically 'modern' elements of Machiavelli's thought, and is even offered as an account of 'the *intention* of Machiavelli's political teaching'.[102] The danger here is not merely that of 'seeing' far too readily the 'modern' elements which the commentator has thus programmed himself to find; there is also the danger that such interpretations may part company with anything that could in principle be a plausible account of what Machiavelli's political writings were meant to achieve or intended to mean. Similarly with Locke, of whom it is so often said (doubtless correctly) that he was one of the founders of the modern empirical and liberal school of political philosophy. Such a characterization readily becomes elided into the claim that Locke was himself a 'liberal' political theorist.[103] This only serves to turn a remark about Locke's significance which might be true into a remark about the content of his works which could not be true. For Locke can scarcely have intended to contribute to a school of political philosophy which, so this fashionable but muddled interpretation suggests, it was his great achievement to make possible.[104] The surest symptom, in short, of this mythology of prolepsis is that the discussions which it governs are open to the crudest type of criticism that can be levelled against any teleological form of explanation: the action has to await the future to await its meaning.

Even when all these necessary historical considerations have been given their due weight, the correct description simply of the contents and arguments of a given classic text still poses a problem. For there is still the possibility that the observer may misdescribe, by a process of historical foreshortening, both the sense and the intended reference of a given work. The result is then a mythology of parochialism. This danger must arise, of course, in any kind of attempt to understand an alien culture or an unfamiliar conceptual scheme. If there is to be any prospect that the observer will successfully communicate his understanding within his own culture, it is obviously dangerous, but it is equally inescapable, that he should apply his own familiar criteria of classification and discrimination.[105] The danger is then that the observer may 'see' something apparently (rather than really) familiar in the course of studying an alien argument, and may in consequence provide a misleadingly familiar-looking description. The writing of the history of ideas is, in fact, marked in particular by two examples of such parochialism. First, there is the danger that the historian may misuse his vantage-point in describing the apparent *reference* of some given statement in a classic text. An argument in one work, that is, may happen to remind the historian of a similar argument in an earlier work, or may appear to contradict it. In either case the historian may mistakenly come to suppose that it was the intention of the later writer to refer to the earlier, and so may come to speak misleadingly of the 'influence' of the earlier work. Now there is no doubt that the concept of influence, while extremely elusive (if it is to be distinguished from a cause) is far from being empty of explanatory force.[106] The danger is, however, that it is so easy to use the concept in an apparently explanatory way without any consideration of whether the conditions sufficient, or at least necessary, for the proper application of the concept have been met. The (very frequent) result – for example, in the history of political ideas – is a story which reads like nothing so much as the first chapters of Chronicles, though without the genetic justification. Consider, for example, the alleged genealogy of Edmund Burke's political views. His aim in his *Thoughts on the Causes of the Present Discontents*, we are told, was 'to counteract the influence of Bolingbroke'.[107] Bolingbroke himself is said to have been under the influence of Locke.[108] Locke in turn is either said – despite appearances – to have been much influenced by Hobbes, to whom he must 'really' have been intending to refer in the *Second Treatise*,[109] or else is said to be concerned there to counter Hobbes's influence.[110] And Hobbes in turn is said to have been influenced by Machiavelli,[111] by whom indeed everyone is said to have been influenced.[112]

Most of these explanations are purely mythological, as can readily be demonstrated simply by considering what the necessary conditions would have to be for helping to explain the appearance in any given writer B of any given doctrine, by invoking the 'influence' of some earlier given writer, A. Such a set of conditions would at least have to include (a) that there should be a genuine similarity between the doctrines of A and B; (b) that B could not have found the relevant doctrine in any writer other than A;[113] (c) that the probability of the similarity being random should be very low (i.e., even if there is a similarity, and it is shown that it could have been A that B was influenced by, it must still be shown that B did not as a matter of fact articulate the relevant doctrine independently). Now consider the example above in terms of this not very stringent model. It is arguable that the alleged influence of Machiavelli on Hobbes, and of Hobbes on Locke, even fails to pass test (a). Certainly Hobbes never explicitly discusses Machiavelli, and Locke never explicitly discusses Hobbes. It is demonstrable that the alleged influence of Hobbes on Locke, and of Bolingbroke on Burke, both fail to pass test (b). (Burke might equally well have found all the doctrines of Bolingbroke by which he is said to have been influenced in a whole range of early eighteenth-century pamphlets.)[114] Locke might similarly have found all the doctrines said to be characteristic of Hobbes in a whole range of 1650s *de facto* political writings – which, indeed, Locke is at least known to have read, while it is not at all clear that he read Hobbes's works.[115] And finally, it is clear that none of the examples cited can be made to pass test (c). (It is indeed clear that the issues raised by test (c) have not even been faced in any of these cases.) It is thus scarcely an exaggeration[116] to say that this whole repertoire of *Einfluss*-studies in the history of ideas is based on nothing better than the capacity of the observer to foreshorten the past by filling it with his own reminiscences.

The other form of conceptual parochialism which particularly marks the history of ideas is that the observer may unconsciously misuse his vantage-point in describing the *sense* of a given work. There is always the danger, that is, that the historian may conceptualize an argument in such a way that its alien elements are dissolved into an apparent but misleading familiarity. This danger arises pre-eminently in social anthropology, of course; there it has become the object of considerable and self-conscious attention by both theorists and practitioners. But it also arises scarcely less seriously in the history of ideas, in which a similar self-conciousness seems damagingly absent. The resulting misinterpretations are many: two very obvious examples must here serve to illustrate the point. Consider, for example, the case of an historian who decides (perhaps quite rightly) that a fundamental feature of radical political thinking during the English Revolution was a concern with the extension of the right to vote. He may then be led to conceptualize this characteristically 'Leveller' demand in terms of an argument for democracy. The danger arises, however, when the concept of a 'philosophy of liberal democracy'[117] is then used as a paradigm for the description and understanding of the Leveller movement. First, the paradigm makes it unnecessarily difficult to account for some of the most characteristic features of Leveller ideology. For if we are programmed to think in terms of the 'republican secularism' of the movement, it is not surprising that their agonizings over the Monarchy and their appeals to religious sentiment begin to look somewhat baffling.[118] And second, the paradigm of 'democracy' will tend to lead the historical investigation in rather inappropriate directions. Some anachronistic concept of 'the welfare state'[119] has to be found in Leveller thought, as well as belief in 'manhood suffrage', which they never in fact held.[120] Or consider, similarly, the case of an historian who decides (again perhaps quite rightly) that the arguments in Locke's *Second Treatise* about the right to resist tyrannical governments are related to his arguments about the place of consent in any decent political community. He may then be led to use the notion of 'Government by consent' as a paradigm for the description of Locke's argument.[121] The same danger then arises. When *we* speak of government by consent we usually have in mind a theory concerned with the best organization of government. It is thus natural, or rather fatally easy, to turn with this conceptualization in mind to Locke's text, and duly to find some such theory rather bunglingly set out there. There is decisive evidence,[122] however, that when Locke spoke of government by consent this simply did not happen to be what *he* had in mind at all. It is now clear that Locke's concern with the concept of consent arises solely in connection with the *origin* of legitimate societies. This is hardly what we should regard as an argument for consent, but it happens to be Locke's argument, and the only result of failing to start from this point is to misdescribe the whole theory, and so to accuse Locke of having bungled an account which he was not, in fact, trying to write. The point is that even when an historian of ideas addresses himself solely to the description of a text, and even when his paradigms reflect genuinely organizing features of the text, the same essential danger still remains: the danger that the very familiarity of the concepts the historian uses may mask some essential inapplicability to the historical material.

The perennial difficulty with which I have been concerned throughout is thus that while it is inescapable, it is also dangerous in these various ways to empirical good sense for the historian of ideas to approach his material with preconceived paradigms. It will by now be evident, moreover, that the point at which such dangers arise is the point at which the historian in effect begins to ignore certain general criteria, logical as well as empirical, which must necessarily apply to the whole enterprise of making and understanding statements. A consideration of the nature of these issues may thus serve to summarize as well as to corroborate the methodological lessons on which I have sought to insist.

The relevant logical consideration is that no agent can eventually be said to have meant or done something which he could never be brought to accept as a correct description of what he had meant or done. This special authority of an agent over his intentions does not exclude, of course, the possibility that an observer might be in a position to give a fuller or more convincing account of the agent's behaviour than he could give himself. (Psychoanalysis is indeed founded on this possibility.) But it does exclude the possibility that an acceptable account of an agent's behaviour could ever survive the demonstration that it was itself dependent on the use of criteria of description and classification not available to the agent himself. For if a given statement or other action has been performed by an agent at will, and has a meaning for him, it follows that any plausible account of what the agent meant must necessarily fall under, and make use of, the range of descriptions which the agent himself could at least in principle have applied to describe and classify what he was doing. Otherwise the resulting account, however compelling, cannot be an account of his statement or action.[123] It will be evident by now that it is precisely this consideration which is so readily ignored whenever a given classic writer is criticized by an historian of ideas for failing to enunciate his doctrines in a coherent fashion, or for failing to enunciate a doctrine on one of the allegedly perennial issues. For it cannot (logically) be a correct appraisal of any agent's action to say that he failed to do something unless it is first clear that he did have, and even could have had, the intention to try to perform *that* action. To apply this test is simply to recognize that many of the questions with which we have been concerned (questions such as whether Marsilius of Padua enunciated a doctrine of the separation of powers, and so on) are not merely scholastic, but strictly speaking void for lack of reference, and so meaningless. For there is no means of reformulating any such questions in terms that could in principle have made sense to the agent himself. (A fourteenth-century anti-papalist pamphleteer can scarcely have been *intending* to contribute to an eighteenth-century French constitutionalist debate.) The same test equally makes it clear that all claims about 'anticipations', all remarks such as the claim that 'we may regard Locke's theory' of signs 'as an anticipation of Berkeley's metaphysics' are meaningless.[124] For there is no point in so regarding Locke's theory if the aim is to say anything at all about what Locke himself was doing. (It can scarcely have been Locke's *intention* to anticipate Berkeley's metaphysics.) And if such historical studies are not to be studies of what genuine historical agents did think (or at least could have thought), then they might as well be turned into fiction by intention, for they must certainly be fiction by attainment. History (notwithstanding a fashionable attitude among philosophers) cannot simply consist of stories: a further feature of historical stories is that they are at least supposed to be true.[125]

The relevant empirical considerations amount to little more than commonplace, but amazingly elusive, facts about the activity of thinking. The first is that it is surely at least a 'fact about many people' (and a fact with which the moralist needs to reckon)[126] that they may *consciously* adopt incompatible ideals and beliefs in different moods and at different times. And even if it is insisted that there may be thinkers whose ideals and beliefs remain in a more or less steady state, there is still a second consideration, that to think at all is surely to engage in an 'effortful activity',[127] and not just to manipulate effortlessly some sort of kaleidoscope of mental images. The attempt to think out problems, as a matter of common introspection and observation, does not seem to take the form of, or to be reducible to, a patterned or even a uniformly purposive activity. It is surely empirically commonplace that we engage rather in an often intolerable wrestle with words and their meanings, that we characteristically spill over the limits of our intelligence and get confused, and that our attempts to synthesize our views may in consequence reveal conceptual disorder at least as much as coherent doctrines. It will be evident by now that it is precisely this consideration which is ignored whenever an interpreter insists on collecting the regrettably 'scattered' thought of some classic writer and presenting them systematically, or on discovering some level of coherence at which the efforts and confusions which ordinarily mark the activity of thinking are made to disappear.

III

It may seem by now that the argument which I have so far presented is open to a crucial objection. To illustrate the various dangers of writing historical nonsense by concentrating on what each classic writer *says* about each given doctrine is scarcely the same, it might be argued, as to prove the conceptual impossibility of writing good history by adopting this approach. It is surely true, in any case, that there are at least *some* writers (Hobbes perhaps springs to mind) who may fairly be said to have articulated a fully coherent set of doctrines, even a 'system of ideas'.[128] If the tendency, moreover, for the study simply of a writer's doctrines to generate mythologies is only to be classified as a *danger*, it is surely one which, with sufficient self-consciousness, the historian may well hope to avoid. And if such dangers *can* be avoided, the demand for a wholly different approach to studying the history of ideas must begin after all to seem somewhat alarmist and unjustified. The answer to such objections is of course that it is not the existence of doctrines in the history of thought which is in question. What is in question − even in the case where a given writer may appear to have articulated a system of doctrines with complete coherence − is the possibility, the conceptual propriety, of treating such a system as a self-sufficient object of inquiry and understanding. In considering this issue, moreover, I now wish to advance a thesis complementary to, but much stronger than, the one I have just argued. I have argued that the danger of writing historical nonsense, in direct consequence of concentrating on the text in itself, is often incurred, and indeed very seldom avoided altogether in current practice. I now wish to claim that even if all the dangers I have outlined could be avoided (as they doubtless could, though they seldom are) the underlying assumption of this whole approach − that one should focus simply on the texts themselves, and study what each classic writer has to *say* about each given doctrine − must necessarily remain a wholly inadequate methodology for the conduct of the history of ideas. I shall seek to argue this claim, moreover, with reference both to intellectual biography, where the doctrines of a given writer are in question, and to 'histories of ideas', where the morphology of the doctrine itself is traced out. It can be shown in both cases that while the study of the texts and their doctrines in themselves may often appear to yield quite satisfactory results, the methodology remains incapable in principle of considering or even recognizing some of the most crucial problems which must arise in any attempt to understand the relations between what a given writer may have *said*, and what he may be said to have meant by saying what he said.

Intellectual biography (as well as the more synoptic histories of thought built on the same model) is subject first of all to the obvious difficulty that the literal meanings of key terms sometimes change over time, so that a given writer may say something with a quite different sense and reference from the one which may occur to the reader. Consider, for example, the reception of Berkeley's immaterialism at the hands of his contemporary critics. Both Baxter and Reid remarked on the 'egoism' of Berkeley's outlook, and it was under this heading that Berkeley appeared in the *Encyclopédie*.[129] It is thus of some consequence to know that if Berkeley's contemporaries had intended to accuse him of what we should mean by egoism, they would have been much more likely to refer to something like his 'Hobbism'. When they spoke of his 'egoism', what they meant was something much more like what we should mean by solipsism.[130] Such reminders perhaps provide the most convenient means of countering the Fregean assumption that meanings must somehow be timeless. A more interesting and intractable objection however to the attempt to make the text in itself a self-sufficient object of understanding is suggested by the various oblique strategies which a writer may always decide to adopt in order to set out and at the same time to disguise what he means by what he says about some given doctrine. Such obliqueness may also be the result, of course, of ignorance or inadvertence. (It is possible, for example, consistently to say something other than what I mean to convey, perhaps due to a misunderstanding of the meanings of the words I use.) Some such examples can be important (for instance in translating), but I shall concentrate here on the central and simpler case of using oblique reference as a deliberate strategy. To take a necessarily simplified example (for the issue itself is plainly very complex), consider the case of the doctrine of religious toleration, as it presented itself to English intellectuals at the time of the English Toleration Act. There is no doubt that the various contributions to the discussion all reflect a common intention and thus a common theme. It could only be as the result, however, of a most sophisticated historical investigation (the character of which remains to be delineated) that we could come to recognize, say, that Defoe's proposed *Experiment* for dealing with dissenters, Hoadly's *Letter* to the Pope about the powers of the Church, and Locke's *Letter concerning Toleration* all reflect a common intention to say something very similar about the doctrine involved. A study simply of what each writer said about the doctrine would more or less guarantee blank misunderstanding of Defoe, and at least considerable confusion about Hoadly. Only Locke seems to say anything resembling what he seems to mean, and even here we might wish (perhaps remembering Swift) to find some means of assuring ourselves that no irony was intended. The problem is not to be resolved, moreover (*pace* Professor Strauss) simply by saying that this must be a case in which the writers were unable to say what they meant (so that their meaning must be decoded by reading between the lines). The problem is rather that we need to understand what strategies have been *voluntarily* adopted to convey their meaning with deliberate obliqueness. And the point is that it is hard to see how any amount of reading the text 'over and over again', as we are exhorted to do,[131] could possibly serve as the means to gain this understanding.

The most intractable form of this problem about oblique strategies – and the form most inimical to the view that a given writer's text can serve as an autonomous object of understanding – arises when there is some question as to whether it is 'historically more credible' to say of a writer that he 'believed what he wrote' than to suggest that what he said was insincerely meant, that he 'wrote with his tongue in his cheek'.[132] It has indeed been recently suggested in an important discussion that 'our conviction as to an author's sincerity' is perhaps the issue with most 'particular relevance' to any discussion about the place of intentionality in the understanding of works of literature. No examples, however, of the issues thus raised were given in this discussion.[133] It seems appropriate, therefore, to give some more consideration to this issue as it arises in practice, especially as the question has recently been posed by historians of ideas in a notable way in the exegetical literature on two important figures, Hobbes and Bayle. In the case of Hobbes, the doctrine he enunciated about the laws of nature included both the claim that the laws of nature are the laws of God, and that men are obliged to obey the laws of nature. It has been traditional to dismiss these overt sentiments as the work of an arch-sceptic slyly pressing a familiar vocabulary into the most heterodox use. The trend in much recent exegesis, however, has been to insist (the form of words is very revealing) that Hobbes must after all have 'meant quite seriously what he so often says, that the "Natural Law" is the command of God, and to be obeyed because it is God's command'.[134] Hobbes' scepticism is thus treated as a disguise: when it is shrugged off, he emerges as the exponent of a thoroughly Kantian doctrine. Similarly with Bayle, whose *Dictionary* contains most of the doctrines appropriate to a Calvinist theology of the most rigorous and unforgiving kind. It has again been traditional to dismiss this overt message by appealing to the presence of a desperate, systematic irony. Again, however, the trend of the best recent literatures has been to insist that, so far from being the prototype of the sneering *philosophes*, Bayle must be seen as a genuinely religious thinker,[135] a man of faith[136] with 'solid roots in the religious tradition'.[137]

I am not concerned here to ask directly which of these interpretations may be said to offer the best account of Hobbes' or Bayle's texts. I am concerned only to point out the inadequacy of the methodology by which these new interpretations have been guided and established. It has been insisted that 'a close study of the texts',[138] a concentration on the texts 'for themselves'[139] will be sufficient to make the case for the new interpretations. It does not seem to have been recognized, however, that the acceptance of these interpretations as textually correct entails the acceptance of some much less obviously correct assumptions about Hobbes, Bayle, and the age in which they both lived. First, both Hobbes and Bayle were accepted not only by the

philosophes as their great predecessors in iconoclasm (a verdict also record-
ed on Hobbes by Bayle himself) but were also understood in the same way by
all their contemporary opponents and sympathizers. It was never doubted
that each had intended to deal both ironically and destructively with the
prevailing theological orthodoxies. (Nor is there any difficulty in principle
about accepting that both had the capacity to deal in sustained irony in the
necessary way. Even if Hobbes' tone in the fourth Book of *Leviathan* is not
certain, there can be little doubt about the ironic form of a work like Bayle's
Various Thoughts on the Comet.)[140] It is possible, of course, though very
difficult, to dismiss this point by insisting on the (very remarkable) coinci-
dence that all of Hobbes's and all of Bayle's contemporary opponents were
all equally, and in exactly the same way, mistaken as to their real intentions.
The point is, however, that to accept this unlikely assumption is merely to
raise a second peculiar difficulty, about Hobbes and Bayle themselves.[141]
Both had particular cause to recognize that religious heterodoxy was a very
dangerous commitment. Hobbes lived for a time in dread (according to
Aubrey) lest the Bishops bring in 'a motion to have the good old gentleman
burn't for a heretique'.[142] Bayle even suffered the ironic fate of having his
professorship at Sedan removed for being anti-Catholic, and later of having
his professorship at Rotterdam removed for not being anti-Catholic enough.
If it is still true, then, that both these writers intended their works to
propagate orthodox religious sentiment, it becomes impossible to understand why neither of them removed from later editions of their works – as
both could have done, and Bayle was even asked to do – those portions which
were apparently so completely misunderstood, and why neither of them
spent any time in attempting to correct the apparent misconceptions which
immediately arose and were publicized[143] about the intentions of their
works. The importance of these implications is of course that they suggest
how far the texts of both Hobbes and Bayle raise issues which a study simply
of the texts themselves then becomes quite inadequate to resolve. If we are
now led by these implications to doubt that the texts do convey in what they
say what they were intended to mean, this is to adopt an interpretation on
the strength of evidence quite outside the texts themselves. But if we now
wish to go on insisting that the texts do mean what they say, we are now
left with the problem of trying to account for the peculiar implications of
this view. The point is that whichever view we now take, the text in itself
is shown to be insufficient as the object of our inquiry and understanding.

Any attempt, in intellectual biography, to concentrate on the texts themselves thus completely fails to deal with the problems raised by what I have
called oblique strategies. I turn now to the analogous type of inadequacy
which marks the method of concentrating instead on the 'idea' itself as a
'unit',[144] and so of 'tracking a grand but elusive theme' either throughout a
period or even 'over many centuries'.[145] The danger that such an approach

may simply engender empirically false claims has already been skilfully pointed out for at least one classic case of this tendency to find what has been called 'spurious persistence'.[146] The mistake which is involved, for example, in trying to insist that the thirteenth century and the Enlightenment were both pre-eminently 'ages of faith' (and thus have much more in common than the *philosophes* themselves would have cared to admit)[147] is clearly the mistake of taking the word for the thing. For to speak of an age of faith, it has been neatly observed, may equally well be to speak of an age of submission (faith rather than argument) or an age of confidence (faith in oneself).[148] The notion that any fixed 'idea' has persisted is spurious. My concern here, however, is not empirical but conceptual: not to insist that such histories can sometimes go wrong, but that they can never go right. My point is that even if we restrict the study of an 'idea' to a given historical period – so that the problem raised by this type of changed connotation is ruled out – there is still an underlying conceptual confusion in any attempt to focus on an idea itself as an appropriate unit of historical investigation.

Consider for example the attempt to write the history of the idea of *nobilitas* in the Renaissance – a quite plausible enterprise, very similar to many that have been carried out. The historian might begin, quite properly, by pointing out that the meaning of the term is given by the fact that it was used to refer to a particularly prized moral quality. Or he might, equally properly, point out that the same term was also used to denote membership of a particular social class. It might not in practice be clear which meaning we are to understand in a given case. When Bacon remarked, for example, that nobility adds majesty to a monarch, but diminishes power, we might, remembering his admiration for Machiavelli, think of the first meaning as readily as we might, remembering his official position, think of the second. A further problem, moreover, is raised by the fact that this ambiguity sometimes seems to have been used by Renaissance moralists in a studied way. Sometimes the aim is to insist that one might have noble qualities even if one lacked noble birth. This possibility that men might rightly be called noble 'more for remembrance of their virtue than for discrepance of estates' is a frequent paradox in Renaissance moral thought.[149] But sometimes the aim is rather to insist that while nobility is a matter of attainment, it happens to be invariably connected with nobility of birth. This possibility, indeed, was understandably even more commonly pointed out.[150] It was always open to the moralist, moreover, to turn the basic ambiguity against the concept of *nobilitas* itself, in order to contrast nobility of birth with accompanying baseness of behaviour. It can be argued, for example, that when More in *Utopia* speaks of the behaviour of the military aristocracy as being fittingly noble, he intends to bring the whole concept of nobility into disrepute.[151]

The example is obviously excessively simplified, but it is still sufficient, I believe, to bring out both the two essential criticisms of the project of studying histories of 'ideas' on which I wish to insist. First, it becomes clear that if we wish to understand a given idea, even within a given culture and at a given time, we cannot simply concentrate, à la Lovejoy, on studying the forms of words involved. For the words denoting the idea may be used, as the example indicates, with varying and quite incompatible intentions. We cannot even hope that a sense of the context of utterance will necessarily resolve this problem. For the context, as Bacon's remark indicates, may itself be ambiguous. Rather we must study all the various situations, which may change in complex ways, in which the given form of words can logically be used – all the functions the words can serve, all the various things that can be done with them. The great mistake lies not merely in looking for the 'essential meaning' of the 'idea' as something which must necessarily 'remain the same', but even in thinking of any 'essential' meaning (to which individual writers 'contribute') at all.[152] The appropriate, and famous, formula – famous to philosophers, at least – is rather that we should study not the meanings of the words, but their use. For the given idea cannot ultimately be said in this sense[153] to *have* any meaning that can take the form of a set of words which can then be excogitated and traced out over time. Rather the meaning of the idea must *be* its uses to refer in various ways.[154]

My second and explicitly critical claim clearly follows from this. If there is good reason to insist that we can only study an idea by seeing the nature of all the occasions and activities – the language games – within which it might appear, then there must be correspondingly good reason to insist that the project of studying histories of 'ideas', *tout court*, must rest on a fundamental philosophical mistake. That this is indeed the case, and that it gives rise in practice to unavoidable confusions, can now be readily illustrated. The underlying confusion itself may perhaps be most conveniently characterized, by adopting an extension of the basic distinction between meaning and use, as the result of a failure to distinguish between the *occurrence* of the words (phrases or *sentences*) which denote the given idea, and the *use* of the relevant sentence by a particular agent on a particular occasion with a particular intention (*his* intention) to make a particular *statement*.[155] To write the history of an idea, it may be said, is obviously to write, in effect, the history of a sentence. It is undoubtedly characteristic of such histories that statement-making agents appear more or less only because the relevant ideas – the social contract, the idea of Utopia, the great chain of being, and so on – can be shown to occur in their works, so that they can be said to have contributed to their development. What we cannot learn from any such history is in the first place what part, trivial or important, the given idea may have played in the thought of any individual thinker who happened to mention it, or what place, characteristic or unusual, it may have taken in the intellectual climate of any given period in which it appeared. We may perhaps learn that the expression was used at different times to answer a variety of problems. But what we still cannot learn – to cite Collingwood's very important point[156] – is *what* questions the use of the expression was thought to answer, and so what reasons there were for continuing to employ it. It follows from this that we could never grasp from such a history what *status* the given idea may have had at various times, so that we cannot eventually be said to have gained any proper historical understanding of its importance and value. And in the second place, we cannot learn from such histories either what *point* a given expression might have had for the agents who used it, or what range of uses the expression itself could sustain. And it follows from this that we can never really grasp from such a history what meanings the given expression may have had, so that we cannot eventually be said to gain from such studies any understanding even of the occurrence of the idea itself.

The nature of the criticism to be made of such histories is not merely that they seem perpetually liable in this way to lose any point. It is rather that as soon as we see there *is* no determinate idea to which various writers contributed, but only a variety of statements made with the words by a variety of different agents with a variety of intentions, then what we are seeing is equally that there *is* no history of the idea to be written, but only a history necessarily focused on the various agents who used the idea, and on their varying situations and intentions in using it. Such a history, moreover, can hardly be expected even to retain the form of the history of an idea. If an historian, for example, who studies the idea of Utopia comes to see that the uses to which the idea has been put are bewilderingly various, then it would seem little more than a very misleading fetishism of words to go on trying to make any sort of historical study out of focusing on the 'idea' of Utopia itself – or progress, equality, sovereignty, justice, natural law, and so on and on. For the persistence of such expressions tells us nothing reliable at all about the persistence of the questions which the expressions may have been used to answer, or of the intentions generally of the various writers who may have used the expressions. The only history to be written is thus a history of the various statements made with the given expression. This – rather than the history of the sentence itself – would of course be an almost absurdly ambitious enterprise. But it would at least be conceptually proper, whereas the sentence itself, apart from the statements which various agents may choose to make with it, is simply not a proper object of study – not even by the logician, it has been argued,[157] and certainly not by the historian.

IV

The second of the two methodologies which I mentioned at the outset may well appear at this point to reveal decisive advantages as a way of studying the history of ideas. If it is conceptually improper, in the ways I have suggested, to concentrate simply on a given idea or a given text in itself, perhaps the best approach does consist – as the methodologists themselves increasingly insist – in recognizing instead that our ideas constitute 'a *response* to more immediate circumstances',[158] and that we should in consequence study not the texts in themselves, but rather 'the *context* of other happenings which *explains* them'.[159] It is true that this alternative methodology has been very consciously resisted, in particular by historians of philosophy and by political scientists, both anxious to insist on the autonomy of textual study. For if the point of studying the classics of these disciplines is conceived in terms of their 'timeless wisdom', then it is absolutely essential, as I have already hinted, to be able to insist that even though they may be 'grounded in the social reality' of their age, they 'are also ageless',[160] 'surpassing' the need to consider any such contingent 'reality'.[161] The whole point is endangered unless the 'historical, biographical, and logical baggage which surrounds the "Great Books"' can if necessary be 'ruthlessly thrown overboard'.[162] Nevertheless, the advantage of insisting instead that the baggage of 'social context' will be crucially needed on the voyage seems clear. To adopt this alternative approach is indeed to put one-self in a position to avoid or even to solve many of the exegetical problems I have sought to raise. A knowledge of the social context of a given text seems at least to offer considerable help in avoiding the anachronistic mythologies I have tried to anatomize. And I have already to some extent invoked the need for such knowledge in considering the conceptual inadequacy of purely textual studies. Thus if it is true that an understanding of any idea requires an understanding of all the occasions and activities in which a given agent might have used the relevant form of words, it seems clear that at least a part of such understanding must lie in grasping what sort of society the given author was writing for and trying to persuade. And if it is true that the understanding of a text presupposes the capacity to grasp any oblique strategies it may contain, it is again clear that the relevant information (as I have already sought to prove in the case of Hobbes and Bayle) must at least in part be concerned with the constraints of the given social situation.

The belief that this method of 'contextual reading'[163] does provide the appropriate methodology for the history of ideas, literary as well as philosophical, appears in practice to be becoming increasingly accepted.[164] It is usual now for even the most synoptic histories of classic texts to include both some concession about knowing 'something of social and political conditions',[165] and some gesture toward paying 'due regard' to 'the historical conditions' which 'produced' the texts themselves.[166] And the systematic adoption of this approach has of course produced its own distinctive and increasingly distinguished literature. In the histories of economic and even scientific thought, the method has been classically applied in the form of the claim that the social context of Puritan attitudes explains the rise both of the spirit of capitalist enterprise[167] and of scientific enquiry[168] in the seventeenth century. Similarly, in the histories of social, ethical, and political ideas, much has been written about the theory that modern developments in these spheres of thought mirrored and followed the changes and developments of the social context. Such histories usually begin with the social structure of the Renaissance,[169] and reach their climax with that of seventeenth-century England. The hero of the story is thus Thomas Hobbes, the first as well as the greatest of the distinctively bourgeois philosophers.[170] And the truth of the story is at this point best corroborated, it is said, by considering the position of James Harrington, the first theorist of the 'opportunity state'.[171] (We are still faced, of course, with the purely historical embarrassment that the commentators have been unable to agree on whether the class of which Harrington was the ideologist was rising or falling in power. But it is essential to recognize that even Professors Tawney and Trevor-Roper agreed on one essential point about the gentry: that Harrington was 'their champion',[172] and that the key to understanding what Harrington must have been saying is thus to be found in the study of the social structure which he analysed.) When this point in the story is reached, moreover, the rest of its development, up to the time when capitalism is said to have caused the characteristic alienation of the intellectuals, typically consists of a story essentially about whether and how far each classic writer accepted and so reflected the new social structure. The explanation of Locke's thought is thus that he accepted the new structure with enthusiasm: this explains what he has to say about property.[173] The explanation of Bolingbroke's thought is that he was more enthusiastic about the social structure which was passing away: this explains his 'politics of nostalgia'.[174] The explanation of Adam Smith's thought is that he accepted the new structure, but for reasons unconcerned with its own ends: this explains the apparent contradictions as well as the real (moral) message of his thought.[175]

If it is true that the relations between the context of any given statement (or any other action)[176] and the statement itself do take the form, in this way, of a relation between antecedent causal conditions and their results, then it is clear that the independent life of ideas in history must be correspondingly in danger.[177] One paradoxical result of the widespread acceptance of this methodology of contextual study has in consequence been to panic the historians of ideas into the suspicion that their subject may not really 'exist' after all.[178] And the main result has been to commit even the best current practitioners to a formula which quite simply begs all the questions: the social context, it is said, helps to cause the formation and change of ideas; but the ideas in turn help to cause the formation and change of the social context.[179] Thus the historian of ideas ends up by presenting himself with nothing better than the time-honoured puzzle about the chicken and the egg, while the more hard-headed historian of 'reality' congratulates himself on having devalued such an unprofitable exercise.[180]

It is my essential contention, however, that none of this panic or equivocation is at all well-judged, since the methodology of contextual reading, in both its Marxist and Namierite versions (they are oddly similar) can itself be shown to rest on a fundamental mistake about the nature of the relations between action and circumstance.[181] Despite the possibility, therefore, that a study of social context may *help* in the understanding of a text, which I have conceded, the fundamental assumption of the contextual methodology, that the ideas of a given text should be understood *in terms of* its social context, can be shown to be mistaken, and to serve in consequence not as the guide to understanding, but as the source of further very prevalent confusions in the history of ideas.

The fact that a knowledge of the context of a given text does *help* in understanding it reflects the fact, surely undeniable, that for the performance of any action – and the making of statements is surely to be appraised as a *performance*[182] – it will always be possible, at least in principle, to discover a set of conditions either such that the action (the statement made) might have been different or might not have occurred in their absence, or even such that the occurrence of the action might have been predicted from their presence. There seems no question that for every statement there must be *some* explanatory context, for every action *some* set of antecedent causal conditions.[183] To concentrate instead on the alleged affective states of the agent as the means to provide an *alternative* (teleological) mode of explanation of a given statement or other action seems at the very least to ignore[184] a good deal of information which is bound to be relevant to any attempted explanation. Conversely, the hypothesis that the context of a text can be used to explain its content may be said to illustrate, but also to gain strength from, the more general and increasingly accepted hypothesis that actions performed at will are to be accounted for by the ordinary processes of causal explanation.[185]

It may well be strenuously doubted, however, whether a knowledge of the causes of an action is really equivalent to an understanding of the action itself. For as well as – and quite apart from – the fact that such an understanding does presuppose a grasp of antecedent causal *conditions* of the action taking place, it might equally be said to presuppose a grasp of the *point* of the action for the agent who performed it. It is a striking fact about current discussions of the claim that actions are caused that they tend to be mounted in terms of such excessively simple and routine examples – always things like putting on one's coat,[186] never things like writing the *Iliad*[187] – that the question of the *point* of the action is very easily made to seem wholly transparent, or quite unimportant. And it is a further striking fact that the examples which have made it seem most plausible to suppose that puzzles about actions may be resolved simply by stating the conditions of their occurrence have often been those in which a lawyer could speak of diminished responsibility and in which we might more colloquially speak of behaving *pointlessly* – cases of being drunk or drugged, of losing one's temper, and so on.[188]

It is true of course that a somewhat scholastic device can be applied at this point to rescue the claim that even fully intended and complex actions are best understood as the results of causes. For a motive or an intention, it is said, is *itself* a cause, in the sense that it is antecedent to and contingently connected with the resulting action.[189] I may intend to do something, but never do it. This is said to discredit any Wittgensteinian notion to the effect that there can be any closer 'logical' connection (perhaps of a syllogistic character)[190] between intentions and actions. This riposte has been regarded as deadly,[191] but it appears to rest on two crucial misconceptions about the procedures by which we may be said to come to an understanding at least of that subset of actions – the making of statements – with which I am here concerned. It is thus my central claim that a consideration of these two misconceptions in turn will serve to discredit the notion that a study of the contextual conditions of making statements can in any sense be regarded as a sufficient or even appropriate methodology for the understanding of statements made.

First, the notion that intentions are contingently connected with actions seems to rest on a pun or confusion between two different senses in which the concept of intention can validly be applied. Suppose that Defoe, in writing about toleration, had stated, as he might have done, his intention to compose a whole series of pamphlets on the subject. As he never did so, what we have here is a stated intention unaccompanied by any resulting action: the best proof that the relation between the two concepts must be of a contingent, and so can be of a causal, character. Suppose, however that Defoe had stated, as again he might have done, that his intention in the pamphlet which he did write on toleration was to promote this cause by parodying the arguments against it. What we have here is an intention not antecedent to and contingently related with his actual statements at all: rather the statement of intention serves to characterize the action itself. And it is purely scholastic to reply that even this intention must precede the action, and thus might still be treated as an antecedent condition. For statements of intention of this kind can quite validly be made to characterize an action *after* it has been performed. The distinction, in short, is between an intention *to do x* which may never successfully issue in an action – though it is not made clear what we should say if such prior statements of intention *never* issued in actions – and an intention *in doing x*, which not merely presupposes the occurrence of the relevant action, but is logically connected with it in the sense that it serves to characterize its *point*. The significance of this claim for my present argument will by now be clear. Every statement made or other action performed must presuppose an intention to have done it – call it a cause if you like – but also an intention in doing it, which cannot be a cause, but which must be grasped if the action itself is to be correctly characterized and so understood.

It might perhaps be claimed, however, that this argument is insufficient to cope with the strongest form of the contextual thesis.[192] It is in effect an argument about what a given agent may have *meant* by making a given statement. But the claim made on behalf of the study of contexts was precisely that they can in themselves serve to yield what the text must mean. This only points, however, to the second mistaken assumption on which this methodology appears to rest, the assumption that 'meaning' and 'understanding' are in fact strictly correlative terms. It has been classically demonstrated, however, by J. L. Austin, that the understanding of statements presupposes a grasp not merely of the meaning of the given utterance, but also of what Austin labelled its intended illocutionary force.[193] This claim is crucially relevant to my present argument in two respects. First, this further question about what a given agent may be *doing* in uttering his utterance is not a question about meaning at all, but about a force co-ordinate with the meaning of the utterance itself, *and yet* essential to grasp in order to understand it.[194] And second, even if we could decode what a given statement must mean from a study of its social context, it follows that this would still leave us without any grasp of its intended illocutionary force, and so eventually without any real understanding of the given statement after all. The point is, in short, that an unavoidable lacuna remains: even if the study of the social context of texts could serve to *explain* them, this would not amount to the same as providing the means to *understand* them.

This central claim – that the grasp of force as well as meaning is essential to the understanding of texts, and yet cannot be supplied from the study of their social context – can readily be illustrated in practice. Suppose an historian comes across the following statement in a Renaissance moral tract: 'a prince must learn how not to be virtuous'. Suppose that the sense and the intended reference of the statement are both perfectly clear. Suppose even that this clarity is the result of a study of the entire social context of the utterance – a study which might have revealed, say, that virtue in princes had in fact led to their ruin at the time. Now suppose two alternative truths about the statement itself: either that such cynical advice was frequently offered in Renaissance moral tracts; or that scarcely anyone had ever publicly offered such cynical advice as a precept before. It is obvious that any commentator wishing to understand the statement must find out which of these alternatives is nearer the truth. If the answer is the first alternative, the intended force of the utterance itself in the mind of the agent who uttered it can only have been to endorse or emphasize an accepted moral attitude. But if the answer is the second, the intended force of the utterance becomes more like that of rejecting or repudiating an established moral commonplace. Now it happens in fact that something like each of these historical claims has been advanced in turn by historians of ideas about the statement to this effect to be found in Machiavelli's *Prince*.[195] Now it is obvious not merely that only one of these claims can be correct, but also that the decision on which one *is* correct will very greatly affect any understanding of what Machiavelli can have been intending to achieve. Potentially the question is whether he intended to subvert or to sustain one of the more fundamental moral commonplaces of political life in his time. But while such a decision may be said to be crucial in this way to understanding Machiavelli, it is neither the sort of decision which could ever be arrived at from studying the statement itself and its meaning (which is pellucid enough), nor from any amount of study of its social context, for the context itself is evidently capable of yielding *both* of the alternative illocutionary acts, and so can hardly be invoked to reject either in favour of the other. It must follow that in order to be said to have *understood* any statement made in the past, it cannot be enough to grasp what was said, or even to grasp that the meaning of what was said may have changed. It cannot in consequence be enough to study either what the statement meant, or even what its context may be alleged to show about what it must have meant. The further point which must still be grasped for any given statement is *how* what was said was meant, and thus what *relations* there may have been between various different statements even within the same general context.

I have illustrated this claim about the insufficiency and even the potentially wholly misleading character of contextual as well as purely textual study only from the simplest possible type of case. But it is also arguable (as I have elsewhere sought to demonstrate)[196] that Austin's own discussion of illocutionary force needs to be extended, in certain more oblique ways, to deal with the identification of less overt and perhaps even non-avowable illocutionary acts. We need, for example, to be able to deal with the obvious but very elusive fact that a *failure* to use a particular argument may always be a polemical matter, and thus a required guide to the understanding of the relevant utterance. Consider, for example, the failure of Locke to use any historical arguments in the *Second Treatise*. Since the discussion of political principles in seventeenth-century England virtually hinged on the study of rival versions of the English past,[197] a strong case could perhaps be made for saying that Locke's failure to mention these issues constituted perhaps the most radical and original feature of his whole argument. As a clue to the understanding of Locke's text, this is obviously important: but it is a clue which the study of the social context (still less the text itself) could never be made to yield. Similarly, we need to be able to cope with the intractable possibility that certain of the classic philosophical texts may contain quite a large number of what contemporaries would instantly have seen to be jokes. Plato and Hobbes perhaps spring to mind: again, this would obviously be an important clue to the understanding of their texts, but, again, it is hard to see how either of the approved methodologies can help. And similarly, questions of allusion and oblique reference generally clearly raise important problems of recognition and correspondingly obvious dangers of misunderstanding any text in which they figure prominently. These and other such problems are obviously too intrinsically complex to illustrate briefly here, but they may already serve to underline the central point, which the simpler examples have, I think, sufficiently made clear: that to concentrate either on studying a text in itself, or on studying its social context as a means of determining the meaning of the text, is to make it impossible to recognize – let alone to solve – some of the most difficult issues about the conditions for understanding texts.

V

If my argument so far has been correct, two positive and general conclusions can now be shown to follow from it. The first concerns the appropriate method by which to study the history of ideas. On the one hand, it must be a mistake even to try either to write intellectual biographies concentrating on the works of a given writer, or to write histories of ideas tracing the morphology of a given concept over time. Both these types of study (not to mention the pedagogic histories of thought which combine their demerits) are necessarily misconceived. On the other hand, it does not follow, as is sometimes claimed,[198] that no particular way of studying the history of ideas is any more satisfactory than any other. My first positive conclusion is rather that the whole trend of my argument points to an alternative methodology which need not be open to any of the criticisms I have so far advanced. The understanding of texts, I have sought to insist, presupposes the grasp both of what they were intended to mean, and how this meaning was intended to be taken. It follows from this that to understand a text must be to understand both the intention to be understood, and the intention that this intention should be understood, which the text itself as an intended act of communication must at least have embodied. The essential question which we therefore confront, in studying any given text, is what its author, in writing at the time he did write for the audience he intended to address, could in practice have been intending to communicate by the utterance of this given utterance. It follows that the essential aim, in any attempt to understand the utterances themselves, must be to recover this complex intention on the part of the author. And it follows from this that the appropriate methodology for the history of ideas must be concerned, first of all, to delineate the whole

range of communications which could have been conventionally performed
on the given occasion by the utterance of the given utterance, and, next,
to trace the relations between the given utterance and this wider *linguistic*
context as a means of decoding the actual intention of the given writer.
Once the appropriate focus of the study is seen in this way to be essentially
linguistic and the appropriate methodology is seen in consequence to be
concerned in this way with the recovery of intentions, the study of all the
facts about the social context of the given text can then take its place as
a part of this linguistic enterprise. The problem about the way in which
these facts are handled in the methodology of contextual study is that they
get fitted into an inappropriate framework. The 'context' mistakenly gets
treated as the determinant of what is said. It needs rather to be treated as an
ultimate framework for helping to decide what conventionally recognizable
meanings, in a society of *that* kind, it might in principle have been possible
for someone to have intended to communicate. (In this way, as I have sought
to prove in the case of Hobbes and Bayle, the context itself can be used as a
sort of court of appeal for assessing the relative plausibility of incompatible
ascriptions of intentionality.) I do not suggest, of course, that this conclusion
is in itself particularly novel.[199] What I do claim is that the critical survey I
have conducted may be said to establish and prove the case for this methodology – to establish it not as a suggestion, an aesthetic preference, or a piece
of academic imperialism, but as a matter of conceptual propriety, a matter of
seeing what the necessary conditions are for the understanding of utterances.

My second general conclusion concerns the value of studying the
history of ideas. The most exciting possibility here, which I cannot now
explore, but which I have touched on in discussing both the causes of
action and the conditions for understanding statements, is the possibility
of a dialogue between philosophical discussion and historical evidence. It is
clear that the distinctions which have been established in the debates over
the causes and meanings of actions are not merely of use to historians, but
essential for historians to grasp, although – with damaging consequences
– they have not so far shown much consciousness of this fact. The
point here, however, is that the converse of this may also be true.
The understanding of statements uttered in the past clearly raises special
issues, and might yield special insights, especially about the conditions
under which languages change. The philosophers have perhaps been rather
slow to take advantage of the possibly very large significance of this fact,
both for the analysis of meaning and understanding,[200] as well as for the
discussion of the relations between belief and action, and in general
over the whole question of the sociology of knowledge.

My main conclusion however, is that the critique I have mounted
already serves to suggest a much more obvious and less remote point
about the philosophical value of studying the history of ideas. On the one

hand, it has I think become clear that any attempt to justify the study of the subject in terms of the 'perennial problems' and 'universal truths' to be learned from the classic texts must amount to the purchase of justification at the expense of making the subject itself foolishly and needlessly naive. Any statement, as I have sought to show, is inescapably the embodiment of a particular intention, on a particular occasion, addressed to the solution of a particular problem, and thus specific to its situation in a way that it can only be naive to try to transcend. The vital implication here is not merely that the classic texts cannot be concerned with our questions and answers, but only with their own. There is also the further implication that – to revive Collingwood's way of putting it – there simply are no perennial problems in philosophy: there are only individual answers to individual questions, and as many different questions as there are questioners. There is in consequence simply no hope of seeking the point of studying the history of ideas in the attempt to learn directly from the classic authors by focusing on their attempted answers to supposedly timeless questions.

This overwhelming element of contingency in the alleged answers provided by the classic texts has frequently been emphasized, but I believe it can be shown, in the light of the critique I have tried to mount, that the precise nature of the point to be made about this issue has been misunderstood by Collingwood as well as by his critics. Collingwood's own misunderstanding derived, I think, from the fact that he chose to link his attack on 'perennial questions' with an excessively strong thesis to the effect that we cannot even ask if a given philosopher 'solved the problem he set himself', since we can only see what the problem was for him if he did solve it. Thus 'the fact that we can identify his problem is proof that he has solved it; for we can only know what the problem was by arguing back from the solution'.[201] But this merely seems to be a version of the confusion I have already sought to point out between an intention *to do* something and an intention *in doing* something. It is true that unless I do perform the action or solve the problem which I intended *to* do, then it can never be known what my problem was – for there will simply be no evidence. It does not follow, however, that you cannot ever know what I intended *to* do unless I did it – for I may have stated, even if not executed, my intention. Nor does it follow that you cannot know what my intention *in* trying to do something was unless I succeeded in doing it – for it is often quite easy to characterize (to decode the intention *in*) an attempted but wholly unsuccessful action. (It may be quite clear, for example, that Defoe intended a parody in writing his *Experiment*, even though the intention was so disastrously misunderstood that we might well say of the intended action that it was unsuccessfully performed.) A further misunderstanding, however, seems to be revealed by those who have criticized this attack of Collingwood's on the idea of perennial problems. It has even been insisted, for example, in an important recent discussion, that when 'Lenin says that every cook ought to be a politician and Plato that men ought to restrict themselves to the exercise of their special function in the state', then this *is* for Plato and Lenin to be concerned with the 'same problem', so that it is merely an *a priori* judgement to deny that any perennial issue is involved.[202] But the claim on which historians of ideas have insisted has not merely been that there may be some semantic sameness of this kind, but that the problem is the same in the sense that we may hope directly to learn from a study of the solution Plato offers of it. It is this sameness, indeed, which is said to constitute the whole reason for studying Plato's *Replublic*.[203] But it is in this sense that the problem simply cannot be the same in both cases at all. For if we are to learn from Plato, it is not enough that the discussion should seem, at a very abstract level, to pose a question relevant to us. It is also essential that the answer Plato gave should seem relevant and indeed applicable (if he is 'right') to our own culture and period. As soon as we begin to study Plato's actual arguments, however, the sense in which the issue of participation is the same for himself and ourselves dissolves into absurdity. What we are most likely to learn from Plato is that the cook should not participate because he is a slave. It is hard to see what problems of participation in modern representative democracies are likely to be advanced by the application of this particular piece of perennial wisdom, decisive though the argument would undoubtedly have seemed to Plato himself.

This reformulation and insistence on the claim that there are no perennial problems in philosophy, from which we can hope to learn directly through sstudying the classic texts, is not of course intended as a denial of the possibility that there may be propositions (perhaps in mathematics) the truth of which is wholly tenseless. (This does not yet amount to showing that their truth is any less contingent for that.) It is not even a denial of the possibility that there may be apparently perennial *questions*, if these are sufficiently abstractly framed. All I wish to insist is that whenever it is claimed that the point of the historical study of such questions is that we may learn directly from the *answers*, it will be found that what *counts* as an answer will usually look, in a different culture or period, so different in itself that it can hardly be in the least useful even to go on thinking of the relevant question as being 'the same' in the required sense at all. More crudely: we must learn to do our own thinking for ourselves.

It is by no means my conclusion, however, that because the philosophical value at present claimed for the history of ideas rests on a misconception, it must follow that the subject has no philosophical value in itself at all. For it is the very fact that the classic texts are concerned with their own quite alien problems, and not the presumption that they are somehow concerned with our own problems as well, which seems to me to give not the lie but the key to the indispensable value of studying the history of ideas.

The classic texts, especially in social, ethical, and political thought, help to reveal – if we let them – not the essential sameness, but rather the essential variety of viable moral assumptions and political commitments. It is in this, moreover, that their essential philosophical, even moral, value can be seen to lie. There is a tendency (sometimes explicitly urged, as by Hegel, as a mode of proceeding) to suppose that the best, not merely the inescapable, point of vantage from which to survey the ideas of the past must be that of our present situation, because it is by definition the most highly evolved. Such a claim cannot survive a recognition of the fact that historical differences over fundamental issues may reflect differences of intention and convention rather than anything like a competition over a community of values, let alone anything like an evolving perception of the Absolute. To recognize, moreover, that our own society is no different from any other in having its own local beliefs and arrangements of social and political life is already to have reached a quite different and, I should wish to argue, a very much more salutary point of vantage. A knowledge of the history of such ideas can then serve to show the extent to which those features of our own arrangements which we may be disposed to accept as traditional or even 'timeless' truths[204] may in fact be the merest contingencies of our peculiar history and social structure. To discover from the history of thought that there are in fact no such timeless concepts, but only the various different concepts which have gone with various different societies, is to discover a general truth not merely about the past but about ourselves as well. Furthermore, it is commonplace – we are all Marxists to this extent – that our own society places unrecognized constraints upon our imaginations. It deserves, then, to become a commonplace that the historical study of the ideas of other societies should be undertaken as the indispensable and the irreplacable means of placing limits on those constraints. The allegation that the history of ideas consists of nothing more than 'outworn metaphysical notions', which is frequently advanced at the moment, with terrifying parochialism, as a reason for ignoring such a history, would then come to be seen as the very reason for regarding such histories as indispensably 'relevant', not because crude 'lessons' can be picked out of them, but because the history itself provides a lesson in self-knowledge. To demand from the history of thought a solution to our own immediate problems is thus to commit not merely a methodological fallacy, but something like a moral error. But to learn from the past – and we cannot otherwise learn at all – the distinction between what is necessary and what is the product merely of our own contingent arrangements, is to learn the key to self-awareness itself.[205]

3

Motives, intentions and the interpretation of texts

The main question I wish to raise is whether it is possible to lay down any general rules about how to interpret a literary text.[1] This presupposes, however, that one is clear both about what is meant by the process of interpretation and why it is necessary to undertake this process at all. I shall begin, therefore, with the briefest possible consideration of these two issues as a preliminary to my main discussion.

What is 'interpretation'? Professor Aiken has complained that the term is habitually used 'with abominable looseness by critics and philosophers of art'.[2] It does seem to be agreed, however, by most literary theorists that when we attempt to interpret a text, what we are basically trying to do is 'to construe it to mean something'.[3] As Bloomfield puts it, 'if we interpret a work of art, we are seeking its significance'.[4] Two words of caution are perhaps in order here. We must certainly be careful to avoid the vulgarity – which philosophers of art are much more prone to than practising critics – of supposing that we can ever hope to arrive at '*the* correct reading' of a text, such that we may speak of having finally determined its meaning and thereby ruled out any alternative interpretations.[5] And we must be careful not to assume too readily that the business of interpretation need always be entirely a reading process.[6] As long as these caveats are borne in mind, however, there seems no objection to saying that the concept of interpretation can briefly be defined as a matter of 'getting at the message' of a text,[7] and of decoding and making explicit its meaning, in such a way that the best reading, rendering what Hirsch has called the 'best meaning', can thereby be attained.[8]

Why is this process necessary? Why do we need to consider the business of interpreting the meaning of a text as a special and indispensable technique?

Two contrasting types of answer have usually been given. One stresses the interaction between the text and the reader, and sees the need for interpretation in phenomenological terms as response to the reader's ever-changing sense of what he has read, and his ever-present need 'to fit everything together into a consistent pattern'.[9] The other, more conventional answer stresses that any literary work of any interest will virtually by definition be an object of considerable intrinsic complexity, characteristically employing such devices as irony, allusion and a whole range of symbolic and allegorical effects. The need for interpretation is thus seen in terms of the need to make the given work 'more accessible to the reader'.[10] According to a well-worn metaphor, the point is that we must be prepared to '*go beyond* the plain literal sense' in order to disclose the full meaning of the work.[11] Or according to an even more seductive metaphor, we must be prepared to probe *below the surface* of a text in order to attain a full understanding of its meaning.

This brings me to the main question I wish to consider. If we grant that the main aim of the interpreter must be to establish the *meaning* of a text, and if we grant that the meaning is to be found 'beyond' or 'below' its surface, can we hope to frame any general rules about how this meaning may be recovered? Or are we eventually compelled to adopt what Hirsch has called the 'resigned opinion' that 'our various schools and approaches' are no more than dogmatic theologies, generating a corresponding 'multitude of warring sects'.[12]

There is one general rule of interpretation which can obviously be stated at once, since it amounts to nothing more than a massive truism. It is that 'good critical practice depends above all on close and sensitive reading' of the text itself.[13] There is a powerful recent tradition of critical theory, moreover, which has been concerned to derive from this truism a second general interpretative rule. Stated positively, this is that the critic must focus on the text and *only* the text in the attempt to interpret it. To cite Cleanth Brooks, the rule is that 'the closest possible examination of what the poem says as a poem' is all that the interpreter needs to undertake.[14] Or to quote F. R. Leavis, the claim is that 'the text, duly pondered, will yield its meaning and value to an adequate intelligence and sensibility'.[15] Stated negatively, and in the form in which this claim has usually been debated, the rule is that the critic should not attempt to pay any attention to biographical matters, to questions about the writer's motives and intentions, in arriving at his interpretation of the work.[16] To move away from the text itself to a consideration of these factors is to commit 'the intentional fallacy'; to interpret the text, the critic must concentrate his attention exclusively on the text itself.

My aim in what follows will be to focus on this second suggested interpretative rule and to comment on the nature and cogency of the arguments which have recently been advanced for and against it.

The rule is: The critic should not attempt to pay any attention to a writer's motives and intentions in the attempt to establish the meaning of his works. The first stage in any attempted analysis of this claim must consist of trying to get clearer about the sense of 'meaning' which is at issue here. For there seem to be at least three discriminable senses of the term which have become assimilated together in most existing theoretical discussions about interpreting 'the meaning' of texts.

The first is that to ask about meaning in this context may be equivalent to asking: What do the words mean, or what do certain specific words or sentences mean, in this work? (I shall call this meaning$_1$.) It seems to be meaning$_1$ which Wimsatt and Beardsley mainly have in mind in their classic essay on the alleged intentional fallacy. They speak of explicating 'the semantics and the syntax' of a poem, 'through our habitual knowledge of the language, through grammars, dictionaries' and so on. When they turn to discuss a poem by T. S. Eliot, they concentrate on the need to decode 'the meaning of phrases in the poem', and in speaking generally about biographical evidence they allow it to be relevant when it provides 'evidence of the meaning of his words'.[17] The second sense is that we may instead be asking: What does this work mean to me? (I shall call this meaning$_2$.) This is the sense which the exponents of the New Criticism usually seem to have in mind when they speak about 'structures of effects' and the need to concentrate on assessing their impact on the reader. The same sense of meaning also seems to underlie the phenomenological approach to literary criticism. When Iser, for example, insists on treating the reading process as a 'realisation' of the text 'accomplished by the reader,' he seems mainly preoccupied with meaning$_2$, especially when he argues that 'one must take into account not only the actual text but also, and in equal measure, the actions involved in responding to that text'.[18] Finally, we may be asking: What does the writer mean by what he says in this work? (I shall call this meaning$_3$.) Sometimes it seems to be this sense of meaning which Wimsatt and Beardsley have in mind. When they speak, for example, of the 'pursuit of full meanings' rendered necessary when a writer has a habit of alluding,[19] they no longer seem to be referring to meaning$_1$, which could scarcely be affected by the specific use of a phrase to allude. It seems they must be referring to meaning$_3$ – to what a writer may have meant by making such a use of that particular phrase. Sometimes it is obviously this third sense of meaning which a literary critic has in mind. It is this sense, for example, which seems to underlie both the account which Bloomfield gives of a work of art having 'a meaning or organisation'[20] and the distinction which Hirsch offers between meaning and significance where 'meaning' is 'defined *tout court* as that which a text is taken to represent'.[21]

I now turn to the nature of the arguments which have been advanced in favour of the claim that a critic should not attempt to pay any attention to a writer's motives and intentions in the attempt to establish 'the meaning' of a text. Two types of argument can be distinguished. One is concerned with the need for purity in critical procedures, and thus with the claim that, even if it may be possible to discover biographical information about a writer, the critic must not allow such information to condition and so contaminate his response to the writer's work. The desire to consider anything other than the information provided by the text itself is thus stigmatized by Wimsatt and Beardsley as a 'romantic fallacy'. The claim, as a recent critic of this outlook has expressed it, is that 'the work of art should provide the data for our understanding, it should be self-explicatory. To call in aid necessary information obtained from biographical or historical sources is a failure of art and criticism.'[22]

The second and main type of argument, however, against any attempt to pay attention to biographical information, derives from two contrasting (indeed incompatible) claims which are habitually made about the concepts of motive and intention themselves. The first is that it is because a writer's motives and intentions stand 'outside' his works, and thus form no part of their structure, that the critic should not attempt to pay any attention to them in attempting to elucidate the meaning of a text. This argument, however, seems to have been mounted in a somewhat confused way. It is necessary to distinguish at least three different reasons which have been given for supposing that it follows from the way in which a writer's motives and intentions stand 'outside' his works that they are irrelevant to their interpretation.

One claim has been that motives and intentions are simply impossible to recover. They are 'private entities to which no one can gain access'.[23] This is the first argument advanced by Wimsatt and Beardsley, who ask 'how a critic expects to get an answer to the question about intention', and who insist that a knowledge of 'design or intention' is simply not 'available' to the critic.[24] The same commitment seems to underlie both Smith's allegation that 'intention is really unknowable' unless we can discover it 'through the medium of the poem'[25] and Gang's comments on 'our inevitable uncertainty about mental processes'.[26] A Cartesian picture of the mind seems at this point to provide the basis for the anti-intentionalist case.

A second claim has been that while it may after all be possible to recover a writer's motives and intentions, to pay attention to such information will be to provide an undesirable standard for measuring the value of what he writes. Wimsatt and Beardsley shift somewhat inconsistently to this ground at an early stage of their discussion of the intentionalist fallacy, claiming that a knowledge of a writer's intentions is not 'desirable as a standard of judging the success of a work of literary art'.[27] Gang also seems to shift to this position when he claims that 'the problem is how far the author's intention in writing a work is relevant to the critic's *judgment* on it'.[28] And so does Smith, when he argues that a concern about intention 'divides the response' of a reader in an apparently undesirable way.[29]

The third claim has been that while it may always be possible to recover a writer's motives and intentions, it will never be *relevant* to pay attention to this type of information if the aim is simply to establish the meaning of a text. Wimsatt and Beardsley eventually shift to this position, insisting that their concern is simply with 'the meaning of a poem' and that the poet's state of mind is a wholly separate matter.[30] An even stronger statement of the same commitment can be found in Ushenko's *The Dynamics of Art*, where it is claimed that 'the intent of the artist is to be counted as one of the antecedents to the aesthetic effect', and that 'an antecedent is no more relevant to the actual work of art than an aftereffect'.[31]

I now turn to the second (and incompatible) claim which is habitually made in this context about the concepts of intention and motive. The reason, it is said, why the critic should not attempt to pay any special attention to these factors is simply that they are 'inside' the work itself, not separate from it, and thus need no separate consideration. A writer, it is said, will normally achieve what he intends to achieve and will normally intend to achieve what he achieves. It follows that all the information we may need to know about these matters will in effect be contained within the texts themselves, and will be revealed by reading them. It is this argument which Hungerland, in criticizing the belief in the intentionalist fallacy, takes to be the main claim of the anti-intentionalist critics. They are claiming that if a writer 'has carried out his intentions successfully, the work itself should show what he was trying to do'.[32] This also seems to be yet another of the grounds on which Wimsatt and Beardsley argue for the irrelevance of intentions to interpretation. They ask how the critic should try 'to find out what the poet tried to do'. And they answer that 'if the poet succeeded in doing it, then the poem itself shows what he was trying to do'.[33] The same view seems to have been adopted by several more recent commentators on the intentionalist fallacy. Smith cites the formula, which he attributes to the influence of Brooks and of Warren, that 'a good poem is one that is successful in fulfilling its intentions'.[34] Gang insists that 'whenever something is plainly and unambiguously said, it hardly makes sense to ask the speaker what he intended his words to signify'.[35] And Hough agrees that 'with a completely successful poem all is achievement, and the question of separately conceivable intention does not arise'.[36]

I am now in a position to ask whether any of these arguments succeeds in establishing, for any of the senses of 'meaning' I have discriminated, that the motives and intentions of a writer can and ought to be ignored in any attempt to interpret the meaning of his works.

The first argument, which derived from the desire to maintain the purity of our critical procedures, appears to rest on a confusion. It may be that a knowledge of a writer's motives and intentions is irrelevant to elucidating 'the meaning' of his works in every sense of 'meaning' I have discriminated. But it does not follow from this that the critic ought to – or will even be able to – ensure that this knowledge plays no role in helping to determine his response to that writer's work. To know a writer's motives and intentions is to know the relationship in which he stands to what he has written. To know about intentions is to know such facts as whether the writer was joking or serious or ironic or in general what speech-act he was performing. To know about motives is to know what prompted those particular speech-acts, quite apart from their character and truth-status as utterances. Now it may well be that to know, say, that a given writer was motivated by envy or resentment tells us nothing about 'the meaning' of his works. But once the critic possesses such knowledge, it can hardly fail to condition his response. The discovery, say, that the work was written not out of envy or resentment, but out of a simple desire to enlighten or amuse, seems certain to engender a new response to the work. This may or may not be desirable, but it seems to some degree inevitable.[37]

I now turn to the various arguments which have been derived from analysing the concepts of motive and intention themselves. The first, to the effect that it is actually impossible to recover such mental acts, seems straightforwardly false. I assert this as obvious, and shall make no attempt to prove it. The second seems to be a misstatement. It would clearly be a mistake to suppose that a knowledge of a writer's motives or intentions could ever supply a standard for judging the merit or success of his works. It certainly will not do, as Cioffi has remarked in a similar context, for a writer to assure a critic that he intended to produce a masterpiece.[38] The third argument, however, seems at least partly correct. I shall concede, that is, that even if it may not be true in the case of a writer's *intentions*, it may well be true in the case of his *motives*, that they may be said to stand 'outside' his works in such a way that their recovery will be irrelevant – for all the senses of 'meaning' I have discriminated – to an understanding of the meaning of his works.

This last claim rests, however, on an implied distinction between a writer's motives and intentions which has not usually been made explicit in the literature on the theory of interpretations, but which my argument now requires me to set out.[39] To speak of a writer's motives seems invariably to be to speak of a condition antecedent to, and contingently connected with, the appearance of his works. But to speak of a writer's intentions may be either to refer to his plan or design to create a certain type of work (his intention to do x) or to refer to and describe an actual work in a certain way (as embodying a particular intention in x-ing). In the former type of case we seem (as in talking about motives) to be alluding to a contingent antecedent condition of the appearance of the work. In the latter type of case, however, we seem to be alluding to a feature of the work itself, and to be characterizing it in terms of its embodiment of a particular aim or intention, and thus in terms of its having a particular point.[40]

We can conveniently corroborate this claim by borrowing the jargon which the philosophers of language have recently developed in discussing the logical relations between the concepts of intention and meaning. They have concentrated on the fact (following J. L. Austin's classic analysis)[41] that to issue any serious utterance is always to speak not only with a certain meaning but also with what Austin labelled a certain illocutionary force. An agent may, in issuing a given (meaningful) utterance, also succeed in performing such illocutionary acts as promising, warning and so on. Austin's usual way of putting the point was that to gain 'uptake' of the illocutionary force of a serious utterance will be equivalent to understanding what the agent was *doing in* issuing that particular utterance. But an equivalent way of putting the same point, which is crucial to my present argument, would be to say that an understanding of the illocutionary act being performed by an agent in issuing a given utterance will be equivalent to an understanding of that agent's primary *intentions* in issuing that particular utterance.[42]

The significance for my present argument of this distinction between motives and intentions, with the isolation of the idea of an intention *in* speaking or writing with a particular force, lies of course in the implication that the agent's motives *for* writing (though not his intentions *in* writing) can indeed be said to stand 'outside' his works, and in a contingent relationship to them, in such a way that their recovery does seem to be irrelevant to the determination of the meaning of the works.

If we now turn, moreover, to the second (and incompatible) claim which has usually been advanced by literary theorists about the concepts of motive and intention, it may seem that we are already committed to saying that this conclusion holds good for the concept of intention as well. I have sought to show that we may speak of a writer's intentions *in* writing, and of these intentions as being in some sense 'inside' his works, rather than 'outside' and contingently connected with their appearance. The contention of the other argument I have cited, however, is precisely that it is because a writer's intentions are 'inside' his works, and not separate from them, that the critic does not need to pay any special attention to their recovery in his attempt to interpret the meaning of any given work.

This claim, however, seems to rest on conflating two different sorts of question we may wish to ask about a writer's intentions in his works. We may revert to the jargon currently used by the philosophers of language in order to make this point. On the one hand, we may wish to ask about the perlocutionary intentions embodied in a work.[43] We may wish, that is, to consider whether the work may have been intended to achieve a certain effect or response – such as 'to make you sad',[44] or to persuade you to adopt a particular view, and so on. But on the other hand we may wish, as I have suggested, to ask about a writer's illocutionary intentions as a means of characterizing his work. We may wish, that is, to ask not just about whether a given writer achieved what he intended and intended to achieve what he achieved, but rather about just *what* he may have been intending to do *in* writing what he wrote.

This brings me to my central contention about the relations between a writer's intentions and the meaning of his works. On the one hand, I shall concede that a writer's perlocutionary intentions (what he may have intended to do *by* writing in a certain way) do not need to be further considered. They do not seem to need any separate study, since the question whether a given work was intended by its author, say, to induce sadness does seem to be capable of being settled (if at all) only by considering the work itself and such clues about its intended effects as may be contained within it. And the question whether it makes sense to impute such intentions to a given writer on a given occasion does not seem to be a question about the meaning of his works so much as about the success or failure of the work's structure of effects. On the other hand, I now wish to argue that in the case of a writer's illocutionary intentions (what he may have been intending to do simply *in* writing in a certain way) their recovery does require a separate form of study, which it will in fact be essential to undertake if the critic's aim is to understand 'the meaning' of the writer's corresponding works.

It now becomes essential, however, if this central contention is to be established, to revert to the three senses of 'meaning' which I began by discriminating, in order to establish the way in which the particular sense of intentionality I have now isolated is in fact relevant to understanding 'the meaning' of a given writer's works.

If we turn first to meaning₁, it must be conceded that an understanding of a writer's intentions in writing scarcely seems relevant to this sense of 'the meaning' of what he writes. To say this is not to take sides on the immense and immensely difficult question whether our statements about the ('timeless') meaning of words and sentences may not ultimately be reducible to statements about *someone's* intentions.[45] It is only to assert the truism that questions about what the words and sentences I use mean cannot be equivalent to questions about my intentions in using them. If we turn next to meaning₂, it must again be conceded that an understanding of a writer's intentions in writing scarcely seems relevant to this sense of 'the meaning' of what he writes. It is clear, that is, that the question of what a given work of literary art may mean to a given reader can be settled quite independently of any consideration of what its creator may have intended. But if we turn to meaning₃, it seems possible to establish the closest possible connection between a writer's intentions and the meaning of what he writes. For it seems that a knowledge of the writer's intentions in writing, in the sense I have sought to isolate, is not merely relevant to, but is actually *equivalent* to, a knowledge of the meaning₃ of what he writes. The stages by which this conclusion can be reached will by now be clear. To gain 'uptake' of these intentions is equivalent to understanding the nature and range of the illocutionary acts which the writer may have been performing in writing in this particular way. It is to be able, as I have suggested, to characterize what the writer may have been doing – to be able to say that he must have been intending, for example, to attack or defend a particular line of argument, to criticize or contribute to a particular tradition of discourse, and so on. But to be able to characterize a work in such a way, in terms of its intended illocutionary force, is equivalent to understanding what the writer may have *meant by* writing in that particular way. It is equivalently to be able, that is, to say that he must have *meant* the work *as* an attack on or a defence of, as a criticism of or a contribution to, some particular attitude or line of argument, and so on. And so the equivalence between these intentions in writing, and the meaning₃ of what is written, is established. For as I have already indicated, to know what a writer meant by a particular work[46] *is* to know what his primary intentions were in writing it.

I wish finally to protect the thesis I have now advanced from two possible misinterpretations. I have argued that we need to know what a writer may have meant by what he wrote, and need (equivalently) to know his intentions in writing, in order to interpret the meaning₃ of his works. This must first be distinguished, however, from the much stronger claim which is often advanced to the effect that the recovery of these intentions, and the decoding of the 'original meaning' intended by the writer himself, must form the whole of the interpreter's task. It has often been argued that 'the final criterion of correctness' in interpretation can only be provided by studying the original context in which the work was written.[47] I have not been concerned, however, to lend support to this very strong version of what Bateson has called 'the discipline of contextual reading'. I see no impropriety in speaking of a work's having a meaning for me which the writer could not have intended. Nor does my thesis conflict with this possibility. I have been concerned only with the converse point that whatever the writer is *doing in* writing what he writes must be relevant to interpretation, and thus with the claim that *amongst* the interpreter's tasks must be the recovery of the writer's intentions *in* writing what he writes.

This thesis must also be distinguished from the claim that if we are concerned with a writer's intentions in this way we must be prepared to accept any statements the writer himself may make about his own intentions as a final authority on the question of what he was doing in a particular work.[48] It is true that any agent is obviously in a privileged position when characterizing his own intentions and actions. It follows that it must always be dangerous, and ought perhaps to be unusual, for a critic to override a writer's own explicit statements on this point. I see no difficulty in principle, however, about reconciling the claim that we need to be able to characterize a writer's intentions in order to interpret the meaning$_3$ of his works with the claim that it may sometimes be appropriate to discount his own statements about them. This is not to say we have lost interest in gaining a correct statement about his intentions in our attempt to interpret his work.[49] It is only to make the (perhaps rather dramatic, but certainly conceivable) charge that the writer himself may have been self-deceiving about recognizing his intentions, or incompetent at stating them. And this seems perennially possible in the case of any complex human action.

I have argued for a general hermeneutic rule which contradicts the one general rule proposed by the New Critics: that the recovery of a writer's (illocutionary) intentions must be treated as a necessary condition of being able to interpret the meanings$_3$ of his works. This in turn suggests a further question about rules of interpretation, which I wish finally to consider: is it possible to state any general rules about how to recover such intentions? There are of course notorious conceptual difficulties involved in the understanding of other people's intentions. I wish to suggest, however, that without eliding these difficulties, at least two such general rules can in fact be framed.

My first suggested rule is: focus not just on the text to be interpreted but on the prevailing conventions governing the treatment of the issues or themes with which the text is concerned. This rule derives from the fact that any writer must standardly be engaged in an intended act of communication. It follows that whatever intentions a given writer may have, they must be conventional intentions in the strong sense that they must be recognizable *as* intentions to uphold some particular position in argument, to contribute in a particular way to the treatment of some particular theme, and so on. It follows in turn that to understand what any given writer may have been *doing in* using some particular concept or argument, we need first of all to grasp the nature and range of things that could recognizably have been done by using that particular concept, in the treatment of that particular theme, at that particular time.

This rule can be applied as a critical as well as an heuristic device, in order to test the plausibility of ascribing any particular intention to a writer in a particular work. It is true that any example of the application of this rule to a work of literature is liable either to look very crude or be very complicated. It can readily be illustrated, however, by considering a simple example from the history of philosophy. Consider the debate about whether some of the English legal theorists of the seventeenth century may be said to have intended to articulate a doctrine of the judicial review of statute.[50] I am arguing in effect that these writers will have been limited, in their intentions in writing, by the range of intentions they could have expected to be able to communicate, and thus by whatever stock of concepts, and whatever criteria for applying them, were generally available. It follows that the question whether the seventeenth-century lawyers were adumbrating a doctrine which was later to become politically important, or whether there is merely a random similarity of terminology, may be settled by settling the question whether the concept of judicial review was a part of the stock of concepts available, in its later and popularized sense, to the audiences for whom the seventeenth-century lawyers were writing. If it was not (as I believe can be shown to be the case) then the question loses virtually any meaning, to say nothing of plausibility.

My other suggested rule is: focus on the writer's mental world, the world of his empirical beliefs. This rule derives from the logical connection between our capacity to ascribe intentions to agents and our knowledge of their beliefs. This rule can also be applied critically as well as serving as an heuristic device. Again, a literary example would necessarily be very complex, so consider another example from the history of philosophy. C. B. Macpherson has recently attempted to interpret John Locke's *Two Treatises of Government* by ascribing a particular intention to Locke in writing: the intention to defend the rationality of unlimited capital accumulation.[51] If this is what Locke was *doing in* writing that work, his mental world must have included at least the following beliefs: that his society was in fact becoming devoted to unlimited capital accumulation; that this was an activity crucially in need of ideological justification; and that it was appropriate for him to devote himself to accomplishing precisely this task. It is a remarkable fact about Macpherson's account that no attempt is made to show that Locke did hold all or any of these beliefs. It has recently been shown, moreover, that there is a good deal of evidence to indicate that Locke did not in fact hold the third of these beliefs, while there is no evidence to show that he held the first two of them.[52] (The first is in any case very doubtfully true.) But if Locke did not in fact hold these beliefs (and perhaps could not in principle have held them), then he could not have had the intention *in* writing which Macpherson's account ascribes to him. It is in this way that this second suggested rule (like the first) has a critical as well as an heuristic point.

I have thus sought to set out two stages to my criticism of the New Critics' attitude towards the idea of general hermeneutic rules. I have tried first of all to argue that in order to be able to interpret the meaning of a text, it *is* necessary to consider factors other than the text itself. I have now tried to suggest just *what* other factors need to be taken into consideration. I thus have been concerned to shift the emphasis of the discussion off the idea of the text as an autonomous object, and on to the idea of the text as an object linked to its creator, and thus on to the discussion of what its creator may have been doing in creating it.

4

'Social meaning' and the explanation of social action

I

A social action may be said to have a meaning for the agent performing it. The acceptance of this rather vague claim represents the one major point of agreement in the continuing debate between those philosophers who wish to assert and those who wish to deny the naturalist thesis[1] to the effect that social actions can sufficiently be accounted for by the ordinary processes of causal explanation. The significance of the fact that social actions have a 'meaning' has of course been emphasized in each of the three main traditions of anti-naturalist opposition to the idea of a social science. The followers of Dilthey, and of the whole tradition which has insisted on the importance of *Verstehen*, stress that the special feature of 'the human studies' is their concern 'with a world which has meaning for the actors involved'.[2] Similarly, the phenomenologists stress that the aim of the social sciences must be to gain 'insight into the meaning which social acts have for those who act'.[3] And the followers of Wittgenstein stress that the 'forms of activity' studied in the social sciences will characteristically be those 'of which we can sensibly say that they have a *meaning*'.[4]

This emphasis on the meaning of social actions has been no less marked, however, in the various strands of thought which have converged in accepting the theoretical possibility of establishing a causal and predictive science of human action. Those who have wished to vindicate a generally 'scientific' approach to the study of social action still concede the need to take account of 'the meaning of people's movements'.[5] Similarly, those who have wished to claim that even an agent's reasons may be the causes of his actions still allow for the fact that such agents will characteristically see 'a point or meaning' in their actions.[6] And even those who have wished to maintain the strictest thesis of positivism, to the effect that an individual action must always be explained by deducing it from some known general law covering such movements, continue to concede that 'what distinguishes a mere bodily movement from an action' is 'the *meaning* of that movement'.[7]

It is in fact possible, as I shall next seek to show, to see the entire debate between the social science naturalists and their opponents in terms of the different conclusions which the two sides of the debate have drawn from their common stress on the fact that 'the acting individual' (as Weber puts it) 'attaches a subjective meaning to his social behaviour'.

The anti-naturalists have traced a logical connection between the meaning of a social action and the agent's motives for performing it. And they have seen the recovery of the agent's motives for acting as a matter of placing the agent's action within a context of social rules. This view of social meaning has led them to the following two conclusions about the explanation of social actions. First, they have claimed that to decode the meaning of a social action is equivalent to giving a motive-explanation for the agent's performance of that action (thesis A). Second, they have claimed that since the recovery of an agent's motives for acting is a matter of placing the agent's action in a context of rules rather than causes, so to cite the social meaning and the motives of an action is to provide a form of explanation which stands in contrast with, and is in fact incompatible with, a causal explanation of the same action (thesis B).

These anti-naturalist conclusions about the idea of a social science have in part derived and have gained great strength from the powerful impact of Wittgenstein's later philosophy upon recent philosophical psychology. This is most clearly evident in a work such as A. I. Melden's *Free Action* – with its stress on 'making sense' of the meaning of actions, its insistence that this is essentially a matter of recovering the agent's motives by way of grasping the 'background against which both the man and his action can be understood', and its conclusion that this process makes causal explanation 'wholly irrelevant to the understanding' of social actions.[8]

There is also a much longer tradition of analysis, however, lying behind this type of anti-naturalist commitment. In the philosophy of history it is best represented by Collingwood's insistence, in *The Idea of History*, that to explain an action is always 'to discern the thoughts' of its agent, and that this study of individual motivation means that the historian who seeks to 'emulate the scientist in searching for causes or laws of events' is simply 'ceasing to be an historian'.[9] This contrast, moreover, between understanding actions in terms of motives and explaining events in terms of causes looks back to Croce and Dilthey, and forward to the development of this argument by Dray, Donagan, and others. And in the philosophy of social science a similar commitment has always informed the Weberian tradition of analysis. Weber himself never wished to suggest that the concepts of *Verstehen* and causal explanation are incompatible. But he did begin *Wirtschaft und Gesellschaft* by discussing motive-explanations, and he did at that point specifically equate the 'understanding of motivation' with the business of 'placing the act in an intelligible and more inclusive context of meaning'.[10] Since then, moreover, a much more strongly anti-naturalist case has been developed by at least two schools of thought which have acknowledged Weber's influence. On the one hand the phenomenologists (such as Schutz, at least in certain moods) have gone on to insist both that an understanding of 'the meaning which social phenomena have for us' is a matter of recovering 'typical motives of typical actors', and that this is a form of understanding 'peculiar to social things'.[11] And on the other hand the Wittgensteinians (such as Winch) have insisted both that 'the notion of meaningful behaviour is closely connected with notions like *motive* and *reason*', and that the explanation of such behaviour, by way of relating the agent's motives to a context of social rules, requires 'a scheme of concepts which is logically incompatible with the kinds of explanation offered in the natural sciences'.[12]

The naturalists, by contrast, have given an account of social meaning from which they have drawn two conclusions opposed to those I have just set out. First, they have claimed that the decoding of the meaning of a social action merely provides a method of redescribing it. And they have insisted that since mere redescription cannot in itself be explanatory, so it must be a mistake to suppose that the placing of a social action in its context, or the decoding of its social meaning, can ever serve in itself as an explanation of the given action (thesis C). Second, they have claimed that if the idea of decoding the meaning of an action is so much extended that it becomes equivalent to recovering the agent's motives for performing it, then there is no incompatibility between the ideas of social meaning and of causal explanation, since the provision of an explanation by way of citing an agent's motive, or even his intentions, is itself a form of causal explanation. They have thus concluded that there is nothing in the fact that a social action may have a meaning or consist of the following of a rule from which it follows that such episodes may not be entirely explicable simply by the ordinary processes of causal explanation (thesis D).

These naturalist conclusions, like those of their opponents, have been in part derived from, and have been greatly influenced by, a recent movement in philosophical psychology. This is the current and increasing movement of reaction against the Wittgensteinian assumption that motives and intentions cannot function as causes of actions. This has already generated some powerful arguments (best stated by Davidson),[13] and has caused several philosophers (notably Hamlyn and MacIntyre) to recant their previously published anti-naturalist views about the explanation of action. The implications of the reaction can be seen at their clearest in an essay such as Ayer's on 'Man as a subject for science' – with its insistence both that to redescribe a phenomenon cannot be 'in any way to account for it', and that to cite either a motive or an intention to explain an action, as we do 'in the normal way', must always be ultimately to point to 'lawlike connections' which are causal in form. The conclusion is that even if we can 'estimate an action in terms of its conforming to a rule', and even if we need to understand such actions 'in terms of their social contexts', these factors affect the agent only as 'part of his motivation', and give us no grounds for doubting that the action can be sufficiently explained 'by means of a causal law'. There is thus said to be 'nothing about human conduct that would entitle us to conclude *a priori* that it was in any way less lawlike than any other sort of natural process'.[14]

As with the anti-naturalist commitment, there is a considerable tradition of analysis lying behind this type of claim. In the philosophy of history the idealist tradition represented by Dilthey and Collingwood has always been confronted by a positivist tradition stemming from the philosophy of science. This is perhaps best represented by Hempel's classic essay on 'The function of general laws in history', originally published in the *Journal of Philosophy* for 1942. The attempt, it is there claimed, to explain the actions of historical individuals in an *ad hoc* manner, in terms of 'the circumstances under which they acted, and the motives which influence their actions' 'does not in itself constitute an explanation'. And the fact, it is claimed, that the historian may concern himself with 'the *"meanings"* of given historical events', as well as with motives and actions, does nothing to vitiate the claim that any genuine explanation of any historical phenomenon will have to consist of 'subsuming it under general empirical laws'.[15] And similarly, in the philosophy of social science, the school of Weber has always been confronted by the school of Durkheim, with his dismissal of the need to study individual intentions and motives, and his insistence (in *The Rules of Sociological Method*) on the 'principle' that 'the determining cause of a social fact', in which he included social actions, 'should be sought among the social facts preceding it, and not among the states of individual consciousness'.[16]

The two opposed theoretical traditions I have now sketched have both been represented in the two most recent volumes of *Philosophy, Politics and Society*. In series II MacIntyre's essay made use of the anti-naturalist approach, and he committed himself to theses A and B.[17] In series III Ayer's essay put the case for the naturalist approach, and argued for theses C and D.[18] My aim in what follows is to reconsider the two opposed theoretical traditions I have now sketched out by attempting to do three things. I shall first try very briefly to make a new start (section II) on the analysis of the required sense of 'meaning', and to give some examples of this analysis in action. I shall then try to show (section III) that if this analysis is sound, then there seem to be some grounds for doubting each of the four theses I have now set out. (Here I shall in part attempt to adapt and apply an account of explaining social actions which I have already published.)[19] Finally, I shall try (section IV) to suggest certain methodological implications of these conclusions for historians and social scientists, at least in so far as they are concerned with explaining the social actions of individual agents.

II

There is a tendency, particularly among the anti-naturalists, to apply the concept of social meaning in a rather over-extended way. (This is perhaps evident from several of the quotations I have already given.) I shall begin therefore by restricting myself to considering the way in which the concept is used in the discussion of a single class of social actions. Later I shall try tentatively to extend the application of this analysis. But at first I shall concentrate on the class of social actions in which the concept of somebody meaning something (in or by saying or doing something) has its clearest and most obvious application, namely in the class of *linguistic* actions.

The classic analysis of the concept of a linguistic action has been provided by J. L. Austin in his William James Lectures, edited and published by J. O. Urmson as *How to Do Things with Words*. Austin's central contention is that any agent, in issuing any serious utterance, will be doing something as well as merely saying something, and will be doing something *in* saying what he says, and not merely as a consequence of what is said. Austin reached this conclusion by way of claiming that to issue any serious utterance is always to speak not only with a certain meaning but also with a certain intended force, corresponding to what Austin dubbed the 'illocutionary' act being performed by the agent in issuing his given utterance. Austin's claim is thus that to gain 'uptake', as he put it, of this element of illocutionary force co-ordinate with the ordinary meaning of the locution will be equivalent to understanding what the agent was *doing in* issuing that given utterance.

A single example will make clear the sense in which the issuing of any serious utterance constitutes, according to Austin, the performance of a type of social action. Consider the case of a policeman who sees a skater on a dangerous pond and issues to the skater the following serious utterance: 'The ice over there is very thin.'[20] Here the policeman is obviously issuing a meaningful utterance: he is saying something and the words mean something. But Austin's further point is that the utterance also has an illocutionary force, corresponding to the fact that the policeman

will be doing something in issuing this meaningful utterance: he may
for example be performing the illocutionary act of *warning the skater*.

I now wish to suggest that this account of linguistic action may be
used to establish two crucial claims about the sense of 'meaning' with
which I am concerned in discussing the meaning of social actions. The
first is that the idea of decoding the meaning of an action seems, at
least in the case of linguistic actions, to be equivalent to gaining uptake
of the nature of the illocutionary act performed by the agent in issuing
that particular utterance. To understand, that is, that the policeman, in
issuing his utterance 'The ice over there is very thin' was performing the
illocutionary act of warning seems equivalent to understanding the meaning
of issuing the utterance itself. It is to understand what the policeman
(non-naturally)[21] meant by performing his given (linguistic) action.

The second point is that to ask about this non-natural sense of
meaning, at least in the case of linguistic actions, seems to be equivalent
to asking about the agent's intention in performing his given social action.
It is perhaps necessary to be more precise, and to stress that to ask this
question is to ask about the agent's *primary* intention. It is arguable
that Austin's way of stating his theory encourages the belief that there
must be a correspondence between single intentions and single actions.
But an agent may well have several different intentions in performing a
single social action, some of which may be less important than others
from the point of view of characterizing what the agent is doing, all
of which may nevertheless form part of a complex set of intentions
which are realized in the given action. It remains true, however, that
to understand (in the example I am considering) that what the policeman
meant to do in issuing his utterance 'The ice over there is very thin' was
to warn the skater is equivalent to understanding what the policeman's
primary intention was in performing that particular (linguistic) action.

It might be doubted, of course, whether this analysis of 'social meaning'
in terms of understanding the intended illocutionary force of an agent's (linguistic) action can possibly be applied in the case of ordinary non-linguistic
social actions. If we accept Austin's own claim, however, that certain
illocutionary acts are invariably performed non-verbally,[22] there seems
some reason to suppose that the analysis can be used at least to decode
the meaning of the 'ritual and ceremonial' acts in which Austin was chiefly
interested, even if many of these turn out to be non-linguistically performed.
If we accept Strawson's argument, moreover, to the effect that the account
which Austin gave of the conventions of illocutionary force may have been
excessively narrow in scope, then there seems some reason to assume that
the analysis can also be used to decode the meaning of a whole range of
ordinary non-ritual as well as non-linguistic actions. Finally, it is relevant
to recall that the main aim of Grice's original discussion of non-natural

meaning was 'to show that the criteria for judging linguistic intentions are very like the criteria for judging non-linguistic intentions', and thus to show 'that linguistic intentions are very like non-linguistic intentions'.[23]

These suggestions may be corroborated by considering some examples of such non-linguistic as well as linguistic actions. Consider first a case of a ritual but non-linguistic social action. (Hollis has popularized the following example.)[24] Certain Yoruba tribesmen 'carry about with them boxes covered with cowrie shells, which they treat with special regard'. Hollis's interest in this example (concerned with the need for the Yoruba to have rational thought-processes) is not relevant to my argument at this point. My interest is in the meaning of this social action and in the nature of the questions we need to ask and answer in order to decode it. In the first place, the crucial question to ask certainly seems to be about what the agent may be *doing in* performing just this action. The answer (Hollis tells us) is that the tribesmen believe 'that the boxes are their heads or souls' and that what they are doing in treating the boxes in a reverent way is protecting their souls against witchcraft. This in turn suggests that to ask and answer this question about the illocutionary force of the action is, as I have suggested, equivalent to asking about the intentions of the agent in acting this way. Notice that we do not learn the nature of the motive which prompts (and perhaps causes) the Yoruba to treat his box with special regard – although we may now infer that the motive is likely to be respect or fear for the power of unknown forces. What we learn is the Yoruba's primary intention in acting in this way – that it is to protect his soul.

Consider next a case of a non-ritual, non-linguistic social action. (I derive the following example from one of the case-histories reported by R. D. Laing and A. Esterson in *Sanity, Madness and the Family*.) An adolescent girl becomes an apparently compulsive reader, 'burying herself in her books' and refusing to stop or allow herself to be interrupted.[25] Laing and Esterson's interest in the case lies primarily in their suggestion that the behaviour can be seen as a strategy, a deliberate social action, and not just as the symptom of an illness. My interest is again in the meaning of the behaviour, and in the appropriate questions to ask in order to determine whether it has any meaning, and if so how it should be decoded. Again it seems that the crucial question to ask is what the girl may be doing in performing just this action. The answer is that she is 'taking refuge' and preventing what she takes to be 'intrusions' by an overdemanding family.[26] And again it seems that to ask and answer this question about the illocutionary force of the action is equivalent to asking about the girl's intentions in acting in this way. Notice again that this does not tell us the motives which prompted (and perhaps caused) the girl's behaviour. Laing and Esterson suggest that the motive may have been a desire for what they call 'autonomy' but one might infer other motives as well – such as a kind of pride, a degree of hatred, and so on.[27] The point is that what we do learn is the girl's intentions in acting in this way – that they are to register a protest against, and to protect herself from, an excessively demanding social situation.

It may still seem, however, that to extend the discussion of non-natural meaning and illocutionary force to deal with such non-linguistic social actions is to give an illegitimate application to Austin's and Grice's theories. Consider finally, therefore, a further case of an ordinary (non-ritual) linguistic action – and not a dummy example this time, but a genuine (and historically important) utterance. Machiavelli, in chapter 15 of *The Prince*, offers the following piece of advice: 'Princes must learn when not to be virtuous.' Several of his interpreters have asked what he may have meant by offering such advice. Here it cannot I think be doubted that the crucial question to ask, in order to answer this question, is what Machiavelli may have been doing in making this claim. One widely accepted answer (suggested by Felix Gilbert) has been that Machiavelli was 'consciously refuting his predecessors' within the highly conventionalized genre of advice-books to princes.[28] Again it seems unquestionable that to ask and answer this question about the illocutionary force of Machiavelli's utterance is equivalent to asking about Machiavelli's intentions in writing this section of *The Prince*. Notice once more that this does not tell us the motives which prompted (and perhaps caused) Machiavelli to offer this advice. Gilbert suggests that the most likely motives might have been a mixture of frustration at the prevailing 'idealist interpretation of politics' combined with a simple desire to shock and a belief in the importance of giving genuinely practical political advice.[29] The point once more is that what we do learn is Machiavelli's intention in writing just what he did write. I do not wish to imply here, of course, that what we learn is the intention lying behind the writing of the particular sentence I have quoted, nor do I wish to imply that Machiavelli need have had any isolable intention in writing just that one sentence. But I do wish to claim that we learn the intention lying behind Machiavelli's argument at this point of his work – the primary intention (and the illocutionary force of his given utterance) being to challenge and repudiate an accepted moral commonplace.

III

I now turn to try to bring out the philosophical interest of these claims. This lies, as I have already indicated, in the suggestion that the argument I have now set out seems to give some grounds for saying that both the theses of the naturalists (C and D) as well as those of the anti-naturalists (A and B) may be mistaken. Consider first the two naturalist theses. Thesis C states that to redescribe an action is in no way to explain it. I have now sought to show, however, that for at least certain classes of social actions there can be a unique form of (illocutionary) redescription which, by way of recovering the agent's intended illocutionary act, may be capable of explaining at least certain features of the agent's behaviour. This conclusion can perhaps be most readily corroborated by reverting to the dummy example of the policeman issuing to the skater the utterance 'The ice over there is very thin'. This episode might be witnessed by a puzzled bystander who for some reason fails to grasp the policeman's primary intention in issuing this utterance. One request for an explanation might then take the form of asking 'Why did he say that?' (Or more exactly, 'Why did the policeman issue that given utterance?') And one reply, providing an explanation of the policeman's action, might be 'He said it to warn the skater'. (Or more exactly, 'The policeman's reason for issuing that given utterance was to give notice to the skater of the potential danger of skating where the ice is very thin.') The illocutionary redescription serves as an explanation of the (linguistic) action.

There seems no doubt, moreover, about the way in which such illocutionary redescriptions may serve as genuine explanations of at least some puzzles about a fairly wide range of social actions. For it is one thing if the bystander understands what the policeman's utterance to the skater means, so that he may be able to give an account of what the policeman said. But it is another and further thing if the bystander understands what the policeman's issuing of an utterance with that meaning was itself intended to mean on the given occasion, so that he may be able to give an account of why the policeman said what he said. Colloquially, we may say that what an illocutionary redescription will characteristically explain about a social action will be its *point*.

Consider next thesis D, that there is nothing in the fact that a social action may have a meaning from which it follows that the action may not be entirely explicable by means of the ordinary processes of causal explanation. I have now suggested, however, that while it may be essential in a wide range of cases to recover the meaning of a social action in order to be able to explain it, to supply this redescriptive form of explanation is certainly to supply something other than a causal explanation. Again this can most readily be corroborated by reverting to the dummy example of the policeman warning the skater. The explanation for the policeman's issuing of his given utterance is supplied by way of recovering what the policeman meant, in the non-natural sense of understanding not just what his utterance itself meant (for as Ziff has stressed it is not even necessary that the utterance should in that sense have a meaning at all) but of understanding what the act of issuing an utterance with that meaning might itself have meant in the given circumstances. This is supplied in turn by way of decoding the conventions governing the illocutionary force attaching to the policeman's utterance itself. But this can scarcely be to provide a causal form of explanation. For this is to focus on a *feature* of the policeman's action, and not on an independently specifiable condition of it, in the way that any causal form of explanation requires. Yet this is still to provide an explanation of the given action. For to know in the required sense what the agent meant is to know how he intended his utterance (or other action) to be taken. But this in turn is to know the agent's intention in performing that action. And this in turn is to know why he performed that particular action. We thus have a genuine form of explanation of the given action, even though it is clear that we cannot construe these sorts of intentions (intentions *in* acting) as causes of which the agent's corresponding actions can then be seen as effects.

Next consider the two anti-naturalist theses. Thesis A states that the reason the concept of social meaning can be explanatory is because it tells us the agent's motives for performing his given action. I have now sought to show, however, first that a sharp line needs to be drawn between an agent's motives and his intentions in acting, and secondly that it is these intentions, and not the agent's motives, which we need to recover in order to decode the meaning of social action.

The possible need for this sharp division between motives and intentions does not seem to have been admitted by any of the anti-naturalist or the naturalist theorists I have cited. The anti-naturalists (such as Melden, Rickman and Winch)[30] as well as the naturalists (such as Ayer, Davidson and MacIntyre in his recent work)[31] write about motives and intentions in this connection – and often about reasons and purposes as well – as if they believe these concepts to be virtually interchangeable. This seems to be a mistake in itself, but it also seems to be a mistake of some consequence when we come to try to explain social actions, since it encourages the elision of what I take to be a necessary stage in the explanation of a certain range of actions. It is this extra stage, and the need to begin by considering it, which I have chiefly been concerned to emphasize – the stage, that is, at which it may be appropriate, before asking either about the agent's motives or about any deeper causes of his behaviour, to ask whether the performance of his given action itself bears any conventional element of (non-natural) meaning or (illocutionary) force.

The possible significance of isolating this extra stage can be conveniently illustrated by reconsidering the main example of a social action which Ayer chooses in his essay on 'Man as a subject for science'. He takes the case of a man drinking a glass of wine, and claims that this action might be explained, according to its context, either as '(1) an act of self-indulgence, (2) an expression of politeness, (3) a proof of alcoholism, (4) a manifestation of loyalty, (5) a gesture of despair, (6) an attempt at suicide, (7) the performance of a social rite, (8) a religious communication, (9) an attempt to summon up one's courage, (10) an attempt to seduce or corrupt another person, (11) the sealing of a bargain,

(12) a display of professional expertise, (13) a piece of inadvertence, (14) an act of expiation, (15) the response to a challenge'.[32]

It is true that my argument is not altogether easy to make good in terms of Ayer's particularly elaborate and eccentric list. In cases (3) and (13) it is not clear that the *explicans* yields the explanation of anything that could be called a voluntary action. In cases (6), (10) and (12) it is not clear how the *explicans* is to be understood. (It is hard to see, that is, how any of these answers could be offered as possible explanations for the action *simply* of drinking a glass of wine.) Furthermore, in cases (1), (7), (9) and (14) it does seem necessary to concede that the question of distinguishing the motives of the agent from his intentions in acting scarcely seems to arise. There scarcely seems, that is, to be any question to ask in these cases about the meaning of the given action, and it seems that, if we were to ask in these cases about the intentions of the agent in performing his given action, this would scarcely explain anything about the given behaviour. This still leaves us, however, with cases (2), (4), (5), (8), (11), and perhaps (15). The explanation in these cases, *pace* Ayer's assimilation of intentions to motives, seems to take the form of a redescription which directs us not primarily to the agent's motives, but rather to his intentions *in* performing the given action of drinking the glass of wine. Thus it does seem possible, at least in these cases, to insist on the need to begin by considering a stage of explanation which is prior to any attempt to elucidate the agent's motives, and which consists of an attempt to recover the unique illocutionary redescription of the action itself, in terms of which the agent's performance of it can be shown non-naturally to mean something. It seems therefore that the anti-naturalists must be mistaken when they equate the recovery of social meaning with the elucidation of the agent's motives for action.

Consider finally thesis B – that to explain an action by citing its meaning and the agent's motives is to provide a form of explanation incompatible with causality. This thesis is contradicted rather than sustained by the way in which I have sought to vindicate the possibility of giving non-causal explanations of social actions. I have sought only to argue that to explain a social action in terms of the agent's intentions in performing it constitutes one stage in the explanation of a certain range of social actions. I have at no point suggested that to provide such non-causal explanations is in any way incompatible with the subsequent provision of further and arguably causal explanations of the same action. One such further stage might be to provide an explanation in terms of the agent's motives. A yet further stage might be to provide an explanation in terms of the grounds for the agent's possession of just those motives. It will normally be indispensable to go on to both these further stages in order to be able to provide anything like a complete explanation of any social action. And I should wish to claim that it is strongly arguable in the case of the first of these further stages, and unquestionable in the case of the second, that to provide these further explanations will be to provide causal explanations for the performance of the given social action.

IV

I turn finally to consider the practical implications of the thesis I have argued. There is a special interest in trying to make this point, first because of the tendency among some recent philosophers of social science to deny that their views about the logic of explanation entail any methodological recommendations,[33] and second because of the more obvious tendency among practising historians as well as social scientists to deny that the acceptance of any particular philosophical viewpoint could possibly have any practical bearing on the study of their subjects. I now wish to suggest that if the conceptual scheme I have set out is sound, it entails at least three methodological recommendations, all of which tend, moreover, to be ignored or even explicitly denied in a good deal of current writing in history and social science. I concede, of course, the difficulty of deriving anything except negative methodological injunctions from my *a priori* arguments. Perhaps any such injunctions, if they are to stand any chance of being sensible as well as sufficiently general to be of practical value, are bound in effect to consist of injunctions not to heed methodological injunctions based on mistaken *a priori* arguments. I hope nevertheless that it may be possible to see in this section the beginnings, if only the negative beginnings, of an answer to those who have refused to accept that the dispute over causal and rational explanations of actions could possibly have anything to do with the methodology of the social sciences.

Consider first the classes (the non-linguistic as well as linguistic classes) of what Austin called 'ritual and ceremonial' actions. There are two methodological recommendations which seem, at least in these cases, to follow from the argument I have advanced. The first is the need to raise questions about the agent's ritual *beliefs* in order to be able to explain such actions. This claim appears to have been explicitly denied in some recent social anthropology,[34] and is certainly bypassed by those who have written as if they believe that ritual actions can sufficiently be explained in terms of their place in a given social structure and by reference to their social effects.[35] It is clear, however, that since there is obviously a crucial logical link between the nature and range of the intentions it makes sense to ascribe to an agent in acting, and the nature and range of that agent's beliefs, it must follow that in order to explain a ritual action by way of recovering the agent's intentions in performing it, we must necessarily be prepared to examine and allude to the ritual beliefs informing the intentions with which the agent performed his given ritual action.

The second recommendation is that as soon as we concede the need to enter the realm of the agent's beliefs in order to explain his social actions it also becomes essential to raise questions about the *rationality* of these beliefs. This has of course been recently stressed, as I have mentioned, by Hollis and others. They have primarily been concerned, however, with the linguistic and logical elements in the concept of rationality. It seems clear, as they have argued, that we must be prepared to make some *a priori* assumptions about the universality of the laws of thought if we are going to be able correctly to identify (and so to translate) the nature of the speech-acts, as well as to explain the nature of the ritual actions, which may be performed in an alien culture. It also seems clear, however, that the analysis of the concept of rationality requires us to consider a further question, concerned with the nature of the procedures which will have to be followed, and the nature of the criteria met, before we can say of a given empirical belief that it is rationally held.

It might be doubted whether my basic theme − that of intentionality in relation to the explanation of action − necessarily requires an examination of this further point. To be concerned, however, with explaining actions, and thus with the examination of intentions as the means both of identifying those actions and of establishing whether they may be said to have a meaning, is to commit oneself not only (as I have just stressed) to examining the beliefs of which such intentional actions form the expression. It is also to commit oneself to asking about the rationality of the agent's beliefs, since the answer to this question must in turn affect our assessment of his intentions and actions.

It is true that the strong influence, until recently, of a positivist theory of knowledge upon the philosophy of social science has made it rather easy to oversimplify, and perhaps to overstress, the significance of this point. It has been usual to define the concept of a rational belief in terms of the agent's capacity and willingness to recognize 'that there is sufficient evidence in its favour',[36] 'that it is based on good evidence',[37] and so on. It is clear however, that this fails to acknowledge something problematic in the very notion of holding a belief in the light of rather than in the face of 'the available evidence', since it fails to acknowledge that the question of what is to count as good or sufficient evidence in favour of holding a belief can never be free from cultural reference. This anti-positivist objection can be developed as follows. We can imagine an alien system of beliefs in which the paradigms used to connect the system together are such that none of the evidence which we should regard as evidence in favour of abandoning those beliefs is taken to count as decisive evidence either for or against them. We can then imagine an agent, operating within this belief-system, who accepts on trust these prevailing paradigms (and these prevailing canons of evidence), recognizing and following only the moves accepted as rational within the given system, but never challenging the rationality of any part of the system itself. It might now be argued, of the beliefs held by someone in this type of situation, that provided they are coherently connected together, and provided the agent recognizes their implications, they may be said to be held in an entirely rational way. There seems to be no space left for this possibility, however, if we insist on defining rational belief in terms of each individual believer's continual willingness to examine 'the available evidence' for and against each belief he holds.

A positivist might still wish to insist, however, that such an agent's beliefs cannot be rationally held, since it cannot be rational for anyone to accept on trust what are to count as the canons of evidence in favour of holding any given belief. Such an answer seems to be given, in effect, even by some of the most recent and avowedly anti-positivist writers on the topic of rationality. MacIntyre, for example, in his most recent essay on the topic, continues to rest his definition of rational belief on the (unanalysed) claim that to hold a belief rationally must be to hold the belief in the light of having engaged in a 'relevant process of appropriate deliberation', conducted according to 'the appropriate intellectual norms and procedures'.[38]

This type of reply, however, scarcely meets the original objection to the positivist way of connecting rational belief with evidence. It is clear that we all accept and act upon a large number of beliefs (particularly of a technical or theoretical character) without ever trying – or even being in a position seriously to try – either to decide in an independent spirit on the 'appropriate procedures' for falsifying them, or to reassess 'the available evidence' in favour of holding them. We accept such beliefs on trust, on the grounds that we know no better, that they look inherently plausible, and that most other people feel the same. There does not necessarily seem, however, to be anything irrational about accepting many of our empirical beliefs on trust in this way, both with respect to the alleged evidence in favour of holding them, and with respect to what should count as evidence. It would indeed be extremely irrational in many cases if we refused to accept a number of such conventional beliefs, and always insisted on the need to try to reconsider for ourselves the status of the alleged evidence for believing them, in order to arrive at our own far more untutored conclusions.

It is true that these sorts of objections to the analysis of rational belief simply in terms of evidence and refutability have gained considerable ground in recent discussions. They have perhaps drawn some of their strength from their apparent connection with Quine's attack on the alleged distinction between analytic and synthetic statements, a distinction which underlies the positivist way of connecting rational belief with the idea of examining the facts of the case. More recently the attack has been popularized in such methodological studies as those of Kuhn and Winch, which have converged in rejecting the assumption that we ever construct or examine our theories in the light of anything like unvarnished evidence. As the idea that our theories really act as paradigms rather than as straightforward conjectures has gained ground, however, a contrasting danger seems to have developed, which the positivists – with their simple application of a correspondence theory of truth to elucidate the concept of rational belief – at least managed to avoid.

This new danger arises with the tendency to suppose that in order to vindicate the rationality of an alien belief-system, *all* the investigator need do is to examine what counts as evidence within the given system, to assure himself that the alleged reasons which the agents may give for acting are genuinely reasons within the system, and in general to assure himself that each particular belief is connected with other beliefs in such a way as to make up a coherent and integrated cultural system. The danger with this type of emphasis lies in the tendency to assume that it must follow from this that there cannot be any trans-cultural or trans-historical criteria for applying the concept of rationality at all. Thus it has been explicitly insisted, for example by Winch, that the attempt to apply any such criteria must be altogether improper methodologically, and in any case 'not open to us', since the result will only be to contaminate our explanations with our own parochial standards of rationality.[39]

This argument between the positivists and these newly fashionable relativists has left the topic of rationality in more or less complete disarray. Perhaps it is by now appropriate, however, to think in terms of trying to make at least a partial defence of a more positivist point of view. It may be proper, that is, first to try to stress the value of attaching *some* weight to the idea of examining and rejecting empirical beliefs in the light of the available evidence, and second to try to show the way in which this approach (however question-begging it may seem) may still yield a methodological injunction to the historian or the social scientist concerned with the explanation of individual social actions.

Suppose it were possible to combine the elements of a correspondence with a coherence theory of truth in the way that such an approach would seem to require. Why would this be worthwhile, from the point of view of trying to explain individual social actions? Because a belief which an agent holds rationally in this sense – in the sense of holding it in the light of considering the evidence available to him for refuting it – will generate a quite different range of social actions from the range generated out of a belief which he holds irrationally, in the sense of holding it in the face of rather than in the light of the available evidence. The reason is that the agent will have a quite different perception in each case of the appropriate action to perform. In the first type of situation, the investigator will need to find the means to assure himself that the agent's beliefs are in fact rationally held. This may require an extremely sensitive analysis of 'the available evidence', since the state of the evidence may be such that the agent's beliefs can be seen by the investigator to be false, and may nevertheless have been rationally held. (Some recent discussions have arguably failed to keep the ideas of rational and of true belief sufficiently separate.)[40] In the second type of situation, a further and different type of investigation becomes necessary if the agent's social action is to be explained. The investigator needs to be able to discover why the agent continues irrationally to hold a given belief if the evidence to refute it is in some clear sense available to him. It follows in each case that if the investigator fails to raise the question of the rationality of an agent's beliefs, in relation to the facts, he will not have established exactly what there is to be explained about the given action. He will thus be unable to avoid the danger of giving a wholly inappropriate type of explanation.

I turn finally to consider the wider class of social actions which I have suggested can in part be explained by decoding the agent's intentions in performing them. I wish to suggest that a further methodological injunction follows in these cases from my general argument. This would be to begin by focusing not on the individual action to be explained, but rather on the *conventions* surrounding the performance of the given type of social action in the given social situation. The sense of grasping what is conventional which is relevant here is not limited to the strict sense in which we speak of understanding that a given action is being performed according to a convention of which the agent is aware, and which he deliberately follows. The relevant sense includes the wider idea of understanding what the established, conventional standards are which we may expect to see followed in the case of various types of social action within a given culture. The methodological injunction then becomes: begin not by trying to recover the agent's motives by studying the context of social rules, but rather by trying to decode the agent's intentions by aligning his given social action with a more general awareness of the conventional standards which are generally found to apply to such types of social action within a given situation.

This injunction appears to hold good even in the case of the type of abnormal social behaviour I have mentioned – such as the example from Laing and Esterson's work on schizophrenia. It seems, that is, that the appropriate injunction to follow, in the attempt to discover whether the apparent autism of an allegedly schizophrenic adolescent may not be a case of deliberate and meaningful behaviour, must be to begin not by making an intensive study of the particular case and its possible aetiology. It must be to begin instead by trying to relate the particular case to other instances of adolescent withdrawal, in order to try to assess the extent to which the given degree of autism may not after all represent a fairly conventional form and degree of adolescent protest, rather than a straightforward set of pathological symptoms awaiting a straightforward causal explanation.

The same injunction applies even more clearly in the case of the types of linguistic action I have mentioned – such as the example from Machiavelli's *Prince*, where there is not only a highly conventionalized genre of writing against which to measure Machiavelli's contribution to it, but also the clear presumption that Machiavelli was aware both of the genre and of the conventions usually applying in it. Here it seems unquestionable that the appropriate injunction to follow, in the attempt to disclose the meaning of such a work, must be to begin not by making an intensive study of the text in itself, but rather by trying to see what relations it bears to these existing conventions.

It is true that this injunction has been explicitly attacked by a prevailing school of historians of social and political thought, who have wished to insist that it must be possible, simply by reading such works 'over and over', to arrive at a sufficient understanding of them.[41] It will be clear by now, however, that to adopt such an approach must usually be to follow an inadequate methodology. It is surely clear (to keep to the Machiavelli example) that the fact that *The Prince* was in part intended as a deliberate attack on the moral convictions of advice-books to princes cannot be discovered simply by attending to the text, since this is not a fact contained in the text. It is also clear, however, that no one can be said fully to understand Machiavelli's text who does not understand this fact about it. To fail to grasp this fact is to fail to grasp the *point* of Machiavelli's argument in the later chapters of his book. It seems then, that some other form of study besides that of reading the text itself 'over and over' must be indispensable to an understanding of it. And it seems that this will at least need to take the form of adding a study of the general conventions and assumptions of the genre, from which the intentions of any particular contributor to it may then – by a combination of inference and scholarship – be decoded.

V

It will be clear by now that my thesis occupies a middle ground which has I believe been somewhat overlooked in the course of the current philosophical debate about the explanation of action in history and in social science. I have not been particularly concerned with exegesis, but I believe my position to be similar, at least in certain important respects, to that taken up – though by a very different route – in Weber's *Wirtschaft und Gesellschaft*. Those who have emphasized (correctly, I believe) the importance of intentions and conventions in the explanation of social action have usually written as though it follows that the attempt to explain such actions causally must represent a confusion, even a 'pernicious confusion'; that it must in any case be 'wholly irrelevant'; and that the whole vocabulary of causality ought accordingly to be 'expunged' from discussions about the explanation of social action.[42] Conversely, those philosophers who have insisted (again correctly, I believe) on the absurdity of this commitment have usually written (as I have shown in the case of all the naturalists I have examined) as though it follows that intentions and conventions must themselves be treated simply as causal conditions of social actions. What I have essentially sought to argue is that neither of these alleged implications follows, and that both these claims seem to be mistaken.

It might finally be asked what relation these conclusions may bear to the issue of determinism with respect to voluntary human actions. This would be a vertiginous question even to broach, were it not that several proponents of the two naturalist theses I have examined seem to suggest that they lend an immediate strength to the thesis of determinism. This belief emerges, for example, at the end of Ayer's essay on 'Man as a subject for science'. It is first pointed out there that we ordinarily explain human action by citing the agent's motives and intentions and the social context of his behaviour. It is then argued that all these conditions must be construed as causes of which the agent's actions are effects. It is then said to follow that there is 'no reason why the reign of law should break down' when we come to explain such actions. This is 'the strength of the determinists'.[43]

I have sought to argue, however, that while there can undoubtedly be successful causal explanations of voluntary human actions, there can also be successful explanations of voluntary human actions which operate simply by recovering the illocutionary redescription of the given action, which are neither causal nor reducible to a causal form. If this argument is sound, then it seems possible to suggest two conclusions about the relations between the naturalist theses I have examined and the idea of the social determinism of actions, without having to commit oneself on the vexed question of the meaning of the thesis of determinism itself. The first, which must obviously be put very tentatively, is that if it is in fact essential for the defence of the thesis of the social determinism of actions that it should be possible to construe all the mental states of agents as causes of their actions, then there may be something inherently doubtful about the thesis. But the main conclusion, which can I think be expressed more confidently, is that in so far as the current arguments in favour of the thesis of social determinism have to depend upon the truth of theses C and D – including the assumption contained in thesis D, that an agent's intentions must always be construed as causes of which his actions are effects – the thesis of social determinism has not yet been strengthened at all.

5

Some problems in the analysis of political thought and action

I am most grateful to Professors Schochet and Wiener not just for their generosity in commenting on my work, but also for their accuracy in reporting my arguments and their perceptiveness as critics.[1] It seems possible to respond to their remarks in one of two ways. One would be to pursue the implications of Wiener's article and try to provide some more historical information about the context of Hobbes' political thought. This strikes me as an attractive alternative, especially since I agree with his suggestion that I ought to devote more attention to analysing the nature of the social pressures which helped to prompt Hobbes and his sympathizers to espouse their peculiar brand of absolutism. (He does not mention, however, that this theme has already been brilliantly explored by K. V. Thomas.)[2] The other alternative is to say something more about my general approach to the study of political theory, of which my work on Hobbes (as Schochet and Wiener both acknowledge) has mainly been intended to serve as an example. This strikes me as even more attractive, and it is this line of argument which I shall pursue.

There are two main reasons for this choice. One is my wish to defend myself against a number of attacks which have recently been mounted on the methodological and philosophical essays in which I have tried to formulate my approach to studying the history of political thought. The first of these was published in 1970 by Dr Leslie in *Political Studies*. This was followed by more technical criticism by Dr Mew in the *Philosophical Quarterly*. Two further critical articles appeared in 1973, one by Dr Parekh and Dr Berki in the *Journal of the History of Ideas*, the other by Professor Tarlton in *History and Theory*. And now Professor Schochet has added a further series of criticisms as the conclusion to the account he has given of my work.[3]

My first aim in what follows will be to discuss these critics, some of whom, I cannot help feeling, have sometimes misstated my case. Parekh and Berki, for example, begin by promising what they call a detailed critical appreciation, but they then go on to concentrate on a single methodological article (for which they give the wrong reference) without ever indicating that it was presented as one of a series or that it was underpinned by a number of historical examples. Although most of my critics have been much more scrupulous, I still feel that what is needed is not the abandonment of my approach (as they all suggest) and still less the acknowledgement of its impossibility (as Schochet in particular demands), but simply an attempt to provide a more careful and less polemical statement of my central claims. I hope this will serve to remove a number of misconceptions, as well as to show that my argument in fact emerges more or less unscathed from the criticisms which have so far been directed against it.

My chief reason, however, for concentrating on these methodological questions is my hope that this may also serve to uncover two implications of my approach, both of which perhaps deserve to be more fully pursued. The first of these (which I shall consider in section I) concerns the question of what precisely ought to be studied in the history of political thought – whether we ought mainly to focus on the traditional canon of so-called 'classic texts', on the leading traditions of political analysis, or perhaps on the entire 'language' of politics at a given time. The other implication I wish to examine (to which I shall turn in section II) is concerned with the intractably large but crucial question of how to analyse the relations between the professed principles and the actual practices of political life. My main aim in what follows is to avoid merely repeating myself in a clearer voice, and to move on – however sketchily – to a consideration of these further points.

I

The aims of my earliest methodological essays, in 1966 and 1969, were avowedly polemical, with the result – which I now mildly regret – that they were written in a tone of 'enthusiasm' for which I have recently been rebuked.[4] My primary concern was to expose the weaknesses of two prevailing assumptions about the study of the classic texts in the history of political thought. One of these, to which Parekh and Berki unrepentantly return, was the belief that 'in some cases the source of a text's intelligibility lies within itself and its understanding does not require the commentator to consider its context'.[5] The other was the belief that a satisfactory history can be constructed out of the 'unit ideas' contained in such texts, or else out of linking such texts together in a chain of alleged influences. As Wiener has indicated, my reason for attacking these methodologies was my sense that they had given rise to a number of exegetically plausible but historically incredible interpretations of the classic texts. I took the case of Hobbes' *Leviathan* and tried to show that this applied both to Warrender's and Hood's interpretations, as well as to Strauss's and Macpherson's accounts of Hobbes' place in seventeenth-century thought.[6]

Although this was intended to be revisionist, there was at least one crucial point at which the assumptions governing my approach were of a wholly conventional kind. As Schochet observes, I assumed throughout that the classic texts were worthy of study in themselves, and that the attempt to understand them ought to be treated as one of the leading aims in any history of political thought. This makes it unfair of Tarlton to claim that the objects of analysis in my proposed methodology remained 'vaguely and arbitrarily specified'.[7] My concern was in fact with the same objects which had always been analysed – the 'select few books', as a recent author has called them, which, for whatever reasons, 'have been raised to the status of "classics"'.[8] My original aim was merely to analyse the nature of the conditions which are necessary and perhaps sufficient for an understanding of any one of these texts. As Wiener points out, I tried to establish that one of the necessary conditions must be the recovery of the historical meaning of the text. I thus concluded that it can never be sufficient in itself (*pace* Parekh and Berki) to be able to supply even the most plausible and coherent internal analysis of their arguments.

This approach has been assailed, however, both for being excessively historical and for not being historical enough. The latter criticism, as Schochet notes, is one which I suggested myself in my earliest methodological article. I should now be more inclined to emphasize it. We can hardly claim to be concerned with the history of political theory unless we are prepare to write it as real history – that is, as the record of an actual activity, and in particular as the history of ideologies. Such a history would have many values, quite apart from providing us for the first time with a realistic picture of how political thinking in all its various forms was carried on in the past. It would enable us to illuminate the varying roles played by intellectual factors in political life. It would thus enable us to begin to establish the connections between the world of ideology and the world of political action. And this in turn would enable us to add an extra dimension to the study of general history which seems at the moment to be missing even in the work of its most distinguished practitioners. (It has become a commonplace, for example, that this is the major weakness of Braudel's attempt to write 'total history'.) It is clear, however, that the chief obstacle to writing such a history of social and political ideas is constituted by our continuing tendency to concentrate on the received canon of classic texts. They impose a distorting perspective when we try to write historically about the development of social and political ideas. And they encourage the adoption of a naive diffusionist account of the relations between the work of leading social theorists and the popular acceptance of new social and political attitudes. As an example of the first danger, consider the attempt of Professor C. B. Macpherson to write the history of 'possessive individualism', and the unhistorical level of abstraction at which the whole work proceeds.[9] As an example of the second, consider the attempts which have recently been made to vindicate the influence of Bentham's ideas on the development of nineteenth-century social policies.[10]

It is possible, however, to endorse this line of criticism (as I do) and still feel that a caveat needs to be entered against the over-enthusiastic adoption of a completely sociological approach, through which the object of analysis becomes nothing less than the whole gamut of 'languages' in which a nation articulates its political experience over time.[11] There is a danger that this new sociology, when writ large, will turn out to be nothing more than the most discredited form of inductivism in fashionable disguise. This danger has already become apparent in the recent historiography of the history of scientific ideas, in which the old, 'internal' history of rational discoveries has tended to be superseded in favour of the attempt to gain 'a full picture of the new science'.[12] The problems this is likely to generate are strictly analogous to those in the history of political ideas, and have recently been excellently discussed.[13] If we try to produce 'the full picture', we are bound sooner rather than later to be reduced merely to colouring-in the most boring and trivial details. We are in any case bound to fail. For the facts are infinite in number, and unless we have some ideas about where to begin and why to begin there, we may literally condemn ourselves to going on for ever. It follows that we must be prepared to make some crucial decisions at the outset about what deserves to be studied and what is best ignored. It will not do, moreover, to accept the solution proposed by Butterfield and the other opponents of 'whig' history, who have argued that, even if we proceed in this way, we must be careful to 'adopt the outlook' and apply only those criteria of significance which were current and accepted at the relevant historical time.[14] It is highly implausible to suppose that there will ever be such an agreement about what matters in any historical period. But even if there happens to be complete agreement amongst their contemporaries that certain writers do not matter, we can scarcely hope to write satisfactory history if we are content merely to endorse such judgements. This would be to leave us, for example, with a history of seventeenth-century ethical theory in which Spinoza is totally ignored, a history of nineteenth-century logical theory in which Frege is barely mentioned, and so on. It seems essential, in short, to place a very strong emphasis on what seems a very obvious point: that the decisions we have to make about what to study must be our own decisions, arrived at by applying our own criteria for judging what is rational and significant.

Once this insight is restored to its rightful status as a commonplace, however, it begins to seem possible both to endorse the value of a strictly historical approach to the study of political thought, and yet to allow that a certain primacy still deserves to be assigned to studying the traditional canon of classic texts. This assumes, of course (as I have always assumed), that to speak of a text as a classic is to imply that there may be special reasons for wishing to understand it. The degree of primacy which this assigns to the classic texts is simply that they become one obvious focus around which it might seem appropriate to organize some of our historical researches. I do not say that they represent the sole or even the most interesting focus we might choose. As I have already hinted, and hope by the end of this article to make clear, I believe that the question of the relations between political ideology and action suggests a wide and more fruitful field for new research. I certainly agree, however, that the classic texts continue to provide us with one potential answer to the inescapable question of where our historical researches ought to begin, and one potential means of investing them with their point.

It may seem, however, that this conclusion merely serves to underline the alternative criticism, to the effect that this represents an excessively historical approach for a political scientist to endorse. This is the main criticism which Leslie makes. My approach is said to involve a paradoxical commitment, since it begins by presupposing the value of seeking to understand the classic texts, but ends by proposing a method of studying which 'threatens to destroy the very treasure we seek, leaving only the dust of scholarship'.[15] Tarlton has repeated the same fear and expressed it as a certainty. My plea for 'strict historicity' is said to make it 'difficult to see how, even if it were workable, anything might issue that would be of any more than the dustiest antiquarian interest'.[16] I fail to see, however, why it should be thought to follow from questioning the immediate relevance of the classic texts that we are bound to be left with nothing but antiquarian scholarship. To proffer these as exhaustive alternatives is simply to discount the point I have been seeking to emphasize: that if we are interested in such issues as the process of ideological formation and change, we cannot avoid involving ourselves in extensive historical enquiries; and if we are genuinely concerned to understand such issues, it seems only sensible to demand that these enquiries should be conducted with as much care and exactitude as possible.

My reply to this second line of criticism is thus the same as before. Although the analysis of political ideology is inescapably a historical subject, it is the merest parochialism to imply that this constitutes a reason for refusing to assign it the place which it clearly deserves in any academic study of politics. It is true that Tarlton professes to find this type of answer 'too thin to be considered an authentic confrontation of the problem'.[17] He gives no grounds for this judgement, however, and in the absence of any such argument I still cannot see what is so unsatisfactory about this conclusion. I originally felt encouraged in reaching it by the fact that a number of social philosophers (for example, Professor MacIntyre) had already made use of a similar set of assumptions in producing some important contributions to ethical and political thought.[18] Since then, I have been heartened to find some congenial arguments presented by a number of political theorists who have no connections with the 'school' which Tarlton castigates for its alleged absorption with itself.[19]

All this brings me to what is obviously the main question: How is the recovery of the historical meaning of a text to be achieved? As Schochet implies, it may be that the polemical organization of my original articles prevented me from stating my positive answer to this question with sufficient clarity. My original answer, however, was a very simple one. I argued that the key to excluding unhistorical meanings must lie in limiting our range of descriptions of any given text to those which the author himself might in principle have avowed and that the key to understanding the actual historical meaning of a text must lie in recovering the complex intentions of the author in writing it.

I should now like to make three qualifying remarks about this doctrine, in the hope of removing a number of misunderstandings of my present views. The first is that its application was always intended to be limited in two ways which I tried to spell out. These are perhaps worth stressing, since some of my critics have chosen to ignore them and have, in consequence, devoted themselves to the demolition of a position which I have never wished to defend. I have been criticized (by Parekh and Berki) for assuming that we can speak as though the author of a complex work had 'a definite "intention" in performing a single action to bring about a definite result'.[20] But I have never made such an assumption. I have rejected it as explicitly as possible, in the hope that this misunderstanding might be avoided (4:86). Second, I have been criticized (again by Parekh and Berki, and also by Tarlton) for assuming that the tasks of recovering and stating an author's intentions may be 'sufficient in themselves for a proper understanding of the work in question'.[21] But again I have never made such an assumption. I have tried to prevent precisely this misunderstanding by insisting as strongly as possible (the italics are in the original) that 'I have been concerned only' to argue 'that *amongst* the interpreter's tasks must be the recovery of the author's intentions'. I have sought to distinguish this argument 'from the much stronger claim which is often advanced' to the effect that 'the recovery of these intentions' must 'form the whole of the interpreter's task' (3:76).

My second remark is that I have never been concerned to suggest that there is anything particularly dramatic or original about my argument.

Tarlton is quite correct to speak of my debt to Mr Dunn's and Professor Pocock's recent writings, and all three of us have in turn acknowledged the influence which R. G. Collingwood has exercised over our methodological studies. It is worth stressing this important common source, for Parekh and Berki have devoted much of their space to 'explaining' how I have come to occupy my present intellectual position, and they allege that the 'most conspicuous tradition' on which I have drawn is 'closely linked with logical positivism'.[22] The fact that I have explicitly pointed to Collingwood as a major intellectual influence, coupled with the fact that Collingwood is unquestionably the leading anti-positivist Idealist in recent English philosophy, is perhaps enough to suggest the preposterousness of their argument at this point.

My final qualification is that I now feel this original statement of my position – on which it happens that most of my critics have concentrated – to have been defective in at least two respects. First, it relied on the idea that every agent has a privileged access to his own intentions, as a way of 'closing the context' on the historical meaning of a text. I now accept that I may have applied this notion too rigidly, as Dr J. W. Burrow has since implied.[23] I have also become more convinced about certain difficulties in the theory itself, which a number of philosophers have more recently explored.[24] I have since become clearer, moreover, that I have no real need to rely on this theory in order to establish my own case, and I have gone on to restate this aspect of my argument in such a way as to leave it free of this fault. The other defect in my original presentation was that I misused the argument which I borrowed from J. L. Austin about the 'illocutionary force' of utterances. I tried to employ it in the course of an attack on the idea that political theories are merely derivations from political practices, an attack which I now feel completely misfired (2:56 – 63). Since then I believe I have made use of this argument in a more satisfactory way (3; 4). I do not feel, however, that I have ever managed to provide a satisfactory reply to the epiphenomenalist case, and for this reason I should like to address myself again to this task in the second half of these present remarks.

Several of my critics (notably Parekh and Berki) write as though I had never made any attempt to repair these defects or to refine and extend the original presentation of my case. As Tarlton very fairly indicates, however, I have since moved on to focus on the concept of a convention, and especially the conventions surrounding the performance of complex linguistic acts, in an attempt to provide a more effective though closely related means of 'closing the context' on the historical meanings of texts. I have sought in particular to ask questions about what a given writer may have been *doing*, and to answer them by appealing to the extent to which his intentions must necessarily have been conventional if they included the intention to communicate and be understood (3). I have also tried to strengthen these purely methodological considerations by locating their foundations in the logic of explanation. I have tried, that is, to show how the recovery of an agent's intentions and the conventions surrounding them can serve to provide a valid (though not a causal) form of explanation for at least some of his voluntary actions (4).[25]

I do not wish to pretend that this somewhat ambitious extension of my original argument has left it entirely free of difficulties. I accept the criticism which Mew has made, by means of some ingenious counter-examples, of my attempt to argue that it must *invariably* be necessary to invoke a set of social as well as linguistic conventions in order to decode the intended force of certain utterances.[26] I am also grateful to acknowledge the refinements which have since been suggested by Dr Close and Professor Hancher in the course of the generally congenial comments which both of them have made about my recent accounts of authorial intentionality.[27] And I should like to emphasize my feeling that before anyone can hope to argue with confidence about these issues, a great deal more work will have to be done on the analysis of the concept of a convention, especially in relation to the idea of someone's meaning something by saying or doing something.[28]

Nevertheless, I see no reason to doubt that my argument in its revised and extended form is capable of sustaining both the main conclusions on which I have sought to insist: that the recovery of the historical meaning of any given text is a necessary condition of understanding it, and that this process can never be achieved simply by studying the text itself. Even Parekh and Berki seem prepared to concede that this is sometimes true, though they insist that in other cases 'the context is negligible and the audience irreducibly general and transhistorical'. They go on to argue that 'perhaps the most obvious case' of a classic text which 'makes eminent sense on its own' and 'has no specific context and no limited and identifiable audience' is the case of Hobbes' *Leviathan*.[29] I agree that *Leviathan* is probably the most plausible candidate, but one of the main purposes of my historical articles about Hobbes has been to establish that even in this case such an assumption would in fact be misplaced. Unless we are prepared to ask questions about what Hobbes is doing in *Leviathan*, and to seek the answers by relating his work to the prevailing conventions of political argument at the time, we can never hope to elucidate the precise character of his counter-revolutionary theory of political obligation, nor can we hope to understand the precise role of his epistemology in relation to his political thought. If we are prepared, however, to consider *Leviathan* in relation to its appropriate intellectual and ideological context, we can readily begin to answer these questions, and in this way to add to our understanding of the work. We can also begin to see the extent to which, even if Hobbes may have had the ambition to speak 'transhistorically' (which I have never sought to deny), his work *was* addressed to a strictly limited and precisely identifiable audience.

My reasons for insisting on these conclusions have been very fairly paraphrased by Wiener, and there is no need to rehearse them here. Since Parekh and Berki evidently reject them outright, I can only conclude that they find my historical arguments in some way grossly defective. It is a disappointing feature of their critique, however, that they offer no comments on the new information which I have sought to present about the context of Hobbes' thought, and in consequence give no reasons for their flat rejection of my claims. They simply insist, on the contrary, that I have never made any attempt to corroborate my general methodological claims by any 'detailed investigation of past thinkers'.[30]

I am prepared to admit, however, that my alleged discoveries about Hobbes may well be controversial in some way, so I shall revert instead to a simpler example, which I have considered before and which can equally well be used to substantiate both my central claims. Locke, in his *Two Treatises*, makes no appeal to the prescriptive force of the ancient English constitution. An examination of the prevailing conventions of debate about political obligation at the time reveals that this was an extremely unusual lacuna for him to have left in his argument. This may well lead us to ask what Locke may have been doing here. We are bound to answer that he was rejecting and repudiating one of the most widespread and prestigious forms of political argument at the time. We may also be led to question whether he may not have had the intention to shift the discussion of political obligation onto a more abstract level at this point, by ignoring the claims of prescription and arguing entirely in terms of the concepts of natural law and natural rights. This seems to substantiate both my central claims. We can scarcely be said to have understood Locke's text until we have considered what he was doing at this crucial stage in his argument. But we can never hope to attain such an understanding simply be reading the text itself 'over and over again' in the way that some commentators have urged.[31]

It is not difficult, moreover, to defend this basic methodological commitment against the chief accusation which has been levelled against it. According to Parekh and Berki, it 'means the denial of the possibility of new insights and experience'.[32] According to Tarlton, it involves denying that some writers 'operate at or beyond the boundaries of established "languages"'.[33] And, according to Schochet, we may become 'blinded to such goals' as innovation and 'creativity' if we follow this approach. This accusation seems to rest on a confusion between the unexceptionable claim that any agent who is engaged in an intended act of communication must be limited by the prevailing conventions of discourse, and the further claim that he must be limited only to *following* these conventions. I have obviously never intended to commit myself to the absurdity of denying that it is open to any writer to indicate that his aim is to extend, to subvert, or in some other way to alter a prevailing set of accepted conventions and attitudes. I am astonished to be told that my approach would make it impossible to map out this kind of innovation and change. It seems to me, on the contrary, that I am providing the means – the only sure means – of exhibiting the precise character of these changes, and of indicating the precise moment at which they actually took place. This can readily be seen if I revert to the example I have just cited from Locke's *Two Treatises*. It is only if and when we have mapped out all the prevailing conventions of political discussion that we can begin to observe the points at which, and the extent to which, Locke may be concerned to breach or repudiate them. So far from denying such moments of creativity, my approach seems in this way to provide the only means of recognizing and illuminating them in a genuinely historical way.

I should like finally to claim one special merit for my approach which I have not previously discussed. I believe it provides a means of avoiding a weakness which otherwise seems endemic in any attempt to take the idea of a 'language' or a tradition as a unit of study in the history of political thought. I am not, of course, hostile to these aims themselves, for my own attempt to focus on the conventions of political argument obviously tends to culminate in a study of genres and traditions of discourse. It would hardly seem necessary to offer this reassurance, were it not that Parekh and Berki have reported me as saying that it can never be justifiable for an intellectual historian to write 'in terms of traditions, periods, schools of thought and the like'.[34] It is hard to see how they have gained this impression. As I have tried to make clear, I share the enthusiasm which they register for attempts such as those of Professor Greenleaf to write about leading traditions of political analysis, even though I cannot entirely endorse their claim (for reasons which I have given at length elsewhere) that Greenleaf has in fact achieved this result 'without any distortion'.[35] (I also find it surprising that they give the wrong title for a book which they single out as so well known.) I do feel, however, that if Greenleaf's stress on traditions or Pocock's on languages are treated as methodologies in themselves, they are prone to generate at least two difficulties. There is an obvious danger that if we merely focus on the relations between the vocabulary used by a given writer and the traditions to which he may appear connected by his use of this vocabulary, we may become insensitive to instances of irony, obliquity, and other cases in which the writer may seem to be saying something other than what he means. The chief danger, however, is that if we merely concentrate on the language of a given writer, we may run the risk of assimilating him to a completely alien intellectual tradition, and thus of misunderstanding the whole aim of his political works.

An obvious example of the first danger is provided by the work of Bayle, as I have sought to illustrate elsewhere (2:51 – 3). An obvious example of the second is provided by the recent discussions of Bolingbroke's political works. It happens to be Bolingbroke, the arch-enemy of the whigs, who supplies in his main political works the clearest summary of a number of radically whig and especially Harringtonian political beliefs. It is, of course, necessary to focus on the political traditions which Bolingbroke was exploiting in order to be able to expose this paradox, and this has been the great strength of the recent commentaries. Their great weakness, however, has been their incapacity to go on to explain or even to comment on this puzzle. They have merely left us with the question-begging observation that 'Bolingbroke, the tory, shows whiggish traits' and with the potentially misleading characterization of Bolingbroke as 'the most spectacular of the neo-Harringtonians'.[36]

I am suggesting that what is needed, in order to be able to carry the argument beyond this rather unsatisfactory point, is not merely to indicate the traditions of discourse to which a given writer may be appealing, but also to ask what he may be *doing* when he appeals to the language of those particular traditions. Since many different things can always be done by different writers with a given 'language', the focus ought not, I think, to be on the language or the traditions in themselves, but rather on the range of things which can in principle be done with them (and to them) at any given time. To cite the prevailing jargon, what we need to go on to ask is what range of speech-acts can standardly be performed by a given writer when he makes use of a given set of concepts or terms. If this further question had been asked in the case of Bolingbroke, for example, I believe it could have been shown that one of his main aims in his political works may not so much have been to articulate a set of political principles in which he necessarily believed himself, but rather to *remind* his opponents of the principles which they professed to believe. (I have recently sought to demonstrate this conclusion.)[37] If we merely focus on the language of Bolingbroke's political works and the traditions with which he appears to align himself, this level of analysis will remain closed off. If we go on to engage with it, however, we may be able to answer the questions which are currently being begged, and so to reach a new level of understanding in our study of these and many other historically important political works.

II

The final outcome of my approach, according to several of my critics, is a refusal to assign any causal role to political ideas or principles in relation to the explanation of political actions and events. It is true that they have sometimes confused this with the rather different accusation which I have already considered, to the effect that my approach is incapable of accommodating the novel insights which are characteristically found in the most creative political works. It is clear, however, that when

Parekh and Berki accuse me of 'not seeing anything else in politics beyond its immediate, pragmatic aspects', what they have in mind is my alleged failure to recognize the influence of general ideological structures upon the world of political events.[38] And Tarlton appears to have the same criticism in mind when he eventually insists on aligning me with those who believe that the world of thought 'merely reflects an underlying and somehow more real world of non-linguistic activity'.[39]

I feel somewhat aggrieved by these criticisms, since one of my main hopes, in proposing a more ideological subject matter for the history of political thought, was that this might enable us more readily to exhibit the dynamic nature of the relationship which I believe to exist between the professed principles and the actual practices of political life (2:56 – 9). I still feel that the suggestion I originally made about the way in which this relationship might be analysed was correct as far as it went – the suggestion that it might be possible to make use of the approach and the insights afforded by the theory of speech-acts. It may well be, however, that I have brought this particular misunderstanding upon myself. For, as I have already conceded, the first attempt I made to formulate and apply this theory was undoubtedly a failure. It is for this reason that I should now like to revert to my original suggestion and attempt to explore it in an entirely new direction.

There seem to be two main types of situation in which a professed principle is capable of making a difference to a social or political action, and *a fortiori* needs to be cited in order to explain it. The most obvious case is where the principle serves as the motive for the action. To explain a voluntary action is normally to cite the end which the agent desires to bring about – corresponding to his motive for acting – together with his belief that the performance of the given action will conduce to the attainment of the desired end. If the agent professes to be acting for the sake of a principle, and if the principle he cites is genuinely his motive for acting, it is obvious that the principle makes a difference to the action and thus needs to be cited to explain it.

The question is whether this simple structure of concepts can ever be applied to analyse the relations between an ideology and a complex course of social or political action. One recent attempt to apply it in this way has been made by a number of historians and political scientists who have been anxious to repudiate the influential scepticism expressed by Sir Lewis Namier and his followers about the role of ideological factors in political life. Professor Holmes, for example, has attempted to construct his massive account of *British Politics in the Age of Anne* around the belief that the political conflicts of the age were not merely concerned with 'power and the quest for office', as all the Namierites have alleged, but were 'concerned with real issues, involving the conflict of sincerely-held principles'.[40] And Professor Kramnick has similarly attempted to analyse the politics of the opposition parties in early eighteenth-century England in terms of the assumption that the protagonists were genuinely motivated by 'political ideals and principles' and not just by 'the common interest of the outsider'.[41]

Despite such recent examples, however, it still seems a safe generalization to say that this sort of attempt to treat principles as sufficient conditions of actions has by now been fairly generally abandoned. One reason might seem to be the doubts which a number of philosophers (particularly some of the followers of Wittgenstein) have expressed about the underlying assumption that motives are causes. I do not myself feel, however, that there is any reason to quarrel with this assumption, the difficulties of which seem to have been somewhat exaggerated (4:86 – 9). The most obvious reason is simply that a number of the most powerful currents in modern social theory have converged in rejecting this way of analysing the *direction* of the causality between principles and actions. This applies not merely to the Namierites, but even more clearly to the Marxists (at least in certain moods) and more recently to behaviourists. They have all insisted, for different reasons, on the same two claims. First, that the principles professed in political life are commonly the merest rationalizations of quite different motives and impulses. As Namier (a great admirer of both Pareto and Freud) puts the common claim, such principles are usually invented *ex post facto*, merely in order to invest political behaviour with a quite spurious 'appearance of logic and rationality'.[42] Second, that *it follows from this* that such principles play no causal role in political life, and scarcely even need to figure in consequence in explanations of political behaviour. As Namier again puts the point, such 'party names and cant' provide us with no guide at all when we are trying to explain 'the underlying realities' of political life.[43]

It is often implied, moreover, that this is the end of the story. This is due to the fact that even those who have sought to oppose these claims have generally accepted the same basic assumption about the nature of the causal relation between political thought and action. They have tended, that is, to concede that what they must show, in order to vindicate the relevance of someone's professed principles in explaining their social and political actions, is that many political agents (as Butterfield insists in his polemic against the Namierites) are in fact 'sincerely attached to the ideals' for the sake of which they characteristically profess to act.[44] But this is simply to endorse their opponents' basic assumption, which amounts to the claim (as Namier's account sufficiently indicates) that the question of the relationship between political thought and action is equivalent to the empirical question of whether an agent's professed political principles ever serve as the motives of his political actions. The result has been to make it seem obvious that political principles have no role to play in the explanation of political behaviour. For as soon as this basic assumption is accepted by the opponents of this sort of epiphenomenalism, they are committed to sustaining the empirical claim (which intuitively may seem rather implausible) that the sincere attachment of political agents to their professed principles actually constitutes their standard motive for political action. And this, in turn, allows their opponents (such as the Namierites) to present the epiphenomenalist case in the form of a simple appeal to realism and common experience. All they have to do is to take their stand on the alternative empirical claim (which is usually taken to be far more plausible) that 'political ideals', as one of Namier's disciples has put it, are 'rarely in themselves the determinants of human action'.[45] Since it is agreed that a principle can only make a difference if it is a motive, and since it is intuitively clear that principles are rarely motives, it is obvious, they conclude, that we do not usually have to refer to an agent's professed principles when we come to explain his actual political behaviour.

It is this shared assumption, however, which seems to be mistaken. Even if we concede that an agent's professed principles are never his real motives, we are still left with at least one type of situation in which they are nevertheless capable of making a difference to his behaviour. This is the situation in which the agent is engaged in a form of social or political action that is (as I shall put it) in some way untoward, and also possesses a strong motive for attempting (in Weberian phrase) to legitimate it. Suppose – to take an example in which Weber himself was interested – the agent is a merchant engaged in some highly profitable commercial enterprise in England at the turn of the sixteenth century. His expected profits supply him with a recognizable and powerful motive for wanting to ensure that he is able to continue with his enterprise. But the social and religious standards of the age ensure that the enterprise itself is bound to appear in a morally and perhaps even a legally dubious light. It is evident that in these circumstances it becomes desirable, perhaps even essential, for the agent to be able to describe his behaviour in such a way as to defeat or at least to override any hostile appraisals of it, and in this way to legitimate what he is doing to those who may have doubts about the morality of his actions.

The suggestion I now wish to explore is that, if we concentrate on the means by which an agent in this type of situation can hope to legitimate his behaviour, we may be able to uncover a further type of causal connection between the principles for the sake of which he professes to act and his actual social or political actions. As a preface to this discussion, however, it is vital to concede that I have characterized the situation in an artificially simple way. I have implied that the sole motive for offering an ideological description of one's untoward social actions will normally be to legitimate them to others who may have doubts about their legality or morality. I have thus implied that there is no reason to suppose that the agent ever needs to offer these descriptions for his own benefit, or even needs to believe in them at all. I have adopted this tactic, however, only in order to avoid having to raise some highly complex and purely empirical questions which in no way affect the validity of my general argument. It is obvious that an agent's motives in this situation will usually be mixed and complicated, and it is arguable that the need to attain an appropriate self-image by legitimating his behaviour to himself and his sympathizers may often be of paramount importance. To preserve the simplicity of the argument, however, I am willing in what follows to concede what is from my point of view the hardest case: the situation of an imagined agent who never actually believes in any of the principles he professes, and whose principles never serve in consequence as the main motives of his actions. My aim is to show that even in this case it still does not follow (as the Namierites, for example, have supposed) that we have no need to refer to this agent's professed principles if we wish to explain his behaviour.

If we now turn to ask how this central task of an innovating ideologist – that of legitimating untoward social actions – can actually be performed, the theory of speech-acts immediately seems to provide an important clue to the answer. A number of recent philosophers of language – having thrown out as an old piece of positivist bric-à-brac the alleged logical distinction between factual and evaluative statements – have been able to concentrate on a group of terms which perform an evaluative as well as a descriptive function in the language.[46] They are standardly used to describe individual actions or states of affairs, and to characterize the motives for the sake of which these actions can be performed. But if the criteria for applying one of these terms can be plausibly claimed to be present in a given set of circumstances, this not only serves to describe the given action or state of affairs, but also to evaluate it in a certain way. The special characteristic of this range of descriptive terms is thus that they have a standard application to perform one of two contrasting ranges of speech-acts. They are standardly used, that is, to perform such acts as commending (and expressing approval, etc.) or else of condemning (and expressing disapproval, etc.) the actions or states of affairs which they are also employed to describe.[47]

To focus on this group of terms is to take over an insight developed by the so-called emotivists in ethical theory, who contrasted the 'emotive' with the 'descriptive' components of the meaning of ethical terms.[48] But as Urmson has pointed out in applying Austin's theory of speech-acts to clarify their account, the emotivists in effect confused what Austin dubbed the 'illocutionary' with the 'perlocutionary' sense in which an agent may succeed in doing something in or by using one of these terms. (Henceforth I shall inelegantly refer to them as 'evaluative–descriptive terms'.) The sorts of perlocutionary effects which an agent may hope to achieve by using these terms are effects such as inciting or persuading his hearers or readers to adopt a particular point of view. But the question of whether he succeeds in realizing such hopes is not primarily a linguistic matter, but simply a matter for empirical investigation. The sorts of illocutionary effects, however, which it is open to an agent to achieve in using these terms, are effects such as evincing, expressing, and soliciting approval or disapproval of the actions or states of affairs which he uses them to describe. The question of whether he succeeds in realizing this sort of intention is essentially a linguistic matter, a matter of applying the relevant terms correctly. And it is this fact which gives them their great analytical significance.[49]

It is essentially by manipulating this set of terms that any society succeeds in establishing and altering its moral identity. It is by describing and thereby commending certain courses of action as (say) courageous or honest, while describing and condemning others as treacherous or disloyal, that we sustain our picture of the actions and states of affairs which we wish either to disavow or to legitimate. This being so, the task of the innovating ideologist is a hard but an obvious one. His concern, by definition, is to legitimate a new range of social actions which, in terms of the existing ways of applying the moral vocabulary prevailing in his society, are currently regarded as in some way untoward or illegitimate. His aim must therefore be to show that a number of existing and favourable evaluative–descriptive terms can somehow be applied to his apparently untoward actions. If he can somehow perform this trick, he can thereby hope to argue that the condemnatory descriptions which are otherwise liable to be applied to his actions can in consequence be discounted.

Two footnotes need to be added at this stage of the argument, one emphatic, the other concessive. The point which perhaps needs to be emphasized is that, however revolutionary the ideologist concerned may be, he will nevertheless be committed, once he has accepted the need to legitimate his behaviour, to attempting to show that some of the *existing* range of favourable evaluative–descriptive terms can somehow be applied as apt descriptions of his own apparently untoward actions. Every revolutionary is to this extent obliged to march backwards into battle. To legitimate his behaviour, he is committed to showing that it can be described in such a way that those who currently disapprove of it can somehow be brought to see that they ought to withhold this disapproval after all. And to achieve this end, he has no option but to show that at least some of the terms which his ideological opponents use when they are describing the actions and states of affairs of which they approve can be applied to include and thus legitimate his own untoward behaviour.

The concessive point is that the situation in the real world is in at least one important respect more complicated than my model has so far implied. It is not simply that the agent tries to apply to his own behaviour whatever favourable evaluative–descriptive terms are in fact best adapted to legitimating it. It is rather that he applies those he happens to believe are best adapted to this purpose. And it is obvious that he may always make a mistake or even an irrational choice in assessing the best means to attain this desired end. Nevertheless, it still seems correct to begin by assuming that the agent will have acted in a rational way. I say this not merely to preserve the simplicity of my general discussion, but also as a methodological precept when it comes to the discussion of actual examples. If we begin by assuming the agent's rationality and find this assumption borne out, this will provide us with an explanation for the agent's apparent belief that he was acting rationally. It will in fact provide us with the best possible explanation – namely, that he *was* acting rationally. Conversely, unless we begin by assuming the agent's rationality, we leave ourselves with no means of explaining his behaviour, or even of seeing exactly what there is to explain about it, if it should happen that he is not acting rationally. To adopt this methodology is thus to remind ourselves of two important lessons. One is that to exhibit a social action as rational *is* to explain it. The other is that to explain why an agent acts as he does must always involve the capacity to explain why he evidently *believed* it was rational for him to perform a particular action when it was not in fact rational for him to do so.

These points can readily be underlined if we revert to the example of those who were concerned in early seventeenth-century England to legitimate their novel commercial and capitalist enterprises. They chose to attempt to legitimate this untoward behaviour in part by seeking to describe it in terms of the concepts normally used to commend an ideal of the religious life. It is clear that this was in fact a rational choice. If they could somehow plausibly apply these concepts to describe their own behaviour, this would obviously provide them with a most powerful legitimating device. It was, moreover, plausible to make such an attempt, since there was a certain element of structural similarity – which they eagerly exploited – between the specifically Protestant ideal of individual service and devotion (to God) and the alleged commercial ideals of service (to one's customers) and dedication (to one's work).

This brings me to the practical question: how is it possible (in the above or in any other case) actually to manipulate an existing normative vocabulary in such a way as to legitimate such new and untoward courses of action? There may be said to be two distinct methods, though they are often confused. (They are systematically confused, for example, by the writers of dictionaries.) The first consists in effect of manipulating the standard speech-act potential of an existing set of descriptive terms. The agent's aim in this case is to describe his own actions in such a way as to make it clear (from the context) to his ideological opponents that even though he may be using a set of terms which are standardly applied to express disapproval, he is nevertheless using them to express approval or at least neutrality on this particular occasion. The point of this strategy is, of course, to challenge his opponents to reconsider the feelings of disapproval or even of mere neutrality which they are standardly expressing when they use these particular terms.

There are two main tactics available to the innovating ideologist in attempting to bring off this first strategy. He may try to introduce some wholly new and favourable evaluative–descriptive terms into the language. There are two possibilities here. One is simply to coin new terms as the descriptions of alleged new principles, and then to apply them as descriptions of whatever apparently untoward actions one may wish to see commended. This seems to be the tactic which most commentators have had in mind when they have discussed the phenomenon of 'altered meanings and new words' in political debate.[50] This is obviously an extremely crude device, however, and it is comparatively rare to find it employed in ideological debate. There is, however, one important instance of it in the case of the ideology I have mentioned. The concept of *frugality* provides an example of an entirely new term which became widely used for the first time at the end of the sixteenth century in order to describe a motive and a form of social action for which approval was beginning to be widely sought. The other and far commoner version of this tactic, however, consists of turning a neutral description into a favourable evaluative–descriptive term (usually by means of a metaphorical extension of its uses) and then applying it in virtue of this extended meaning to describe some course of action which one wishes to see commended. There are many cases of this sort of transformation in the ideology I have mentioned. The metaphorical (and, hence, evaluative) uses of such terms as *discerning* and *penetrating*, for example, make their first appearance in the language at the relevant time in order to describe a range of talents which many people had come to have a special reason for wishing to see commended.

The second and bolder tactic consists of varying the range of speech-acts which are standardly performed with an existing set of unfavourable evaluative–descriptive terms. Again there are two possibilities here. The more usual is to apply a term normally used to express disapproval in such a way as to neutralize this speech-act potential. The agent thus makes it clear that he intends the action which the term is being used to describe to be appraised on this occasion in a wholly neutral way. One clear and ultimately successful instance of this tactic is provided by the concept of *ambition*. It was only at the start of the seventeenth century that this term began to acquire its current neutral uses. It had previously been applied exclusively to express the strongest possible disapproval of whatever courses of action it was used to describe. The other and more dramatic possibility is actually to reverse the standard speech-act potential of the existing and unfavourable evaluative–descriptive term. An equally clear and successful example of this tactic, again from the same ideology, is provided by the concept of *shrewdness*. Again, before the start of the seventeenth century, this term had been used exclusively to express disapproval. During the ensuing generation, its potential was completely reversed, giving it the standard use which it still fulfils as a term of approbation.

It is, of course, conceptually possible, though it seems to be empirically less usual, to employ a mirror-image of both these tactics as a means of trying to bring off this first strategy. It is possible in the first place to coin new and unfavourable evaluative–descriptive terms, and apply them to describe familiar forms of social behaviour which one may have come to wish to see condemned. This happened in the case of the ideology I have been citing with the concept of *squandering* and of being a *spendthrift*. Both these terms became widely used for the first time at the end of the sixteenth century in order to describe and express a new disapproval of the aristocratic ideal of conspicuous consumption. It is also possible to turn existing neutral descriptive terms into unfavourable evaluative–descriptive terms by means of a metaphorical extension of their uses. Two examples from the same ideology are provided by the concepts of *errant* and *exorbitant* behaviour, both of which first attained their metaphorical (and hence evaluative) meanings at the start of the seventeenth century. And, finally, the standard application of an existing evaluative–descriptive term to express approval can also be reversed – as happened with the concept of acting *obsequiously*. The term was standardly used until the end of the sixteenth century to express approval and only afterward became a term of disapprobation.

I now turn to the second strategy, which is both much simpler and of far greater significance as a legitimating device. This consists, in effect, of manipulating the criteria for the application of an existing set of favourable evaluative–descriptive terms. The ideologist's aim in this case is to insist, with as much plausibility as he can muster, that, in spite of any contrary appearances, a number of favourable evaluative–descriptive terms can in fact be applied as apt descriptions of his own apparently untoward social actions. The point of this strategy is to challenge his ideological opponents to reconsider whether they may not be making an empirical mistake (and may thus be socially insensitive) in failing to see that the ordinary criteria for applying an existing range of favourable evaluative–descriptive terms may be present in the very actions they have been condemning as illegitimate.

The attempt to make this move is, of course, ideological in the most pejorative sense, since it depends on the performance of a linguistic sleight-of-hand. The aim is to argue that a favourable evaluative–descriptive term is being applied in the ordinary way, while trying at the same time to drop some of the criteria for applying it, thereby extending the range of the actions which it can properly be used to describe and commend. (Again, the mirror-image of this strategy is to try to limit the application of existing unfavourable evaluative–descriptive terms.) This will fail if too many of the criteria are dropped, for in this case the fact that the term has undergone a 'change of meaning' will become too obvious. But it will also fail if not enough are dropped, for in this case the capacity of the term to cover and thus to legitimate new forms of social action will not have been extended after all.

Despite these difficulties, this probably represents the most widespread and important form of ideological argument. It was extensively employed in the case of the ideology I have been citing: by means of it an attempt was made to connect the principles of Protestant Christianity with the practices of commercial life. Consider, for example, the use of the two most important evaluative–descriptive terms in the religious vocabulary of the age, the term 'providence' and the term 'religious' itself. By the end of the sixteenth century, it began to be suggested by those who wished to legitimate the characteristic interest of the commercial classes in being foresightful in monetary affairs that this apparently miserly (and, hence, untoward) pattern of behaviour ought really to be seen as a commendable working of providence and thus as a provident form of action. They also began to suggest that their characteristic interest in punctuality and exactitude ought not to be condemned as excessively rigorous and severe, but ought rather to be appraised and thus commended as a genuinely religious form of commitment. The best proof of the ideological motives at work in these new patterns of social description and evaluation is provided by the fact that the meanings of these key evaluative–descriptive terms soon became stretched and confused. The concept of providence began to be used in good faith (as it is still used) to refer simply to acting with foresight about monetary affairs, while the concept of acting religiously came to be used simply to refer to cases of exact and punctual behaviour. The standardization of these new meanings both date, as one might expect, from the start of the seventeenth century.

My main conclusion, which these examples serve to underline, is that all those who have argued about the relations between social and political thought and action in the manner of Namierites or the behaviourists have in effect been involved in a non sequitur. It does not, as they have tended to suppose, follow from the fact that an agent's professed principles may be *ex post facto* rationalizations that they have no role to play in explaining his behaviour. As I have sought to emphasize, this argument ignores the implications of the fact that any agent possesses a standard motive for attempting to legitimate his untoward social or political actions. This implies first of all that he will be committed to claiming that his apparently untoward actions were in fact motivated by some accepted set of social or political principles. And this in turn implies that, even if the agent is not in fact motivated by any of the principles he professes, he will nevertheless be obliged to behave in such a way that his actions remain compatible with the claim that these principles genuinely motivated him. To recognize these implications is to accept that the courses of action open to any rational

agent in this type of situation must in part be determined by the range of
principles which he can profess with plausibility. There is both a general
and more specific conclusion to be drawn out here. The general conclusion
derives from the fact that any course of action is inhibited from occurring
if it cannot be legitimated. It follows that any principle which helps to
legitimate a course of action must also be amongst the enabling conditions
of its occurrence. The more specific conclusion derives from the fact that
the nature and range of the evaluative concepts which any agent can hope
to apply in order to legitimate his behaviour can in no case be set by the
agent himself. Their availability is a question about the prevailing morality
of the society in which the agent is acting; their applicability is a question
about the standard meaning and use of the terms involved, and about how
far these can be plausibly stretched. These factors serve as rather specific
constraints and directives to the agent about what precise lines of conduct
afford him the best means of bringing his untoward actions in line with some
accepted principle, and thereby legitimating what he does while still gaining
what he wants. He cannot hope to stretch the application of the existing
principles indefinitely; correspondingly, he can only hope to legitimate a
restricted range of actions. It follows that to study the principles which
the agent finally chooses to profess must be to study one of the key determinants of his decision to follow out any one particular line of action.

Even if these conclusions seem acceptable, however, it may still be felt that
I have chosen to illustrate them with an unfortunate example. It has become
a commonplace amongst historians to repudiate any suggestion that the
principles of Protestant Christianity played a causal role in the development
of capitalist practices. As Trevor-Roper has put it, any such theory 'is
exploded by the simple fact' that 'large scale industrial capitalism' already
existed before the Protestant reformation.[51] It is true that if Weber imagined
that a pre-existing Protestant ethic later helped in such a direct way to cause
the rise of capitalism, then his theory is refuted by showing that the emergence of capitalism predated the rise of Protestantism. It is hard to believe,
however, that he intended only to suggest such a crude and easily discredited
connection. It seems more plausible to construe him as having intended to
argue that the Protestant ethic was particularly well adjusted to *legitimating*
the rise of capitalism, and in this way helped it to develop and flourish. My
own argument can thus be read as an attempt to reinterpret what I take to
have been Weber's real meaning. I do not wish, however, to press this point
of interpretation here. I only wish to emphasize that even if Trevor-Roper's
criticism can be shown to point to a real weakness in Weber's argument, it
cannot be shown to point to any weakness in the argument I have myself
been concerned to advance. My suggestion that the role of Protestantism
was to legitimate the rise of capitalism is obviously based not on ignoring
but on assuming the fact that capitalism predated Protestantism. What I

have tried to show, however, is that it does not follow from this fact, as Trevor-Roper and others appear to conclude, that Protestantism had no causal role to play in the development of capitalism. As I have sought to argue, this ignores the fact that the earliest capitalists lacked any legitimacy in the moral climate in which they at first found themselves, and so needed – as one of the conditions of being able to flourish and develop – to find some means of legitimating their behaviour. As I have sought to illustrate, one of the most valuable means they found was to appropriate and apply to themselves the normative vocabulary of the Protestant religion – greatly to the horror, in this case, of all sincerely religious Protestants, who naturally found no difficulty in seeing through the trick. But there is no doubt that the trick worked: the vocabulary of Protestantism not only helped to increase the acceptability of capitalism, but arguably helped to channel its development in specific ways – in particular towards an ethic of industriousness. The relative acceptability of this new pattern of social behaviour then helped in turn to ensure that the system developed and flourished. It is for this reason that, even if the emergence of capitalism predated the emergence of its ideology, and even if the professed ideology never provided the capitalists with any of their real motives, it is still essential to refer to the ideology in order to be able to explain how and why the system developed.

6
Language and social change

What can we hope to learn about the processes of social innovation and legitimation by studying the key words we use to construct and appraise the social world itself? This is the question I hope to confront in the course of the following remarks. The question is obviously a vast one, however, and in order to make it manageable I shall concentrate on one recent and highly influential study which has focused on the links between linguistic and social change. The work I have in mind – which I intend to use as a stalking horse in what follows – is Raymond Williams's *Keywords*.[1] It is Williams's central contention that a study of 'variations and confusions of meaning' may help us to improve our understanding of matters of 'historical and contemporary substance'.[2] If we take 'certain words at the level at which they are generally used', he suggests, and scrutinize their developing structures of meaning 'in and through historical time', we may be able 'to contribute certain kinds of awareness' to current social and political debates, and in particular an 'extra edge of consciousness'.[3] But what precise kinds of awareness can we hope to attain from studying the histories of key words? And how should we conduct our studies in order to ensure that this awareness is duly attained? These are the questions I should like to examine at somewhat greater length.

I

Before proceeding, however, we need if possible to neutralize one serious doubt. It might be objected that, in singling out 'a shared body of words', we are focusing on the wrong unit of analysis altogether.[4] Williams' aim, he tells us, is to illuminate 'ways not only of discussing but at another level of seeing many of our central experiences'.[5] But if we wish to grasp how someone sees the world — what distinctions he[6] draws, what classifications he accepts — what we need to know is not what words he uses but rather what concepts he possesses.

It is true that this objection may appear a purely verbal one. For it might be replied — and the claim has often been made — that possessing a concept is equivalently a matter of knowing the meaning of a word. This certainly seems to be Williams's own view, for in discussing the term *nature* he equates 'the word and the concept', and in speaking of *democracy* he explains how the 'concept' is 'embodied' in the word.[7]

However, to argue for any such equivalence is undoubtedly a mistake. First of all, it cannot be a necessary condition of my possessing a concept that I need to understand the correct application of a corresponding term. Suppose, for example, that I am studying Milton's thought, and want to know whether Milton considered it important that a poet should display a high degree of originality. The answer seems to be that he felt it to be of the greatest importance. When he spoke of his own aspirations at the beginning of *Paradise Lost*, what he particularly emphasized was his decision to deal with 'things unattempted yet in prose or rhyme'. But I could never have arrived at this conclusion by examining Milton's use of the word *originality*. For while the concept is clearly central to his thought, the word did not enter the language until a century or more after his death. Although a history of the word *originality* and its various uses could undoubtedly be written, such a survey would by no means be the same as a history of the concept of originality — a consideration often ignored in practice by historians of ideas.

Moreover, it cannot be a sufficient condition of my possessing a concept that I understand the correct application of a corresponding term. There is still the possibility (explored by Wittgenstein as well as Kant) that I may believe myself to be in possession of a concept when this belief is in fact mistaken. Consider for example the difficulties raised by certain highly general terms such as *being* or *infinity*. A whole community of language users may be capable of applying these terms with perfect consistency. Yet it might be possible to show that there is simply no concept which answers to any of their agreed usages.

What then is the relationship between concepts and words? We can scarcely hope to capture the answer in a single formula, but I think we can at least say this: the surest sign that a group or society has entered into the self-conscious possession of a new concept is that a corresponding vocabulary will be developed, a vocabulary which can then be used to pick out and discuss the concept with consistency. This suggests that, while we certainly need to exercise more caution than Williams does in making inferences from the use of words to the understanding of concepts and back again, there is nevertheless a systematic relationship between words and concepts to be explored. The possession of a concept will at least *standardly* be signalled by the employment of a corresponding term. As long as we bear in mind that 'standardly' means neither necessarily nor sufficiently, I think we may legitimately proceed.

II

If our aim is to illuminate ideological disputes through the study of linguistic disagreements, the first issue we need to clarify – as Williams acknowledges – is obviously this: what exactly are we debating about a word when we find ourselves debating whether or not it ought to be applied as a description of a particular action or state of affairs?

Unfortunately, Williams's answer is confusingly vague. 'What is really happening in such encounters', he claims, is a 'process' whereby 'meanings are offered' and are then 'confirmed, asserted, qualified, changed'.[8] All such debates are thus taken to be about 'meanings'; about the 'historical origins and developments' which have issued in the 'present meanings' of the terms involved.[9]

This question-begging tendency to speak without further explication about 'changes of meaning' is due, I believe, to the fact that Williams at no point tries to isolate and describe the class of terms in which he is chiefly interested – the class of what he calls the 'strong' or 'persuasive' words, the words which 'involve ideas and values'.[10] No consistent account of how certain words come to 'involve values' is ever presented. But it seems clear that, if any further progress is to be made in discussing the phenomenon of meaning change in ideological debates, the provision of such an analysis will have to be treated as a crucial preliminary step. As it happens, this is a less Herculean task than might be feared. A great deal of attention has lately been paid by theorists of language as well as moral philosophers to isolating and commenting on precisely these terms.[11] Drawing on their accounts, we may say, I think, that three main requirements need to be met if such terms are to be understood and correctly applied.

First, it is necessary to know the nature and range of the criteria in virtue of which the word or expression is standardly employed. Suppose, for example, that I am unaware of the meaning of the appraisive term *courageous*, and ask someone to explain to me how to use the word properly. He (or she) will most naturally reply by mentioning various criteria that serve to mark off the word from similar and contrasting adjectives, and so provide it with its distinctive role in our language of social description and appraisal. When listing these criteria, he will surely have to include at least the following: that the word can only be used in the context of voluntary actions; that the actor involved must have faced some danger; that he must have faced it with some consciousness of its nature; and he must have faced it heedfully, with some sense of the probable consequences of the action involved. Summarizing these criteria (in what is only apparently a tautology), we may say that the conditions under which the term *courageous* can be applied are such that the action involved must have been a courageous one.

Next, to apply an appraisive term correctly I also need to know its range of reference. I need, that is, to have a clear sense of the nature of the circumstances in which the word can properly be used to designate particular actions or states of affairs. The concept of reference has often been taken to be an aspect or feature of the meaning of a word. But it is perhaps more helpful to treat the understanding of the reference of a word as a consequence of understanding the criteria for applying it correctly. To grasp these criteria is to understand the sense of a word, its role in the language, and thus its correct use. Once I have acquired this understanding, I may expect in consequence to be able to exercise the further and more mysterious skill of relating the word to the world. I may expect, for example, to be able to pick out just those actions which are properly to be called courageous, and to discuss the sort of circumstances in which we might wish to apply that particular description, or might wonder whether we ought to apply it rather than another one. For instance, someone might call it courageous if I faced painful death with cheerfulness. However, it might be objected that strictly speaking no danger is involved in such circumstances, and thus that we ought not to speak of courage but rather of fortitude. Or again, someone might call it courageous if I stepped from the circus audience to deputize for the lion tamer. But it might be countered that this is such a heedless action that it ought not to be viewed as courage but rather as sheer recklessness. Both these arguments are about the reference (but not the meaning) of *courageous*: both are concerned with whether a given set of circumstances – what a lawyer would call the facts of the case – are such as to yield the agreed criteria for the application of the given appraisive term.

To apply any word to the world, we need to have a clear grasp of both its sense and its reference. But in the case of appraisive terms a further element of understanding is also required. We need in addition to know what exact range of attitudes the term can standardly be used to express. (To adopt J. L. Austin's jargon: it is necessary to know what type of speech-acts the word can be used to perform.) For example, no one can be said to have grasped the correct application of the adjective *courageous* if they remain unaware that it is standardly used to commend, to express approval, and especially to express (and solicit) admiration for any action it is used to describe. To call an action courageous is at once to describe it and to place it in a specific moral light. I can praise or rejoice at an action by calling it courageous, but I cannot condemn or sneer at it by describing it in this way.

If these are the three main things we need to know in order to isolate the class of appraisive terms and apply them correctly, we can now return to the question raised at the beginning of this section. I asked what we might be debating about a key word if we found ourselves asking whether or not it ought to be applied in a particular case. As we have seen, Williams's answer is that such arguments must be about the senses or meanings of the words involved. As I have sought to show, however, we might be disagreeing about one of at least three different things, not all of which are self-evidently disagreements about meaning: about the criteria for applying the word; about whether the agreed criteria are present in a given set of circumstances; or about what range of speech-acts the word can be used to perform.

III

So far I have tried to isolate the main debates that arise over the application of our appraisive vocabulary to our social world. I now turn to what I take to be the crucial question: in what sense are these linguistic disagreements also disagreements about our social world itself?

I have suggested that one type of argument over appraisive terms centres on the criteria for applying them. Now this is certainly a substantive social debate as well as a linguistic one. For it can equally well be characterized as an argument between two rival social theories and their attendant methods of classifying social reality.

As an illustration of such a dispute, recall the way in which Marcel Duchamp liked to designate certain familiar objects (coat-pegs, lavatory bowls) as works of art, thereby causing them to be framed and hung on the walls of galleries. Some critics have accepted that these are indeed significant works of art, on the grounds that they help us to sharpen and extend our awareness of everyday things. Others have insisted that they are not works of art at all, on the grounds that we cannot simply *call* something a work of art, since works of art have to be deliberately created.

This disagreement arises at the linguistic level. It centres on whether or not a certain criterion (the exercise of skill) should or should not be regarded as a necessary condition for the correct application of a particular appraisive term (*a work of art*). But this is certainly a substantive social dispute as well. What is at issue is whether or not a certain range of objects ought or ought not to be treated as having a rather elevated status and significance. And it is obvious that a great deal may depend on how this question is answered.

A number of the arguments in *Keywords* are primarily of this character. For example, the essays on 'literature' and 'science' largely fit this analysis, as does the useful discussion of 'the unconscious', where Williams actually points out that 'different theories' have generated 'confusions between different senses' of the term.[12] Moreover, Williams is surely right to claim that in these cases the argument is in fact about the senses or meanings of the words involved. It is true that powerful voices have lately been raised against the contention that, if we introduce a new theory relating to a given subject matter (for example, what constitutes a work of art) this will inevitably give rise to changes in the meanings of the constitutive terms.[13] And there is little doubt that Paul Feyerabend and other post-empiricists have tended to employ this assumption with an altogether excessive enthusiasm. Certainly we cannot readily say that every change of theory brings about a change in the meaning of all the words involved (if only because nouns and adjectives shift in meaning so much more readily than, say, conjunctions). Moreover, it seems unduly anarchistic to claim that the meaning of a word must have changed if we simply change our beliefs about whatever the word is customarily used to denote (although it is admittedly very hard to think of clear cases in which meanings have in fact remained constant in the face of changing beliefs).[14] However, it does seem that if someone is mistaken about the criteria for applying a term, then he cannot be said to know its current meaning. And since I have argued that the question of whether Duchamp's coat-peg is a work of art is (at one level) an argument about the criteria for applying the term *a work of art*, I agree with Williams that in this type of argument about key words the disagreement really is about the meaning of the word concerned.

What Williams misses, however, in his account of these disputes is their almost paralysingly radical character. He remains content to suppose that in all discussions about 'meaning' we can 'pick out certain words, of an especially problematical kind' and consider only 'their own internal developments and natures'.[15] This fails to recognize the implications of the fact that a term such as *art* gains its meaning from the place it occupies within an entire conceptual scheme. To change the criteria for applying it will thus be to change a vast deal else besides. Traditionally, the concept of art has been connected with an ideal of workmanship, has been opposed to the 'merely useful', has been employed as an antonym for *nature*, and so on. If we now endorse the suggestion that an *objet trouvé* or a manufactured article can count as a work of art, we at once sever all these and many other conceptual links. So an argument over the application of the term *art* is potentially nothing less than an argument over two rival (though not of course incommensurable)[16] ways of approaching and dividing up a large tract of our cultural experience. Williams appears in short to have overlooked the strongly holistic implications of the fact that, when a word changes its meaning, it also changes its relationship to an entire vocabulary.[17] What this tells us about such changes is that we must be prepared to focus not on the 'internal structure' of particular words, but rather on their role in upholding complete social philosophies.

IV

Even if we agree about the criteria for applying an appraisive term, I have suggested that a second type of dispute can arise over its use: a dispute about whether a given set of circumstances can be claimed to yield the criteria in virtue of which the term is normally employed. Again, such a disagreement will certainly be a substantive social one, not merely linguistic in character. For what is being contended in effect is that a refusal to apply the term in a certain situation may constitute an act of social insensitivity or a failure of social awareness.

As an illustration of this second type of argument, consider the contention that wives in ordinary middle-class families at the present time can properly be described as suffering exploitation, as being an exploited class. The social argument underlying this linguistic move might be spelled out somewhat as follows. It ought to be evident to all persons of goodwill that the circumstances of contemporary family life are such that this strongly condemnatory term does indeed (if you think about it) fit the facts of the case. Conversely, if we fail to acknowledge that the application of the term *exploitation* – in virtue of its agreed criteria – is indeed appropriate in the circumstances, then we are wilfully refusing to perceive the institution of the family in its true and baleful light.

This is clearly a dispute of an entirely different character from the first type of argument I singled out. Nevertheless, there has been a persistent tendency among moral and political philosophers to conflate the two. Consider, for example, the analysis Stuart Hampshire offers in *Thought and Action* of an imagined debate between a Marxist and a Liberal in which the latter is 'startled to find that actions of his, to which he had never thought to attach a political significance, in his sense of "political", are given a political significance' by his Marxist opponent.[18] As the above quotation already indicates, Hampshire classifies this kind of disagreement as one about the 'sense' of the word 'political'; as 'a disagreement about the criteria of application' of the term.[19] If this is a genuine argument, however, it is obviously crucial that the Marxist should be able to claim with some plausibility that he is employing the term in virtue of its *agreed* sense. It is not clear that he can even be said to be arguing with the Liberal if he is simply content to point out that, as Hampshire puts it, he has a different concept of 'the political', with the result that he and the Liberal are both confined to 'the largely separated worlds of their thought'.[20] It is even less clear, if this is all that he wishes to point out, why the Liberal should feel in the least affected by the argument, given that it amounts to nothing more than a declaration of an intention to use a certain appraisive term in an idiosyncratic way. If the Marxist is genuinely seeking to persuade the Liberal to share or at least acknowledge some political insight, he needs in effect to make two points. One is of course that the term *political* can appropriately be applied to a range of actions where the Liberal has never thought of applying it. But the other, which his application of the term challenges the Liberal to admit, is that this is due not to a disagreement about the meaning of the term, but rather to the fact that the Liberal is a person of blinkered political sensitivity and awareness.

The same confusion appears to afflict many of Williams's discussions about key words. He gives historical examples of debates about, for example, whether a certain procedure can be appraised as *empirical*, whether a particular kind of household can be called a *family*, whether someone can be said to have an *interest* in a particular state of affairs, and so on.[21] In each case he classifies the dispute as one about the 'sense' of the term involved. Again, however, it seems essential to the success of the social argument underlying such linguistic debates that the appraisive words in question should be offered in virtue of their accepted senses as an apt way of describing situations which have not hitherto been described in such terms.

It is true that, as a consequence of such arguments, new meanings are often generated. But the process by which this happens is the opposite of the one Williams describes. When an argument of this nature is successful, the outcome will hardly be the emergence of new meanings, save that the application of a term with a new range of reference may eventually put pressure on the criteria for applying it. The outcome will rather be the acceptance of new social perceptions, as a result of which the relevant appraisive terms will then be applied with unchanged meanings to new circumstances. It is only when such arguments fail that new meanings tend to arise.

This contention can readily be supported if we consider some of the ways in which a failure in this type of argument is capable of leaving its traces on the language. It may be that, when a social group seeks to insist that the ordinary criteria for applying a particular appraisive term are present in a wider range of circumstances than has commonly been allowed, the other users of the language – not sharing the underlying social perceptions of the first group – may simply assume in good faith that a 'new meaning' has indeed been 'offered', and may then accept it. The history of our culture (and in consequence our language) has been punctuated with many such misunderstandings. One fruitful source has been the continuing efforts of the proponents of commercial society to legitimate their undertakings by reference to the most highly approved moral and spiritual values. Consider, for example, the special use of the term *religious* that first emerged in the later sixteenth century as a way of commending punctual, strict, and conscientious forms of behaviour.[22] The aim was clearly to suggest that the ordinary criteria for applying the strongly commendatory term *religious* could be found in such actions, and thus that the actions themselves should be seen essentially as acts of piety and not merely as instances of administrative competence. The failure of this move was quickly reflected in the emergence of a new meaning for the term *religious* in the course of the seventeenth century – the meaning we still invoke when we say things like 'I attend the meetings of my Department religiously'. It seems clear that the need for this new lexical entry originally arose out of the incapacity of most language users to see that the ordinary criteria for *religious* (including the notion of piety) were in fact present in all the circumstances in which the term was by then beginning to be used.

There are many recent instances of the same phenomenon, some of which are cited in *Keywords*. For example, many industrial firms like to claim – with reference to their own business strategies – that they have a certain *philosophy*; and firms regularly promise to send their *literature* (meaning only their advertising brochures) to prospective customers. Again a crude attempt is clearly being made to link the activities of commercial society with a range of 'higher' values. And again the failure of such efforts often gives rise to genuine polysemy. Hearing that a firm has a certain philosophy, most language users have assumed that a new meaning must be involved, and have gone on to use the term accordingly; they have not in general come to feel that corporations can indeed be said to have philosophies in the traditional sense of the term.

The language also supplies us with evidence of such ideological failures in a second and more decisive way. After a period of confusion about the criteria for applying a disputed term, the final outcome may not be polysemy, but rather a reversion to the employment of the original criteria, together with a corresponding obsolescence of the newer usages. This can be observed, for example, in the history of the word *patriot*. During the eighteenth century, the enemies of the ruling oligarchy in England sought to legitimate their attacks on the government by insisting that they were motivated entirely by their reverence for the constitution, and thus that their actions deserved to be commended as patriotic rather than condemned as factious. This at first bred such extreme uncertainty that the word *patriot* eventually came to *mean* (according to one of Dr Johnson's definitions) 'a factious disturber of the government'. With the gradual acceptance of party politics, however, this condemnatory usage gradually atrophied, and the word reverted to its original meaning and its standard application as a term of praise.[23]

Finally, the same form of argument can also have a more equivocal outcome, one which the language will again disclose. It may be that, after a similar period of semantic confusion, the original rather than the newer usage becomes obsolete. At first sight this may seem to indicate a success in the underlying campaign to change people's social perceptions. For this certainly makes it harder to invoke the primitive meaning of the word in order to insist that its newer applications may be nothing more than a deformation of its basic sense. But in fact such changes again tend to be indexes of ideological failure. For the standardization of a new set of criteria will inevitably carry with it an alteration of the term's appraisive force. Sometimes the power of the word to evaluate what it is used to describe may be retained in a different (and usually weaker) form, as in the well-known case of the word *naughty*. But often the process of acquiring a new meaning goes with a total loss of appraisive force. A good example is provided by the history of the word *commodity*. Before the advent of commercial society, to speak of something as a commodity was to praise it, and in particular to affirm that it answered to one's desires, and could thus be seen as beneficial, convenient, a source of advantage. Later an attempt was made to suggest that an article produced for sale ought to be seen as a source of benefit or advantage to its purchaser, and ought in consequence to be described and commended as a commodity. For a time the outcome of this further effort by the earliest English capitalists to legitimate their activities was that *commodity* became a polysemic word. But eventually the original applications withered away, leaving us with nothing more than the current and purely descriptive meaning of *commodity* as an object of trade. Although the capitalists inherited the earth, and with it much of the English language, they were unable in this case to persuade their fellow language users to endorse their attempted eulogy of their own commercial practices.

V

Even if we agree about the criteria for applying an appraisive term, and also agree that a given set of circumstances can properly be said to answer to those criteria, I have suggested that still a third type of dispute can arise: a dispute, that is, about the nature and range of the speech-acts it can be used to perform. Once again this can certainly be characterized as a substantive social dispute and not merely a linguistic one. For in this case what is at issue is the possibility that a group of language users may be open to the charge of having a mistaken or an undesirable social attitude.

We can distinguish two main routes by which an argument of this kind will be likely to issue in a contentious use of evaluative language. First, we may dissent from an orthodox social attitude by employing an appraisive term in such a way that its standard speech-act potential is weakened or even abolished. This can in turn be achieved in one of two ways. If we do not share the accepted evaluation of some particular action or state of affairs, we may indicate our dissent simply by dropping the corresponding term from our vocabulary altogether. There are many instances of this move in current social debate. Among terms which have hitherto been used to commend what they describe, this seems to be happening in the case of *gentleman*. Among terms previously used to express an element of condescension or patronage, this already seems to have happened with *native*, at least when used as a noun.

The other method of registering the same form of protest is more challenging. While continuing to employ an accepted term of social description and appraisal, we may make it contextually clear that we are using it merely to describe, and not at the same time to evaluate what is thereby described. Again, there are many contemporary instances of this move. Among terms previously used to evince condescension or even hatred, the classic example is provided by the word *black* (used as the description of a person), whether employed as an adjective or a noun. Among terms previously used to commend, we may note the new and carefully neutral applications of such words as *culture* and *civilization*. As Williams himself observes,[24] these latter usages appear to have originated within the discipline of social anthropology, but have now come to be very generally accepted by those who wish to disavow any suggestion that one particular civilization may be more deserving of study than another.

The other main way in which we can use our evaluative language to signal our social attitudes is more dramatic in its implications. It is possible to indicate, simply through our use of appraisive terms, not that we dissent from the idea of evaluating what they describe, but rather that we disagree with the direction of the evaluation and wish to see it reversed.

Again there are obviously two possibilities here. We may use a term normally employed to condemn what it describes in such a way as to make it contextually clear that, in our view, the relevant action or state of affairs ought in fact to be commended. As Williams points out, one interesting example of this reversal can be seen in the history of the word *myth*. In a more confidently rationalist age, to describe an explanation as mythological was to dismiss it. But in recent discussions the term has often been used to extol the mythological 'version of reality' as 'truer' and 'deeper' than more mundane accounts. [25] Conversely, we may dislike a form of behaviour now regarded as praiseworthy, and indicate our disapproval by making it contextually clear that, although the term we are using is standardly employed to commend, we are employing it to condemn what is being described. Once again, there are many instances of this kind of struggle in current ideological debates. One only has to think of those politicians who are regularly praised by one group of commentators as *liberal* while others employ the same term in order to denounce them.

Williams surveys a large number of disagreements that fall within this third general category, and in many cases his comments on them are extremely interesting and shrewd. But his discussion suffers throughout from a failure to distinguish this type of argument from the first type we considered, in which the primary point at issue was the proper sense or meaning of the terms involved. Indeed Williams not only fails but refuses to distinguish between these two types of argument. For example, he insists that the change involved in the move from condemning myths to commending them must be construed as a change in the 'sense' of the word *myth*.[26]

It would be perfectly possible, however, for both the sense and the reference of *myth* to remain stable in the face of the sort of changes in the use of the word that Williams is concerned to point out. It may be that all (and only) those theories and explanations which used to be called mythological are still called mythological, and that the *only* change involved in the use of the term derives from the shift from condemning myths to commending them. It is true that such a variation of speech-act potential will be very likely in due course to affect the sense (and in consequence the reference) of the word. But it is a mistake to suppose that this type of argument is primarily (or even necessarily) concerned with sense. What is changing – at least initially – is nothing to do with sense; what is changing is simply a social or intellectual attitude on the part of those who use the language.[27]

VI

I have now tried to furnish at least a preliminary response to the very large question I raised at the outset. I asked what kinds of knowledge and awareness we can hope to acquire about our social world through studying the vocabulary we use to describe and appraise it. I have answered that there are three main types of insight we can hope to gain: insights into changing social beliefs and theories; into changing social perceptions and awareness; and into changing social values and attitudes. I have thus attempted to supply at least a sketch of what seems to me most seriously lacking in Williams's book: an account of the sort of methodology we need to develop in order to use the evidence of our social vocabulary as a clue to the improved understanding of our social world.

This in turn suggests a further and even more vertiginous question: are we now in a position to say anything about the nature of the role played by our appraisive vocabulary in the process (and hence in the explanation) of social change?

Williams clearly thinks that we are, and conveys this sense by alluding repeatedly to the image of language as a mirror of social reality. The process of social change is treated as the primary cause of developments in our vocabulary; conversely, such developments are treated as reflections of the process of social change.[28] Describing the emergence of capitalism as 'a distinct economic system', for example, Williams remarks that this gave rise to 'interesting consequent uses of language'.[29] And in commenting more specifically on 'the economic changes of the Industrial Revolution', he notes that these produced a 'greatly sharpened' and extended 'vocabulary of class'.[30]

There is no doubt that this image serves to remind us of an important point. Where we encounter a wide measure of agreement about the application of key social terms, we must be dealing with a strikingly homogeneous social and moral world; where there is no such agreement, we can expect chaos. But it is arguable that the metaphor is also misleading in one crucial respect. It encourages us to assume that we are dealing with two distinct and contingently related domains: that of the social world itself, and that of the language we then apply in an attempt to delineate its character. This certainly seems to be the assumption underlying Williams's account. He sees a complete disjunction between 'the words' he discusses and 'the real issues' in the social world. And he sometimes speaks as if the gap between the two is one we can barely hope to bridge. 'However complete the analysis' we offer at the linguistic level, he maintains, we cannot expect that 'the real issues' will be fundamentally affected.[31]

To speak in this way is to forget something that Williams emphasizes at other points in *Keywords* with striking force: the fact that one of the most important uses of evaluative language is that of legitimating as well as describing the activities and attitudes of dominant social groups. The significance of this consideration can be brought out if we revert for a moment to an example already cited – the entrepreneurs of Elizabethan England who were anxious to persuade their contemporaries that, although their commercial enterprises might appear to be morally doubtful, they were in fact deserving of respect. One device they adopted was to argue, as we have seen, that their characteristically punctual and conscientious behaviour could properly be seen as religious in character, and hence as motivated by pious and not merely self-seeking principles. Their underlying purpose was of course to legitimate their apparently untoward behaviour by insisting on the propriety of describing it in these highly commendatory terms.

Now it may seem – and this is evidently Williams's view – that this sort of example precisely fits the metaphor of language as a mirror of a more basic reality. The merchant is perceived to be engaged in a more or less dubious way of life which he has a strong motive for wishing to exhibit as legitimate. So he professes just those principles, and offers just those descriptions, that serve to present what he is doing in a morally acceptable light. Since the selection of the principles and their accompanying descriptions both relate to his behaviour in an obviously *ex post facto* way, it hardly seems that an explanation of his behaviour need depend in the least on studying the moral language he may elect to use. For his choice of vocabulary appears to be entirely determined by his prior social needs.

As I have tried to hint, however, this is to misunderstand the role of the normative vocabulary which any society employs for the description and appraisal of its social life. The merchant cannot hope to describe *any* action he may choose to perform as being 'religious' in character, but only those which can be claimed with some show of plausibility to meet such agreed criteria as there may be for the application of the term. It follows that if he is anxious to have his conduct appraised as that of a genuinely religious man, he will find himself restricted to the performance of only a certain range of actions. Thus the problem facing the merchant who wishes to be seen as pious rather than self-interested cannot simply be the instrumental one of tailoring his account of his principles in order to fit his projects; it must in part be the problem of tailoring his projects in order to make them answer to the pre-existing language of moral principles.[32]

The story of the merchant suggests two morals. One is that it must be a mistake to portray the relationship between our social vocabulary and our social world as a purely external and contingent one. It is true that our social practices help to bestow meaning on our social vocabulary. But it is equally true that our social vocabulary helps to constitute the character of those practices. To see the role of our evaluative language in helping to legitimate social action is to see the point at which our social vocabulary and our social fabric mutually prop each other up. As Charles Taylor has remarked, 'we can speak of mutual dependence if we like, but what this really points up is the artificiality of the distinction between social reality and the language of description of that social reality'.[33]

The other moral is that, if there are indeed causal linkages between social language and social reality, to speak of the one as mirroring the other may be to envisage the causal arrows pointing in the wrong direction. As the example of the Elizabethan merchant suggests, to recover the nature of the normative vocabulary available to an agent for the description and appraisal of his conduct is at the same time to indicate one of the constraints on his conduct itself. This in turn suggests that, if we wish to explain why our merchant chose to concentrate on certain courses of action while avoiding others, we are bound to make some reference to the prevailing moral language of the society in which he was acting. For this, it now appears, must have figured not as an epiphenomenon of his projects, but as one of the determinants of his actions.

To conclude with these morals is to issue a warning to literary critics and social historians alike to avoid a prevalent but impoverishing form of reductionism. But it is also to suggest that the special techniques of the literary critic have – or ought to have – a central place in the business of cultural criticism which a book like Williams's *Keywords* has scarcely begun to recognize.

PART III

Critical Perspectives

7

Say it with flowers

Martin Hollis

The historian has only the husks of action, the traces of what once were episodes played out between past and future. To recover these passing moments he relies on texts of all sorts, on utterances in ink and stone, metal and ash, which once had meaning for his blank skeletons. Even written, reflective texts are not as if the tape-recorded voices of actors prevented by death from uttering them in person, since they were addressed to other audiences, couched in other idioms and fired by other concerns. The historian must read in before he can read out and there is a plain danger of his finding what he put there himself. Even written texts are not just strings of propositions. In uttering them, their authors were acting and interacting and the historian must interpret the actions as well as the words. Here lie circles of the most daunting kind but Quentin Skinner has braved them before and I seize the chance to dissect them with him.[1] It goes without saying that what so visibly troubles him in the dark of the archives also afflicts anyone trying to understand the social meaning of action.

To broach a huge topic, I shall assume that historical actors have at least some autonomy within a context which both enables and constrains them; that their actions are their solutions to problems set by circumstance and other actors; and that their skill is crucial in interpreting their actions. Ideally I should like to defend this picture but, since Mr Skinner shares it and space is short, I shall concentrate on the puzzles it poses. The first part of the paper will fill it in for action by individuals, which can readily be seen as manoeuvre within a context but not without encountering some wicked circles. The second part will try to extend the idea to the combined action of persons in groups, where the context is no longer wholly external to the actors. Here some snags in the logic of collective action are added to the previous circles and I shall hand the resulting knots over to Mr Skinner with relief. The clue to these puzzles of meaning and explanation is to be the notion of rationality but I cannot pretend that it is an easy clue to read.

I

'Say it with flowers', the florists urge. Very well, let us do so in a story intended to sketch an approach to historical interpretation which Skinner will recognize as his own, to exhibit the circles which arise and finally to usher in the one disagreement between us. Let us suppose that, soon after the balcony scene of some real-life *Romeo and Juliet*, Romeo sends Juliet a bunch of red orchids with a card inscribed, 'A beauteous flower for when next we meet.' This episode is the text and I shall be using 'text' to refer not just to speech but to any act whose author intends others to understand something by it. What is its interpretation? The question is ambiguous between meaning and explanation and I introduce the elements of our discussion by splitting it into four. First, there is the overt meaning – in the case of speech 'What did he succeed in saying?' Second, there is the covert meaning – 'What did he intend to say and intend in saying it?' Third, there is the overt explanation – 'Why was the utterance apt?' Fourth, there is the covert explanation – 'What was his motive in uttering the text?' The historian's primary task, according to Skinner, is to answer the first three parts of the question but not the fourth. Having extolled the subtlety of this approach, I shall nevertheless insist that the question of motive be answered too.

The division into overt and covert has to do with the importance of context. It is not as if the sending of the flowers means just whatever Romeo means by it. 'In "action" is included all human behaviour', says Weber, 'in so far as the acting individual attaches subjective meaning to it.' The dictum is not to be read as saying that subjective meaning is all. Romeo cannot succeed in meaning what he pleases by the flowers. The gesture is taken from stock, its meaning restricted to a conventional list. It may be a mark of love, respect, gratitude or sympathy, perhaps, but not of hate, scorn or support for the Verona football team. (I ignore hidden codes or conventions, like irony, which exploit conventions.) This is just as well, since utterances constituted wholly by subjective meanings would be quite beyond the historian's reach. So let us suppose the episode to be one in courtship, expressing something conventionally said by lovers. What exactly is said is then determined by the message on the little white card, provided that it is within the list of proper meanings. (If the card reads 'The cat sat on the mat', Romeo succeeds in meaning nothing by the flowers.) A sort of social grammar is at work.

Here, then, is one notion of context, where the actors engage from socially recognized positions, attended with normative expectations. We may call it the *normative context*, the set of rules governing what a man must, may and shall not do in each social capacity. The rules both constitute and regulate. Romeo is not Juliet's lover at all, unless he stays within the rules of courtship; he is a sorry lover, unless he courts her with grace, unselfishness and fervour. Admittedly, the notion of a norm is an elusive one, witness my swift transition from 'position' to 'capacity', and requires a tricky distinction between what is publicly and tacitly permitted. But the idea that social action is constituted and regulated by rules for what is legitimate is clear enough to accept.

It has been held that the normative context exhausts both meaning and explanation. Although Romeo has more than one option as a lover, he also has other social positions and capacities, which together determine a uniquely legitimate course of action. This approach is known to sociologists as normative structuralism and its claim depends on seeing norms as the social category of the last resort and on absorbing the actor into them. By refusing the first move, on the ground that norms have further social determinants, we get a notion of *structural context*; by refusing the second, on the ground that actors also express inner states, in a way governed by rules which are not normative, we get one of *expressive context*.

In speaking of structural context, I am thinking of structure in a manner typified by Marx's distinction of structure and superstructure. But I shall leave the topic unexplored, since, even if there is an all-encompassing structure, the normative context is still intermediately important enough to keep us busy. In the same cavalier way, I shall ignore other external factors of, for instance, geography, biology and even technology, presuming them to enter the interpretation of social action only through the normative context and the actors' consciousness. These are pieces of ontological impudence which lack of space demands.

The expressive context, however, is as crucial as the normative. Romeo's flowers are not just a lover's insignia, like the wig on a judge. They are red for passion, expressing fire within. This is a symbol, not a natural sign, and belongs to a language of the heart. Romeo's gesture in its normative context is that of a suitor; in its expressive context it is that of a man in love. The expression of feeling is governed by rules too and, in doing what is normatively proper, Romeo also conveys a claim to inner sentiment. That the claim can be false shows that there is an external and enabling context for it.

By citing the normative and expressive contexts, the historian gives the overt meaning of the text. But, if that is what the flowers mean, it does not exhaust what Romeo means by the flowers. Or so it will seem to anyone who denies that actors are mere vehicles of norms and sentiments.

Romeo also intends his gesture to be read in particular ways and intends to achieve something by it. In part, no doubt, he means what the flowers mean, uttering their overt message with the intention that others recognize this intention. But, anticipating Henry James, he can be addressing several messages to several audiences with the one text. Conscious perhaps of Lady Capulet's intercepting eye, he intends the formality and the plush orchids to bespeak an admirer of solid substance but slight acquaintance – an intention likelier to succeed if it goes unnoticed. At the same time he intends Juliet to catch the echo of her own words on the balcony:

> This bud of love by summer's ripening breath
> May prove a beauteous flower when next we meet.

He intends her to relish the incongruity of these intentions. He means, in a common sense of that nimble term, whatever he intends others to understand. That is the covert meaning of the text.

The overt explanation is got by parading the overtly legitimate elements of the covert meaning and showing why the actor was justified in context in acting as he did. Much is forgiven a man in love and much can therefore be achieved by laying successful claim to the title. Exactly what needs doing to regain the sense of an action in the eyes of contemporaries for the benefit of posterity will depend on the particular case. In Skinner's hands the idea that texts are to be interpreted by recovering the context, the actors' intentions and their legitimating reasons becomes a sharp tool, as the articles cited at the start bear witness. What does not depend on particular cases, however, is his contention that the historian should not tackle, still less prejudge, questions of motive. Hence the overt explanation stops strictly with what is legitimate. We are not meant to infer that it tells us by what the actor was really moved. For the principles and sentiments which a man professes in action are the key to explaining his actions in context, whether or not he expresses them sincerely. The crucial point is that an actor cannot succeed in his actions without legitimating them.

So when, fourthly, we ask whether Romeo's intentions were honourable, the answer is that we neither know nor need to know. He is sighing like a furnace, his orchids are aflame, he is every inch a man on fire; yet it may all be sound and fury, signifying nothing. Actors are neither mere creatures of norms nor mere vehicles of sentiments. They are being conceived at a distance not only from what their actions mean but also from what they mean their actions to mean. Once the historian has found them sufficient reason to have acted as he did, the historian can penetrate no further but he has done enough. To sum up schematically, Romeo illustrates this picture:

	overt	covert
what?	rules	intentions
why?	reasons	motives

The four boxes correspond to the opening four questions and, in strong, ingenious support of Collingwood's dictum that all history is the history of ideas, Skinner offers to do history with the first three only.

We are now ready for the circles which beset any hermeneutic account of understanding. They arise because rules, reasons, intentions and indeed motives are inter-related both ontologically and epistemologically. Ontologically, the rules of courtship are those binding lovers in the expression of love; lovers are persons subject to the rules because they are in love; love is the sentiment expressed by observing the rules of courtship. Are these relations constitutive? The case for saying so is that love is surely not a universal condition which people catch like colds in all climes and contexts and then express in what happens to be the local idiom; that, even if courtship rules from many cultures are all so classified because they govern expression of the same sentiments, the sentiments are the same because their expression is governed by courtship rules; that in general the covert is a discrimination of the overt, no less than the overt is an expression of the covert. But I merely mention this daunting issue, since there is an epistemological circle in any case.

Epistemologically, to be warranted in ascribing an intention to express love, the historian must know that the relevant rules are those of courtship and that the actors are lovers; and hence must already be warranted in ascribing the intention. He understands the overt as the context of the covert and the covert as what the actors mean by the overt. Nor can he take the problem as an empirical one, to be overcome by tacking back and forth from overt to covert in advancing zig-zags, since apparent success will not guard him against a charge of imputing what he purports to discover. The problem is a theoretical one of conceiving the relation between rules, actors and intentions in such a way that the merit of rival interpretations can be judged. Even if he knows it is soluble, on the ground that the actors succeed in interacting with each other, the exact solution makes a difference and he does not yet have one.

The way in, Skinner and I agree, is to make the actors as rational as possible. But here we part company. In his version to deem a man rational is to say that he knows how to legitimate and so achieve his intentions. The idea is to treat meaningful action as a text which, construed with an apparatus of locutions, illocutions and perlocutions and on the assumption that it was rationally uttered, is its own explanation. The attraction is that the historian can spin his yarn, knit the actor a cap and, if a critic doubts whether the actor was actually wearing the cap, retort that we need not ask. A rational actor, in recognizing good reasons for acting, makes those reasons his own. Motives are not needed where the actor in his context would have acted in the same way from more than one motive. For instance Romeo would have sent the flowers, whether he was sincerely in love or merely bent on an alliance with the house of Capulet; so we want a form of explanation which leaves the matter of motive open.

I claim to detect two non sequiturs and a lacuna. First, if the actor emerges with more than one possible motive, it does not follow that the matter of motive is left open. If the actor is rational, then motives which would have led him to act differently are thereby ruled out and so the matter of motive is only partly open. Second, just because two possible motives would yield the same action in the context, it does not follow that explanation can proceed without deciding between them. To know a man acted as he did involves knowing how he would have acted in other conditions, for instance those where the two motives would move him along differing paths. It involves knowing too when a man wanted but failed to achieve, as opposed to when he seemed to want but covertly was not really trying. So it looks as if motive does matter – a suspicion confirmed by noticing that the actor has as yet no reason for action at all. He has legitimating, overt reasons but his being rational depends on his having a covert reason for taking advantage of them. His intention cannot be this reason, nor can his expressions of principle and sentiment, while all are being conceived as tactical devices. There is thus a lacuna when we ask why he wants what he is overtly pursuing and it must be filled, if his tactics are to be interpreted as those of a rational man.

Motives do matter then but, in the face of the hermeneutic circles, they must be the sort of item which can move a rational man. The heart has its reasons; yet not such as reason knows nothing of. Mere wants will not do. Someone may complain that whether there is a reason for Romeo to send flowers is one thing and whether Romeo himself has a reason another, the difference depending on whether he has a motivating desire. I reply that having a desire to do something does not in itself make it rational to do it, even when no other stronger desire would thereby be frustrated. The rational man not only has good reasons for his actions, given his desires and projects, but also has good reasons for his desires and projects. What makes the difference between there being good reason for him to act and his having good reason to act is recognizing the good reason, which he thereby makes his own. The point needs proper argument but it is enough for the moment that a vicious circle occurs without it. If we are to discover Romeo's motive by asking what desires he must have had for his action to be rational, we cannot then hold that whether his action was rational depends on the desires he happened to have. An action which is the incompetent effecting of one want is wrongly interpreted as the competent effecting of another. Hence we can find the rational man's motive only on the assumption that it is a rational one.

There is now no case for assuming that all action is always equally rational. Indeed there never was in the eyes of anyone who finds subjective logic-of-the-situation explanations vacuous. But the rationality postulate still stands, now revealed as an ideal-type assumption and a yardstick for assessing what needs to be explained. Fully and objectively rational action is explained by showing how it matches the ideal case; imperfectly rational action needs a further account of why it fell short. Either way, the historian starts by trying an intellectual interpretation and, even where only partial explanation results, he will have determined what is missing. This is what is involved in making the actors out to be as rational as possible.

As soon as we insist on rational desire for rational actions, we embark on a theory of real interests, *eudaimonia* or some such unnerving concept. But there is no turning back and, if Skinner jibs at the notorious problems thus set, I shall retort that he is already covertly relying on one himself. Indeed I have always hoped that I find his writings rational because I know that he writes as a rational man who rationally desires to find the truth. Not pretending that the notorious problems are illusory, however, I look to him to help their discussion forward.

So far, then, we have a slightly revised scheme for interpreting individual action:

	overt	covert
what?	action's meaning	actor's meaning
why?	legitimating reasons	actor's good reasons

The emended version retains the idea that legitimating reasons are crucial, whatever the actor's true motive, and still tries to elicit what is covert by treating the actor as an objectively rational man. It differs only by insisting on motive after all, but in the face of the hermeneutic circles, recasts motives as reasons, in so far as the actor has good reasons for his desires. The proviso leaves a large issue unresolved, however, as will be seen presently.

II

Any success with Romeo can be generalized to small groups confronted with a given context and either wholly of one mind or wholly under the command of one member. But these are tight conditions and do not apply even to an individual actor with any power over the context. Since the power exists not only for wielders of law or force but wherever norms are fluid or ambiguous, and since historians are crucially interested in groups, movements and classes in transition and imperfect unity, Romeo cannot be pressed straight into further service. To see why not, let us first try treating group action as the combined action of individuals.

The usual shape of this idea is that groups form and act through, or as if through, a bargain among the members. Then, in parallel with the unemended scheme before, it seems at first not to matter just what motive each member has for joining in, provided that each gets more from belonging than membership costs. To be rational, group action need not succeed, since there will be opposing groups and other constraints, nor need it best further the collective aim of the group, since this aim ascribes a notional identity to the group which the analysis denies to be real; but it must offer the members individually the largest likely return on their costs, either directly or with a promise of a later *quid pro quo*. In assuming rationality, the historian sets out to apply such an analysis as far as it will go.

The sharper the edge of the conceptual tool, the smaller its scope. Sharpness comes from keeping strictly to cost-benefit terms; scope exists only where the benefit could not have been gained at lower costs. Hence, to borrow a famous line of argument, the tool works only where benefits are confined to those who pay and are proportional to how much is paid. Otherwise it is always more rational to let others take the burden. The history of the British trades union movement, for instance, cannot be explained in this way. Members, especially leaders, bore all the risks and hardship, while benefits went to workers as a whole. Since no single worker could significantly affect the outcome, each had a choice between benefit with cost and benefit without cost. Admittedly, had everyone acted rationally, there would have been no benefits for anyone; but it is still true that costs-plus-no-benefits is a worse choice than no-costs-plus-no-benefits. Admittedly too, early unions were often Friendly Societies, thereby offering some benefits to members only; but the story would still have been very different without the brave thousands who acted irrationally in cost-benefit terms. The logic of collective action seems to show that individuals are rarely rational in their collective bargains.

A likely retort is that the fault lies not in deeming men rational but in dubbing them egoists; that the paradox arises only if self-seeking is the sole rational motive. Trades union history is intelligible enough, granted that the pioneers were altruists, who recognized the need to combine to gain their altruistic ends.

The retort is plausible and instructive. It shows that motive does matter, if what is irrational from one motive is rational from another. But it does so misleadingly, since egoism and altruism are not motives in the sense of good reasons. Egoists and altruists, like everyone else, have specific reasons for specific intentions, for instance demanding manhood suffrage as a way of increasing the political power of unions. These specific reasons are not fixed in advance. They emerge from debate and theorizing and take shape only as the movement progresses. Yet the historian needs to know what they are, since his knowledge of who would have done what in what circumstances depends on them and since his claims to interpret depend, as we saw with Romeo, on such counterfactuals. He is not dealing with a fixed motive, like 'altruism', which spreads as the campaign gains adherents. An altruist is someone with specific reasons for actions which are his reasons because the actions will benefit others. That said, however, it does seem plausible to reject the universal egoism often assumed by economic theories of collective action. Yet it is not thereby shown more rational to be an altruist than an egoist and a step in the argument is still missing.

Putting the point aside for later, we must next insist on a fundamental difference between individuals and groups. While Romeo and Juliet act singly, the likely response of each is an external factor in the planning of the other. When they join forces, they acquire a joint power to decide what both will do. Since what was external to each becomes internal to both collectively but not to either, the power of joint decision is an emergent property. Since it can include deciding the rules of their relationship, context is no longer the external, fixed frame which it has been hitherto. With larger groups in permanent and more embracing alliance, there starts to be a control not only over relations within the group but also over some of the external norms which enabled and constrained its growth. Rational manipulation of context emerges as a possibility and much of what was *explicans* becomes *explicandum*.

If we want to take the idea of emergence seriously yet also to retain the scheme of meanings and reasons, we might try regarding the group as if it were a single actor. The most promising line is perhaps a Marxist one, with the crucial units as classes, the overt being analysed through a theory of ideology and the covert a matter of *praxis* and class interests. I shall not discuss the merits of the line here, however, since it involves rejecting the analogy between single actor and unitary group. There is no sufficiently analogous process of deliberation and decision. If the actor's real reasons are those he would give to himself correctly and in secret, the group's are not those it would agree on in private session. The private session, although similarly closed to outsiders and although determining the public stance of all the members, remains an internally public session of individual members. Debate about what the group should do reflects not only uncertainty about strategy and tactics but also uncertainty about manoeuvre within an alliance of actors with conflicting covert motives. So the puzzle of recovering Romeo's reasons is translated not into that of laying hands on the private-circulation-only minutes of the meeting but into that of recovering the various reasons of the several members present.

The impasse stands. To interpret the overt utterances and actions of a group, we need access to real reasons. If the real reasons are those of individual actors and if we conceive the actors as pre-social atoms, real reasons are irrecoverable. If the real reasons are those of the emergent group and if we conceive the actors as deriving their human identity from membership of groups, we lose the thematic analogy between individuals and groups. So we still need a way to conceive actors so that, provided they are rational, it is possible for us to discern the reasons for which they act. And we still need to show how groups of actors can be judged rational or irrational in their manipulation of context.

Someone will protest that there is an impasse only because I have insisted that rational action has objectively good reasons; whereas *perceived* reasons will surely suffice. But, however great the difficulties, I remain unrepentant. How a man perceives his situation is presumably meant to be a variable the value of which is to be settled empirically. To settle the value we must know how rational the man is. How rational he is is either given vacuously by the proposition that everyone always does what seems to him a good idea at the time or depends in part on how accurately he perceives his situation. To cut into this circle, we must treat rationality as a skill in judgement which can be ascribed *a priori* in some measure to anyone capable of communicating with others. If the actors are not basically rational, it is impossible to know how accurate or inaccurate their perceptions are. In a longer script I would try to say what the basic measure must include but I hope the point can be made in principle without going into detail.

How then are the actors to be conceived? If their identity is not to be derived from that of definitive groups, we must still try to show how what is collectively rational is so because it is rational for those taking part. Since the puzzles arise when the actors are conceived as egoists, the solution is to break the earlier tie between egoism and rationality. Yet other motives cannot just be tacked on to rational-man models. It does not make the self-sacrifice of Victorian trades unionists rational merely to point out that they were moved by moral commitment. Nor is self-sacrifice made rational by invoking, as a selective incentive, the calm of a clear conscience which comes from a sense of commitment discharged. Once we have insisted that rational action needs objectively good reasons, we must show how commitment can be rational. The question then becomes what it is about human beings (or some at least) which makes it rational for them to act uneconomically.

The objection to egoism is not that it predicates the wrong motive of the right subject but that it wrongly abstracts the actor as a timeless universal monad. So the corrective which will tempt a historian is to give human nature more substance by having it vary with place and time. If different cultures are peopled by different sorts of men and women, it is a historian's job to know what sort he is dealing with. The point of assuming rationality is then to let him discover by asking what kind of man would find it rational to act as he did. To a charge of relativism he replies that he still has an objective criterion of rationality to determine what it would be rational for a specific sort of man to want and to try to achieve in a specific context. But now the assumption of rationality helps him only if it is rational for the sort of actor a culture creates to accept the aims and ethos it prescribes. Hence he can account for contextual change only as the adjusting of a discrepancy between prescribed aims and permitted means. And he is still confined to meanings and legitimating reasons, with the circular results discussed earlier.

It seems to me, then, that actors must be conceived in a timeless, universal way, so that historical explanation is given enough *a priori* to avoid the circles. The fault in attributing egoism to these actors is that to do so is to think of them as monads. The alternative, I suggest, is that they create their human identity through using social capacities in social relations. They succeed not by achieving any old equipoise between desires and norms but by creating a rational identity, one which expresses what it is rational to value. It has to be rational to be virtuous, and virtuous to act as a person bound to others. Here the argument crosses the border into ethics and I cannot pursue it. But I do urge that combined action is rational only when it helps each participant to live as he should and that the historian who judges the rationality of contextual change is also judging its worth.

Having flaunted my colours, I shall end more soberly with some summarizing questions to Mr Skinner. His admirable method works well with Romeo and other single actors, especially when they happen to be authors of written texts. I object solely that the historian needs their motives or, rather, since what is needed must be recoverable, their real reasons. But the method seems at first no help in interpreting combined action. This can hardly be because action in concert is never rational for those taking part and the problem is to find a logic for collective action. When and why is it rational for individuals to incur the costs of banding together? When and why is it rational for groups to try to change the norms internal and external to them? These are the ontological questions – the former being acute for Skinner, if he still wishes to be silent about motive, and the latter, if social meaning and explanation always require a given context.

Epistemologically, the daunting circles can be broken only by assuming that actors are rational enough for even their irrational acts to be intelligible. But it needs to be more than a platitude that the social world makes sense when interpreted and the assumption must have an edge. The edge comes from an objective, not a subjective, notion of rationality, which involves the historian in judging how well the actors did. Rational action is a skill. At what? Is it just the effective translation of consistent preferences into the most promising course of action? I have claimed that the rationality of motives is needed in judging that the actors' real reasons were good reasons. Yet the puzzle set by ascribing a universal egoism to pre-social individuals is not removed by tacking other, more benevolent motives on to the same model of man. A fresh way of conceiving the actors is required. Since a vicious relativism results if human nature is made to vary empirically with historical context, I hold out for something universal. Here metaphysics and ethics run together and I expect that the mixture will be too much for Mr Skinner's historian to stomach. Yet, if rational action is its own explanation, every historical explanation judges and partly endorses. Where, I ask finally, do Mr Skinner's endorsements stop short of moral approval?

'Wherefore art thou Romeo?', Juliet exclaimed. If the rational actor aims at what it is rational to become in an historical setting, she has posed the hardest question.

8

How do illocutionary descriptions explain?

Keith Graham

In the years since Austin coined the term *illocutionary act*[1] the concept has been widely discussed and employed in theoretical linguistics. It could hardly fail to be of interest, however, in the broader context of theories of behaviour in general, and more recently it has received growing attention in this connection. At the centre of such discussion is the work of Quentin Skinner. He has discussed the idea of illocution and its connection with behaviour in a whole series of methodological papers, employed it in his historical work on Hobbes and in his wide-ranging *Foundations of Modern Political Thought*, and has been justly influential on other historians and philosophers.[2] What I wish to examine here is the contribution which an awareness of illocutionary force[3] makes to our understanding of social phenomena. Skinner has argued (4) that a proper understanding of the concept of illocution gives us grounds for assessing different (and rival) theories of social explanation. I shall attempt to show that the explanatory power which illocutionary force carries is different from what it is taken to be by Skinner. This will doubtless affect the inferences we can draw about various theories of social explanation, but I am principally concerned to clarify just what difference it does make to acquire information about illocutionary force in particular cases.

What is an illocutionary act? On Austin's original account it is an act performed *in* saying something. This is to be distinguished both from acts *of* saying something (the making of noises, or marks, belonging to a language) and from acts of bringing something about as a *consequence* of saying something. In short, illocutionary acts are to be distinguished from locutionary and perlocutionary acts.[4] Doubts may be raised about how clear-cut and well-defined Austin's category of illocutionary acts is,[5] but at least we have the intuitive idea provided by the examples he gives when he first introduces the term (e.g., *asking or answering a question, giving some information or an assurance or a warning, pronouncing sentence*), the long lists he provides by the end of his lectures, and the discussion in between.

It would be fair to say that in general critics have found that discussion to be at least in need of supplementation. Strawson and Searle have tried to provide the supplementation by marrying Austin's theory of illocution with Grice's theory of meaning, and in this they are followed by Skinner.[6] Questions about the illocutionary acts performed in issuing a given utterance are, he suggests, equivalent to questions about what the utterer non-naturally meant in issuing his utterance (4:83),[7] and this is identified with a kind of social meaning (4:84). Thus, in the case of historical texts, an investigation into the authors' meaning will enable us to characterize 'what their authors were *doing* in writing them'.[8] It is claimed, moreover, that on this understanding of illocutionary force such force can be ascribed to a whole range of non-verbal voluntary actions (4:85–6). We are also given a particular theory of the best way of going about recovering an utterer's Gricean intentions, the details of which need not concern us here.[9]

According to Skinner, when we have the information not merely that someone issued a given utterance but that in doing so he performed, say, the illocutionary act of warning, then this further information itself constitutes a 'mode of explanation' (4:86).[10] It does so specifically because it furnishes an answer to the question 'Why did he say that?'. The illocutionary redescription of the episode serves as an explanation of the utterer's behaviour; it takes us beyond the knowledge of what the utterance itself meant to knowledge of how the utterer meant it. Colloquially, illocutionary redescription explains certain features of an action by getting at its *point* (2:59; 4:87).[11] This, he contends, is a species of explanation distinct from causal explanation, on the familiar grounds that intention as involved here cannot itself be regarded as an antecedent causal condition.

Finally, Skinner claims that the stage of recovering illocutionary force is a *necessary* stage not just in explaining utterance but in explaining a range of actions. He explicitly dissociates himself from the view that the need to recover illocutionary force is incompatible with subsequent causal explanation of the action in question (4:89),[12] but he insists that an explanation of the illocutionary type is *required* in some cases, that it is a necessary stage of explanation which should not be conflated with a further account making reference to the agent's motives or other causes of his behaviour, however important that further account may itself be to a full understanding (4:88–9).

We have here, then, a theory of illocution, and one from which substantive consequences are held to follow for the explanation of social behaviour. The recovery of illocutionary force is seen as a necessary step in understanding behaviour, and one with its own special features as a mode of explanation.

It is not the claim about the non-causal status of illocutionary explanation which I wish to contest (though I should in fact challenge the ground on which Skinner holds it). However, it provides a useful starting point for my own argument. Consider, then, a possible objection to Skinner's position. Someone might say that he can show that the ascription of illocutionary force is non-causal only at the cost of accepting that it is non-explanatory altogether. Gricean intentions are definitive of illocutionary force for Skinner, and hence the recovery of the appropriate kind of intention serves to *identify* that which requires explanation, rather than itself providing any such explanation.

This is a tangled question[13] and no doubt such an objection will not do as it stands. I shall now use it, however, to develop an alternative account to Skinner's of what is going on when the illocutionary force of an utterance is recovered. I do not endorse that alternative account, but with its aid I hope to highlight both the strengths and the weaknesses in Skinner's own account.

Let it first be allowed that there is an analytical distinction between 'mere' utterance and substantive behaviour. There will be no such separation in reality, as we know from Austin's original discussion. Any actual issuing of an utterance will constitute the performance of a locutionary act and will therefore involve such behaviour as expelling air through the teeth, or drawing a graphite-filled tube across a piece of paper, and so on. And of course we are taking it for granted in the present context that most if not all[14] such issuings will also constitute the performance of some illocutionary act.

I presume that it is an important fact about language that we are able to *abstract* from all this and consider an utterance merely *as* an utterance. Thus, I may know only that Jones issued a given utterance ('The last train for London left five minutes ago') and have no knowledge whatever of any acts he performed, whether he opened his mouth, waved two flags, etc. (except, trivially, that he performed the act of issuing an utterance); but, regardless of that, I am now possessed of a piece of knowledge which will govern my own subsequent behaviour in important ways. I take it this ability to focus exclusively on the utterance and its content is what makes efficient and sophisticated communication possible. (It is also, of course, what makes a theory of the recovery of illocutionary force necessary.) Here we have a species of acts whose features *qua* acts may not, from one point of view, occupy our attention at all, and this makes them quite unlike other kinds of act.[15]

Bearing this point in mind, consider now the move from

(a)   X issued the utterance U (Jones said 'The ice over there is very thin')

to

(b)   X performed the illocutionary act I (Jones warned)

According to Skinner's account, this move (which we accomplish when we arrive at the speaker's intentions as a result of attending to various facts about context and convention) is explanatory of behaviour. According to the alternative account this cannot be so. The move cannot be explanatory of *behaviour*, in the first place, since what we begin with is merely an utterance. What the ascription of illocutionary force then does is to reallocate the utterance to the appropriate category for an explanation-of-behaviour type of explanation. That is, it subsumes it *for the first time* under an *action* description instead of a mere utterance description. But what this further suggests is that the move from (a) to (b) is not explanatory *at all*. It involves, rather, a kind of categorial transformation: the phenomenon mentioned in (a) is reclassified in (b) into a category for which a given range of subsequent explanatory moves will then be appropriate. According to this alternative account, therefore, the move is essentially descriptive, or more accurately redescriptive.

Consider now an obvious line of objection to this account. Surely, it may be said, it rests on the false assumption that description and explanation exclude each other, and this is one of the assumptions which Skinner presents his own account precisely to argue against (cf. 4:82).[16] As a related case, I might replace the description

(c)   John is waving his arms about

with the description

(d)   John is calling for another drink

But this second description functions at one and the same time as an explanation, and there is no general objection available to construing the move from (a) to (b) in the same way. Moreover (this objection continues), it is plain not only that (b) can function both as a description and as an explanation but that it does. Supposing that the case is one where a policeman utters the words 'The ice over there is very thin' to a skater, then as Skinner points out (4:87):

it is one thing if the bystander understands what the policeman's utterance to the skater means, so that he may be able to give an account of what the speaker said. But it is another and further thing if the bystander understands what the policeman's issuing of an utterance with that meaning was itself intended to mean on the given occasion, so that he may be able to give an account of why the policeman said what he said.

How should we respond to this objection? First, I think it should be conceded that there is indeed no general reason against the fusing of redescription and explanation into one operation. Accordingly, though we may wish to preserve a distinction between answers to the questions *what?* and *why?* we shall be hard pressed to make a *sharp* distinction in the area we are concerned with.[17] But notice that the objection in fact serves to reinforce my earlier distinction between utterance and behaviour and to concede that we are given an explanation of an utterance: we pass to knowledge of why the utterer issued the *utterance* which he did. Skinner's account has therefore to be modified in one respect: recovery of illocutionary force is a mode of explanation of utterance, not of behaviour.[18]

It may be thought that a change so small could not carry any real significance. I am not convinced of this, however. I take it that something may well turn on the description under which – certainly the *categorial* description under which – a given event can be explained; or to put it another way, even if we can explain a given event under the true description e_1 it does not follow that we can explain it under the true description e_2.[19] Compare the related case of *anomalous monism* and Davidson's claim that psychological events are physical events, that as such they fall under deterministic laws, but that it does not follow that those events fall under such strict laws *when described as psychological events*.[20] But whether devoid of such further consequences or not, Skinner's claim must be modified in the respect I have described.

I now go on to argue for a further, and more fundamental, modification to Skinner's account. From that last quotation of Skinner's, it is fairly plain that the utterer's intention is required not only to fix the illocutionary force but also to carry the explanatory burden. Effectively, in the kind of transition which interests us, (b) has to be replaced by

(b′) X intended to I or X meant U as an I

This would be a matter of indifference if intention and illocution were indissolubly linked in the way Skinner's analysis requires. I suggest that they are not, with further consequence for his claims about the explanatory power of illocution.

In his methodological papers Skinner continually identifies what a speaker is doing in issuing an utterance with what he means or intends to be doing – illocutionary force with intended illocutionary force.[21] There is an initial oddity in this, as though illocutionary acts, acts realized in language, could escape the ills which all action is heir to, as Austin might put it. Austin himself urges that in the case of illocutionary, as of any other, acts we must distinguish between doing x and attempting to do x (*How To Do Things With Words*, p. 105), and this seems reasonable enough. How could there be a whole range of actions such that an agent succeeds in performing an action of that kind if and only if he intends to? How could we have such luck? Further reflection suggest that we do not, and that for a variety of reasons someone may issue a given utterance intending it to have a particular illocutionary force which fails to materialize. For example, he may issue an utterance meaning it as a warning but fail to warn because his audience is deaf, or stupid, or foreigners unacquainted with the language (all very different cases); or, again, because the circumstances in which he issues it are such that no one could reasonably be expected to construe it as a warning; or the speaker may be rather opaque and not realize that, though the circumstances are right for a warning, the issuing of his particular utterance will not do; or he may simply come out with the wrong words.[22]

Now it may be replied that this is too easy a dismissal of Skinner's theory. It is all very well to gesture towards skeletal examples of this kind, but if we tried to flesh them out we could not suppose a speaker capable of formulating just any *outré* intention he chooses, given actual circumstances. A more charitable reading of his point would therefore be that a speaker performs a given illocutionary act if and only if he intends to, in circumstances which allow the formulation of the intention as a realistic possibility; and of course it is one of the central aims of Skinner's account to show how prevailing conventions act as a constraint on what an agent *can* sensibly intend. Hollis argues in connection with meaningful actions that they are 'taken from stock' and their meaning is 'restricted to a conventional list'.[23] Skinner concurs, holding that for many types of social action 'the recovery of the agent's intentions must be secondary to recovering the meaning of the action itself, since the agent can only mean by the action what his action means, and will be in danger of meaning nothing at all unless he expresses himself through the medium of the action's conventional significance'.[24] Surely what applies for actions applies even more clearly for utterances?

There is something in this reproach, and certainly in his historical work Skinner has done much to demonstrate the importance of examining the intellectual milieu as a means to understanding, and as a constraint upon, what an author can be taken to be trying to do. But the point is an ill-chosen one for rebutting my claim that illocution and intention can fall apart. For what it helps us to notice is that the detachment can be effected in the opposite way to the one I have mentioned. My intentions, in performing an action or issuing an utterance, are limited by knowledge of the conventional significance which may be attached to it. But as I have argued elsewhere,[25] and as Hollis and Skinner in any case seem to accept, there will typically be a *range* of possibilities here. But then one of those possibilities may be realized even though it is not one I intend: I may perform an illocutionary act in the absence of the appropriate intention. To take what is in fact a rather special case, conventions may be so strong, or of such a kind, that in the appropriate circumstances it becomes true that I have performed a certain action by virtue of the fact that I am regarded as having done so in speaking as I do.[26] In these cases something akin to the legal notion of strict liability applies. Thus, a bridge-player who lets slip the word 'redouble' without intending to redouble nevertheless does thereby, in the appropriate circumstances, redouble.[27] There may be some dispute about how far the idea of unintended illocutionary acts can be extended beyond such highly conventional cases, but there are grounds for saying that a wide range of actions which Austin counts as illocutionary can be performed unintentionally – acts like warning, revealing, calculating, assuming, and so on.[28] It seems, therefore, that just as I can intend to perform an illocutionary act and fail, so I can perform an illocutionary act without intending to.

Once again, this may be thought a relatively small change to Skinner's own account. All that has been shown, it may be said, is that there can be marginal and parasitic cases where an unintended illocutionary act is performed: nothing has been said which will threaten in general the links between illocutionary act, convention and intention.

Two comments in reply. First, even this degree of loosening of the links may be significant for the employment of illocutionary theory in historical investigation. A case which Skinner has mentioned on a number of occasions is C. B. Macpherson's claim that Locke's *Two Treatises* has the force of a defence of the rationality of unlimited capital accumulation (3:78). Skinner objects that it is a logical requirement of Locke's intending to give such a defence that he should hold certain beliefs, for example that unlimited accumulation was in need of defence; and that, as a matter of fact, Locke is not likely to have held them. But if illocutionary acts are sometimes, even exceptionally, performed unintentionally, we may have such a case on our hands here. Hence, evidence as to Locke's possible intentions will simply not settle the question whether his text carried the illocutionary force of such a defence. It may be that the text had this force whether Locke intended it to or not.

Second, it may in any case be that the links should be loosened still further. So far, we have considered cases where an illocutionary act may be performed unintentionally, but where at least its description is picked up by conventions prevailing in the context where it is performed; indeed, it is precisely the attitude of an audience which displaces the priority normally given to the agent's intentions. But once it has been conceded that the agent's view of the matter is not necessarily authoritative, similar doubts can be raised about the authoritativeness of the audience's view.[29] That is to say, we may wish to read back into an historical situation illocutionary acts the description of which was not even available in the contemporary context. Thus, a text might have the force of expressing the aspirations of an ascendant social class in circumstances where there was barely a recognition that the class in question existed (or where, perhaps, the concept of social class was itself unavailable). If so, then the gap between actual illocutionary force and any intentions which the agent might have had will be considerable.[30]

Before I connect these points with Skinner's view of the explanatory force of illocution it may be as well to point out that illocutionary acts may be, in two different ways, intentional – even *essentially* intentional – but in ways which will not serve Skinner's purpose. On a Gricean view, a proper account of the locutionary content of an illocutionary act will have to relate it back to the speaker's intentions; and whether Gricean theory is correct or not, there is some force in saying that intentions are necessary to at least the central notion of utterance, the sense in which a human being can, but a parrot or tape recorder cannot, issue an utterance. Secondly, on a Davidsonian view of action, illocutionary acts will be intentional under some description merely by virtue of being acts.[31] But of course it by no means follows from either of these claims, that they will be intentional *under their illocutionary description*, and that, surely, is what Skinner needs to establish.[32]

What, finally, follows from all this for Skinner's claim about illocution and explanation? Take the case where someone issues an utterance intending to perform a particular illocutionary act and fails. Then we should notice that the move from (a) to (b') is impugned in no way whatsoever as an explanatory one. It remains a (partial) explanation of why the speaker issued his utterance to say that he meant it as a warning, even though *ex hypothesi* he did not warn. But since the explanatory power remains the same whether or not the illocutionary act was performed, it seems to follow that illocutionary redescriptions are, as it were, explanatory only *per accidens*, when and because they constitute the recovery of the speaker's intentions. The fact that a man did or did not warn in issuing his utterance adds nothing by way of explaining why it is that he issued the utterance he did in the circumstances he did. And that is as good as to say that the illocutionary description *by itself* provides nothing to explain why the agent said what he did.

It may now look as though nothing at all is left of Skinner's claim that illocutionary redescription is a special mode of explanation of behaviour. (The claim that it explained *behaviour* was earlier challenged, and now the claim that illocution as such *explains* has been challenged.) That is not my conclusion, however. I have tried to locate the truth somewhere between Skinner's account and the alternative account which I described, and I now have to push the pendulum slightly once more to arrive at an acceptable point of equilibrium. In doing so I draw together some points already implicit in my discussion.

What is acceptable in the alternative account is the idea that recovery of illocutionary force involves some kind of categorial transformation; what is unacceptable is the idea that this carries with it no explanatory punch. What is acceptable, after all, in Skinner's account is the idea that recovery of illocutionary force does explain something; what is unacceptable is the idea that it answers any question 'why?' It is the latter which I have argued against in the last part of my discussion, rather than against the idea that illocution is explanatory in some way or other. The shared assumption, underlying both Skinner's and the alternative account, is that *if* illocution is to have explanatory value it must answer a 'why?' question, and it is that assumption which I think must be rejected. There are other questions — for example 'what?' or 'how?' – to which an answer will count as an explanation. In this sense there can be explanations of the rules of chess, or the structure of DNA or even the function of the liver which do not necessarily answer any question 'why'.[33] And it is surely as an explanation-what that illocutionary description comes into its own, precisely by virtue of effecting the categorial transformation earlier described. It is one step in explanation, productive of a corresponding increase in understanding, to know that a human being's producing some noises on a given occasion was not merely that but also the issuing of an utterance or the saying of something. It is then a further step to know that this same event was also the performance of some illocutionary act or other. We have significantly increased our understanding of what was going on in the world on that occasion, even if we are none the wiser about why anything occurred or what anyone's intentions were. There is a strong case, moreover, for saying that this step is an *essential* one at least in the case of utterances. If we understand what someone said on an historical occasion but do not understand what he was *doing* in saying it then our understanding is in a very obvious way incomplete.

Two comments in conclusion. First, this account of how the recovery of illocutionary force enlarges our understanding fits in well with some of Austin's original aims. One of his chief targets is the traditional 'statement' which he regards as an abstraction, and one of the morals he wishes to suggest is that 'The total speech act in the total speech situation is the only *actual* phenomenon which, in the last resort, we are engaged in elucidating.' Hence, 'the words used are to some extent to be "explained" by the "context" in which they are designed to be or have actually been spoken in a linguistic interchange'.[34] But that kind of placing in a context is likely to lead to a new understanding precisely of *what* the actual phenomenon is. In a similar way (to take a familiar case), the further information that a man who left some sacks of potatoes outside my door was *delivering* them provides a categorial reclassification which itself helps to explain what happened.

Second, although the account diverges from Skinner's it is also consistent with one of *his* central aims. Echoing Austin, he argues against the school of historians of thought who believe it is possible to achieve a full understanding of a text simply by reading it over and over (4:95). He is surely right to do so, for the text itself is an abstraction and in its historical context it will constitute a number of other things besides the utterance of a string of statements. Accordingly, the value and importance of Skinner's own historical work is in no way impugned, on this score, by adopting a different account from his own. To put it one way, I have simply tried to arrive at a more accurate picture of what it is that Skinner is doing in recovering the illocutionary force of particular historical texts.

9

An historicist critique of 'revisionist' methods for studying the history of ideas

Joseph V. Femia

Man, bound and determined by the reality of life, is set free not only through art – as has often been set forth – but also through the understanding of history.

Dilthey

We must use the criterion that a philosophical position should be criticized and evaluated not for what it pretends to be, but for what it really is . . .

Gramsci

I

What are the correct procedures to adopt in the attempt to arrive at an understanding of a past work of philosophy or political thought? In the past decade or so traditional approaches to the history of ideas have been subjected to severe and fundamental criticism by a handful of scholars who, while not agreeing on all particulars, generally laud one another's work, depict themselves as methodological innovators, and constitute what we might loosely call a 'revisionist school' within the field of intellectual history. The nucleus of this school – Quentin Skinner, J. G. A. Pocock and John Dunn – all complain about the lack of historicity in the treatment of linguistic artefacts from the past. Their *bête noire* is the prevalent notion that the whole point of studying 'great' works of philosophy is to extract the 'timeless elements' or 'dateless ideas' with universal (and therefore contemporary) application. In striving to appropriate the 'classical texts' to the present, the orthodox historians of ideas, it is contended, have generated both mistaken empirical claims and conceptual confusion; they have ignored the uniquely historical question of what the various thinkers intended to say, and have, instead, deployed interpretative techniques which are not properly historical. As an alternative, say the revisionists, it is necessary to develop 'a truly autonomous method, one which offers a means of treating the phenomena of political thought strictly as historical phenomena and – since history is about things happening – even as historical events: as things happening in a context which defines the kind of events they were'.[1] In essence the alternative urges a theory of interpretation which stresses the recovery of an author's *intention* to mean a particular thing in writing what he wrote at a particular time. The 'intentional' approach, it is said, offers the best hope of restoring the study of past thought to a sound historical footing.

In what follows, I shall challenge some basic assumptions of this recent critique and methodology. The revisionists have, of course, been attacked before, but not from the perspective I adopt – the 'absolute historicism'[2] expounded by Antonio Gramsci. Rejection of the conventional 'timeless approach', I shall argue, by no means commits us to the arbitrary brand of historicism espoused by the revisionists. For reasons of economy and convenience, my criticism will concentrate on Skinner's famous article, 'Meaning and understanding in the history of ideas' (2), the classic of the genre which established its author as the foremost representative of the methodological point of view I am concerned to assess. It has not escaped my notice that Skinner has, in subsequent papers, sought to refine and develop his position,[3] but, since he has never repudiated the basic points made in the 1969 article,[4] it is perfectly fair to use this as our focal point. Anyhow, it is not my aim to trace the development of Skinner's thought but to examine the work which most forcefully articulates a specific (and, in my view, grotesquely mistaken) approach to the history of ideas.

As will be seen, Skinner (and others like him) advance the following propositions: (1) In the sphere of political/social reality, there are no universal truths or perennial questions; all systems of ideas correspond to specific phases and orders of experience. (2) Past thought must be completely dissolved into its precise context (culture, situation, and so forth); it possesses no capacity for independent life. (3) The intellectual historian should not concern himself with the validity or present significance of past ideas; texts must not be regarded as vehicles for the exercise of the analyst's own preoccupations. (4) Historicity demands that we focus on what an author consciously intended to say. And (5), no subsequent account of a thinker's enterprise could survive the demonstration that it is itself dependent upon the use of anachronistic criteria of description and classification – criteria which, in other terms, would have been unintelligible to the thinker himself.

Historicism, I hope to show, only commits us to proposition (1) (and that only in modified form). Skinner apparently believes that propositions (2) – (5) follow logically from proposition (1), but he is wrong. Indeed, propositions (2) – (5), if taken seriously, would reduce the history of thought to little more than a sterile celebration of intellectual pedigree. Following Gramsci, I argue that: (a) ideas may enshrine much that is of permanent value, even though they are themselves untrue or obsolete; (b) thinkers do indeed work within intellectual traditions, which – *to some extent* – transcend particular contexts; (c) all history is 'contemporary history', dictated by the interests of the historian; study of the past is valuable only in so far as it throws light on present problems or needs; and (d) it is neither necessary nor desirable, from an historicist perspective, to understand a body of thought purely or even primarily in terms of the author's conscious designs.

II

Let us now take a closer look at the new 'intentional' approach. The revisionists' debt to the historicist tradition has never received the attention it deserves. While historicism traces its origins back to Vico's seminal, but indigestible and long-ignored writings, it was only in the nineteenth century that we witnessed the triumphant emergence of *history* as a distinct manner of understanding and explaining events. The historicist outlook, though hardly uniform, characteristically comprises four logically interconnected features: (1) Men transform themselves by their own efforts to understand the world and adapt it to their needs, both physical and spiritual; there is, then, no fixed, unchanging human nature, common to all men everywhere at all times, no static psychological structure from which universal goals and principles can be logically deduced. (2) Truth and goodness are not universal and immutable Platonic forms existing in some super-sensible, timeless heaven; consequently, there are no absolute standards in terms of which things and persons can finally be evaluated; 'the historical consciousness lives in the comprehension of all ages', writes Dilthey, 'and it observes in all creativity of individuals, the accompanying relativity and transience'.[5] (3) All ideas and values are products of a given historical epoch, of a specific civilization, or even of definite national collectivity; every philosopher is a child of his time; he uses the symbols or language at his disposal and deals with the problems unique to his age. (4) Forms of human experience, including works of art or philosophy, must be understood and assessed not in terms of eternal principles, valid for all men in all circumstances, but (essentially) in relation to the scales of values and rules of thought appropriate to their own specific time and environment; human achievements must always be interpreted with reference to the particular network of practices and institutions in which they are embedded.[6]

While Skinner scarcely acknowledges his debt to the historicist tradition, his affinity with it (or with an extreme variant of it) clearly underlines his methodology (2:64):

> [I]t has I think become clear that any attempt to justify the study of [the history of ideas] in terms of the 'perennial problems' and 'universal truths' to be learned from the classic texts must amount to the purchase of justification at the expense of making the subject itself foolishly and needlessly naive.

'Great' texts, he believes, do not highlight any universal political predicament; they are not to be viewed as perennially important attempts to set down universal propositions about political or social reality (2:64 – 5).

> Any statement . . . is inescapably the embodiment of a particular intention, on a particular occasion, addressed to the solution of a particular problem, and thus specific to its situation in a way that it can only be naive to try to transcend . . . there simply are no perennial problems in philosophy: there are only individual answers to individual questions, with as many different answers as there are questions, and as many different questions as there are questioners.

Since the authors of the 'classics' were not discussing eternal questions in an eternal language, but writing in a particular situation, addressing their arguments for particular purposes to a particular audience, it must be mistaken to read them as though they were speaking to our present concerns – in even the most oblique manner.

Having dismissed the possibility that past ideas can survive translation into the language of disparate cultures, long after their own worlds have passed away, Skinner can treat the ideas of our ancestors as purely historical phenomena, forever locked into their determinate contexts. Does this amount to the sort of determinism which seeks to reduce linguistic acts to an underlying, more 'real' world of production or social reality? Not at all. The revisionists, especially Skinner, are infatuated by what Husserl called the 'intentionality of experience'. The 'essential aim' in any attempt to understand past texts, must be to ascertain the 'complex intention on the part of the author' (2:63). As Dunn puts it: 'The problem of interpretation is always the problem of closing the context. What closes the context in actuality is the intention (and, much more broadly, the experiences) of the speaker.'[7] Priority is very much accorded to *what the writer in question consciously wished to communicate* to his listeners or readers. Herein lies the key to discovering the actual historical meaning of a text.[8] Once again, the similarity to (at least certain strands of) historicist thought is striking. Dilthey, for example, maintained that historical understanding must be firmly based in a reconstruction of the subjective experience of

historical actors. Human beings – unlike stones and trees – reflect on
what they do; they interpret the situations they are in, set themselves
deliberate goals and plans for the future. On this view, any study of
man's behaviour which ignores intentionality and purposiveness thereby
leaves out of account the most important features of the human condition.

How, then, do we go about recovering the intentions of past thinkers?
How can we decode what they meant to convey? What are the criteria
for evaluating alternative interpretations? As the quotation from Dunn
indicates, it is necessary to examine the *context* in which a writer
formulated his thought, in order to specify the range of meanings which
his words could have had for him. For Skinner, the relevant context is the
prevailing set of *linguistic* conventions, the stock of concepts and symbols
available to a writer and his audience. This linguistic context should be
'treated as an ultimate framework for helping to decide what conventionally
recognizable meanings, in a society of *that* kind, it might in principle have
been possible for someone to have intended to communicate' (2:64). In
urging us to immerse ourselves in the historical context (however defined),
the revisionists express their distaste for the textualist orthodoxy, insisting
as it does 'on the autonomy of the *text* itself as the sole necessary key to
its own meaning' (2:29, 51). In demanding that the historical meaning of a
statement be identified with (or reduced to) the intention of the writer in
uttering the statement, they also join issue with the so-called 'contextual
methodology' (2:59), which holds that 'it is the *context* "of religious,
political, and economic factors" which determines the meaning of any given
text' (2:29). The core assumption of this approach, 'that the ideas of a
given text should be understood *in terms of* its social context', is – according
to Skinner – fundamentally erroneous. Knowledge of the antecedent causal
conditions of an action is not equivalent to *understanding* the action, for
such understanding presupposes 'a grasp of the *point* of the action for the
agent who performed it' (2:59). For Skinner, 'real understanding' of
any statement is tantamount to uncovering its 'intended illocutionary force'
(2:61). Indeed, any characterization of past utterances that goes beyond
subjective intentions is, to use his word, 'meaningless'. If historical studies
are not to be studies of what genuine historical agents did think 'then they
might as well be turned into fiction by intention, for they must certainly be
fiction by attainment'. It cannot be a correct appraisal of any agent's action
to say that he did (or failed to do) something 'unless it is first clear that he
did have, and even could have had, the intention to try to perform *that*
action' (2:48). For example, we cannot, *à la* Macpherson,[9] describe Locke
as a defender of unlimited capital accumulation unless we can establish that
this is actually how he viewed himself when enunciating certain propositions
at particular points in his work.[10] With its presumption that philosophical
systems can be understood primarily in terms of underlying economic forces

or constraints rather than conscious designs, Marxist discourse particularly offends Skinner's sensibilities. But Marxism is only the most obvious villain. *Any* form of historical interpretation predicated on a distinction between the 'manifest' and 'latent' content of a body of thought is dismissed as 'fiction'. No thinker can be said to have meant or done something which he himself would not accept as a correct description of what he had meant or done.

Failure to reduce the meaning of a text to authorial intentions can only breed what Skinner calls 'historical absurdity' (2:32, 35). This absurdity is ultimately caused by the historian's foolish habit of projecting his own interests, views and preoccupations onto the author he is discussing. In so doing, he employs a number of misguided strategies, inexorably producing a succession of fantastic claims about what the thinker in question was doing. What strategies, then, raise the ire of Skinner and his friends?[11] The list is extensive. Here I shall mention only those relevant to my subsequent argument.

First, there is the 'mythology of coherence' (2:38), the assumption that it is the historian's business 'to furnish his author with a degree of coherence he did not in fact achieve'.[12] If there is no coherent system readily accessible to the exegete, his duty, by this 'mythology', is to find one – even if this forces him to rummage through one work after another, imposing a high degree of consistency on the whole corpus. Because of this tendency, laments Dunn, 'it is often extremely unclear whether the history of ideas is the history of anything which ever did actually exist in the past'. Instead, it becomes 'a history of fictions – of rationalist constructs out of the thought processes of individuals, not of plausible abridgements of these thought processes'.[13]

Closely connected with the 'mythology of coherence' is the 'mythology of doctrines', the main form of which consists of 'converting scattered or quite incidental remarks by a classic theorist into his "doctrine"' on a theme close to the heart of the analyst. This leads to 'sheer anachronism', whereby a given writer is 'discovered' to have held a view, because of some chance similarity of terminology, on a subject to which he either did not or could not have meant to contribute. For example, on the basis of some typically Aristotelian remarks concerning the executive role of a ruler compared with the legislative role of a sovereign people, Marsilius of Padua is often said to have possessed a 'doctrine' of the separation of powers, even though the ideas and suggestions making up this doctrine were 'first canvassed some two centuries' after his death. Marsilius himself 'was not even concerned with the issue of political freedom' – which issue is central to the 'separation of powers' thesis. It is improper, Skinner concludes, to suppose that the Paduan '*could* have meant to contribute to a debate the terms of which were unavailable to him, and the point of which would have been lost on him' (2:32 – 3). Even 'more insidious' is the danger of '"reading in" a doctrine which a given writer might in principle have meant to state, but in fact had no intention to convey'. An example here is J. W. Gough's inflation of Locke's scattered remarks on trusteeship into nothing less than Locke's doctrine of 'the political trust' (2:34).

Skinner is also resolutely opposed to all attempts to praise or fault past theorists on the basis of our own standards or interests.[14] As historians it is our duty only to relate and explain, not to pronounce verdicts: the historian is not a judge but a detective. Indeed, Skinner conveys the distinct impression that *all* evaluative judgements of past works are ludicrous — regardless of whether or not the 'judge' purports to be engaged in the activity of writing history. Commentators, we are warned, must refrain from criticizing, say, Plato's *Republic* for omitting the influence of public opinion or Hobbes' *Leviathan* for overlooking the social basis of political power or Locke's *Second Treatise* for failing to set out a clear position on universal suffrage. These alleged 'failures' are illusory. Since 'failing presupposes trying', and since neither Plato nor Hobbes nor Locke had any intention of dealing with the subjects mentioned here, it is simply illogical to castigate them in this way.[15] But this is not all. Neither should we, like Leo Strauss, presume to condemn Machiavelli's teaching as evil and irreligious, a disastrous deviation from true ethical standards. Such a tone of moral disapproval has no place in historical investigation (2:36). Conversely, it makes no sense at all to *praise* past thinkers for either their moral insights or their analytical innovations. It is therefore absurd, for example, to applaud Montesquieu for sowing the seeds of the welfare state or Machiavelli for destroying medieval illusions about the actual conduct of politics (2:35).

Another (related) 'absurdity' which draws Skinner's fire is the tendency to point out earlier anticipations of later doctrines and to credit each writer in terms of this 'clairvoyance'. Thus, it is false to maintain, as does one observer, that 'Locke's theory of signs is notable "as an anticipation of Berkeley's metaphysics"'. Such statements are, in fact, literally 'meaningless' (not just unhistorical) because 'it can scarcely have been Locke's *intention* to antici-pate Berkeley's metaphysics' (2:35, 49). Unless Skinner is simply making a pedantic point about the 'misuse' of the verb 'to anticipate', we must assume that he is also against all transhistorical comparisons (for example, *comparing* Locke and Berkeley on various metaphysical and epistemological questions). Such purism would, in any case, seem to follow from his notion that philosophical statements can in no way transcend their specific contexts, as well as from his unrelenting focus on intentions. (Locke cannot have *intended* his work to resemble Berkeley's in X, Y and Z respects.)

All these erroneous strategies and tendencies, in Skinner's opinion, ignore a fundamental consideration: namely, no 'acceptable account of an agent's behaviour could ever survive the demonstration that it was itself dependent on the use of criteria of description and classification not available to the agent himself' (2:48). There would be no temptation to deviate from this criterion if it were realized that past texts are completely without modern relevance: the 'classic texts cannot be concerned with our questions and answers, but only with their own' (2:65). Interpreters are driven to anachronism and absurdity by the hope that, through reflection on the worth or significance of past ideas, they can arrive at a clearer understanding of our present predicament. To Skinner, at least, this hope is vain: 'We must learn to do our thinking for ourselves' (2:66). This, then, is the basic assumption of his purification exercise.

III

Earlier I enumerated five propositions advanced by Skinner, four of which, it was contended, are not necessarily entailed by the historicist perspective – which I take to be essentially correct. Using Gramsci as our point of departure, let us examine these propositions in turn.

According to proposition (1), in the sphere of political/social reality, there are no universal truths or perennial questions; all systems of ideas correspond to specific phases and orders of experience. On this point Gramsci was adamant:

> [I]t is necessary to deny the existence of 'absolute philosophy', abstract and speculative; that is, philosophy which 'emerges' out of preceding philosophy and inherits from it so-called 'supreme problems' ... Precedence passes to practice, to the real history of changes in social relations, from which ... emerge (or are presented) the problems that philosophy resolves and elaborates.[16]

Ideas do not fall from heaven – like all products of human activity, they are formed in given circumstances through the action of definite needs. Conceptions of the world are responses 'to specific problems posed by reality'.[17] As such, 'every "truth" believed to be eternal and absolute has had practical origins and has represented a "provisional" value'.[18] Gramsci's desire to 'historicize' or 'relativize' all philosophies or systems of thought (including Marxism) was explicitly derived from Croce, one of his early mentors, who rejected the notion of a static, transcendent conception of ultimate truth, corresponding to an ideal model outside the human mind. Philosophies, along with the problems they attempt to solve, are – to Croce – expressive of nothing but the historical reality in which they are produced. Without the historical conditions which call it forth, no set of ideas would be what it is:

> The Kantian philosophy was impossible at the time of Pericles, because it presupposes, for instance, exact natural science, which developed from the Renaissance onward. And this presupposes geographical

discoveries, industry, capitalist or civil society, and so on. It presupposes the scepticism of David Hume, which in its turn presupposes the deism of the beginning of the eighteenth century, which in its turn is connected with the religious struggles in England and in all Europe in the sixteenth and seventeenth centuries, and so on. On the other hand, if Kant were to live again in our time, he could not write the *Critique of Pure Reason* without modifications so profound as to make of it, not only a new book, but an altogether new philosophy . . .[19]

But does not the historicist approach go too far? Surely, *some* problems are perennial, in the sense of always underlying thought about certain ranges of concrete particulars, and such problems *do* tend to recur as explicit focuses of concern. Acceptance of this point does not, I think, require us to abandon the historicist framework – provided certain distinctions are maintained. Vico himself conceded that we could abstract what is common to various phases of culture – parallels and correspondences of psychological and social structure common to individuals remote from one another in space and time, race and outlook. Accordingly, he refers to 'uniform ideas originating among entire peoples unknown to each other', ideas transcending 'variations of detail'; to 'the universal and eternal principles . . . on which all nations were founded and still preserve themselves'; and to 'the human necessities or utilities of social life', upon which the science of human affairs can be established.[20] Exactly what Vico means is not spelled out but reasonable inferences can be drawn. Men have physical needs and sexual impulses, suffer from fear, are capable of using symbols, must work together in groups to satisfy mutual needs, and so forth. Human beings at all times become aware of needing such things as food, shelter, security, language, sexual satisfaction, and human companionship. Thus, any group of people living in a defined territory and interacting with one another must devise social forms and cultural products to meet these basic requirements. This is the *permanent substratum* of all philosophizing and political thinking. It is this substratum, I submit, that accounts for the recurrence of certain questions in the history of political thought; questions such as *who* should rule, *why* and *in what manner*. Likewise, the problems of social order and social change have been enduring preoccupations. On a deeper level, all major political or social theorists in the Western tradition have been concerned, implicitly or explicitly, with the nature of man and of the good life. But, it may be asked, does not a given problem receive its true meaning only in relation to its surrounding context? In relations to the criteria of rationality, systems of values and social structures in which it is embedded? The historicist need not answer in the affirmative: crucial here is the level of abstraction at which we pitch our discourse. When we claim that there are no 'permanent problems' in philosophy, we mean that the *forms* taken by certain *abiding* (assuming they are abstractly framed) questions will be determined by the particular culture or period. Formulating the position in this way is not merely an exercise in semantic hair-splitting. For to accept that there are universal 'necessities or utilities of social life' is to concede that past institutions, customs, works of art and philosophies will speak to us – and may have some bearing on the present. It seems, then, that we must reject proposition (2) – past thought must be completely dissolved into its precise context. Gramsci, it is evident, does just this.

While he never directly discusses any permanent substratum of human needs and concerns,[21] much of what he says becomes incomprehensible and self-contradictory unless we attribute to him some such conception. For while he insisted that past ideas be firmly located in their socio-historical contexts, and not uncritically applied in divergent circumstances, he never attempted to *dissolve* these ideas into the historical process. In the final analysis, social practice determines what is thought; it does not follow, however, that what is thought cannot, in some senses and in varying degrees, transcend its context. In this connection, Gramsci makes two separate points. First, he notes that particular authors usually think and write in a way that they regard as relevant to what their predecessors wrote; they seek, in other words, to elaborate, reshape, or rebut their predecessors: 'each philosopher cannot ignore the philosophers who have preceded him and, indeed, usually acts as if his philosophy were a polemic against or a development of preceding philosophies'.[22] It need scarcely be pointed out here that Gramsci is right. To take one obvious example, Marsilius of Padua plainly borrows arguments from Aristotle when countering papal claims to secular authority (for example, the self-sufficient nature of the political community and its possession of all necessary means for the maintenance of internal peace and order). Gramsci goes on to draw the following conclusion: once we eliminate what is 'social' from a work of philosophy, there still remains a 'residue' – to use his word – which cannot be explained by the historical context. Although philosophies are 'expressions of real historical development',[23] social exigencies are conceived by particular philosophers in 'an individual and personal manner', and the 'importance' of this is not to be denied.[24] Elsewhere, he refers to this 'individual' element as the 'ahistorical' part of a philosophical system, in the sense that it does not correspond to 'contemporary conditions of life'.[25] It is also true, says Gramsci (and this is the second way in which theoretical products may transcend their historical contexts), that the 'actuality' or 'fecundity' of certain ideas survives the demise of their social precipitants; but the extent to which this is so can only be established by empirical investigation:

> The question arises whether a theoretical 'truth' discovered in correspondence with a specific practice can be generalized and

deemed universal . . . The proof of its universality consists precisely in that which it can become: (a) a stimulus to know better the concrete reality of a situation different from the one in which it was discovered (this is the prime measure of its fecundity); (b) when it has stimulated and helped this better understanding of concrete reality as if it were originally an expression of it.[26]

In keeping with this approach, he declaims against those who hold 'that the whole heritage of the past must be rejected'. On the contrary, there exist certain 'instrumental values', capable of being 'elaborated and refined',[27] and these must be distinguished from 'the transient philosophical values that have to be rejected outright'.[28] What are these 'instrumental values'? Among them, Gramsci includes concepts or ideas like natural rights, the 'intrinsic value' of which is *'limited'* by their historicity, 'but *not negated'*.[29] He was, in fact, intrigued by the possibility of using the splendid ideals of the French Revolution to undermine the bourgeois hegemony. Such ideals were clearly capable of rising above the social order and social classes which spawned them:

> The ideas of quality, of fraternity, of liberty excite passions among those strata of men who see themselves neither equal, nor brothers of other men, nor free in their social interactions. Thus it happens that in every radical movement of the multitude, in one manner or another, in the mould of particular ideologies, these claims are put forward.[30]

Needless to say, Gramsci, as a good Marxist, was not suggesting that Enlightenment ideals could be taken over in their original form, still less that we could accept the underlying conceptual framework from which they arose. This framework, as is well known, conceived man in abstract fashion; that is, individuals were emancipated by logical abstraction from their historic connections and from every social necessity; the concept of society was reduced to its atomic constituents, to the sum of the individuals composing it. Abstract categories of individual psychology, it was thought, sufficed for the explanation of all human facts. It is hardly surprising that this notion of the individual as prior in some sense to the society originated in the early bourgeois epoch, because seeing oneself in this manner is a necessary part of the form of life of the entrepreneur in a regime of free enterprise. For the entrepreneur the rest of society is an agglomeration of individuals with whom he must interact in such a way as to realize a profit, and with whom he can enter into contractual relations. Society, according to this view, is created by the voluntary agreement of free and independent individuals to protect their property. Here we find the foundation of modern concepts of 'rights' and 'freedom'. As the economy became more integrated, nationally and internationally, as work situations became more socialized, and as new discoveries in the social sciences pointed to the profound effects of environmental conditioning, the underlying assumptions of classical liberal theory lost much of their force. To present them as eternal verities is to fail to realize that ways of looking at the world are organically linked to concrete modes of activity. And yet, as Gramsci indicates, ideas and values integral to this theory represent an advance for mankind and still carry conviction. Even if Hobbes and Locke did provide a political doctrine corresponding to (and sanctioning) incipient capitalist economic relations, as well as the state structures necessary to maintain these, much of what they said is still valuable and worthy of being 'absorbed' into modern theorizing.[31]

Let me add an example of my own to help illustrate this general point. Consider Aristotle. The system he constructed was determined in its most essential characteristics by the conditions prevailing within the confines of ancient Greek society. The postulates of his thought were: the general superiority of the Greeks, the natural justice of slavery as a basis of social organization, and the incompatibility of bread-winning pursuits with the moral and intellectual attributes of good citizenship. All these ideas now strike us as outmoded, if not patently ridiculous. Yet Aristotle also enunciated principles which, justifiably, are still features of political analysis: for instance, his notion that social stability is most to be found where extremes of wealth and poverty are unknown and the middle class is strongest; his analytical distinction between the underlying causes of revolution and the immediate factors which trigger it. Interestingly enough, the one example Skinner offers to 'prove' that past thought is irrelevant to our own culture and period is based on a gross simplification of Plato, whose views on democracy and participation are 'historicized' as follows (2:66):

> As soon as we begin to study Plato's actual arguments, however, the sense in which the issue of participation is the same for himself and ourselves dissolves into absurdity. What we are most likely to learn from Plato is that the cook should not participate because he is a slave. It is hard to see what problems of participation in modern representative democracies are likely to be advanced by the application of this particular piece of perennial wisdom.

Regardless of what Plato said about cooks and slaves, and notwithstanding the strange myth about people being born with different 'metals' in their souls, the fact remains that his justification of hierarchy embraces arguments that still enjoy currency: the need for expertise, the tendency for democracy to produce cultural mediocrity, the conception of society as a system of interlocking needs and functions requiring a strict division of labour. Whether or not we agree with Plato, we must allow that at least some of his concerns and arguments are neither alien to us nor impossible to incorporate into our own political thinking.

The goal of historicism, properly conceived, is not to devastate the entire philosophical legacy of mankind, but (primarily) to ensure that positions of the past are not arbitrarily detached from their explanatory context and simply reproduced in the present, without due regard for subsequent intellectual discoveries or changed social conditions. For example, no historicist would, like Nozick in *Anarchy, State and Utopia*, try to revive wholesale modes of theorizing appropriate to the seventeenth century. What is 'dead' in the thought of our ancestors must always be presumed to outweigh the part which is 'living'. But the historicist need not operate on the facile assumption that past ideas are *entirely* and *inextricably* bound up in a straitjacket of particular circumstances, particular questions and particular intentions. Skinner writes of the history of political thought as if it were merely a series of disconnected intellectual events. But if every historical utterance and action is a unique event, historical inquiry itself becomes impossible. The historian must, unavoidably, pursue analogies, make comparisons, identify regularities, and use general concepts. If all historical events are *sui generis*, then we cannot write history; we can only pile up documents. But this argument raises a tricky question the centrality of which to the whole debate does not prevent it from being curiously ignored: namely, what is history? The revisionists refuse to recognize this as a matter open to dispute: history is what they *assume* it is, and that is the end of it. Thus they can issue solemn pronouncements on what is 'historically correct' and what is 'historically illegitimate'[32] in the absence of any serious examination of the concept of history itself. What is its nature? Its purposes? We shall briefly consider these questions next, in the course of our consideration of proposition (3) – the intellectual historian should not concern himself with the validity or present significance of past ideas; texts must not be treated as vehicles for the exercise of the analyst's own preoccupations.

The positivist theory of knowledge rests on a complete disjunction of subject and object. Facts, like sense impressions, impinge on the observer from outside and are independent of his consciousness. The process of reception is passive: the external world of fact 'speaks for itself', and man's knowledge only translates, or reflects, what takes place in the primary world of 'given' things. While it was once fashionable to base historical research on such epistemological suppositions, they have, with good reason, fallen into general disrepute. To speak plainly, purely descriptive history is impossible. More than one construction can always be placed on a given collection of data. From the welter of perceptible things, we must choose, and this requires abstraction. The historical observer never confronts a bare and simple fact, unrelated to a broader context. Every fact has significance for him only because it fits into a system of ideas he has already formed. The historian must organize historical phenomena according to categories. But whence does he derive these categories? His *practical preferences and attitudes* will inevitably influence the questions he asks, the facts he selects and the connections he perceives; and such preferences and attitudes will ultimately mirror the historian's own culture. Historical narrative is always dependent on the culture in which and from which it springs. This conception of the historian's enterprise seems compatible with the historicist endeavour to discover the unique features of any given event or utterance – those that can be comprehended only with reference to the specific historical context. Even Dilthey realized that the historian's understanding is necessarily limited by his own experience, his own 'customs, habits, political circumstances and religious processes'.[33] The point is, as Croce rightly notes, 'that only an interest in the life of the present can move one to investigate past fact'. Therefore, 'this past fact does not answer to a past interest, but to a present interest'. This is the reasoning behind his famous dictum: 'every true history is contemporary history'. History, that is to say, 'if it means something and is not an empty echo', responds to problems that 'come forth from the bosom of *life*'.[34] *Historical* enquiry, in contrast to mere chronicle, must be governed 'by the practical and scientific needs of a definite moment or epoch'.[35] An event conceived as having no relation to present life would have no historical value. True, a full understanding of worlds remote from our own can never be achieved through the myopic application of our own ideas and valuations; on the other hand, the historian can view the past only through the ideas of the present. And, if he is practising 'true history', he brings the past into relation with our contemporary life not merely as an act of comparison, but as an actual widening of our apprehension of the present.

Gramsci accepted all of this. For him, as for Croce, 'history is always contemporary history', guided by the practical interests of the historian.[36] History, as opposed to dead chronicle or source material, is always relevant to our present needs and situations. The story of the past, he declares, 'cannot but be written with and for present interests'.[37] In fact, Gramsci attacks all claims for a 'disinterested' historiography; that is, an historiography purporting to exemplify an 'external "objectivity"'.[38] Such claims are found wanting on two counts. In the first place, they presuppose the notion that such objectivity is possible. But, according to Gramsci, the analysis of reality *must* be filtered through *a priori* theoretical assumptions – a set of categories and a hierarchy of values, which are culturally determined.

An investigation into a series of facts to discover the relations between them presupposes a 'concept' that permits one to distinguish that series of facts from other possible ones. How can there occur a choice of facts to be adduced as proof of the truth of one's own assumptions if one does not possess a pre-existent criterion of choice? But what will this criterion of choice be, if not something superior to each single fact under investigation? An intuition, a conception, which must be regarded as having a complex history, a process that is to be connected with the whole process of the development of culture.[39]

Even if it were possible, argues Gramsci, 'external' or 'disinterested' history would be undesirable. The purpose of history *should be* to make men more self-conscious and effective as political actors. Knowledge of the past is of use only in so far as it illuminates the present.[40] Gramsci is not, of course, saying that historical reality *authoritatively prescribes* solutions to practical problems; it simply serves to make action more rational by clarifying the historical origins of contemporary dilemmas, by indicating the range of realistic choice, and by providing a treasure trove of ideas and insights, models and analogies.

But if interpretation always emerges from an encounter with the practical concerns of the interpreter, does it not to become a matter of political taste or even whim? The answer is no. To argue that the study of history is axiological, an enterprise wherein facts are selected and questions formulated from the standpoint of values, is not to offer a license for anarchy. The influence, however profound, of theories or perspectives on men's perception and understanding is one thing; the (extreme relativist) claim that historical facts are purely the product of theory and therefore incapable of distinguishing reality from fiction, truth from falsehood, is quite another. Gramsci, despite his rejection of empiricism, was animated by the spirit of empirical inquiry; for him, generalizations and theoretical constructs are worthless unless tested against the real world of observed experience, of 'hard' facts.[41] While (on his view) the interpretation of the past is always a practical endeavour, conducted from within the horizon of the present, by no means does it follow that the interpreter is justified in mutilating the evidence to suit his preconceptions or political passions.

In the prison notebooks, Gramsci's attitude towards history is well revealed in those pages he devotes to an interpretation of Machiavelli.[42] The Sardinian felt that his own situation was in a sense parallel to Machiavelli's, and, as one commentator has perceptively observed, 'meditation upon this historical connection helped him to formulate his own position'.[43] What is the 'connection'? Machiavelli was concerned with the seizure of power by Renaissance princes and the unification of Italy; Gramsci with the revolutionary activities of the Marxist Party and the building of socialism. Both men wanted to mobilize the Italian people for a common purpose and develop a theory (and technique) of politics enabling the 'outsiders' to overturn the established order. Gramsci's own thought certainly bears the imprint of various Machiavellian ideas: among them, the belief that *fortuna* can yield to men bold enough to conquer her, and the 'principled realism' which fuses concern for 'what ought to be' with clear-eyed appreciation of the limits imposed by the extant constellation of forces.

Does this dialogue with the Florentine's ghost constitute a deviation from historicist principles? Not in Gramsci's eyes. While 'Machiavelli is a man wholly of his period', whose 'political science represents the philosophy of his time',[44] it is nevertheless possible to use his observations and precepts as a reference point for reflection on contemporary society. To Gramsci, then, it is perfectly legitimate for the intellectual historian to treat the great texts as vehicles for the exercise of his own preoccupations – so long as this does not result in outright distortion or disregard for historical 'conditions and exigencies'.[45] (In any case, the particular interpretations he arrives at will *inescapably* be influenced by these very preoccupations.)

There is nothing unhistorical about this contemporary approach. To preach otherwise is to misconceive the character of historical inquiry. To repeat, we cannot understand the human past save in terms of its relation to ourselves and our world, unless we trace it backwards from the present. Skinner himself shows some recognition of this necessity: 'We must classify in order to understand, and we can only classify the unfamiliar in terms of the familar' (2:31). The full implications of this statement, however, apparently elude him.

We are now in a position to consider propositions (4) and (5) together. They are, respectively: historicity demands that we focus on what an author consciously intended to say; and no subsequent account of a thinker's enterprise could survive the demonstration that it is itself dependent upon the use of anachronistic criteria of description and classification. Once all the above points are recognized, the case for these two propositions vanishes; and many of the methods or practices Skinner and other revisionists hope to banish from the sphere of historical explanation appear perfectly proper – indeed *necessary*. A quasi-religious fixation on intentions can only impoverish our approach to the history of ideas, diminishing our capacity to learn from our forebears (and let it be noted that we can learn from their failings as well as their successes). Consider the 'mythology of coherence'. Sometimes intellectual historians do seem determined to inflict a coherence 'at all costs' (2:39) on the object(s) of their study. Many are loath to admit that the theorists they have chosen for analysis may have contradicted themselves or simply changed their minds over time. Such admissions make it difficult to enclose a thinker within a tidy and exciting formula. But this pursuit of a spurious coherence is only the diseased variant of two related (and quite healthy) interpretative strategies, both of which are arbitrarily rejected by the revisionists. The first is the attempt to impose system or order on a disjointed body of thought. Some thinkers just never got around to arranging their ideas in logical sequences or coherent wholes, and if we are to expound or assess their respective contributions, the ordering process is left to us. The end products may be 'rationalist constructs', which never did actually exist in the form we have given them, but so what? How, for example, could we even begin to comprehend Gramsci's fragmented and disorganized *Quaderni* if we did not endeavour to elaborate his notes 'to a degree of formal intellectual articulation which there is no evidence that they ever attained'?[46] The second strategy is to search for an 'inner coherence' underlying (and perhaps explaining) apparent contradictions. Skinner is especially scathing about all such attempts, which he dismisses as 'metaphysical' (2:40 − 3). Now (as noted above), in certain cases, the desire to detect an inner coherence has degenerated into a misguided attempt to iron out even genuine inconsistencies in the name of some higher unity. But the fact that such misguided attempts exists does not mean, *pace* Skinner, that all attempts to find hidden consistency must be misguided. This apparent flaw in his logic is explained by his failure to accept that what an agent is in fact doing in performing an action may have little or no connection with his actual intentions. There is a crucial difference between an idea and the bout of thinking it reflects. Although an idea is the product of the thinking which went into it, it also transcends that thinking. There may be logical relations between a person's ideas which do not correspond to any psychological relations between the thought processes which led respectively to those ideas − logical relations of which he may be unaware. Which brings us to a general observation: not all thinkers understand the full theoretical or logical implications of what they say. Assume, for the sake of argument, that Locke did not *intend* to furnish an ideological justification of capitalism. If the historian lets the matter rest there, he has not succeeded in telling the whole story. For, by removing all natural-law limitations on the private appropriation of property, Locke *necessarily* conferred moral legitimacy upon the emergent capitalist order − an order incompatible with such limitations and founded on massive concentrations of private wealth. Otherwise stated, a defence of capitalist economic relations is *inherent* in his doctrine of property rights. If he was unconscious of this fact, then he, quite literally, did not know what he was doing.

That a thinker might misconstrue or simply remain blind to the logic of his own ideas is, one would think, intuitively obvious; but Skinner and his disciples are advocating a form of historical analysis which is contrary to common sense and ordinary experience. In everyday conversation we leap from expression to expression, filling gaps, removing apparent inconsistencies, drawing inferences, and so develop an intellectually elaborated result, which is our understanding of what the other person has said. Moreover, when we try to understand an individual *as such* − his character, his thoughts, and so on − it never occurs to us to confine ourselves to his own self-image; on the contrary, we strive to uncover the *hidden premises* (psychological or social) as well as the *consequences* (logical or practical) of his behaviour and statements. What the revisionists never do is to explain why the procedures needed to gain an understanding of historical actors must so diverge from the procedures we manifestly use to acquire an understanding of our contemporaries. To be sure, an historian may be able to give an explanation of unconscious influences on a thinker which illuminates his ideas in a way he himself did not understand. This, of course, is a commonplace of Marxist historiography, but is by no means confined to it. Built into Dilthey's concept of hermeneutic exegesis, for example, is the idea that we should seek to understand an author better than he understood himself. Because expressions may contain more than the agent is aware of, the analyst can never, in his quest for understanding, concentrate exclusively on a reconstruction of conscious purposes.[47] Furthermore, a thinker can fail to grasp the *potentialities* of his thought. For example, many who have contributed to the shaping of the modern secular consciousness had no intention of doing so. The Reformation thinkers (who helped to shift the focus of religious thought from contemplation of the divine to man's temporal needs and concerns) are a case in point. Now Skinner does not deny that we can be legitimately interested in the retrospective significance of a philosophical work; he only wishes to claim that this significance has nothing to do with the *historical meaning* of the work and is therefore a peripheral (if not actually extraneous) object of historical investigation (2:43 − 5). But this is merely an arbitrary assertion. Dilthey's approach to 'meaning' (and the tasks of the historian) seems much more plausible. For him, a particular act 'gains meaning from its relationship with the whole, from the connection between past and future, between individual and mankind'.[48] Unearthing the historical meaning of an action, on this conception, is not equivalent to discovering its 'intended illocutionary force' (though this is a valid *starting point*); it involves, above all, an apprehension of the *importance* or *impact* (at various levels) of the action in question.[49]

All the above considerations point to this: what an author is doing in composing a text or set of utterances cannot be understood solely or even mainly in terms of his intention(s). Thus (assuming sufficient textual evidence can be found) there is no historical impropriety in saying that Rousseau's *Social Contract* amounts to a theoretical justification of totalitarianism, or that Locke's *Second Treatise* embodies a defence of exploitation and unlimited capital accumulation, or that Machiavelli's *Prince* − and here we quote Gramsci − contains '*in nuce* both the separation of powers and parliamentarism'.[50] Although such statements disregard subjective intentions, they may nevertheless be accurate *and* help us to assess the limitations or strengths of the works in question. Of course, in Skinner's opinion, attempts to evaluate past ideas are pointless, if not literally meaningless. But he overlooks an important consideration emphasized by Gramsci: the intellectual historian ignores the mistakes of past philosophies only at our peril, for these mistakes 'although made in the past', have a nasty habit of being 'reproduced in the present'.[51] World views that correspond to previous phases of historical development have 'left stratified deposits in popular philosophy', and for this reason, the evaluation of past thought is much more than an academic exercise: it becomes a voyage of self-discovery, in which the historian/critic lays bare the deeply rooted assumptions of his own (and his culture's) mode of thought. 'To criticize one's own conception of the world', Gramsci tells us, 'means criticism of all hitherto existing philosophy.' He then adds,

> The point of departure of critical elaboration is the consciousness of what one really is; it is 'knowing thyself' as a product of the historical process, which has deposited in each of us an infinity of traces, without leaving an inventory ... *Philosophy cannot be separated from the history of philosophy.*[52]

If we follow Skinner's instructions, we can never produce 'contemporary history' – historical knowledge that has as its sounding-board and measuring rod contemporary preoccupations and concerns. The methods and practices denounced by Skinner are precisely the methods and practices which enable us to separate what is valuable from what is erroneous or transient (tied to a determinate social form) in the philosophical works of the past. How, it may be asked, can we ever learn from past thought unless we allow historians to criticize, to examine historical trends, to make transhistorcal comparisons, to impose system where there is none, to uncover subterranean or unconscious assumptions, to pose artificial questions – our questions – to draw out implications? For Skinner, as we have seen, this is a pseudo-problem, because he simply assumes that the ideas of our ancestors are, for all intents and purposes, extinct. Each generation, he seems to be saying, must begin over again all the work done since the childhood of humanity. But political ideas cannot be created *ex nihilo*: we are crucially dependent on our philosophical tradition. Innovation in political thought rarely, if ever, consists of unprecedented originality. Rather, it is a matter of extending and rearranging old ideas, shifting emphasis among them, playing variations on them and so forth. We expand our range of vision and crystallize our own political thinking by meditating on our philosophical predecessors. If Skinner really believes that we can 'do our thinking for ourselves', then he entertains an implausible view of political conceptualization.

IV

Skinner's exhortation to students of past philosophy to practise austerities so that they might be delivered from all temptations to violate his canons of historicity is to render intellectual history gratuitously barren. It is, I would contend, one of the functions of history 'to cast', in E. H.

Carr's words, 'a beam of the past over the issues which dominate present and future'. Revisionist intellectual history can, at best, issue in what Labriola called 'the empiricism of a boundless erudition'.[53] At the conclusion of his famous article, Skinner remarks (2:67):

> [I]t is a commonplace – we are all Marxists to this extent – that our own society places unrecognized constraints upon our imaginations. It deserves, then, to become a commonplace that the historical study of the ideas of other societies should be undertaken as the indispensable and the irreplaceable means of placing limits on those constraints.

But it is precisely this estimable goal which is rendered unattainable by his curious methodological strictures.

10
Method in intellectual history: Quentin Skinner's *Foundations*

Kenneth Minogue

Quentin Skinner's *The Foundations of Modern Political Thought* is primarily of interest to philosophers not for its excellent account of European thought about the state but for the self-conscious philosophy which has gone into it. It is a rare historian who pauses to get his philosophy in order before he embarks on a major enterprise, though such a policy is possibly less unusual in intellectual history than in other fields. In Skinner's case, however, this order of doing things has been pushed so far that he counts as a philosopher in his own right, rather than as merely someone who is unusually careful to think about what he is doing. The publication of this present major work thus provides a convenient opportunity to make a few remarks about the relation between historical theory and practice.

I

Professor Skinner's fundamental belief is that the development of intellectual history depends upon an appropriate philosophical understanding. We learn from the preface that the *Foundations* exemplifies 'a particular way of approaching the study and interpretation of historical texts',[1] and he goes on to link the virtues of the method with the virtues of the book. In more recent contributions to the philosophical field, subsequent to the publication of the *Foundations*, he has pleaded for further work on method since otherwise the disciplines of the human sciences 'will continue to suffer from their present conceptual disarray'.[2] At its most extreme, this position seems to amount to saying that no hitherto written intellectual history is satisfactory, since he tells us that if the approach he champions were practised with success, 'it might *begin* to give us a history of political thought with a genuinely historical character'[3] (my italics). There is no doubt that Skinner is prepared to press hard on the view that the correct method is a necessary[4] condition of good practice.

He also recognizes two implications of this view, and we may begin to explore the position by considering them. The first is that whatever virtues an intellectual history has will be attributable to good method, and this appears in the preface to the *Foundations*[5] where Skinner asks if any new discoveries have come out of the new method. He cites two. Earlier intellectual historians had not adequately realized how much the political thought of the Renaissance had been influenced by the Stoics. And another discovery: 'it has not I think been sufficiently recognized that the theories they [Calvinist revolutionaries] developed were almost entirely couched in the legal and moral language of their Catholic adversaries'.[6] These are historically interesting contentions, but it will be immediately apparent that there is nothing in them which necessarily results from the use of the philosophy of speech-acts or an immersion in hermeneutic theory. The examples given do not even provide inductive support for the principle asserted.

The second implication is that bad intellectual history results from bad or intellectually incoherent method. The central target of Skinner's criticism has been something called 'the textualist approach' which was described and anatomized in his first important contribution to the methodology of intellectual history 'Meaning and understanding in the history of ideas' (2). Most of the critical elements of his theory are here laid out in the form of a syllabus of errors resulting from a belief in timeless answers to perennial questions; in implausible coherences to be detected in a writer's thought; in seeing a thinker as 'anticipating' ideas which were not formulated till later, and much else. Critics of Skinner have often seen this controversy in terms of a conflict between political theorists, who tend to immerse themselves in the great texts of political thought, and historians whose tendency is to dissolve writings in the wider context of events to which they belong.[7] All the political theorists wanted was to be left alone with their books (thus John Plamenatz: 'Is there to be no division of labour?'),[8] grateful if historians should correct their odd historically implausible misreading of their texts. But the Skinnerian programme seemed at times to be a war *à outrance* in which only one of these academic activities could survive the great debate. One must emphasize 'seems' here, partly because the issues were never entirely clear, and partly because Skinner's position was often modified towards a common-sense accommodation in the course of its development. Sometimes, indeed, modified too far. Thus, in a flank-guarding exercise towards the end of 'Meaning and understanding in the history of ideas' he tells us that his position 'is not even a denial of the possibility that there may be apparently perennial *questions*, if these are sufficiently abstractly framed . . . it will be found that what *counts* as an answer will usually look, in a different culture or period, so different in itself that it can hardly be in the least useful even to go on thinking of the relevant question as being "the same" in the required sense after all. More crudely: we must learn to do our thinking for ourselves' (2:66). Now one might, perhaps, deny that there is any such thing as a perennial question, but if one admits such a thing (or even 'apparently' perennial questions!) then there must also be perennial answers, since the cultural specificity of the answers must unavoidably affect the questions as well. And it is, of course, the youthful incaution of that 'we must do our thinking for ourselves' which dismayed the political theorists. For when, say, social psychologists take off from Machiavelli in setting up a typology of high machs and middle machs – or when, for example, Miss Anscombe sets off in a discussion of future events from Aristotle's discussion of the sea-battle – they are certainly not abdicating their thought to Machiavelli or Aristotle. They are merely using materials which, although from one point of view they may be historical records, can also be used in a non-historical way. Just as one finds aesthetic value in the Parthenon, the Sistine Chapel, and *The Magic Flute* (though these are also historical survivals which can tell us something of the period) so one may also find philosophical value in works of earlier writers.

It is certainly true that historians will find some very strange things said in political studies whenever historical personages are referred to. But, as Skinner would no doubt agree, in reading another writer one must be sensitive to his intention in saying what he does, and this salutary rule is often ignored in the course of the enthusiastic[9] trawl of errors which constitutes the first part of 'Meaning and understanding in the history of ideas'. To take a couple of examples: Robert A. Dahl earns his place as believing in a universal human nature on the basis of a couple of casual sentences appended in a bibliographical note to a chapter of his *Modern Political Analysis* (2:38).[10] Again, Robert Armstrong falls under anathema for using the unhistorical idea of 'anticipation' in connecting Locke with Berkeley. All he is actually doing is, at the end of an article, pointing to an abstract affinity between the two writers: 'Berkeley's metaphysics, then, may be regarded as a development of an idea suggested by Locke. Or we may regard Locke's theory as an anticipation of Berkeley's metaphysics' (2:49).[11] To indict a man's historical credentials on the basis of an odd throwaway line is, I think, pretty clearly to ignore the intention of the writer; and if one were to take this practice seriously, one would have to infer that Skinner is affirming some such unlikely doctrine as: 'All past objects must be understood as evidence for historical understanding, and they must be understood in no other way whatever.' One has merely to state this view in its extreme form to recognize that it could not possibly be held; and indeed, if ever held, it was smartly abandoned.

It should now be clear that an important clarification is needed before one could even begin to decide the question of whether bad intellectual history results from bad method. In his long critical essay, Skinner lights upon many instances of remarks which must indeed be recognized as bad history; and he attributes them to false methodological assumptions about coherence, perenniality and the rest. This argument is totally invalid unless these writers are asking historical questions. Skinner does, on occasion, recognize that philosophers may have found in timeless abstraction an exemption from his historical strictures; but this is not enough. Telling stories is an important part of the explanatory practices of all societies and in many activities; in some domains, there are no other forms of explanation. A great deal of political argument takes place in terms of 'historical' analogies, and the word 'historical' here has to be protected by quotation marks because the references in this type of argument are historical in the popular sense of referring to the past, but not historical in the sense of being contributions to the academic problem of attempting to understand some passage of events in a properly historical manner. Again, in a world of incessant controversy, our understanding of 'the classic texts' is a valuable resource for naming and signposting ideas. This is part, though only a part, of the form of literature named (and perhaps misnamed) the 'history' of political ideas. It is easy to demonstrate that the whole thing is historically an absurdity. But, clearly, important and interesting arguments have been advanced within this curious *genre* by people like Wolin, Strauss and Arendt.[12] Most of the criticism of Skinner by political theorists consists essentially in howls of anguish that this lovable old absurdity should be so shoddily treated.

One might, indeed, take this argument one step further. There are evidently two ways of interpreting a work like Hobbes' *Leviathan*. One is to put it in a context of Hobbes' other writings and see it as a work of philosophy; another way (which is licensed by some of Hobbes' remarks) is to see it within a context of the events of the time. In understanding Hobbes, we are not bound to employ either way exclusively, and each may be sensible according to the questions that concern us. Each way has its dangers. There is evidently a danger that in understanding a work as a response to a context, for example, we may underestimate that less evident concern which philosophers and other serious writers have to maintain the consistency of their thought. And it is possible that a history of political ideas written in this latter manner will allow the context systematically to cannibalize each writer, who will be represented only by those bits of his thought which appear to be relevant according to our conjecture – and it can hardly be more – of the practical problem he was responding to. As a tendency to distort a writer's coherence arising from too gross a concern with context, we might, after Skinner, call this the 'mythology of fragmentation', and some critics have seen this as characteristic of the

Foundations.[13] This fallacy may be seen in Skinner's treatment of Hobbes, whom he attempts to assimilate to the *de facto* theorists of the Engagement Controversy. 'It is clear . . . that there is nothing unusual or even particularly original about Hobbes's most characteristic political beliefs'[14] is a remark that assumes that a 'belief' is merely the practical conclusion arrived at; whereas we might suggest that the real belief is in part constituted by the reasons for it, which were certainly highly original. Understood whole, Hobbes cannot be thus so easily assimilated to the polemicists of his day. Hobbes did, we are told, make 'it quite clear that he both saw and intended his great work precisely as a contribution to the existing debate about the rights of *de facto* power. It goes without saying that *Leviathan* is much else besides.'[15] Well, it doesn't have to go without much saying because Hobbes said it himself, and pretty decisively. He said that he was the founder of civil science. And while it picks up some stray remarks Hobbes made, to say that Hobbes was 'contributing to the debate' is quite to miss the tone of Hobbes' thought. He was bent on *ending* the debate,[16] not contributing to it. To go further along this path would be a diversion; but the conclusion I draw is that the claim that historians can correct what political theorists say about the great thinkers of the past is, while far from being absurd, much less evidently illuminating than Skinner habitually claims.

II

Still, to suggest that Skinner is an exponent of historical fundamentalism is unjust to him because he is really a philosophical imperialist in historical disguise. It is a transforming method which lies at the heart of his concerns. We thus seem to have a chain of influence by which the philosopher develops the concepts by which we understand human action, to the benefit of the historian, whose results can in turn rule out of court the errors resulting from the textualist approach of the political theorist. Further, history studied in this way reveals how little understanding can come from the abstractions by which we ordinarily try to leap across cultural and temporal boundaries. Humility on this point is one of the promised fruits of the method, with just possibly the hope that the new method will broaden our imaginative horizons (2:67).

Thus we find ourselves confronted with the project of putting intellectual history on solid philosophical foundations. Such a project runs into immediate difficulties, because it transfers all discussion of general ideas in history to a more abstract methodological level. The focused talk of practitioners, usually found in *obiter dicta* scattered through their histories, is judged, and often misjudged, as the advancing of methodological propositions. Confusion occurs here even at the philosophical level. Thus Herbert Butterfield remarks that in interpreting, for example, the sixteenth century, we ought not to see it in anachronistic terms such as 'progressive' against 'reactionary' but ought rather to 'adopt the outlook' of the sixteenth century upon itself.[17] Skinner takes these sensible words as being one possible solution to a question that Skinner himself is posing, and proceeds to pepper the remark with pleasantries about its entailing a seventeeth-century history of ethics without Spinoza, and a nineteenth-century history of logic without Frege (5:100). But Butterfield, writing in a less desperately methodological idiom, meant nothing remotely like this; and indeed, what he did mean is endorsed by Skinner only two pages further on.[18] A related danger of confusion arises when historical method is imposed on those who have other interests. Thus the unfortunate John Plamenatz, into whose protesting hands a banner marked 'the textualist approach to intellectual history' is regularly thrust immediately prior to condign punishment being meted out, is simply not concerned with Skinner's questions. Thus Skinner is very much interested in whether or not Locke, by ignoring prescription and historical argument in the *Second Treatise*, 'had the intention to shift the discussion of political obligation on to a more abstract level' (5:105). This is an interesting question, though it does not follow, as Skinner goes on to claim, that 'We can scarcely be said to have understood Locke's text until we have considered what he was doing at this crucial stage in his argument.' This is a little odd even in terms of the Skinnerian argument, since he has already put to rest our suspicions that his work is haunted by some notional goal of a complete or full understanding of a text (5:100). Hence, there are many things to understand about Locke's text, and one of them is the cogency of the abstract arguments he did present, leaving aside the question of whether he was *also* intending to produce a kind of paradigm shift in the terms of English political argument. What Plamenatz does is to remark, rather mildly, that there are some writers of whom it can be said that 'we learn more about their arguments by weighing them over and over again than by extending our knowledge of the circumstances in which they wrote'.[19] Skinner assimilates Plamenatz to Skinner's own question, remarking that 'we can never hope to attain such an understanding simply by reading the text 'over and over again' in the way that some commentators have urged'. Plamenatz, of course, never said you could. Altogether, there is a lot of loose talk about approaches, and not enough concern with *what* it is that is being approached.[20]

It is thus one disadvantage of transposing all talk about intellectual history into the project of a search for the one correct method that a great deal of contingent misunderstanding is likely to take place. But leaving these difficulties behind, let us consider what an appropriate methodology of intellectual history would look like. I take it that intellectual history is a circumstantial explanation of the ideas of earlier times. We ask about

Luther's ideas, and understand them by relating them to his theological preoccupations and the political tensions of his time, so that what he did and thought becomes an intelligible outcome of a human situation. Now a methodology of intellectual history must be an abstract set of ideas in terms of which one is guided to asking all of the questions necessary to eliciting such an explanation. There must be a one to one relationship between the questions that must be asked of a passage of intellectual history, on the one hand and the distinctions and concepts of the methodology on the other. A fully satisfactory methodology would guide the historian in every question he asks, and its justification lies in the suggestion that the unguided historian is in fact already guided, but only in a confused and irregular way, by a jumble of approaches which leave many of the subtleties of human action unobserved. The beginning of intellectual history lies in asking: What did X mean? What was the point of his act or utterance? Now early on in his quest for a method, Skinner came upon the Austinian theory of speech acts, which allowed him to transpose these questions into the philosophical language of locutionary and illocutionary acts. To understand Luther, for example, we must look for the illocutionary force of his utterance. And the reasons that this transposition constitutes an advance is, presumably, because, while there is little general elaboration that can be done with the idea of the 'point' of an action or utterance, there is a great deal of conceptual elaboration actually going on to render the speech-act theory a subtle and coherent theory of great range and application.

So far so good, at least in the sense that what the skilled historian will instinctively do can at least be redescribed in the language of the speech-act. And no doubt this might well be valuable in stimulating the imagination and awareness of the historian. But, as Skinner is perfectly aware, the advice: Look for the illocutionary acts being performed by personages of history, is radically incomplete. We have already noted that he is impressed by the fact that one of the most important features of Locke's *Second Treatise* may consist in what he did *not* say. What, then, is the illocutionary force of a silence? Indeed, how does one even detect *a* silence, since all of us are silent about an infinite number of things? It is clear that this is a point where the methodology won't help, for even if we try the obvious ploy of generalizing about all other writers of a period, and seeing which of the generalizations are not true of X, we shall still be dependent upon instinct to guide us in finding that silence which might deserve our attention. Again, it is an important part of an illocutionary act that it depends upon the prevailing conventions by which such an act may be performed. But then, as Peter Strawson has pointed out,[21] some illocutionary acts involve social conventions in a way that others do not. Skinner is well aware that the theory of speech acts goes on ramifying according to the theoretical interests of philosophers, and it is far from clear which of these branches, if any, will be of any use to historians. We need not doubt that the philosophy of speech acts, like hermeneutics, belongs to the wider cultural field of which intellectual history is a part; and that the latter will benefit from contact with psychology, or anthropology, and much else. It all depends on the contingent matter of putting acute and penetrating questions into the heads of intellectual historians. Hence there is room to doubt whether they ought to sympathize with Skinner in feeling 'an increasing need to look for renewed philosophical help'.[22]

The test of the general contention would be to produce specific problems in intellectual history where a block to the understanding had been removed, and also could only have been removed, by the application of a philosophical doctrine. It is one of the virtues of Skinner's work that he is constantly aware of this test, but it cannot be said to have produced any notable successes. Thus he observes that there are some questions to be good' which cannot be answered by the closest of textual attention. be virtuous' which cannot be answered by the closest of textual attention. Nor, he adds, will fishing in the social context help much. And, formulating the issue in the simple terms of whether Machiavelli was merely repeating a commonplace piece of cynicism, or trying to subvert an established moral truth, between which we must come down on one side or the other, he gets us to a formal statement of what he thinks the nature of the problem is: 'The further point which must still be grasped for any given statement is *how* what was said was meant, and thus what *relations* there may have been between various different statements even within the same general context' (2:62). And there we are left, rather high and dry, without any ideas of quite how this puts us ahead of an intelligent student of Machiavelli pondering the question in his own way.

And how would such an innocent think about the problems of intellectual history? Well, we can bring philosophy here to something of a test by considering how J. W. Allen, writing back in the pre-methodological days of the 1920s, deals with what Skinner calls 'the mythology of coherence' which occurs when historians succumb to the temptation to 'find in each of [the] texts the coherence which they may appear to lack' (2:38). Allen, as it happens, wrote a history of political ideas in the sixteenth century on a similar scale and covering some of the ground of the *Foundations*.[23] Dealing with the problem of understanding Machiavelli, he writes:

> In reading Machiavelli with intent to grasp his thought as a whole, we have constantly to make correlations that he did not distinctly make, to take note of implications about which he is silent and to give some degree of definition to what he has left indefinite. The result must, to some extent at least, be to give his thought a fullness and coherency which his writings afford no solid ground

for supposing that it possessed. The whole process is fallacious and, if we adopt it, it is only by the greatest care that we can hope to avoid gross misrepresentation ... We are bound to look for a unity which, however loosely articulated, must have been there. We cannot know for certain how much of what he left unexpressed was actually in his mind, but it is certain that he left much unexpressed.[24]

Someone who writes like this would no doubt approve of what Skinner has to say, but there doesn't seem much to teach him. And it is here, in the talk of practitioners as they reflect on the problems raised by their specific questions (rather than one set of questions thought universally relevant to all intellectual historians) that we find a different kind of methodology. To improve on this is a bit like trying to make Groucho Marx a better comic by drilling him in Freud on wit and Bergson on laughter.

For the point about intellectual history is that it is, of almost all academic activities, one of the most resistant to reduction to form. With a sonnet, or a scientific hypothesis, there is a clear sense of form and thread of relevance, and hence there may (or may not) be lots of work for various general methods to do. In intellectual history, by contrast, the nexus of problems and solutions is extraordinarily diffuse, and the historian is to be found giving us information, supplying background, pointing out analogies, and in general providing us with (in Skinner's terms) an 'outline account'[25] of much that was written and done. Hence the rhetoric is extraordinarily vulnerable at every point. Thus in the *Foundations* (and why, one may wonder, are they plural?) Skinner takes us through the acts and responses of Europeans over several centuries, only to arrive at a point outside history when we have acquired an unhistorical something called '*the* modern concept of the state'.[26] Suddenly at this point, we move into analysis and schema, and Skinner has abandoned history. Again, history unfolds continuously, but one of the attractive features of Skinnerian exposition is the deft use he makes of literary devices like the flashback. The very title of the work – containing, as it does, the metaphor of foundations – might pedantically be indicted in terms of an error which Skinner calls the 'mythology of prolepsis', (2:44) since it implicitly understands its personages as contributing (another dangerous word) to a building which was no part of their experience or their intentions.

Consider, further, the difficulty of avoiding anachronistic terminology which will distort the intention of the people being studied. We have noted that Herbert Butterfield thought that 'progressive' and 'reactionary' were distorting words to use, and it is evident that Skinner avoids modern political words. But he still feels the need to make some sort of judgement of the same kind, and hence he is much addicted to words like 'conservative', 'radical' and even 'subversive'. Those Lutheran and Catholic writers who advocate passive obedience to the rulers are 'conservative' while constitutionalists and those who find reasons for resistance to rulers are 'radical'. This makes perfectly good sense if one assumes a long-term historical drift towards democracy, in which case radical is anything that co-operates with this drift and conservative that which opposes it. But in the England of 1535, for example, it was King Henry VIII who was being radical – he was, after all, tearing up the religious establishment by the roots – while 'the king's good servant, but God's first' Sir Thomas More was, in his resistance, being profoundly conservative.[27] Skinner seems to think that advising the people not to resist the edicts of their rulers was equivalent to advising them to sit around passively munching their feed like sheep, which is a typically modern prejudice. Since this was a population which nearly tore Europe apart with its violent addiction to its own prejudices and its limitless lust for innovation, one can only wonder what they would have got up to if their preachers had not ceaselessly fixed their minds upon the contents of chapter 13 of the *Epistle to the Romans*. One wonders this rather in the spirit of Lenin pondering what the vegetarian George Bernard Shaw might not have achieved had he eaten a beef-steak.

I conclude that the search for the one correct methodology is often unilluminating because it imports a good deal of confusion into the discussion of how to do history. What it generates will necessarily be incomplete, partly because even an endless elaboration of distinctions will never properly replicate the subtle responses of the historian to his material; and also for the familiar reason that no method can prescribe the terms of its own application. It is unnecessary because intellectual historians (especially when they are not lumped in with political theorists and other related species) have long shown themselves to be aware of most of what has so far emerged from the methodological discussion: on this point, we ought no doubt to wait in patience for the possibilities of future breakthroughs, but there is room for a little preliminary scepticism. And one may perhaps add that a great deal of the philosophy of speech-acts is irrelevant, since even were philosophers definitively to settle such questions as whether reasons can be reduced to causes – a supposition of stunning improbability – it will have no effect whatever upon the procedures of the intellectual historian, who will be searching out reasons anyway.

This is perhaps enough. But I think we can go further, and suggest that the project is, additionally, pernicious.

III

The problem at the heart of intellectual history arises from the fact that ideas have two aspects. They are abstract and universal, and it is in virtue of this character that they allow communication to bridge such gulfs as person to person, epoch to epoch and culture to culture. But the thinking of any idea is also a specific occurrence which has a spatio-temporal location and a social context. Philosophers are interested in the abstract ideas, historians in the individuality of the utterance, and the problem of the intellectual historian is how to negotiate this extremely interesting and poorly demarcated frontier.

One solution to this problem, valuable for its single-minded clarity, was A. O. Lovejoy's theory that the intellectual historian follows the adventures of unit-ideas which underlie the thought and writing of each epoch, ideas which pass from time to time and genre to genre, recombining as they go, rather like randy chemical elements in an unstable soup.[28] This must, I suppose, be the most unhistorical account it is possible to give of the basis of a history of ideas, since the only historical work that seems to be left reduces to identifying the unit-ideas underneath the circumstantial variation, and the chronological matter of who said what to whom, when and where. Yet it did not prevent Lovejoy and many of those he influenced from producing some excellent history.

The intellectual historian's practical problem is: where should he find his thread of relevance? Lovejoy had based his theory on the universal element of the idea. The great chain of being,[29] for example, appears in Plato and goes through many transformations to resurface in Pope's *Essay on Man*, where it is ready to pass on to further impersonations. The actual context of such ideas was, for Lovejoy, a tiny hook suitable for chronological docketing and identification. Since that time, theory (though not invariably practice) has gone entirely in the other direction. An idea *is* how it functions in its context; and what was a tiny hook in Lovejoy becomes the essence of the idea for later writers, leaving the universal element shrunk very close to vanishing point. Such is the process which underlies Skinner's equivocal remarks on perenniality. Ideas must become, as it were, historio-degradable: dissolvable into circumstance. The practical consequence of this reversal has at times been that historians of ideas have avoided philosophical writers, who don't easily dissolve in history, and sought for their material among publicists and pamphleteers. Skinner's earliest forays reveal this bias of attention very clearly, for 'Meaning and understanding in the history of ideas' began its life as a scintillating conference paper called 'The unimportance of the great texts in the history of political thought'.

Now whether to look to the text or the context is not a very serious question for an intellectual historian: he will answer it according to the question he is asking, and methodological prescriptions which try to give a general answer are so much waste of time. As so often happens in this field, there is remarkably little that can profitably be said in general. But the intellectual historian who accepts the project of getting help in his (usually non-existent) perplexities from philosophers will soon find himself pretty confused. Lovejoy seems to be encouraging him to go around pulling off the false noses and assumed wigs by which time and circumstance disguise the fundamental unit-ideas that underlie thought. John Pocock thinks he ought to take off from languages and some political equivalent of Kuhnian paradigm.[30] Sir Karl Popper is eager to rescue him from some rather unlikely misunderstandings by invoking his ontological theory of World 3, in which 'psychological relations' are replaced by 'the analysis of third-world relations'.[31] And meanwhile, Skinner is dazzling him with excursions into speech acts and hermeneutics. Even if he merely flips a coin in order to choose between these and other forms of methodological salvation being marketed, the historian will find that he has taken on-board a cargo of philosophical theory on which validity – not easily testable – his work as a historian will be dangerously dependent.

Indeed, he will be lucky if it is only a philosophical theory he is lumbered with, for philosophy's attempt to rescue the historian from excess abstraction can often be stopped half-way, and as a result lumber him with, additionally, a sociological theory. At its crudest, the insistence that writers don't write in a vacuum and that every thinker is the product of the society he lives in leads directly on to the idea that the writer is merely the epiphenomenon of deeper tensions or transitions in the society. Thus Plato turns into an apologist for the aristocracy,[32] Hobbes a sensitive reed vibrating to the perception that the society around him is turning into capitalism.[33] There is obviously enough theory here to sink a historian, whose primary task is to regain a pre-theoretical innocence about general trends so that he can respond to the actual evidence before him. Skinner is in general a stern critic of these excesses in all their forms. The general thrust of his methodological interests has been to appropriate for history those intellectual objects which were being converted into somewhat pointless philosophical currency, and in this objective he represents a salutary development of ideas about intellectual history following Lovejoy's work. His awareness of the problem can be seen in such remarks as his insistence that we must beware of the 'over-enthusiastic adoption of a completely sociological approach, through which the object of analysis becomes nothing less than the whole gamut of "languages" in which a nation articulates its political experience over time' (5:100). Here the target of criticism is John Pocock, but much more vulnerable objects can easily be thought of. The problem is that the methodologist who may perhaps save us from timeless essences may, if he is not careful, involve us with no less disastrous postulates about a changeless society. It is not, of course, that anyone thinks that societies don't change; rather, that the idea of social change is often essentially unhistorical. It is a matter of systems, stages of evolution, process, transition and similar abstract ideas. Now an insistence on 'the social' is part of the way Skinner has moved from texts to contexts, however subtle he has been in construing this relationship. The illocutionary act depends on the conventions by which communication takes place. Focus on the prevailing conventions, is the advice he gives, since 'to understand what any given writer may have been *doing in* using some particular concept or argument, we need first of all to grasp the nature and range of things that could recognizably have been done by using that particular concept, in the treatment of that particular theme, at that particular time' (3:77). Now what the historian wants to know is what the man was *actually* doing in using the particular concept. He may or may not hit upon the answer. But the advice that he should go off on a detour of setting up 'the nature and range of things that could recognizably have been done by using that particular concept' is not only to involve him in an impossible task, but also one that requires endless theorizing. More generally we may say that the whole idea of 'the prevailing conventions' will tend to import a static fixity into the work of the historian which can only tempt him into sociological shortcuts. Modern philosophy is rightly sceptical of the view that science is an expanding body of proven fact and theory; and philosophy itself is all the more subject to continuing change and revision. It would seem, then, that the more the historian lives – self-critically – within his own resources of evidence, the better.

A further aspect of the danger may be illustrated by some of the curious notions that currently infest this literature. Students of hermeneutics sometimes write of 'textual strategies' as if the text were a hostile animal to be trapped and disarmed; and it is remarkably common in this field for philosophers to talk about 'decoding' the social meaning of a speech-act, as if communication involved a special form of scrambling to prevent its meaning being known to outsiders. Skinner himself has picked up this strange way of speaking, and imports it into Strawson's standard example of the skater to whom the policeman remarks that the ice over there is very thin, an utterance which Skinner thinks has to be decoded by the skater in order to discover its meaning. And here, by contrast with the more selective theory advanced by Leo Strauss to the effect that political philosophers sometimes conceal from outsiders the real kernel of their doctrine, *everything* is taken to be a matter of decoding. As well as the risk of error, then, there is the risk of picking up the modish distortions common in most fields of theorizing, and this is an additional hazard.

The standard objection to my line of criticism takes the form of pointing out that the historian necessarily takes a lot for granted, and the more self-conscious he is about this, the better. No doubt he does, though we shall see in section IV, below, that there is often less to this than meets the eye. But what is useful to the historian is to realize that what he is actually taking for granted in some specific bit of thinking about past argument, and remarkably little can be contributed here by general theories about conventions, society, classes and the rest.

Fundamentally, then, an intellectual historian ought to be an epistemological *naif*, and the less he thinks he knows in advance, the better. Now it is one of the things that Skinner knows that the history of political thought must be written as a history of ideologies. Indeed, only such a history appears to be recognizable as 'real history', (5:99) presumably because the word 'ideology' has been taken to mean thought in response to a situation, by contrast with thinking about timeless essences. Being a sophisticated exponent of this view, Skinner does at times contrast the 'theoretical' and the 'ideological' significance of thought; among his more valuable contributions to the philosophy of intellectual history has been to find convincing ways of explaining why political doctrines are not mere instruments of justification. And in the *Foundations* he is dealing with a time when philosophical achievement was not great and when most political theory can be seen as having a pretty clear practical purpose. Yet it remains possible to wonder whether the idea does not at points clog his understanding.

Our doubts may initially focus upon the dominant metaphor of 'a large arsenal of ideological weapons available to be exploited by the revolutionaries of late sixteenth-century Europe'.[34] This is a typical and recurring phrase. But the metaphor is curiously inappropriate, since an ideological weapon cannot destroy an enemy position by bombardment from the outside, as it were, but can only act as a kind of fifth column by co-operating with the enemy's genuine convictions in destroying his position. It is in virtue of what sixteenth-century men shared – reverence for authority, Christianity, etc. – rather than of what divided them, that the political doctrines of the period were effective in persuasion. In terms of argument, it is the shared rather than the contested which is always fundamental, and in seeing merely an exchange of weapons, Skinner seems to me to be taking over one of the dominant features of the political realism of our age: the assumption that conflict is more fundamental than co-operation in human life. The effect of this assumption is to create a gap in his history. We learn in the *Foundations* much about arguments advanced by this writer or that, but hardly anything about the audience. People, however, do not as a rule rush forward to be devastated by weapons: they rush forward to engage with them because these arguments, far from being merely weapons to destroy conviction, also answer questions which the readers must have found puzzling or worrying. The audience is the great missing character of the *Foundations*, especially in the second volume. It does make occasional appearances. In 1554, we learn, John Knox put some deeply troubling questions about the limits of obligation to Heinrich Bulling[35] and in 1530 Lutheran theologians are found still completely unable to overcome their scruples about the idea of forcible resistance. But mostly we follow the speakers rather than the listeners. No doubt part of the reason for this is (as so often in history) that we have plenty of records

of the utterers and few of the hearers. Yet the result is that we come away
without any real sense of the *strangeness* of the world he is describing.

There is a further way in which the abstract thesis that the history of
political ideas must be a history of ideologies inhibits Skinner's sensitivity to
his material. The early Lutheran arguments he deals with are recognizably
moral, developed from shared premises, which are usually theological. Some
of the later Calvinist arguments, however, are of a distinctly different
character: instead of asking what people ought to do, these arguments
are concerned to redefine the world. Thus a Calvinist called Goodman
is said to arrive 'at his most revolutionary political claim: since the ruler
. . . is nothing more than a felonious private citizen, he may be lawfully
resisted by any or all of his own subjects, since God at this point "gives
the sword into the people's hand"'.[36] Now this transportation of moral
argument into pseudo-philosophical redefinition is what we sometimes
distinguish as 'ideological' in another sense of that very slippery term.
The methodological postulate of the ubiquity of ideology dulls the sense
that something interestingly new is here happening to human thought.

IV

I wish to conclude by developing the point about excess theoretical
baggage. What is the significance of theorizing thought in terms of
speech-acts, conventions, contexts and the rest? In part, as we have
seen, it is to allow history to get a grip on properly historical materials
rather than sliding off the glassy surface of abstractions. Such theories
stress the dependence of a thinker on his society to the exclusion of
the independence which thought also exhibits, and which is why thoughts
change. The effect of the theory invoked by Skinner is to emphasize the
limitations on thought. How far is he prepared to push these limitations?

The point may be illustrated by Skinner's use of a familiar type of
modern argument:

> Consider the following imaginary but familiar social situation: a
> public meeting at which one delegate is repeatedly prevented from
> speaking by the chairman and eventually leaves before the meeting is
> concluded. The action constitutes the 'text' we are asked to explain.
> Confronted with this request, we might well be tempted to theorize
> about the agent's likely emotions and to explain his act of leaving
> the room as the outcome of anger or frustration. This account only
> 'makes sense', however, in the light of two further assumptions
> about the situation which are left inexplicit in this type of motive
> explanation. One is that to invoke anger as the motive refers us

to the general idea that this particular emotion (or something like it) constitutes a natural or fitting response by the agent to the circumstances. The other is that the agent's action constitutes a natural or fitting expression of this emotion in the circumstances.[37]

If we do make sense of our hypotheses in this way, we shall, as Skinner recognizes, find ourselves 'moving in an interpretive circle'[38] and hardly a circle (we may add) worth the dalliance at that. If, however, we were historians, we would hardly bother with intuitions about the fitting at all, because we know that people often don't do the fitting thing. But we would be extremely wary about the important point which is taken for granted in Skinner's account: namely, that there is some connection between the agent's being prevented from speaking and his walking out of the room. It is precisely this sort of connection which historians often get wrong, and which no amount of methodology will automatically correct. My main point here, however, is to observe Skinner's tendency to assimilate acts to social forms: we are confident in this case, he tells us, in seeing 'a recognizable (and virtually conventional) form of protest'.[39] Is an actor actually *limited* to such forms in his behaviour? It sometimes seems that he is: for it is 'an unexceptionable claim that any agent who is engaged in an intended act of communication must be limited by the prevailing conventions of discourse' (5:105). But languages and conventions are in fact resources of speech and action, as Skinner seems to recognize immediately by going on to say that agents are not limited merely to *following* conventions since they may also extend them, or subvert them or alter them. But if this is true, why say that conventions *limit* people at all?

One answer might be that it is convenient to the historian to have such fixed rules because they give him a handle in explaining otherwise puzzling acts. Convenience, of course, is not necessarily a good guide to truth, and anyway, a more portentous explanation would seem to emerge from Skinner's writings. Consider a remark from 'Meaning and understanding': 'it is a commonplace – we are all Marxists to this extent - that our own society places unrecognized constraints upon our imaginations. It deserves, then, to become a commonplace that the historical study of the ideas of other societies should be undertaken as the indispensable and irreplaceable means of placing limits on those constraints' (2:67).

This is, of course, one of those odd doctrines which cannot even be exemplified without refuting itself, since if someone tells me a specific something I cannot imagine here in the twentieth century, then he has already imagined it. It would indeed be absurd to think that at any time we could imagine everything (whatever that might mean) and it is certainly true that men of earlier centuries and cultures did not imagine many things; and perhaps we may even, in retrospect, discover patterns in the things which their imaginations did encompass. But that the reason for this is that they were subject to a 'limitation', and that this limitation was imposed on them by something called 'society' is not a doctrine that can be extracted from history; and it would seem bad sociology and worse philosophy, according to how it might be construed. We would do better to emphasize – as Martin Hollis does in his discussion with Skinner – that conventions, and the stock of culture at any time, constitute a resource, something which enables rather than restricts (7:135).

There seems little doubt, then, that Skinner has consistently cultivated a sense of supposedly inescapable limits within which men must act, and that this interpretation is shared by those most closely associated with him. Thus John Dunn's reading of the *Foundations* emphasizes a doctrine which is hardly explicit in the pages of the history itself:

> The European intellectuals whom Skinner studies pace restlessly, century after century, the bounds of a narrow imaginative cage. The conceptual materials available to them derive from a tiny range of intellectual resources: Roman history, Roman law, Augustinian theology, Greek moral philosophy, Roman literature; and the political importunities which confront them never let them rest . . . more sophisticated thinking, in the face of these importunities, proves just as much as before to be thinking under very fierce constraints.

And then we learn that, while the likes of Machiavelli and Bodin 'in some measure' escape from the cage, we ought to consider the possibility that we too are also constrained.[40]

The form in which this ceaseless preoccupation surfaces in Skinner's methodology is relatively innocent because it refers to a world of ultimate deterministic explanations: 'While our explanation needs to start with meanings and motives, it only ends when we have identified the underlying conditions which caused Romeo [in the example being discussed by Skinner and Hollis] to come into the possession of the motive which then prompted him (caused him?) to act.'[41] There are some perfectly good historians who think that everything that happens falls out according to God's providential ordering; and there are also historians who believe that ultimately all thoughts emerge from the class-determined dynamics of the social system. These are harmless bees in the bonnet so long as such historians do not substitute such convictions for the under-labouring work of actually studying the circumstances and events that concern the historian. Skinner's metaphysical determinism seems to function in the same way, and we may be grateful that it ticks away harmlessly in the form of a conviction about ultimates. It is no doubt responsible for that occasional messianic tone in which he assumes his methodology to have provided 'the means – the only sure means – of explaining change and innovation' (5:106) and in which he seems to be summoning us to a promised land of historical understanding as yet merely glimpsed. But we should essentially be grateful for an historical sense which, while discovering 'ideological superstructures' in the past goes on to insist that one cannot 'treat these ideological superstructures as a straightforward outcome of their social base'.[42] Most of his methodology emphasizes the free and creative aspects of thought responding to the world, rather than becoming entangled in tendentious convictions about base and superstructure which would only bow the neck of a serious historian. There is some excess baggage in the hold, but fortunately he mostly works from his cabin bag.[43]

11

Quentin Skinner's method and Machiavelli's *Prince*

Nathan Tarcov

In his most extensive methodological writing, Quentin Skinner concluded that 'the classic texts cannot be concerned with our questions and answers, but only with their own', and that there is therefore simply no hope of learning directly from their 'attempted answers to supposedly timeless questions' (2:64). But he still found an 'essential philosophical, even moral, value' in the classic texts in that they 'help to reveal – if we let them – not the essential sameness, but rather the essential variety of viable moral assumptions and political commitments' (2:66). He thus paradoxically claimed that 'to discover from the history of thought that there are in fact *no such timeless concepts* . . . is to discover *a general truth not merely about the past but about ourselves*' (2:67). This may sound merely like the parochial assertion that the (historicist) commonplace of our society is a timeless truth whereas the (non-historicist) commonplaces of other societies were false. But Skinner made a wise distinction: between demanding from the history of thought a solution to our own immediate problems ('not merely a methodological fallacy, but something like a moral error') and learning from it what we cannot otherwise learn at all – 'the distinction between what is necessary and what is the product merely of our own contingent arrangements . . . the key to self-awareness' (2:67). If, however, we can distinguish the necessary from the contingent, then so might have the classic authors, who may therefore help us to do so more directly, not only by their contingent errors but by their perceptions of necessity. If some things are necessary and not contingent, then we may be able to separate the permanent from the transient in the classic texts. Skinner's warnings about the pitfalls of textualism are salutary in so far as they protect us from assumptions that would prevent us from understanding texts, but detrimental in so far as they forbid us to learn from them. Skinner seems to share with his textualist foils the notion that belief in the text as 'the self-sufficient object of inquiry and understanding' is 'logically tied' to the justification of studying it for its timeless wisdom and conversely that 'to suggest instead that a knowledge of the social context is a necessary condition for an understanding of the classic texts is equivalent to denying that they do contain any elements of timeless and perennial interest' (2:30 – 1; 56 – 7). This non sequitur offers us a false choice between refusing external aid necessary to understand a text and refusing to learn directly from it. A text may instead contain both timeless and timely elements and be neither self-sufficient nor irrelevant.[1]

In his preface, Skinner declares that *The Foundations of Modern Political Thought* has 'three main aims': first, to offer an up-to-date 'outline account of the principal texts of late medieval and early modern political thought'; second, 'to indicate something of the process by which the modern concept of the State came to be formed'; and third, to exemplify his method (ix–x).[2] He presents the third aim at greatest length (x–xiv). He repeats his earlier call for 'a history of political theory with a genuinely historical character' (xi). He means by this that he begins with the social context, then considers the intellectual context, and tries to write 'a history centred less on the classic texts and more on the history of ideologies' than did 'the more traditional method' (x–xi). This approach helps us 'to understand earlier societies' by drawing 'a more realistic picture of how political thinking in all its various forms was in fact conducted' and to establish 'closer links between political theories and political life', specifically, how the available 'normative vocabulary' constrains the behaviour of political actors (xi–xiii). But the 'main reason' Skinner gives here for the 'study of ideologies' is 'to construct a general framework within which the writings of the more prominent theorists can then be situated', indeed to 'return to the classic texts themselves with a clearer prospect of understanding them' (xiii).[3]

It is appropriate, therefore, to ask whether Skinner's work provides us with a clearer understanding of the classic texts. In particular, Machiavelli's texts dominate nearly a third of the work. The interpretation of *The Prince* is the culmination of the account of princely theory (113–38), as the interpretation of the *Discourses* caps that of late Renaissance republicanism (139–90), for which the first chapters, on scholasticism and humanism (3–112) provide the context (cf. 144).

The political context which Skinner provides and Machiavelli clearly recognizes is the foreign invasions of Italy starting in 1494 and the 'extension and consolidation of increasingly despotic forms of princely rule', including that of the Medici in Florence (113–15). The princely triumph 'helped to bring about' a return from the primacy of activity to that of contemplation, from Cicero to Plato, while political concern returned to advising rulers, princes and courtiers (115–18). This genre of advice books, especially those of Pontano, Patrizi and Castiglione (117–28), is treated as 'the precise intellectual context within which' Machiavelli was writing *The Prince* (129).

Skinner deliberately begins by showing the extent to which *The Prince* was characteristic of the genre (118–28) before attempting to assess its originality (128–38). He claims that Machiavelli clearly endorses the genre's concern for glory as the reward of virtue. Evidence is supposed to be Machiavelli's pointing to Ferdinand of Aragon as 'worthy of imitation' and 'conversely' his 'contempt' for Agathocles of Sicily, whom he 'refuses to hold . . . up as an example of princely *virtù*' because 'the criminal methods he invariably employed "can win a prince power but not glory"' (119–20; 137–8). This dichotomy and the moral Skinner infers from it are far from clear. First of all, Agathocles *is* held up as an example for imitation. He is one of two examples given of ascending to a principality by some wicked and nefarious way 'for whoever may be necessitated, to imitate them' (chapter 8; cf. also 2.13).[4] Conversely, Ferdinand of Aragon, 'the first king of the Christians', appears at least equally criminal, committing 'a pious cruelty, chasing out and despoiling his kingdom of the Marranos', an example which 'cannot be more miserable or more rare' (chapter 21; cf. also chapter 18). Skinner points out that Machiavelli shares with the genre and its *quattrocento* humanist predecessors the opposition of *virtù* to *fortuna*, but is 'something of an exception' to their connection of educational and political advice, save in so far as *The Prince* itself is the best education (119–23).

According to Skinner, the advice-books depart from the civic humanists in turning from liberty to security as the purpose of government, and Machiavelli follows this departure, making the two-fold recommendation that the ruler 'attend to his own "security and strength"', while ensuring at the same time that his subjects are 'stabilized and made secure' (123–4). The two quotations from the end of chapter 19 of *The Prince* that Skinner employs here do not in context distinguish the security of subjects from that of their ruler. The first refers to 'the security and strength of his kingdom'; the second to 'a state which may be already stabilized and firm'. Given Skinner's view that security is the 'basic value' of *The Prince* in contrast to liberty in the *Discourses* (156–7), it is a disappointment that he does not provide even the sketchiest account of Machiavelli's subtle treatment of security and a more precise notion of its implications for popular liberty. There is indeed a hint of two-fold security as the end of government at the end of chapter 8: Machiavelli recommends concentrated cruelty, what he calls 'cruelty well used', done from the necessity of securing oneself, because it enables one to assure men and enables them to assure themselves of one (cf. also the end of chapter 5 and the role of the French *parlement* in chapter 19). But, as one might expect of a security provided subjects by a policy of concentrated cruelty, it is a security of a peculiar sort. In chapter

3, Machiavelli recommended keeping men quiet by leaving them, on the one hand, unharmed, and, on the other, afraid. Similarly, Cesare Borgia made the Romagna peaceful and united by making the people not secure exactly but instead 'satisfied and stupefied' (chapters 7 and 17); where the soldiers are more powerful than the people, it is necessary to divide satisfaction and stupefaction between the soldiers and the people, respectively (chapter 19). Machiavelli explains that a wise prince makes his citizens always have need of the state and of him (chapter 9, end); men unite most with their prince when their houses are burned and their possessions ruined in his defence (chapter 10). The character of security is clearest in the dictum that it is better to be feared than loved, which means leaving men secure in their property and family but fearful for their lives (chapter 17; cf. also chapter 19, beginning, and chapter 21 end), or in the recommendation that a prince should not be served by men with 'too much security' (chapter 20).

According to Skinner, Machiavelli departs from the genre's general preference for monarchy in that he 'prefers to hold in tension two contrasting views about the rival merits of princely and popular regimes' – the necessity of 'the strong rule of a single man' to restore virtue in case of corruption and 'his own personal preference' for liberty and republicanism (124). Machiavelli is supposed to join the genre in distinguishing the virtue of princes from that of citizens, attributing to princes 'an astonishingly creative force' and to peoples a 'benign passivity', but, of course, he 'dissociates himself as sharply as possible' from the genre's understanding of princely virtue as a combination of the Christian and the classic virtues, especially justice, faith, liberality, clemency and truth telling (125–8).

Skinner recognizes that, while 'the format, the presuppositions and many of the central arguments of *The Prince* make it a recognizable contribution to a well-established tradition of later *quattrocento* political thought', Machiavelli 'may have had the further intention to question or even to ridicule some of their values' (129). For Skinner, Machiavelli's critique of humanism consists in his 'strong emphasis on the role of sheer force' in politics and his denial that princely virtue consists in the Christian and classic virtues (129–31). Whereas in an earlier methodological article, Skinner reports that 'the fact that *The Prince* was in part intended as a deliberate attack on the moral conventions of advice-books to princes cannot be discovered simply by attending to the text, since this is not a fact contained in the text', here he notes that 'we have Machiavelli's own assurance on the point – that he saw himself as a self-conscious critic of several key elements in the existing literature of advice-books for princes'. This turn to Machiavelli's own statement for his own understanding of how far his intention reached is a welcome addition to the method of generic juxtaposition. The page Skinner cites for this assurance might refer to either the end of chapter 14 or the beginning of chapter 15. At the end of chapter

14 Machiavelli recommends that a prince read histories and, above all, do what some excellent man has done before, who has imitated someone before him, 'as one says that Alexander the Great imitated Achilles; Caesar, Alexander; Scipio, Cyrus'. Machiavelli specifies only that it was Xenophon's life of Cyrus that Scipio imitated, leaving Homer and the writer of the life of Alexander unnamed – not to mention the writers who in turn tell us of these imitations, such as Plutarch and Cicero. This passage, however, would not seem to display self-conscious criticism of the literature, were it not for Machiavelli's subsequent criticism of Scipio (cf. 133), who conformed so closely to 'those things that were written by Xenophon of Cyrus' (cf. chapter 17). Xenophon is indeed the *only* writer of advice-books for princes we have Machiavelli's explicit assurance that he was conscious of in writing *The Prince*. Xenophon is not mentioned in *The Foundations of Modern Political Thought*! Pontano, Patrizi and Castiglione are not mentioned in *The Prince*, nor does Skinner offer any external evidence for Machiavelli's concern with them. The resemblances between his topics in *The Prince* and theirs are strong enough to persuade us that Machiavelli may have intended a critique of them but not to persuade us that such a critique exhausted his intentions. At the beginning of chapter 15 – more probably Skinner's intended reference – Machiavelli admits he knows that 'many have written' of how princes should deal with subjects and friends, and that he departs especially from the orders of the others. He goes straight to 'the effectual truth' of the thing, whereas 'many have imagined republics and principalities which have never been seen or known to exist in truth'. But nothing in this famous statement assures us that Machiavelli was specifically criticizing the contemporary advice-books to princes. The mention of republics indeed indicates a broader concern. When Machiavelli means to single out his contemporaries, he is perfectly capable of doing so, as in his attack on an opinion of 'the wise of our times' (chapter 3).

Skinner's account of the much-vexed question of Machiavelli's understanding of *virtù* and the problem of politics and morality is very difficult to make out (131–8). This is only partially because 'the exact nature' of Machiavelli's position is 'a little obscured by his love of paradox' (131; cf. 137). It is also because Skinner seems to waver from page to page in what he wants to say about Machiavelli's position. Skinner first presents three Machiavellian claims (131–4). (1) Machiavelli 'sometimes seems' to claim that 'in order to act as virtuously as possible' princes must sometimes act other than virtuously. (2) Machiavelli also claims that only the appearance of virtue matters, which not only permits viciousness but requires deception. (3) His 'most heterodox claim' is that the conventional virtues bring ruin and the vices success. This last claim in particular leads him to attack the virtues of the advice-books, especially liberality, clemency and faith. Skinner asserts that the 'heart' of Machiavelli's message consists in (2) and (3) (132). Since these two claims are 'scarcely less paradoxical' than the first, it is hard to see why Machiavelli's love of paradox should have obscured which of them he wished to defend.

Skinner then turns to consider the interpretation by Croce, Chabod, and others, that Machiavelli 'divorces politics from morality' (134–5), and offers instead the interpretation by Berlin and others, that Machiavelli embraces a 'very different morality' from Christian morality. The rejected interpretation of Machiavelli embodies 'a misunderstanding of the relationship between his outlook and that of his contemporaries'. He shared their view of princely goals as maintaining one's state and glory, but found their Christian morality an inappropriate means. Here is a case where Skinner's understanding of Machiavelli's context is supposed to pay off by arbitrating between conflicting interpretations. But first one wonders how this view of Machiavelli's rejection of his contemporaries' means to agreed ends shows that he accepted a different morality rather than divorcing politics from morality. Skinner seems to mean not that Machiavelli regarded a certain set of qualities, such as Hannibal's 'inhuman cruelty', as constituting the new non-Christian morality, but rather that he intended the prince to acquire whatever qualities 'his situation dictates' without any one given set of moral qualities (cf. 138). If that would not be a divorce, it would at least be a separation from morality, if it is not rather the subjection or reduction of morality to politics or the denial of morality for politics. Second, the specific example Skinner gives of Machiavelli's 'fundamental criticism of his contemporaries', that 'they' admire Hannibal's achievements but condemn the 'inhuman cruelty' that made them possible, has no such specific reference to contemporaries. Machiavelli criticizes simply 'the writers' (chapter 17. In 3.21, 'all the writers' admire the most great advantage resulting from Hannibal's being held impious, a breaker of faith, and cruel; he does not say they all condemned these qualities – cf. Polybius 9.22–6). As many writers in our times have noticed, Machiavelli alludes here to Livy, who wrote that Hannibal's virtues were equalled by his enormous vices, including his 'inhuman cruelty' (21. 4. 9), which Machiavelli in contrast calls a *virtù*. It is not only Christian morality and not only his contemporaries that Machiavelli has in mind.

Skinner seems to begin over again with an admission that the advice Machiavelli offers princes about morality is 'not presented with complete consistency' (135–6). This time Machiavelli 'sometimes . . . seems' to say that 'although the princely virtues may be good in themselves, there is no place for them in political life', so one should only appear to have them and actually 'abandon them altogether' and prefer being feared to being loved. But the 'main thrust' of his advice now 'does not generally involve him in abandoning the conventional moral norms with so much readiness', 'the most accurate summary of his advice' being to do good if possible and evil if necessary. This account is startlingly close to the precise reversal of the earlier claim that the heart of Machiavelli's message is in claims (2) and (3) rather than (1).

Finally Skinner turns to consider the 'note of horrified denunciation' in discussions of Machiavelli's works from the sixteenth century to Strauss (136–8). According to Skinner, Strauss 'insists in his *Thoughts on Machiavelli* that the doctrines of *The Prince* are simply "immoral and irreligious", and that their author can only be characterised as "a teacher of evil"' (137). The identification of the illocutionary act that Strauss performs as 'insisting' and the claims that he views Machiavelli's doctrines as 'simply' immoral and irreligious and their author 'only' as a teacher of evil are Skinner's gratuitous additions, as is the view that Strauss's characterization applies specifically to *The Prince*. Skinner quotes from the notorious first sentence of *Thoughts on Machiavelli*: 'We shall not shock anyone, we shall merely expose ourselves to good-natured or at any rate harmless ridicule, if we profess ourselves inclined to the old-fashioned and simple opinion according to which Machiavelli was a teacher of evil.'[5] Without dwelling on the conditional character of that profession of inclination,[6] one should note that Strauss, far from simply insisting on that 'simple opinion', writes of its 'deficiency'. He allows that it may inadequately articulate and therefore misinterpret the most important thing about Machiavelli and recommends 'the considerate ascent from it'. Far from insisting that Machiavelli's teaching is 'simply' immoral and irreligious, Strauss writes in that passage of 'what is truly admirable in Machiavelli: the intrepidity of his thought, the grandeur of his vision, and the graceful subtlety of his speech'.[7]

Skinner concedes that sometimes Machiavelli 'likes to affect a self-consciously cool and amoral tone' and 'speaks in a purely technical way about issues with obvious moral significance'. He admits 'the shocking tone that Machiavelli tends to employ', and 'his undoubted fondness for throwing off shocking asides'. But he insists that 'it seems something of a vulgarisation of Machiavelli's outlook to label him a preacher of evil. He is far from wishing to take evil for his good, and he seldom says anything to imply that the conventional virtues should not be regarded as admirable in themselves.' Skinner characterizes Machiavelli's tone as 'shocking' but refuses to be shocked by it. Not everyone will agree that one cannot call immoral what Skinner (132) labels as the heart of Machiavelli's message: claim (2), teaching that only the deceptive appearance of virtue matters and, claim (3), recommending that princes learn the vices that bring security. In his commitment to the power of the conventional context, Skinner seems to believe that what an author like Machiavelli 'seldom' says can be safely disregarded, in contrast to Strauss, who offers the 'rule' that 'the real opinion of an author is not necessarily identical with that which he expresses in the largest number of passages'.[8]

Skinner immediately retreats to an admission that Machiavelli 'is not completely consistent on this point, and generally prefers to stress the importance of acquiring a reputation for the virtues rather than the virtues themselves. But he is equally capable of insisting without equivocation that "everyone realises how praiseworthy it is" for a prince "to be straightforward rather than crafty in his dealings."' Here Skinner seems to adopt the opposed interpretative principle that what an author 'generally prefers to stress' can be subordinated to what he is 'equally capable of insisting' on without equivocation. But Skinner's identification of Machiavelli's unequivocal insisting is as spurious as his identification of Strauss's. Far from being 'without equivocation', the statement Skinner quotes from the first sentence of chapter 18 continues, like so many of Machiavelli's provisional concessions to morality and religion, with its next word a 'nevertheless': 'nevertheless one sees by experience in our times those princes to have done great things who have held little account of faith and have known how to cheat the brains of men with craft; and in the end have overcome those who have founded themselves on loyalty'. Even without the 'nevertheless', the statement is far from an unequivocal insistence. What 'everyone realizes' is not Machiavelli's standard of truth. The chapter Skinner quotes from (entitled 'How faith should be observed by princes') culminates in the explanation: 'Everyone sees what you appear, few feel what you are . . . the vulgar are always taken by what appears and the event of the thing; and in the world there is nothing but vulgar.' Skinner (136) makes similar use of Machiavelli's other reference to vulgar opinion, that 'everyone will confess that it would be a most praiseworthy thing to find in a prince all the qualities written above that are held good' (chapter 15). Finally, that everyone realizes 'how much' (*quanto*) it is praiseworthy in a prince to keep his faith and live with integrity does not tell us whether it is very much so or very little (for both the ambiguity of *quanto* and Machiavelli's attitude toward universal opinion, see 2. 17). Skinner here invokes again Machiavelli's 'disapproval' of Agathocles, whom Skinner calls 'the tyrant of Sicily' and Machiavelli calls 'king of Syracuse' who 'liberated' Syracuse (cf. 137–8 with chapter 8). Skinner tells us that, for Machiavelli, 'a man of completely vicious character, like Agathocles, can never be considered a man of true *virtù*' and cannot be celebrated among the most excellent men, but does not tell us that Machiavelli speaks of his *virtù* of mind and body and ranks him with the 'most excellent captain', considering his *virtù* in entering into and exiting from dangers and the greatness of his mind in bearing and overcoming adversity. Nor does Skinner mention that Machiavelli's last word on Agathocles is that by cruelty well used he could remedy his position with God and men. Skinner contrasts Agathocles here with Severus, who, though extremely cruel and rapacious, was 'a prince "of so much *virtù*" that "he reigned successfully to the end" in spite of countless difficulties', but he does not tell us that Agathocles 'lived a long time secure in his *patria*'.

For Skinner, Machiavelli's *virtù* 'cannot possibly be equated with viciousness' and 'cannot possibly exclude viciousness' (138). His 'final sense of what it is to be a man of *virtù*' is a man of 'flexible disposition', capable of 'varying his conduct from good to evil and back' according to circumstances. Even Skinner must conclude that this is a 'highly original sense' of princely *virtù* distinct from 'the conventional virtues' (by which Skinner seems to mean the classical and Christian virtues). But Skinner does not wish to admit that such a disposition, though it may occasionally issue in acts in conformity with those virtues, is, if taken seriously, incompatible with regarding those virtues as 'admirable in themselves' and, if they are taken seriously, is a form of immorality.

Skinner's interpretation of Machiavelli is superficial, confused and poorly documented. Perhaps one must take for granted misleadingly simplified and selective treatment of complicated and difficult works in any outline or survey. Skinner himself warned that 'to write a textbook in the history of ideas, of course, is simply to fall prey systematically' to the temptation to abstract 'messages' from works, with the result that 'textbooks in the subject are not merely poor things, but are actively misleading' (2:39). What is remarkable is rather the particular ways Skinner simplifies and selects, the ways dictated or permitted by his method. Skinner interprets Machiavelli's statements as either contributions to or critiques of traditions which Skinner does not otherwise show were Machiavelli's major concerns. He does not pay much attention to Machiavelli's own statements and indications of his intentions, addresses and targets, whether distant or immediate. Everyone knows that Machiavelli says things not said by the previous classic texts, some of which still come as a shock to us; Machiavelli himself emphatically declares this originality (chapter 15). To know that these things were at least as contrary to what Machiavelli's contemporaries or immediate predecessors were saying adds something, but not something of the greatest importance. That judgement of importance depends ultimately on whether we turn to Machiavelli primarily for historical information about the sixteenth century and for his contribution to our concepts, or primarily for an alternative way of understanding politics. Skinner is less interested in Machiavelli's contradicting the Bible, Plato, or us, than in his contradicting Pontano or Patrizi. Skinner's use of quotations too often assists his method of generic juxtaposition only at the cost of doing violence to their textual context. He tends to smooth away the rough edges of the text from which other sorts of interpretation begin. He does not take the issues seriously enough to press them, to see what positions are incompatible, or to assess what is at stake. For the same reason, he cannot be shocked by the shocking. Skinner seems to have no method for identifying the unequivocal when confronted with the paradoxes, contradictions, and equivocations of the text. Sometimes he pallidly imitates them by his own wavering; sometimes he takes the most frequent statements, sometimes the rare ones, sometimes the provisional first ones; usually he substitutes an unbalanced, simply conventional, or simply counter-conventional selection for Machiavelli's paradoxical and thought-provoking complexity. He does not try to solve these problems by examining the structure of the text or by identifying Machiavelli's authorities and criteria of truth. It is the boast of Skinner's method not to seek to learn from Machiavelli or to confront him with our context. But the result is not merely to assimilate Machiavelli's originality to conventional sixteenth-century contexts or to construe it in their terms, but to assimilate it in our context – to make it less seriously concerned with the political problems posed by theology and morality.

Skinner both points out the great difficulty of properly attributing influence (though he ultimately accepts the usefulness of cautious attribution) and provides useful warnings against rashly assuming past writers to have had doctrines on what we consider the requisite subjects, to have met our standards of coherence, to have intended later results, or otherwise to correspond to what is familiar to us. These warnings are an articulation of good historical method: we should not impose our themes or notions on the thinkers of the past but strive to understand their thought as they understood it themselves. An awareness of these dangers is helpful, but escaping the familiar is easier said than done. Skinner does not seem to doubt whether it is possible or explain how it is done other than by acquiring familiarity with contexts. There is a danger, moreover, that his strictures and proposals may lead to the opposite mythologies: to assumptions that philosophic writers of the past could not in principle have had coherent doctrines, addressed posterity, intended ambitious results that have come to pass, or surpassed the confused intelligences or limited imaginations of twentieth-century scholars and thereby have something to teach us. Attention to their social and linguistic contexts and especially to their indications of how they themselves saw those contexts, need not result in a view of them as confused and merely timely. It may help us to distinguish their accommodations to those contexts and prevent those accommodations from obscuring our vision of the coherence and importance of their thought.

12

More theses on the philosophy of history

John Keane

1. Political argument, it is often observed, comes into its own only during crisis conditions, when conventional beliefs and unargued assumptions begin to disintegrate and to be questioned. It is recognized less often that crisis periods also prompt awareness of the crucial political importance of the past for the present. As a rule, crises are times during which the living do battle for the hearts, minds and souls of the dead. They are also times in which controversies erupt about the prevailing definitions of *how* to understand the past in relation to the present. The belief that history is simply history tends to be undermined during crisis periods, as is the belief in the neutrality of methods of accounting for the past. *How* the past is understood and explained comes to be seen as a crucial determinant of *what* is supposed to have happened in the past.

2. Recent controversies surrounding 'the history of political thought' are exemplary of this rule. Since the 1960s, in Anglo-American political philosophy circles at least, established methodologies for interpreting the history of political ideas have been subjected to intensive scrutiny and rethinking. Quentin Skinner's 'new history' of political ideology has played a prominent role in catalysing this development. His contributions have prompted many historians of political thought to reflect upon the methodological status of their own inquiries. They have also forced many historians, often for the first time, to take seriously the linguistic turn in philosophy, as it has developed during the past half-century in the writings, say, of Heidegger, Wittgenstein, Kuhn and Feyerabend. Inspired by the new history, old historiographies of political thinking – for instance, C. B. Macpherson's historical materialism and Leo Strauss's predilection

for 'understanding authors as they understood themselves' – have been put into question. They are being replaced by an emphasis on understanding past political thought as political argument, as the discourse of particular historical actors situated in specific contexts, which are subject to reinterpretation, fierce arguments and political transformation.

The success of the new history in facilitating this shift of emphasis is no small achievement. Yet the confident and often self-congratulatory posture adopted by some of its supporters – the suggestion, for instance, that the new history has effected something of 'a revolution in the historiography of political thought'[1] – is unwarranted. While the new history indeed broaches the possibility of reformulating genuinely interpretive approaches to understanding the political past from the standpoint of the present, it is also crippled by several fundamental weaknesses. This self-crippling character of the new history weakens its credibility and undermines its stated ambition to be *the* proper method for studying political ideas in a genuinely historical way.

I

3. The weaknesses of the new history project are evident in all three of its central propositions. The first of these propositions might be termed 'the intentionality claim'. This is indebted to a basic insight of speech-act theory: In as much as agents both say and do something through their performative utterances (and objectify them in, say, the form of a political treatise), the historian's understanding of such utterances necessitates a grasp of their illocutionary force (Austin). Such force corresponds to what agents saw themselves as doing in issuing those performative utterances. The proclamation of the death of the author[2] is declared to be wholly premature. Against the idea of the author-subject as an ideological construction and texts as autonomous, 'worldless' objects whose meaning is produced through the interplay of their inner structures and shifting themes, Skinner invokes a promising hermeneutic rule: Historical interpretation is synonymous with explications of what authors were self-consciously attempting in their creative acts of writing (2:63 – 4; 3:74, 76, 78; 5:102). According to the new history, texts do not speak, only authors do. This means that writers are not merely prisoners of the discourse within whose boundaries they take pen in hand. Nor are they transcendental egos. Authors always exercise a certain (developed) 'practical' consciousness of the conditions and possibilities in the field of action within which they write.

This intentionality claim is directed against not only textualist theories of meaning. It is pointed equally at the 'New Criticism' of Leavis and others.[3] It is argued that texts, duly pondered *as* texts, never yield their secret meanings to their interpreters' intelligence. Texts are not authorless entities which produce their own meaning. On the contrary, they are intentional objects of their creators. Thus, to know what writers saw themselves as doing in issuing utterances in the form of a text is *equivalent* to understanding their performed illocutionary speech-acts (of promising, warning, criticizing, etc.). When searching for the meaning or 'message' of texts, the historian's range of descriptions must focus on what 'motivated' authors' speech-acts, that is, on what they were intended to mean and how this meaning was intended to be taken. Skinner often speaks casually about the 'dynamic' relationship between writers' professed principles and the actual practices of political life, (2:56 – 9; 5:107 – 8) but the implication is clear: Professed intentions (which serve either as genuine motives for actions or as legitimating rationalizations of given or recommended states of affairs) make a crucial difference to the production and reproduction of political life and *a fortiori* must therefore be cited in order to explain that life.

4. It should be noted in passing that the intentionality claim presupposes two highly problematic points, the implications of which cannot be pursued fully here. In the first place, the new history's methodology rests on the exaggerated claim that agents always have a privileged access to the significance of their own intentional utterances. This assumption is vulnerable before the insights of the work of Hirsch and others on the unconscious, symptomatic meanings that typically escape the self-understanding of agents.[4] Such work is indebted to the insights of classical psychoanalysis, for which dream analysis is central: the dream is understood as an ensemble of disguised and substitute representations which have been formed on the boundary between the impulses and civilization, and recovered through the deformed utterances of the dreamer.[5] The idea of deformed utterances is alien to the new history. At best, it can admit of the possibility of intentional deception, of authors attempting to legitimate their untoward claims through commendatory or cunning language.

A second presupposition of the intentionality claim is equally vulnerable to criticism. The new history assumes that language, far from displaying a 'productivity' of its own, comes in the form of transparent wrappings within which intentional utterances are enclosed and issued. To be sure, Skinner cleverly censures defenders of the fallacy of the absolute text by insisting that any political text is always a discourse told by somebody, said by someone to someone else about something. Yet this point results in a misleading *volte face* – it exposes itself to the old and telling criticisms of the intentional fallacy by structuralist theories of the text, which in turn draw on the classic Saussurean distinction between *langue* and *parole*. Ricoeur's distinction between the subjective and objective moments of meaning is helpful in clarifying this point. The new history focuses only on the former – on the utterer's meaning, in the three-fold sense of the self-referencing of speech-acts, their illocutionary dimension, and the author's intention of receiving audience recognition for his or her utterances. The consequent subjectivist bias of the new history results in the eclipse of the objective dimension of authors' utterances, or what has been called the semantic autonomy of their texts. This autonomy (which is expressed in the commonplace distinction between what authors intend to say and what their texts mean) is conditioned by the logic of textual intersignification, that is, by the cluster of 'objective' generative rules and devices which preside over authors' intentions, the formal structure of their discourse and their reception by readers.[6]

5. These serious difficulties within the first argument of the new history can be set aside, in order to consider its second guiding claim: the thesis of authors' dependency on a field of conventions (3:77).[7] In Skinner's view, to redescribe the intentions guiding authors' utterances is to anticipate an explanation of their meaning. Historical interpretation, in this view, consists in the recovery of agents' intentions as they are expressed in relation to an ensemble of extra-textual conventions of political argumentation, within which these agents already and necessarily stand. The speech-acts of authors consist in their meaning something by saying or doing something in relation to others. Speech-acts are not simply 'precipitates' of their context (as Skinner points out convincingly against the reductionist treatment of language in Raymond Williams's *Keywords*) (6:130 – 2). Speech-acts are nevertheless always 'situated' or conventional, in the sense that they standardly intend to communicate arguments to others and therefore must be recognizable *as* intentions. In so far as they are addressed to strictly limited, precisely identifiable audiences, all works of political argument are bound up – though never absolutely so – with the established universe of permissible communication.

This reasoning does *not* bring into play (as Parekh and Berki have claimed)[8] the simplistic and erroneous assumption that prevailing conventions are immutable. In principle, Skinner's new history admits correctly of the possibility of inventive discourse, of writers consciously or unintentionally extending or even subverting radically prevailing conventions of political argument. The new history's concern with conventions is even more subtle than this. In the process of understanding the past, it is argued, contexts serve as courts of appeal for assessing the plausibility of interpretations of speech-acts which have a polysemic and sometimes obscure character. That is to say, through the invocation of contexts, the historian can more readily understand the extent to which a particular situated author intentionally ignores, criticizes or wilfully apologizes for prevailing political conventions. The relationship between an author's text and its context is an instance of the hermeneutic circle: particular authors' utterances can be explicated as 'meaningful' only if it is recognized that they always allude 'outside themselves' to prevailing assumptions, local styles of argumentation and contemporary or past political personalities, groups and struggles. Written discourse both refers back to its writer at the same time that it alludes beyond itself to the wider world of political action. This means that a text's meaningfulness cannot be conceived as immanent within that text, a meaning that can be unearthed by reading the text 'over and over again' (to repeat words once used by Plamenatz).[9] Through the thesis of conventions, Skinner seeks to question the commonplace fetishism of texts which have been elevated in mysterious ways to the status of 'classics' and 'masterpieces'. As Skinner's own work on Hobbes has tried to demonstrate,[10] and as he repeats against Mesnard and Sabine in the methodological introduction to *The Foundations of Modern Political Thought*, an historical approach which dwells abstractly on the 'classics' must be decentred. (It is another matter whether this claim is contradicted by Skinner's actual historical research. *The Foundations of Modern Political Thought* contains surprisingly 'classical' biases, omitting any reference, for instance, to La Boétie's *Discours de la servitude volontaire*, or to texts in the 'utopian' tradition, such as Campanella's *La città del sole*.) At most, according to the new history, 'classic' texts are to be treated as foci around which redescriptions of the range of intentional meanings of past political discourse can be organized.

6. The new history's two inter-related claims – that the hermeneutic appropriation of texts must recognize their status as codified objects intentionally produced within a horizon of extra-textual conventions – presuppose a third claim: The aim of the history of political ideologies is the sympathetic recovery or redescription of the *mentalité* of past phases of political life. Skinner submits that honest historians of political thinking must set themselves the modest goal of reproducing 'real history' through a 'strictly historical approach' which provides 'realistic pictures' of how 'actual' political speech acts unfolded in the past (5:99).[11] Interpreters must cast themselves in the role of good-natured and unbiased observers bent (as Skinner's more recent methodological writings stress (5:107 – 18)) on establishing the complex connections between the history of political ideology – understood in the positivist sense of an action-orienting *Weltanschauung* – and its implication within conventional situations of political action. The new history is concerned to identify the logic of processes of ideological formation and transformation through careful, patient and exact descriptions of the past. The iniquitous *imposition* of 'distorting perspectives' on this past must be avoided. 'The business of the historian . . . is surely to serve as a recording angel, not a hanging judge [and] to recover the past and place it before the present, without trying to employ the local and defeasible standards of the present as a way of praising or blaming the past.'[12] Writers' conventionally mediated intentions must be treated

as both self-explicatory and capable of 'recovery' through the initiation of a mental process called understanding. Armed with this proposition, the new history confidently berates its opponents for their unfaithfulness to the past: Walzer's account of the origins of the Calvinist theory of revolution is said to misjudge anachronistically the impact of the radical conciliarism of d'Ailly, Gerson and others; C. B. Macpherson's history of possessive individualism is judged for invoking 'rank anachronisms' and proceeding at a fundamentally unhistorical level of abstraction; and so on.

7. For the new history, then, the task of interpreting the past is posited as a process of mimetic reproduction of the immediately given intentions of actors within their respective conventional fields. The new history invokes the idea (drawn from Colllingwood's maxim that historians must re-enact past experience)[13] that there can be an untrammelled identity between present-day knowers and past producers of political argument. In principle, it is argued, intentionally produced utterances are capable of being re-enacted fully. Here the new history embraces a covertly positivist model of interpretation – a model long since abandoned within the most sophisticated circles of interpretation theory. This copy model presumes that valid understanding is identical with the loyal reproduction of the intentionally produced and meaningful utterances of others. It thereby revives a form of objectivism, against which the project of the new history has consistently (and convincingly) rallied from the beginning.[14] For the empathy model of imitating or 'recovering' the meaning of others' utterances, of empathetically looking them in the eye and stepping into their shoes, rests on the supposition of an initially uninvolved observer whose specific identity and prejudices can be selflessly repressed in the act of interpretation.

II

8. At least two inter-related arguments can be adduced against this model of the empathetic historian with innocent eyes. Both counter-arguments cast serious doubts on the viability of the new history. In the first place, a theme common to hermeneutics since Heidegger ought to be reaffirmed: Not only those whose utterances are to be interpreted, but interpreters themselves are always situated within a field of historically bound conventions and practices mediated by ordinary language. It is surprising that this point is missed in Skinner's account – especially given his references to Gadamer, Ricoeur and Habermas, the occasional (yet never developed) hints that interpreters' 'experience and sensibility' are a necessary precondition of interpretation,[15] and, finally, the rather different claim (directed against Butterfield)[16] that 'realistic pictures' of past political thinking are possible only in as much as interpreters structure their

interpretations through prior choices about 'what deserves to be studied and what is best ignored' (5:100).[17] The vital point which is merely hinted at here is that interpreters are always implicated within, and must always draw upon, the universe of linguistically structured activities within which their own subjectivity has been formed. This is true even in the most elementary sense that historians live, socialize and work within forms of everyday life enmeshed in an ordinary language framework, which in turn shapes their aesthetic judgements about which narrative and explanatory structures to adopt for the purpose of simplifying and rendering intelligible to their fellow historians the infinite quantity of 'raw historical material'. Indeed, this framework and its tacit conventions serve as a hermeneutic point of departure, a condition of *possibility* of generating historical interpretations in the first place. Interpreters always already stand within this field of intersubjectively shared conventions and 'preunderstandings', with the necessary 'bias' of which they approach the past. They cannot jump freely over the boundaries of this field and walk contentedly on the *terra firma* of the past. There can be no 'contemplative' or 'presuppositionless' understanding of the past or present speech and action of others.

This is not to insist, fallaciously, that interpreters are cast necessarily in the mould of situated spectators surveying an alien past. The interpretive understanding of the past is neither identical with its immediate, empathetic grasp (as the new history suggests) nor with the simple and 'motivated' subjection of this past to the situated concerns of the present-day interpreter. The logic of interpretive understanding defies such a dualism. Here the new history overlooks a second crucial insight, which it ought to have sensed from first-hand experience: Historical interpretation is possible only through the mutual participation of interpreter and interpreted in the medium of a common language that provides 'access' to the forms of life activity with which it is intermeshed. In order to understand their past, interpreters at the very least must have mastered its language, a mastery which in turn allows that past to be rendered into the words and actions of the present. This shared, ordinary language framework permits, through the medium of intersubjectively valid symbols, the negotiation of the meaning of past actors' speech-acts. In spite of the inerasable difference between past and present which results from the flux of historical time and space, interpreters are always (in the rudimentary sense mentioned above) 'members' of the universe of communication that they seek to understand. This *a priori* participation of 'prejudiced' interpreters within the realm of past communication under interpretation is concealed by the old-fashioned positivism of Skinner's new history. Its presupposition of selfless researchers who are (initially) detached from their object of interpretation fails to consider that, in order for interpretation to be possible at all, both must already be conjoined in and through a shared linguistic *point de départ*, in accordance with the generative devices and rules of which interpreters are able to proceed with their interpretive acts.

This line of argument implies that historians' understanding of past political speech-acts is possible only in so far as they assume the role of partner in dialogue with those acts. The actual meaning of past texts is always co-determined by their presently situated interpreters. Voltaire's quip (in his *Essai sur les moeurs et l'esprit des nations*) that history is a pack of tricks played by the living on the dead still contains a profound grain of truth. All historical interpretation is inescapably 'subjective'. Whether they recognize it or not, historians in every age encourage the dead to perform whatever tricks they prefer or deem necessary. To be sure, the proper relationship between interpreter and interpreted is not one of an absolute subject who stands as 'authority' over and against its 'object' (authors engaged in speech-acts). It is, rather, a relationship between situated (if unequal) partners conjoined through the medium of a common language. In this sense, the interpretive understanding of the past is a form of interlocution or communicative action. It is an instance of the dialectic of distanciation and appropriation (Ricoeur) – of the endless struggle between the alien otherness of a spatially and temporally distant past and the appropriation of precisely this past that is separated from us – and therefore unfamiliar and alien. In other words, historical interpretation effects what Gadamer has called a fusion of horizons (*Horizontverschmelzung*). This fusion of the world horizons of the reader with the writer rescues the meaning of his or her text from the threat of distanciation only by placing it in a new proximity to those in the present. (In this respect, as has been argued within the hermeneutic tradition from Heidegger's *Sein und Zeit*, the historian's acts of interpretive understanding are neither a mere 'method' nor a privileged mode of enquiry; rather, they are a more systematically articulated form of what is in fact practised routinely by situated subjects living, socializing and working within any particular society.) Contrary to the new history's unconvincing attempts to revive Collingwood, interpretation cannot be conceived as a reproductive act which rehabilitates a primal or original past. The annexation of the past always assumes the form of a *productive* achievement (an *inventio*) that draws on *present* meanings.[18]

9. If it is the case that every attempted recognition of what has been written or said is a newly produced understanding mediated by the social horizons and language of the interpreter, then the new history overlooks two additional methodological points of considerable significance. First, Skinner's conviction that the meaning of a text is equivalent to redescription of what situated agents saw themselves to be doing in issuing certain utterances must be revised thoroughly. It cannot grasp the fact that unintended consequences are a chronic feature of all speech-acts, past and present. Against the new history's intellectualist precept that agents always

act in a 'rational' manner (3:76), it must be emphasized that the meaning of such utterances *always* goes beyond their authors' intentions, in the specific sense that the meaning of these intentions, to repeat an earlier thesis, must be co-determined by the interpreter. The significance of a past author's action is never over and done with, for the restitution of its meanings is possible only to the extent that they are reconstructed and expressed 'in other words', and by way of their interpreters' judgements. Accordingly, there can be no absolute knowledge of a text. It is part of the fate of any text that its meaning is dependent on an indefinite number of readers and, hence, of multiple interpretations. Each age must therefore understand a transmitted text in its own way. History, as Burckhardt observed, is always the record of what one age finds worthy of note in another. In spite of their best intentions, those in the present are always parochial with respect to their indefinite interpreters in the indeterminate future. Conversely, as Habermas has remarked, present-day historians are always cast uncertainly and temporarily in the role of the ultimate historians.[19]

10. The uncritical character of the new history constitutes a second consequence of its disavowal of a negotiation model of interpretation. If the understanding of the past is a productive achievement of a situated interpreter, then the new history's assumption that the tasks of explicating and evaluating the past can be separated in favour of the former is false, and must be rejected. As might be expected, this assumption derives from Skinner's prior claim that historical interpreters can assume the role of detached and selfless chroniclers —'recording angels' — who look at the past with innocent eyes. On the basis of this implausible claim, historians' critical reflection on the power of tradition is ruled to be illegitimate. Complacent political theorists are allowed to breathe easily: texts must be accurately understood first, and then (in accordance with their readers' whims) judged only later, if at all. It seems clear that the (unintended) effect of this rule is to celebrate the power of the past over the present. The new history suffers from a definite lack of critical imagination, as several critics of its 'dusty antiquarianism' have intimated.[20] It seeks to maximize the quantity of treasured 'reproductions' of the political past for those living in the present. It thereby forgets the need, in certain cases, to shake off the legacies, burdens and distortions of the past. In other words, it devalues the historian's capacity to question critically and weaken the grip of 'realistic' interpretations of the past over the present, self-consciously to appropriate, preserve or break up tradition, and therefore to enhance the (potential) subjectivity of those living in the present. (The false sobriety of the new history can be contrasted with the energetic and critical powers evidenced within some contemporary works of feminist political theory, such as Hanna Pitkin's *Fortune is a Woman* or Carole Pateman's *The Problem of Political Obligation*, or with the stimulating and iconoclastic

works of contemporary historical reinterpretation, such as Carlo Ginzburg's *The Cheese and the Worms* or Michel Foucault's *Histoire de la folie*. None of these contributions claims to be a sober reproduction of our historical past, and yet each contributes to fundamental shifts in our shared sense of the past, present and future).

The pseudo-detached 'contemplativeness' of the new history is at least consonant with the ideological positions of both liberalism and conservatism (as Mannheim observed in another context)[21] and it is reinforced by the presumption (discussed above with reference to the intentionality claim) that agents always have a privileged access to the significance of their utterances. The new history turns a blind eye to the important dictum that unrecognized power is everywhere, that (at least in all hitherto existing societies) relations of command and obedience have become routinized or 'sedimented' in the institutionalized forms of life within which speaking and acting subjects are formed. Political argument is presumed to be a fully transparent play of self-conscious intentionality. It is supposed to be unhindered by 'invisible' relations of power, interest and ideological self-deception. As a consequence, the new history fails to account for the possibility that particular authors may unconsciously or half-consciously 'rationalize' their power-ridden forms of life as universal. (Throughout *The Foundations of Modern Political Thought*, for example, various authors' defence of 'the people' against absolutism is treated at face-value; this results in the false impression that these authors included women, the propertyless, the indigent, the colonized and others within their universal category of citizenry.) Conversely, it fails to ask the familiar set of questions concerning the relationship between given utterances of authors and their clarification and explanation through the listing of probable causal antecedents.[22] True, Skinner acknowledges the need for an explanatory account of past actors' self-declared intentions. Yet the form of explanation he has in mind is flaccid and uncritical, and accepting of the immediacy of these intentions. In Skinner's view, to explain authors' utterances is to redescribe their guiding intentions (3:76; 5:107ff., esp. 112 – 13). Notwithstanding an allusion to the explanatory significance of judging the *rationality* of agents' utterances and motives (4:90 – 4), he maintains, misleadingly, that to know what authors meant is to know how they intended their utterances to be taken and, therefore, *why* they performed their particular speech-acts. The post-Enlightenment insight that we cannot so simply judge an age and its constituents on the basis of their *own* understanding is thereby lost.

III

11. It may be objected that the arguments raised here against all three premises of the new history are self-contradictory, in that they secretly

lay claim to a 'true' historical methodology which is wholly at odds with their avowed rejection of attempts to generate indisputable knowledge of the past. This suspicion would be unjustified, since no such claim in support of a fundamental interpretive standard is intended or presupposed. The methodological proposals of the new history can be interpreted in a *variety* of ways – as a survey of the contributions to this volume confirms. The particular interpretation defended here does not lay claim to be exhaustive or comprehensive. It has been concerned neither to summarize exhaustively the new history in its own terms nor to extract from it systematic and irrefutable generalizations. It has instead pursued a modest type of hermeneutic approach, one which has aimed to reconstruct and interpret the deliberately organized arguments of the new history, in order to indicate the ways in which they 'wander' from, and sometimes contradict, the arguments advocated by its author.[23] In foregrounding these 'adventures' of the new history's arguments, this particular approach has not overlooked the heteromorphous and wholly conventional nature – and therefore irreducible *plurality* – of interpretive language games. On the contrary, it covers itself against being trapped in a performative contradiction of this kind by relying on the logic of occasion, as it is found, say, within the writings of Greek sophism. The unique feature of this logic of argument is its rejection of claims in support of one universal truth by pointing to the ways in which both itself and these claims are only individual cases of the logic of the particular, of the special case, of the unique occasion.

12. This methodological reliance upon the logic of particularism in matters of historical interpretation is well-suited to modern conditions. In modern capitalist societies, at least those in which a measure of democracy still prevails, the old presumption that there can be one true historical methodology – a presumption evidently still embraced by the new history – has worn thin. In modern democratic societies, the shared sense of the past – as well as the foundations of social and political order – are permanently unstable. These societies severely weaken the efficacy of forms of life whose legitimacy draws on either transcendental standards (such as God) or beliefs in a naturally given order of things (as in traditional societies). Modern democratic societies also begin to pluralize the prevailing definitions of the past. It is not only – as supporters of the new history might claim – that the nineteenth-century efforts of professional historians to explain the riddles and laws of motion of history, or to distinguish between scientifically based 'proper history' and common-sense beliefs about the past, have become wholly unconvincing. Professional historians also come to quarrel openly about both the substantive meaning of the past (i.e., about historical 'facts' and their meaning) and *how* to interpret the past. It slowly becomes evident in modern democratic societies that the specific tactics used by historians – their initial designation of certain historical 'facts' as important; their favouring of certain plot

structures to narrate sequences of past events as significant; their choice of particular forms of explanation of 'what happened in the past' and their normative judgements about these past events – are entirely conventional, and therefore highly variable in scope and number. Consequently, the belief among historians that 'history is history' is replaced gradually by the sense that history is always history as it is narrated, interpreted, explained and judged by particular historians with particular interests and concerns.

These quarrels about the methodology and meaning of history are consonant with the broader tendency of modern democratic societies to destroy slowly all reference points of ultimate certainty. This tendency encourages social actors within these societies to doubt the reality of 'reality'. They begin to perceive, in other words, that they are not in possession of any ultimates (based on knowledge, conviction or faith), and that they are continually, and forever, forced to define for themselves the ways in which they wish to live. Modern democratic societies are in this sense the first (potentially) historical societies. Marked by a deep socio-historical indeterminacy, these societies are permanently in crisis. Their members begin to perceive, if only dimly and sporadically, that the ends (and corresponding means) which they set themselves are neither ultimate nor incontrovertible, and that these goals and techniques are therefore subject to debate, conflict and resistance and, hence, to temporal and spatial variation.

13. The self-revolutionizing, self-questioning character of modern democratic societies no doubt renders them vulnerable to morbid attempts to restore absolute historical certainty. It also makes them prey to sickly forms of nostalgia, the negative political effects of which (such as blind complacency or fervid nationalism) can be checked only through the diffusion of *memories*, through the active interplay of a *plurality* of definitions of the past. This is why history ought to become a field of study *without* a consensus about which narrative strategies to adopt, which explanatory approaches to rely on, and which normative commitments should guide the enquiries and findings of historiography in the first place.[24] Historical memories can be prevented from becoming History only by preserving a variety of historical methodologies and, thus, by extending votes to the most disenfranchised of all constituencies – our silenced ancestors. Democracy among the living requires democracy among the dead. A genuine plurality of historiographical approaches and substantive accounts of the past – including highly non-conformist approaches – is a *sine qua non* of democratic societies.[25]

14. In his 'Theses on the philosophy of history' (1940), Walter Benjamin urged that history had until now been written from the standpoint of conformists and conquerors.[26] Following Nietzsche's advice on the need for 'critical history',[27] he insisted that prevailing definitions of the past are always those of the oppressor and that, in so far as the dead are not safe from

their clutches, official 'History' must be doubted, interrogated and rejected. Arguably, Benjamin's proposals for rewriting history against the dominant power groups and in anamnestic solidarity with the oppressed of the past and present are illusory in certain respects. His theses on the philosophy of history depend, for instance, on the mythical assumption (gleaned from historical materialism and Romanticism à la B. G. Niebuhr, Michelet and Carlyle) that the dead voices of lost generations can be resurrected, that the viewpoint of the downtrodden classes can be recovered fully by their politically motivated allies living in the present. Benjamin's proposals for rescuing and critically redeeming the lost past rested on several other unconvincing premises: a theory of language as representational naming; the positing of a golden past, in which there was not yet a need to struggle with the discursive dimensions of language; and the belief (derived from Goethe) that historical interpretation is capable of redeeming the authentic origins of the discordant elements of contemporary life.

Notwithstanding these difficulties, Benjamin's rejection of the stubborn belief in progress among his contemporaries remains compelling, as does his advice on the need to remember the dismembered, to recollect fragments of the broken past. Every image of the past that is neglected by the present can disappear forever into oblivion or the dusty obscurity of archives and museums. This is why every democratic society requires constant efforts to pluralize definitions of history, to break the power of the officially recognized dead over the living. It is also why, conversely, there is a need to awaken those souls who are dead, buried and forgotten, to 'rescue' those authors, texts and events that can increase our affection for democracy, despite the fact that they have been pushed aside (as 'irrelevant', 'confused', 'bourgeois' or 'obscure') or incorporated falsely into the prevailing definitions of history.[28] In an age threatened by growing state authoritarianism and a multiplicity of other anti-democratic trends, this goal of rescuing beleaguered democratic traditions can be realized only through the struggle to make 'foreign' what has become habitually 'our own', to distance ourselves from the conventional accounts of 'real history'.

It has been argued above that the process of understanding the past defies the logics of subjection and simple reproduction, and that it is better analysed as a form of interlocution. If this argument is plausible, then non-conformist historical interpretations must explore the possibility of developing a type of critical history which orients itself to past authors, texts and contexts, in order that their conformist definition and consequences can be buried through an active, future-oriented process of forgetting and remembering. Analogous to the self-understanding of psychoanalysis, a non-conformist historiography must strive to break the grip of 'the past' over the present – by way of a defence of a possible, if indeterminate, future that is sustained by certain past memories.

By contrast with this task of defining a future-oriented memory which brushes history 'against the grain', the new history's misguided quest to grasp descriptively what past authors 'could in practice have been intending to communicate' is implicitly conformist. Its aim of producing a 'real history' of political ideologies more closely resembles an official history that unwittingly defends the spell-binding hold of past ideologies over the present. In spite of its modest and detached intentions, the new history clings to an old and suspect motto: *Tout comprendre, c'est tout pardonner.*

13
The hermeneutics of conflict

Charles Taylor

Quentin Skinner has staked out an interesting and challenging position in the field of political theory. It centres around his view of what it is to give an account of the political theory of a given thinker or epoch. But this is in turn connected with an arresting and in some ways original conception of the bases of modern political thought, and indeed, of modern civilization. Skinner has been able to explore this connection, instead of just remaining in the realm of methodological generalities as so many philosophers do, because he is also, in fact first and foremost, an historian. He has been able, as it were, to work both sides of the fence, methodological and historiographical, and this is what has made his work exceptionally rich and suggestive.

Of course, just because of this breadth and richness, a question can arise about the unity of this work. Skinner's theoretical reflections relate to and partly arise from his actual practice as an historian, and as always when this is so, an issue can arise about whether there are features of this practice which are not fully captured by the theory. In taking up some issues in Skinner's methodological views, therefore, I may not be questioning the practice, at least not in the same way and to the same degree. Coming to grips with this practice in its full range would be an eminently worthwhile endeavour. But it would be beyond my powers to do justice to this in the short space I have at my disposal, if indeed I could ever do it. Here I want to confine myself to raising some issues about the methodology, starting in fact not from Skinner's own statements, but from the useful and concise summary that James Tully has offered.[1]

In fact, I want to raise a set of related questions about Skinner's methodology which deeply puzzle me. They do so because I am still confused and uncertain about the underlying matters that they address.

But I think that I am not alone in this confusion, and therefore that it's worthwhile trying to deal with them in this chapter. I have spoken of a set of questions with a number of facets, or of directions of approach.

The first approach could be put this way: where does the historian stand in accounting for the thought of a given writer or epoch? Tully formulates one of the basic tenets of Skinner's method: to find the 'historical' meaning of a text, look for what one might call its 'illocutionary force'.[2] Try that is, to see what the author was trying to accomplish in his political context in writing it. Read the text as action in context.

Now we need a language to talk about texts in this way. Skinner suggests that we understand the context as a language of politics, one that in the manner adumbrated by Wittgenstein, is woven into and helps constitute a given political way of life, helping to define the limits of the acceptable, the good and the bad, the obvious and the problematical. This can perhaps be referred to in short as an 'ideological context', or 'ideology'.[3]

The text-as-action can then be understood not only against the background of this context, but also as directly relating to it. What a writer is striving to *do* in producing a text is reinforce or change his ideological context, strengthen or weaken rival elements of it, preserve a certain form of it intact against assault, or on the contrary give it a new twist or direction. The motives for such action can be understood in relation to the political battles of the epoch, and the importance of the text-as-action can be measured by how it contributed to the outcome of these battles.

The context of action is one of struggle. Political battles in history, which from time to time tip over into military conflicts as Clausewitz reminds us, are also always battles for the 'hearts and minds' of those who can affect the outcome. In this latter theatre, the texts of political theory are weapons. The pen becomes a sword, and indeed, a very powerful one, as Tully's title avers.

A persuasive picture, as far as it goes. Who of the great political theorists was not concerned to combat some historical forces of their day and further others? But it leaves one important set of questions unaddressed: what is the truth value of the theories the texts expound? The texts are seen as moves in an attempt to bend and shape the terms in which people argue and justify themselves. They are attempts to manipulate the terms of debate in which the political identity of a society is established and continued.[4] But they can be identified as such as independent of any judgement of their truth or validity. Of course, the terms in dispute had to be thought valid by the civilizations in which they were disputed. Otherwise the battle would have no point. And it is quite likely that one of the reasons for a writer to try to alter these terms is that he believes his revision to have greater validity – although even this is not necessary: he may have other motives for wanting to manipulate the language of debate. But it doesn't appear as though the *historian* need take a stand on this issue in order to identify the manipulative intent of the text. The context of struggle can be kept separate from the context of truth.

Or can it? Is there an issue about where the historian stands, which he cannot evade except at the cost of muddle? I believe that there is, and that the bracketing of the issue of truth is never successfully achieved. The attempt to sidestep it just leads to a confused prejudging of it; it always returns to haunt us. But I could be wrong about this, and Skinner's work could be one of the things which prove me wrong. I am uncertain about all this: uncertain whether Skinner wants to bracket the question of truth, and unclear, if he does, on what basis.

Perhaps I can explore this issue usefully by trying to build the case that this bracketing is impossible. I want to build it polemically, by looking at some of the inadequate reasons which have justified it in the past.

The first is the notorious belief of positivist social science, that one could separate 'facts' and 'values'. This positivist variant of value-freedom – very different from Weber's doctrine [5] – justified the historian or social scientist in not taking a stand on the issues raised in the texts on the very simple grounds that these were not issues of truth. The various combatants in the ideological struggles of history took value positions. But values cannot be arbitrated as to truth, and so the historian has no call to intervene. By contrast, issues of historical explanation, of identifying the motives and effects of historical action, raised questions of fact. The scientist does his business of getting at the truth, and leaves the quite distinct issue of what is right and good (on which he undoubtedly also has views) out of account.

Now this doctrine has fewer friends today, and certainly Quentin Skinner is not one of them. He has rather helped to show how inextricably entwined the explanatory and the evaluative are in all languages of politics. My point in evoking it is simply to show what follows from negating it. Once you drop positivism, you lose any *a priori* grounds for situating your own explanatory language on a different level from the language you are trying to study and explain. The language in which I explain the politics of the Middle Ages, the Renaissance, the French Revolution, is not of an utterly different kind from the language of Aquinas, Machiavelli, Hobbes or Hegel. These are all conceptual schemes which serve inseparably to classify political realities, to describe them, explain them and evaluate them. To the extent that they are different and uncombinable, they are rivals.

So when we account for what a thinker was doing in writing his text in terms which he would have found strange, which he would no sooner understand (if this were possible) than repudiate, we are involved in revision. We are *ipso facto* challenging his picture of things and putting our own in its place. We are not bracketing the question of truth, but taking a negative stand on that issue in relation to this thinker's work. Positivism was in deep conceptual confusion partly because it was in fact profoundly revisionist in relation to the greater part of the history of thought but in ways that it couldn't ever understand or admit to itself.

To admit this revisionism is to call to mind a brace of theories which share much of the naturalist philosophical background of positivism, but which have made much stronger explicit claims. 'Materialist' theories, like Marxism (under one interpretation) and contemporary socio-biology, offer another type of ground for separating the historian from the subject of historiography. This is no wishy-washy pretence of neutrality, but the claim to have got the language of politics right. These theories purport to tell us what is really going on, what the real driving motives of people have been, and hence the nature of the actions they performed and the changes they brought about. Where historical languages deviate from this picture, and offer an incompatible view of action, they are just wrong, illusory, 'ideological'. So theologies of the Reformation can be understood as moves in a struggle over new forms of production, and marriage codes can be understood as reflections of the evolutionary success of pair-bonding among hominids in the Pleistocene.

Of course, these particular theories are widely thought to be reductionist and implausible. But the question arises whether any historian isn't forced to make claims which at least are of this kind, even though they will usually be much less confident, sweeping and presumptuous. To write history is surely to claim, at least implicitly, to have identified the level of description of at least some significant action. And where this identification enters into conflict with those of one's subjects, one is inescapably challenging and revising these latter. The difference between more cautious and sensitive historiography and the 'materialist' theories above lies in their lack of *a priori*, metaphysical assurance that the historian is on a different scientific level from his subjects, in virtue of having found the 'key' to human action. Here the last motive for segregation breaks down, and one is forced to see the subject as a rival and potential interlocutor. I am revising his language and redescribing his action, but I have to be aware of how this move is inherently itself open to challenge, including from a defender of something like his position. It is as relevant to my enterprise to make clear where I stand as it is to expound where he stands.

Against this background, I am puzzled by James Tully's claim: 'The question with which [Skinner] approaches his study is not "What is politically true and right?" It is rather . . . "What counts as politically true or right, or as grounds for testing political knowledge claims, in different ideologies and contexts?"'[6] Of course, one can set out to address one of these questions rather than the other. But I don't see how you can hope to answer the second without taking some stand, implicit or expressed, on the first. Tully calls the focus on the second question 'historical pragmatics', and he believes that Skinner's work provides a justification of this direction of enquiry as an exclusive focus, bracketing the issue of truth or validity. But as he spells this out, one begins to wonder whether it shouldn't be seen in a different light.

The justification is a thesis about the political ideas which have come to dominate our western societies. The terms of modern political discourse are in fact a precipitate of earlier battles, in which the protagonists attempted to establish certain expressions as canonical, for understandable reasons in terms of the political issue of their day. The dominant ideology today centres on a conception of the state and of legitimate state power, and makes crucial use of such key terms as 'sovereignty', 'law' and 'rights'. Tully calls this outlook the 'juridical ideology'. But this ideology hasn't arisen as a single coherent body of thought, following a single consistent train of reasoning. Rather what we live with today is

> the unintended and unrecognized product of four hundred years of political thought and action. Each tactical manipulation of a convention within local ideological controversies, and each use of this as an artifice in parochial political struggles are shown, from the perspective of the present, to add in effect an element in the construction of the juridical form of political representation.[7]

It follows, Tully reasons, that our modern political outlooks 'whether juridical or humanist, lack rational foundations, and this is because we lack a language, each convention of which has been independently grounded, in terms of which we could assess all the conventions of our ideologies'.[8]

It isn't clear whether this claim is meant in a narrow scope, to apply just to the ideology of the present age, or whether the dominant ideology of today is just being singled out as an example of what is generally true of any age. Starting from Skinner's thesis about the origin of reigning ideologies (they are the outcome of conflicts over the terms of political discourse), and adding some more plausible premises about most periods in history (they are the scene of a number of related conflicts, and the outcomes of these has a high component of unintended consequences), we generate the expectation that most ages will have a dominant ideology consisting of rather heteroclite elements.

I'm not sure what the reasoning is here, whether it is meant to follow from the fact that a political outlook is a compound of disparate origin that it is without rational foundation. This consequence doesn't seem to hold. To see this, imagine what an ardent supporter of modern liberal democracy could say when we tell him that the elements which make up his outlook are of very different origins. We explain to him that the notion of rights stems from the late Middle Ages, with its rather special legal ideas and distribution of power. He learns that Magna Charta was the instrument of a class of greedy and oppressive magnates, that the ideology of universal-suffrage democracy would have seemed like subversive madness to them, and the utilitarian premise that government ought to maximize happiness and minimize pain despicable if not incomprehensible. After the initial separation trauma from the edifying platitudes of his high school civics course, he could surely construct for us a justification that made sense to him today of the way of life in which all these figure as elements. The fact that it wouldn't be the same as the one that appealed to the barons at Runnymede, nor the one which enthused officers of the New Model Army, nor what Robespierre or even perhaps Jefferson thought, wouldn't have to worry him. As a matter of fact, it is not even excluded that one could construct a single unified justification, from one coherent theory of philosophical anthropology, even though historically we all know that liberal democracy didn't arise that way.

This being so, perhaps we should understand that basic argument in another way. Perhaps the basic claim is that just because dominant ideologies are decided by the outcome of conflicts, it will generally be the case that they are only randomly related to what is true or valid in relation to the needs of the people who live under them. I have put this thesis in the broad form, because only in this form would it justify our bracketing the issue of truth. If we held a thesis of this kind just about our contemporary outlook, it would be inseparable from a plea to revise it to bring it more in line with the truth. But if one held that in general, ideas rise and fall as a result of struggles in which their truth plays little or no deciding role, then one could argue that the historical explanation of their fate could indeed be separated from judgements as to their validity, for it involves factors of a very different kind.

Now Tully seems to be suggesting something of this kind in the third thesis which he attributes to Skinner, which he dubs 'the primacy of war': 'Effectual changes in European political thought and action are the consequences of war and secondarily the outcome of the ideological response to the legitimation crises engendered by the shifting power relations that give way to battle.'[9] It follows from this that, however political theorists conceptualize their activity, it 'is unavoidably caught up and etched into more fundamental political relations that are relations of war.'[10] And Tully invokes Clausewitz here, whose dictum is reversed while being adapted: instead of seeing war as a continuation of politics, we see theory as a phase of war.

Now if this is the argument, we can begin to understand why it might seem plausible to bracket off the issue of truth. After all, no one expects the outcome of armed clashes in history to bear a close relation to any of the other basic standards of valuation we cherish. Certainly not to right and justice. We all know that we are lucky that Hitler over-extended himself, and we in the west are lucky that we didn't have to be delivered from Hitler by Stalin. So why should truth be on the side of the big batallions either?

Is this neo-Clausewitzian thesis Skinner's? I'm not sure it is. If so, one could certainly see how he might hope to insulate questions of historical explanation from those of truth. But this kind of thesis, to the effect that the arbiter of ideas is a kind of power which is no respecter of truth, is in fact a radical one, and has far-reaching consequences. Tully's invocation of Clausewitz puts one in mind of Foucault, a theorist whom Tully sees as moving along the same lines as Skinner. And Foucault in turn puts us in mind of Nietzsche, and another quite different way of bracketing the question of truth, quite unlike either positivism or classical materialism. Nietzsche in some of his writings wanted to present the will to truth itself as a manifestation of the will to power. And Foucault has drawn on Nietzsche to develop his notion of 'regimes of truth', established within relations of power, and between which there is presumably no rational arbitration.

I am not sure whether Nietzsche really did bracket the question of truth, as Foucault tried to do. I am even less sure whether, if he did, the attempt is ultimately coherent. But I haven't got space to go into these issues here.[11] I want rather to make a few remarks about a slightly easier question: whether this neo-Clausewitzian thesis is at all plausible.

In a sense we might see it as the antithesis of Hegelianism, at least as vulgarly understood. Where Hegel seems to be saying that the real is the rational, and that truth will eventually bring about its own realization, the view I'm calling neo-Clausewitzian holds that it is without effect, and that what happens is quite unrelated to it. The first view is rightly discredited today. But is the second any more plausible?

In a sense I am coming around to my basic puzzlement from a different line of approach. I started off asking: where does the historian stand? Can he avoid taking a stand on the truth of the ideas he is examining? I have been arguing that a language of political explanation is on all fours with the historical theories it is called on to explain, that they are potential rivals, and thus that certain explanations are inseparable, from affirmations or negations of what we are explaining. We need some special plea to put ourselves on a different level from our subjects. Marxism offers one such: the theorist finally has 'science'. Now neo-Clausewitzianism offers another: the relevant factors in explaining how ideas become prevalent or die away have nothing to do with truth.

But this brings us to another puzzlement, about the language of explanation which is being offered. On one level, the thesis sounds very plausible. Different languages, and different variants of tradition-ally recognized languages, are in competition. Their protagonists are in struggle. But there is no single focus, the struggle is carried on in a multitude of different contexts on a great many levels, through the history of a society. The reigning language of any epoch is the provisional outcome of this multi-layered struggle as it stands at that moment.

As a general thesis it sounds undeniable. And to flesh it out with military metaphors sounds quite unexceptionable. But then a crucial ambiguity comes to light. Is the military language just metaphorical? Or does it rather betoken that actual armed struggle, and the political structures and disciplines which have been built to wage or deter armed struggle, are the paradigm contexts in which the issue is decided? Tully interprets Skinner in this second way; and he explains his use of military language thereby.

But this is a much less plausible thesis. As much as the first interpretation is easy to accept, even approaching a truism, the second is highly dubious and questionable.

Let us take one component of the 'juridical ideology' as an example. The modern age developed the notion of sovereignty, and foundational to liberal democracy is the view, also generated out of early modern developments, that this sovereignty ultimately resides in the people. The seventeenth century adds the crucial extension, that the people themselves, as a collective body, are to be seen as constituted by the consent of individuals. This notion, which was expressed in terms of social contract theories, survives today even when some of the quasi-historical beliefs which accompanied it have gone, and even though the contract is no longer invoked in disputes about legitimation. Its continuing importance can readily be seen in the great impact of post-Kantian theories of the social contract as an 'as if' construction, most notably in our day with Rawls.

Now I am far from being able to offer a detailed account, but it seems to me very likely that this strength of political individualism – the notion that rights pertain to individuals, and that the legitimacy of a system hangs to a large degree on how it deals with individuals – is connected to the saliency of individualism in other forms and other aspects of our culture. That it is connected, for instance, with the rise of our modern conceptions of marriage and the family, of human fulfilment in the companionate marriage (or more latterly 'relationship'), which have helped to make the nuclear family or its surrogate the most important basic unit of social life. That it is connected with post-Romantic notions of 'fulfilment', with all the accompanying ideas of individual difference and the corresponding crucial importance of being true to myself. It has become a banality that it is connected with free-enterprise forms of capitalist entrepreneurship. And the list could be continued.

Now while it may seem plausible that the prevalence of political individualism on its own be attributed to the fortunate outcome of politico-military struggles in history – including some decisive armed conflicts, such as the American Revolution and the Second World War, not to speak of the dominance of imperial powers the political culture of which was based on these values – it is much less obvious that the hold on us of the reigning images of sexual love and personal fulfilment is to be explained in the same terms. We can indeed speak of these emerging through a struggle. But this has partly been the struggle of daily life, in which individuals and couples strive to make sense of their lives and give shape to their hopes, fears and aspirations. No one can underestimate the great impact that war, conquest, mass migrations, expulsions, imposed industrialization, and many other such founding events of modern civilization have had. But these condition and don't displace the struggle to give form to one's daily life.

And while it is easy to believe, where the fate and prevalence of ideas is decided in war, that this is only randomly related to their truth and validity, it is a different proposition to hold that those self-interpretations which emerge out of the daily struggle for self-understanding are quite unrelated to their validity for us. To put it most simply, we may have to explain their rise at least partly in terms of their fit with what we have become, rather than explaining in the reverse direction, where what we become is a function of the language which has been imposed on us by strategies of power.

In short, only if we could show that relations of domination, and the strategies which create and sustain them, have totally invaded the world of everyday self-understanding could we adopt the narrow, neo-Clausewitzian interpretation above, and make all dominant ideas the outcome of conflicts which centre on war and the struggle for power. If we cannot, then the neo-Clausewitzian thesis ceases even to be plausible for our political ideas, granted the close interweaving between them and the other languages of our culture. The reality of historical change would be a much more complicated and messy business, in which the truth of ideas is neither decisive nor totally irrelevant to their fate, since this truth would have very different weight in different facets of what was nevertheless a single interconnected culture.

I confess that this messy picture seems to me close to the reality of things. But I recognize that Michel Foucault made a strong case for the invasion of everyday understanding by relations of power. If this case could be made good, then indeed, the neo-Clausewitzian perspective would appear tremendously plausible. Tully is right, granted his interpretation of Skinner, to relate him closely to Foucault. For Foucault provides the indispensable philosophical underpinning for a Skinner who really wanted to go this route.

But does Skinner really want to go this route? I am still uncertain. In a sense, what I have been trying to do here is relate Skinner's methodology to a requirement that seems to me inescapable for any historian or social scientist: confronting one's own language of explanation with that of one's subjects' self-understanding. The different avenues of questioning I've explored here converge on this central demand. We can meet it by asking what our language of explanation entails about the truth of our subjects' beliefs. Or we can get at the same issue via another route by asking how we ought to describe their actions and thoughts.

In the last few paragraphs I have been trying this second line of approach. The challenge here as it relates to Skinner's methodology could be put in this way: telling us to identify what the author of a text is doing, how he is intervening in the conflicts of his day, is not enough. We can't take it for granted that we already know how to do this for an age sufficiently different from our own. Perhaps we need to learn more about the kinds of conflicts there were, what was at stake in them, the kinds of moves you could make, and what represented victory or defeat. The war model seems to make things easy, because in one way this kind of extreme conflict is understandable wherever we meet it in human history. We know right away what it is to win and lose. Thus the operations of the European state system from early modern times, in so far as this was concerned with war, the preparations for war, the acquisition of the sinews of war, and the like, seems readily comprehensible to us. We find our feet right away in conflicts of this kind. We would have much more trouble understanding the conflicts of the pre-twentieth-century Balinese state system. Thanks to the penetrating and sensitive work of Clifford Geertz, we can get some sense of what was at stake here.[12] But we have a lot to learn – and specifically, *inter alia*, from their self-descriptions – before we can find our feet here.

Now the reference to Bali might be thought irrelevant in a discussion of Skinner's work. In fact, he has been concerned with the origins of modern western thought, and it is precisely the European state system which has played a major role in this. But the issue arises here in another form. We are confident that we can understand the goals and methods of a Richelieu, and in earlier centuries of a Medici or a Sforza. But what is it to understand the conflict in which Luther, Eck, Zwingli and Contarini were engaged? This is highly relevant to the modern age, since however great the difficulty in formulating the connection exactly, we are clearly in a number of ways the spiritual heirs of the Reformation.

Now the conflict over the Reformation was central to the struggles of the European state system in its formative period. And the actual spread of the Reformation churches was obviously largely decided by the balance of political and military forces. Would Luther have avoided the fate of Hus without the Elector of Saxony? These centuries abound with examples of the cynical use of power.

But it doesn't follow from this that the important place of the legacy of the Reformation in our lives is to be explained in terms of the outcome of the struggles, intrigues and strategies in the chancelleries of those times. One modern *idée force* which I believe we owe to the Reformation is what I call the affirmation of ordinary life, the belief that the central point of human existence and human fulfilment is to be found in the life of production and reproduction, or work and the family, or labour and sexual love. In various forms this has been one of the great revolutionary forces of modern culture. It gained this position as a result of struggle, in some sense of this term. And one of the phases of this struggle was the spiritual battle for hearts and minds of the sixteenth century. But I think we still have some way to go before we understand the terms and nature of this struggle. I don't think that war and the preparations for war of the European state system even begin to give us the key.

Now the demand I've been talking about, namely that we confront our language of explanation with the self-understanding of our subjects, is nothing else but the thesis of hermeneutical theory. Tully at the end of his paper wants to contrast Skinner's approach with a hermeneutical one. Skinner's path runs parallel with hermeneutics for a long way, but then he diverges where the hermeneutical theory falls into error. But the error that Tully identifies here, namely 'that it continues to encourage and underwrite the view that the language [of the subjects themselves] must be the best, and often the only guide to the activity it describes',[13] is not part of contemporary hermeneutical theory, not at any rate since Gadamer. That one must confront one's language with that of one's subjects doesn't involve accepting this language. It may of course. But the upshot can also be that one judges oneself to have a perspective that they couldn't share, and so far forth revises their beliefs. The point is the issue must be faced, one way or another, or muddle will prevail.

We can all too easily be over-quick in concluding that we understand what is going on in some distant place or century. And modern European scientific thinking has a tendency to focus on and make primary just those aspects of social life which seem closest to invariant across different cultural contexts: war; the reproduction of the material means of life; the conditions of ecological survival; the presence or absence of civil strife. Perhaps the neo-Clausewitzian thesis is an exciting new insight, but perhaps it is also another case where we cede to this old temptation.

A number of questions arise from all this for Skinner's methodology, to some of which I might have the answers if I understood it better, or had a better grasp of modern history. I am all too aware that these questions represent largely stages of my incomprehension of the tremendously rich and interesting body of work which Quentin Skinner has been laying out before us.

PART IV

Afterword

14

A reply to my critics

Quentin Skinner

INTRODUCTION: FOR METHOD

I am not sure where to begin. Reading my critics, I am perplexed to learn that I am at once an idealist, a materialist, a positivist, a relativist, an antiquarian, an historicist, and a mere methodologist with nothing of substance to say at all.[1] The last charge is mainly pressed by Minogue, who declares in chapter 10 that any attempt to offer general prescriptions about historical method is 'so much waste of time' (10:186). But Minogue is not alone among my critics in suggesting that my theoretical writings are completely superfluous. Gunnell complains that they have already been discussed more extensively than is warranted, especially in view of their futility as a guide to practice.[2] Tarlton, and more recently Levine, have similarly claimed that there is nothing at all in my essays of the least practical value for political theorists or intellectual historians.[3]

On reflection, this seems the right place to begin. It is certainly unpardonable to waste one's colleagues' time. So it will be best to start by investigating the grounds these scholars have given for objecting that this is all I have done.

One reason they offer is that so many different questions can legitimately be asked by intellectual historians that general prescriptions are bound in effect to function as straitjackets.[4] Among contributors to the present volume, Minogue puts forward this criticism in general terms (see 10:179 – 80,

185 – 87), while Femia concentrates on the fact that my grotesquely mistaken approach involves the arbitrary rejection of any study of the potentialities or consequences of systems of thought (9:157, 171, 173).

Femia does not mince his words; but nor does he follow my arguments. I have never denied the obvious fact that we can and do turn to major works of moral and political philosophy for all sorts of reasons, some of which may carry us far beyond the works themselves and the intellectual milieu within which they were conceived. My own concern, however, has solely been with the question of how best to approach such works if our aim is, in Dunn's luminous phrase, to recover their historical identity.[5] I have exclusively been concerned, that is, with how we should proceed if we wish to gain an understanding of the utterances that go to make up such texts, and hence an understanding of what their authors may have been saying and doing in issuing just those utterances. To put the point more polemically, I have sought to argue that, if our aim is to acquire this kind of understanding, we have no option but to adopt an historical and intertextual approach.

It would be a relevant and devastating criticism if it could be shown – as Deconstructionist critics claim to show – that this project embodies an impossibility, since there is nothing determinate to recover and understand. This objection I shall have to consider at a later point. But it can hardly be a relevant criticism to observe that we may approach a text with many other questions in mind besides the one I have singled out. I do not *arbitrarily* exclude these other questions: I exclude them on the grounds that they are unconnected with – and must not be confused with – the hermeneutic enterprise in which I am alone interested.

Even those who have understood the scope of my arguments have often insisted that the precepts I put forward are, as Minogue remarks, probably pernicious and at best unnecessary (10:185, 186, 188). Minogue himself offers a number of different reasons for this discouraging conclusion. One is that the recovery of meaning is not a proper subject for rules and precepts at all. The claim he has in mind here is far stronger than the indisputable one mentioned by several other commentators, including Tarcov in the present volume: that even if we follow the best methodological precepts, we can never hope by such means alone to turn ourselves into good historians.[6] (Tarcov seeks in chapter 11 to demonstrate that my own historical practice illustrates this melancholy truth.) Minogue's is the more radical contention (echoed by Gunnell)[7] that it is a mistake to suppose that philosophical reflections about the concepts of meaning and explanation have any bearing upon the intellectual historian's task of recovering the meaning and explaining the occurrence of past utterances. As Minogue puts it, 'there is remarkably little that can profitably be said in general' about such issues. The moral is that 'an intellectual historian ought to be an epistemological *naif*', remaining as far as possible in a state of 'pre-theoretical innocence' (10:186 – 7, 189).

This position strikes me as self-defeatingly incoherent. The claim that philosophical argument cannot give rise to any useful precepts about historical method is itself a philosophical argument from which a strongly legislative methodological precept is said to follow: namely, that we ought to be 'against method'. But even if we endorse the complete separation between theory and practice enjoined by Gunnell and Minogue, it remains a jolting non sequitur to suppose that we can hope to remain in a state of pre-theoretical innocence simply by treating philosophical ignorance as bliss. The result of doing so will inevitably be to condemn ourselves to making unselfconscious use of whatever intellectual tools may happen to be lying around in our environment. Why this should be thought preferable to engaging in self-conscious reflection about the nature of those tools and their suitability for the kinds of tasks we want to perform is something these epistemological anarchists never pause to explain.

It is true that this response does nothing to establish the positive value of connecting theory and practice in the manner I propose. But I can see no other way of doing this than by offering up to Minogue and his ilk the whole of the rest of this reply. In the course of it I shall try to defend a series of philosophical arguments about interpretation, to show how these can be couched in the form of precepts about method and to suggest how these can in turn serve to provide us with a helpful guide to practice. By my fruits I must ask to be judged.

A number of my critics have given a second and contrasting reason for supposing that the precepts I put forward amount (in Minogue's phrase) to nothing more than excess baggage (10:193). Minogue himself raises this further doubt, even though this introduces an obvious inconsistency into his argument. If, as he puts it, we think of an intelligent student pondering the problems of interpretation in his own way, we shall find that 'there doesn't seem much to teach him' (10:183, 184). (So there *was* something to know?) As Levine similarly suggests, there are of course general rules of good interpretative procedure, but 'the ordinary historian' already knows and practises them.[8]

There is one version of this criticism I feel perfectly willing and indeed anxious to endorse. As Levine, Wootton and several others of my critics have stressed, there has never been anything particularly novel about my arguments on historical method.[9] I am far from supposing otherwise. My first essays owed an obvious debt to the theoretical writings of Pocock[10] and Dunn,[11] and a still deeper debt to the approach embodied in Laslett's scholarship on the history of political thought.[12] One way of describing my original essays would be to say that I merely tried to identify and restate in more abstract terms the assumptions on which Pocock's and especially Laslett's scholarship seemed to me to be based.[13] I was further aided in this task, moreover, by the philosophical writings of J. L. Austin and, even more immediately, of R. G. Collingwood. To the latter, indeed, I am directly indebted for what remains my fundamental assumption as an intellectual historian: that the history of thought should be viewed not as a series of attempts to answer a canonical set of questions, but as a sequence of episodes in which the questions as well as the answers have frequently changed.[14] I hope I have never sought to minimize these intellectual debts, and I am happy to acknowledge them once more.

I should add that in this present reply I am still more conscious of standing on the shoulders of others. I have learnt so much in recent years from those with whom I have discussed the problems of interpretation[15] that I doubt whether my views about how to formulate the issues are truly my own, still less my views about the issues themselves. It is even probable that I have unwittingly borrowed some turns of phrase from those to whom I am most indebted. But this merely underlines the obvious fact that I am not trying to claim any novelty for the remarks that follow. The most I want to claim for them is that they are (so far as I can see) true.

I confess myself less happy with a second version of the same criticism. Doubtless it is the universal fate of those with the temerity to write about historical method to find their conclusions dismissed as obvious where they are not dismissed as false. But to claim as Levine has done that I merely inform 'ordinary historians' of what they already know seems to me insensitive to the character of the intellectual milieu into which I originally launched my bromides. When I published the essay reprinted here as chapter 2, I was surely able to show, if nothing else, that a number of historians were practising their craft in violation of what I proposed as canons of good historical method. I am not denying that I may have been wrong to propose those canons, and that the historians I criticized may well have been right to ignore them. I am only observing that my proposals were far from universally embodied at the time in ordinary historical practice.

In any case, it has never been my intention simply to offer what Levine calls 'a method for doing the history of ideas'.[16] As I have indicated, my aim has been to articulate some general arguments about the process of interpretation itself, and to draw from them a series of what I take to be methodological implications. As a result, I have been forced to confront, however ineptly, a number of central issues in the theory of meaning and the logic of explanation. And these issues are surely worth considering at any point, regardlesss of whether the implications I seek to draw from them happen to be in or out of favour with practising historians.[17]

Minogue at least recognizes that, in spite of my 'desperately methodological idiom', I am 'really a philosophical imperialist in historical disguise' (10:180). But this leads him to yet a further reason for concluding that my precepts about historical method are worse than useless. What if the philosophical theory from which they are drawn should itself prove untenable?

The trusting but luckless historian would then be sunk. Better off, Minogue concludes, without incurring such dangerous dependence (10:187).

I agree that this is the heart of the matter. It is true that Minogue himself makes no serious attempt to show that my views about interpretation are in fact constructed out of philosophically faulty materials. But most of the contributors to the present volume have gone for the jugular by concentrating on just that point. I think it may be said without undue oversimplification that in doing so they have focused on two main difficulties. One concerns the relationship between explaining beliefs and assessing their rationality or truth. The other relates to my understanding of the theory of meaning and speech-acts. No one could be more conscious than I am that, if I now try to address these issues, I shall at once find myself out of my depth, not waving but drowning. However, there can be no doubt that these are the issues most worth addressing. So there seems no alternative but to take the plunge.

Before I jump, however, I should like to add one last word in my own defence. This is that, in one important respect, the severely limited nature of the following remarks is deliberate. I have tried so far as possible to avoid repeating anything I have already said. I do not think I have actually contradicted any of my earlier arguments. But I have certainly rephrased and extended them in many ways. It is true that several of my critics have already deplored my willingness to introduce what Boucher calls equivocations and changes of emphasis.[18] But I do not see that this propensity need be the cause of any confusions or difficulties. If there is anything in the following remarks which does in fact conflict with anything I have already said, I should like what follows to be taken as the statement of what I actually believe.

ON DESCRIBING AND EXPLAINING BELIEFS

Though words be the signs we have of one another's opinions and intentions; yet, because the equivocation of them is so frequent according to the diversity of contexture, and of the company wherewith they go (which the presence of him that speaketh, our sight of his actions, and conjecture of his intentions, must help to discharge us of): it must be extreme hard to find out the opinions and meanings of those men that are gone from us long ago, and have left us no other signification thereof but their books; which cannot possibly be understood without history enough to discover those aforementioned circumstances, and also without great prudence to observe them.

Thomas Hobbes, *The Elements of Law*

I

I turn first to consider the relationship between the explanation of beliefs and the assessment of their rationality and truth. Among contributors to the present volume, these problems are raised most acutely by Charles Taylor in chapter 13. Should an historian try to avoid 'taking a stand on the truth of the ideas' he or she is examining? (13:224). Is it desirable, or even possible, 'to insulate questions of historical explanation from those of truth'? (13:223). Taylor, like Shapiro,[19] rightly observes that I have failed to make clear what view I take about this question of 'bracketing' truth, and they both ask me to explain myself.

I am not altogether clear what Taylor means when he speaks about 'bracketing' truth (e.g. 13:220). Sometimes he seems to be asking whether an historian should somehow seek to discount or set aside the fact that he or she holds certain beliefs to be true and others false. If this is Taylor's question, then my answer is that I am sure no historian can ever hope to perform such an act of forgetting, and that in any case it would be most unwise to try.

Consider the fact that so great a political philosopher as Jean Bodin believed there to be witches in league with the devil.[20] Or the fact that so great an empirical scientist as Aristotle believed that bodies change quality whenever they change place.[21] Living in the late twentieth century, we are likely to feel, and unlikely to be able to repress the feeling, that these claims are simply false. But we are also likely to find our interest quickened by the discovery that such eminent authorities, capable of saying so many things that seem straightforwardly true, were also capable of entertaining such apparent absurdities. If we begin by focusing on such beliefs, we shall provide ourselves with the best possible starting-point for investigating the structure of Aristotle's or Bodin's thought. For here at least we come upon something that cries out to be explained. We shall also provide ourselves with the best possible means of ensuring that our eventual explanation takes a sympathetic and non-anachronistic form. For whatever account we provide will have to include an explanation of the fact that such admittedly bizarre beliefs nevertheless commended themselves to such unquestionably distinguished minds.[22]

At other points, however, Taylor seems to be asking a different question: whether the views that historians take about the truth-value of the beliefs they expound ought to affect the types of explanation they give of them (13:219). My answer is that this depends on what is meant by speaking about the truth-value of beliefs, a topic on which Taylor writes in an ambiguous way.

Sometimes the issue he raises is whether our explanations ought to vary – or are bound to vary – with our sense of whether the beliefs we are investigating are 'true or valid in relation to the needs of the people who live under them' (13:223, cf. also 226). This question – seemingly inspired by Gadamer – appears to me to embody an unhelpfully wide, even metaphorical, extension of the concept of a true belief. But if this is the issue on which I am asked to comment, then my answer is that of course I agree that our explanations are bound to vary with whatever judgements we make about truth in this extended sense. If we encounter an ideology which we find to be true to the needs of the society living under it, we are sure to treat that very fact as part of the explanation for its success. If we come upon an ideology which is demonstrably untrue in this extended sense, we shall certainly be obliged to explain its success in a very different way. (But unless we find that the society in question is on the point of dissolution, we are surely more likely to conclude that we cannot hope to explain such a phenomenon at all.)

At most points, however, Taylor speaks about true beliefs in a more familiar and restricted way. When he asks whether we should take account of the fact that a particular belief is true when seeking to explain it, what he generally seems to be asking is whether we should take account of the fact that the belief in question accords with our own best current beliefs about the matter at issue. I am not of course (nor is Taylor) offering this as a definition of truth. I am only observing, uncontentiously I hope, that this is how we generally use the term.[23] (Though the moral of this, as Davidson has suggested, may well be that we ought not to ask for a definition.)[24] I take it, accordingly, that the question with which Taylor is principally occupied is this: whether we as historians can or ought to avoid asking ourselves whether we endorse the beliefs we are seeking to explain.

Taylor himself maintains that it is undesirable and probably impossible to bracket truth in this way (13:220). This conclusion aligns him with a considerable number of recent writers on social explanation, including Jarvie, Lukes, MacIntyre, Newton-Smith and especially Macdonald and Pettit.[25] It also aligns him with several other critics of my own work, including Graham, Shapiro, and Hollis in chapter 7 of the present volume.[26]

When Taylor states his grounds for this judgement, however, he remains deliberately tentative. He explores a number of reasons given by positivist philosophers for supposing that the issue of truth can be bracketed, and seems to me to dispose of these without difficulty. But he makes no mention of the arguments put forward by the philosophers I have just cited for supposing that the question of truth must always be raised. Instead he emphasizes that he remains puzzled and uncertain about the issue, and 'could be wrong' about it altogether (13:218, 220).

Perhaps the best way to proceed will accordingly be to attempt a more direct confrontation of the issue. Among the philosophers I have mentioned, two main reasons have been given for supposing that the question of truth can never be bracketed. One argument, stressed in particular by Macdonald and Pettit, derives from Davidson's theory of radical interpretation.[27] The suggestion is that, unless we begin by assuming that the holding of true beliefs constitutes the norm among the people we are studying, we shall find ourselves unable to identify what they believe. If too many of their beliefs prove to be false, our capacity to give an account of the subject matter of those beliefs will begin to be undermined. And once this begins to happen, we shall find ourselves unable even to describe what we hope to explain. The implication, as Davidson himself puts it, is that 'if we want to understand others, we must count them right in most matters'.[28]

I cannot see that this view of radical interpretation possesses the relevance for historians that some of Davidson's more enthusiastic followers, such as Macdonald and Pettit, have supposed. Davidson is merely proposing a general strategy for using assertions to get at underlying beliefs, the strategy of beginning by assuming general agreement. It may well be that we need to start with some such assumption if we are to find another culture intelligible. If I am to identify the nature of Bodin's beliefs about witches, or even to establish that they are beliefs about that particular subject matter, it certainly seems plausible to assume that Bodin and I must share a considerable number of ancillary beliefs.(It is in any case clear that the beliefs we share with our Renaissance ancestors are literally infinite in number.) But it hardly follows from this (nor do I imagine that Davidson thinks it does) that I need to assume that Bodin's beliefs specifically about witches are mainly true before I can be sure of identifying them as beliefs about witches. It may be that practically everything Bodin says about that particular topic is false. But by learning his language (an easily recognizable form of French) and by seeing what concepts he uses and how he reasons with them, I can nevertheless hope to identify without much difficulty where he is talking about witches and what he thinks about them. It is true that, if I am to keep up with his arguments, it may be necessary for him to reassure me at various points that he is still talking about witches. As long as he continues to make it clear that this is so, however, there seems no reason to fear that I may suddenly feel obliged to conclude that he must be talking about something else, even if practically everything he is saying strikes me as patently absurd.[29]

I turn to the second reason often given for supposing that the issue of truth must never be bracketed. False beliefs, it is said, point to failures of reasoning, and failures of reasoning require additional explanations of a kind not needed in the case of true beliefs. This appears, for example, to be the thought underlying Graham's contention that we shall be acting 'in a spirit of ill-judged humility' as historians if we fail to consider the points at which the social beliefs we investigate are 'flawed or inadequate'.[30] A similar thought clearly underlies Lukes' discussion of the special explanatory problems he takes to arise in connection with the need to 'identify the mechanisms that prevent men from seeing the falsity' of their beliefs.[31] Finally, the same commitment clearly emerges from Macdonald and Pettit's more extended analysis of the way in which judgements about truth and falsity are bound to enter into 'the kind of explanation one gives' of alien beliefs.[32] When a belief under investigation proves to be true, they assert, no further explanation seems to be required. But when a belief is 'manifestly false' or 'obviously incorrect' there is something further to be explained. We need in particular to consider the kinds of 'social function or psychological pressure' that could have prevented the agent in question from recognizing 'the mistaken nature of the belief'.[33]

If this is the argument on which I am asked to comment, then my response is that I think it fatal to introduce the question of truth into social explanation in this way. To do so is to assume that, whenever an historian encounters a belief which he or she judges to be false, the explanatory problem must always be that of accounting for a lapse of rationality.[34] But this is to equate the holding of rational beliefs with the holding of beliefs that the historian judges to be true. And this is to exclude the obvious possibility that, even in the case of beliefs that nowadays strike us as manifestly false, there may have been good grounds for holding them true in earlier historical periods.

Having gestured at the concept of rationality, I ought to stress that I intend nothing very grand or precise by that much-abused term.[35] When I speak of agents holding rational beliefs, I mean only that their beliefs (what they hold to be true) should be suitable beliefs for them to hold true in the circumstances in which they find themselves. A rational belief will thus be one that an agent has attained by some accredited process of reasoning. Such a process will in turn be one that, according to prevailing norms of epistemic rationality, may be said to give the agent good grounds for supposing (as opposed to merely desiring or hoping) that the belief in question is true.[36] A rational agent will thus be someone who, as Lewis puts it, believes what he or she ought to believe.[37]

None of this implies that rational agents need to hold any particular beliefs, save for those which may be indispensable to bare survival.[38] So this means in effect that a rational agent will be someone whose beliefs are held in the light of a certain attitude towards the process of belief-formation itself.

This attitude must certainly include an interest in consistency. Rational agents want their reasons for holding their beliefs to bear upon their truth. But to espouse a given belief as well as its contradictory is to hold at least one belief that must be false. A rational agent will thus be concerned, at least in seriously troubling cases, to identify and eliminate any such obvious inconsistencies.

Above all, rational agents must be interested in the justification of their beliefs.[39] They must be concerned with the kinds of coherence, and where appropriate the kinds of evidence, that give them grounds for concluding that their affirmations of belief can in fact be justified. They will thus be concerned, at least to some degree, to view their own beliefs critically, to consider whether they really can be justified by considering the degree to which they may be said to fit with each other and with their perceptual experiences.

It seems difficult to go further. In particular, it seems positively erroneous to try to arrive at a single criterion, and hence a method, for discriminating rational beliefs. The relations between the ideal of rationality and the practices that may be said to manifest it seem far too complex and open-ended to be captured in the form of an algorithm.

It is true that recent epistemology has been much concerned to discover such procedures or sets of rules. Among positivist philosophers, this at first gave rise to the proposed test of verifiability. But this seems much too strict. Apart from other difficulties, it provides the historian with a potentially anachronistic – and in any case a far from perspicuous – notion of direct observational evidence as the basis for justifying beliefs. This in turn appears to overlook the fact that it may be rational to hold a given belief, even in the absence of any such evidence, as long as it can be plausibly inferred from other rationally held beliefs.[40]

The enemies of positivism later proposed an alternative criterion, that of falsifiability. But this seems even less satisfactory. As I have suggested, it appears a minimal characterization of rational agents to say that the reasons they give for their beliefs should be reasons for holding them to be true. But on the one hand, the fact that a given hypothesis may have resisted attempts to falsify it scarcely gives us any grounds for supposing it to be true.[41] And on the other hand, the application of such a test has the effect of excluding as irrational a number of otherwise well confirmed and well justified beliefs.[42]

This, then, is as much as it seems appropriate to try to say about rationality in general terms. I now turn to explain why it seems to me fatal to satisfactory social explanations to exclude the possibility of holding a false belief in a wholly rational way. My reason is an obvious and familiar one. It is simply that the kinds of explanations we offer for beliefs we judge to be rationally held are of a different order from the kinds of explanations we feel obliged to offer if we once come to doubt whether a given belief is held in a rational way. To equate the holding of false beliefs with lapses of rationality is thus to foreclose, in advance of knowing whether this is appropriate, on one type of explanation at the expense of another.

This is not to claim – as Hollis does in this volume – that rational belief is its own explanation (7:140, 144). One problem with this thesis is that it overlooks the gap between demonstrating the rationality of a belief and explaining why it was held. Even if we can show that it was rational for a particular agent to accept a certain belief, the explanation of why he or she accepted it may always be independent of that fact.[43] Hollis's formulation also conveys the impression that, once a given belief is exhibited as rational, there will be nothing further to explain. It is certainly true that we find the phenomenon of rational belief less puzzling than blatant lapses from rationality. But therein lies the danger. For it remains true that the attainment of rationality will always be an achievement. So an enquiry into the conditions that enable us to attain that state will never be any the less legitimate – and may in some cases be no less necessary – than an enquiry into the conditions that may prevent us from attaining it.

Nor am I claiming – as Hollis, MacIntyre and others have done – that the forms of explanation appropriate to rational and irrational belief must differ because 'rational belief cannot be explained in causal terms'.[44] I see no reason to doubt that, if there is a sufficient reason for an agent to accept a given belief, this may function as a cause of its acceptance. I agree, that is, with the proponents of the so-called 'strong programme' that it seems appropriate to adopt what Bloor has called a requirement of impartiality in the explanation of beliefs, a requirement that they should all be approached and explained in the same causal terms.[45] But I see no reason to suppose, as the exponents of the strong programme have added, that this requirement is incompatible with making judgements about rationality.[46] To insist on the relevance of such judgements is not to deny that we ought to be looking for causal explanations of the capacity to achieve rationality no less than of failures to achieve it.

When I insist on the need to ask whether a given belief is or is not rational as a preliminary to explaining it, my reason is rather that the different cases raise explanatory puzzles of different kinds. Even if we assume that our explanations will in each case be causal in form, the causes of someone's following what are taken to be the relevant norms of reasoning will nevertheless be of a different order from the causes of their violating them. It follows that, unless we begin by enquiring into the rationality of the belief concerned, we cannot be sure of correctly identifying what it is that needs explaining, nor in consequence of directing our investigations along appropriate lines. If the belief proves to be one that it was rational for the agent to have held, we shall need to investigate the conditions of that achievement. If it was less than rational or palpably absurd to have held it, we shall need to enquire into the very different sorts of conditions that may have inhibited or prevented the agent from following accepted canons of evidence and argument, or perhaps supplied the agent with a motive for defying them.[47]

To reject this line of argument, as the advocates of the strong programme have done, it is necessary to insist not merely on a requirement of impartiality in the explanation of beliefs, but also on what Bloor has called a requirement of symmetry.[48] This further principle, as Barnes expounds it, claims that we must reject any contention to the effect that one belief can be stigmatized as more 'ideological' than another in consequence of being in some way 'unsatisfactory' or insufficiently grounded.[49] We have to recognize that all our beliefs are socially caused in such a way that, to some degree, their objects remain masked from us. It follows that all of them must be approached and explained in one and the same way.

If this is nothing more than a stipulation about how we ought to use the term 'ideological', then perhaps it will do no harm. But if it is a proposal about how we ought to set about the business of explaining beliefs, then it seems to me fatal for just the reasons I have sought to give. It deprives us of an indispensable means of identifying the most appropriate lines of enquiry to follow in any given case.

It may be helpful to offer an illustration of what I mean by speaking of the fatal consequences of failing to ask in this way about the rationality of beliefs. Consider the influential explanation of witchcraft beliefs offered by Le Roy Ladurie in his classic study, *The Peasants of Languedoc*.[50] Ladurie starts by stressing that such beliefs are of course manifestly false, a mere product of 'mass delirium'.[51] He proceeds to infer that they could never have been rationally held. As he explicitly asserts, those who espoused them were simply 'slipping savagely into the irrational in belief and behaviour'.[52] The effect of this commitment is to direct Ladurie's attention as an historian in one particular way. He assumes that what he must be looking for is an explanation of a breakdown in normal reasoning, a situation in which 'the peasant consciousness suddenly broke loose from its moorings'.[53] The question, as he puts it, is how to account for such an upsurge of obscurantism, such an epidemic of pathological beliefs.[54]

Part of Ladurie's answer is that, with the progress of the Reformation, the peasantry began to fear a loss of their traditional spiritual help. 'Far from their priests, the peasants found themselves alone with their anxieties and their primordial fears – and abandoned themselves to Satan.'[55] But his main hypothesis is that they felt a deep sense of frustration at the collapse of the social upheavals associated with the Reformation. With the failure of social reform, their continuing desire to improve their lot took on a 'mythical dress', being forced to express itself in the 'chimerical and fantastic revolt of the witches' Sabbath, an attempt at demonic forms of escape'.[56]

I am not concerned with Ladurie's actual explanations, although it hardly seems an incidental consequence of his approach that they turn out to be so dizzyingly speculative. I am solely concerned with the fact that, by treating it as self-evident that a certain set of beliefs could never be rationally held, Ladurie leaves himself no space to consider a quite different sort of explanation. He cannot allow that the peasants may have believed in the existence of witches as a result of holding a number of other beliefs from which that particular conclusion might reasonably have been held to follow.

To consider only the simplest possibility, suppose that the peasants held the belief – widely accepted as rational and indeed indubitable in sixteenth-century Europe – that the Bible constitutes the directly inspired word of God. If this was indeed one of their beliefs, and if it was rational for them to hold it, then it would have been the height of irrationality for them to have disbelieved in the existence of witches. For the Bible not only affirms that witches exist, but also that witchcraft is an abomination and that witches must not be suffered to live.[57] To announce one's disbelief in the existence of witches would thus have been to announce a doubt about the credibility of God's word. And what could have been more dangerously irrational than that?[58]

Ladurie excludes in advance the possibility that those who believed in witches may have done so as a result of following out some such recognizable chain of reasoning. But this means that he not only puts forward an explanation of witchcraft beliefs which, for all he knows, may be completely irrelevant; it also means that he bypasses a range of questions about the mental world of the peasants which it may be indispensable to answer if their beliefs and behaviour are to be properly understood.

A common objection to the above line of argument has been that it presupposes an excessively objectivist conception of rationality. Disciples of the later Wittgenstein such as Peter Winch, as well as exponents of the strong programme such as Barnes and Bloor, have all converged on this point. As Barnes puts it, echoing and endorsing Peter Winch's case, to claim that we can assess and criticize the rationality of beliefs is to presuppose 'external standards' of rationality of an 'objective' kind.[59] But we have no access to any such 'super-cultural norm', and in consequence no prospect of being able to 'discriminate existing belief-systems or their components into rational and irrational groups'.[60] The very idea of assessing the rationality of beliefs is thus dismissed as nothing better than an intrusion, a forcible imposition of our own epistemic standards on an alien 'universe of discourse' or 'form of life'.

This objection is I think totally misconceived. But my reason for saying so is not that I imagine – as Hollis does – that we can hope to vindicate a substantial and objective conception of reason and employ it in the assessment of beliefs.[61] It is rather that the abandonment of any such project does not preclude the idea of assessing beliefs for their rationality. If an historian stigmatizes the upholding of a particular belief within a particular society as irrational, this judgement need never flow from the application of an allegedly objective conception of what can or cannot properly count as rationality. The historian need only be claiming that he or she has uncovered the prevailing norms for the acquisition and justification of beliefs in that particular society, and that the belief in question appears to have been upheld in the face of, rather than in the light of, those norms themselves. The historian need only be claiming, that is, that the agent in question fell short of – or perhaps abandoned, manipulated or in some other way deliberately defied – some generally accepted standard of epistemic rationality.

If historians were to adopt this approach, they would be engaging in the assessment of beliefs in just the manner I have recommended. But at no point would they be applying an 'external' standard of rationality in an intrusive way. They would not be asking themselves whether the belief in question is rational according to their own standards (still less *the* standards) of epistemic rationality. They would merely be reporting that it was not an appropriate belief for that particular agent to have espoused in that particular society at that particular time.

It might seem that this is bound to deprive the concept of any cutting edge. This is certainly the inference drawn by Rorty, who assumes that once we give up the idea of rationality as a concept 'floating free of the educational and institutional patterns of the day', we shall have to admit that we cannot hope to employ the notion in the assessment of beliefs.[62] We shall find that practically everyone is capable of putting their desires and opinions together in such a way as to satisfy a purely pragmatist test of rationality. So the idea of asking whether it was in fact rational for them to hold their resulting beliefs becomes devoid of content.[63]

A number of intellectual historians have recently endorsed the same viewpoint. Once we discover the inner coherence of a given system of beliefs, they maintain, we can hardly fail to count it rational for the system to have been upheld.[64] So the project of assessing the rationality of individual beliefs again drops out of sight. 'If ways of thinking are recreated sympathetically, then one never refutes but always sustains' whatever beliefs are identified.[65]

I concede that accusations of irrationality must only be hurled in the last ditch, if at all. We need to begin by recreating as sympathetically as possible a sense of what was held to connect with what, and what was held to count as a reason for what, among the people we are studying. Otherwise we are sure to commit the characteristic sin of the 'whig' intellectual historian: that of imputing incoherence or irrationality where we have merely failed to identify some local canon of rational acceptability. I cannot see, however, why it should be supposed to follow that our interpretative charity must always be boundless. On the contrary, there may be many cases in which, if we are to identify what needs to be explained, it may be crucial to insist, of a given belief, that it was less than rational for a given agent to have upheld it.

As an illustration of what I have in mind, consider one of the beliefs fundamental to Renaissance political philosophy, the belief that the quality of *virtù* is indispensable to military and political success. It was owing to their loss of this quality, Machiavelli particularly insists, that the

Florentines of his own age became so disastrously incapable of defending themselves. In his earlier writings Machiavelli merely asserts this belief, but in the course of his *Florentine History* he supports it with some dramatic examples. Describing the battle of Anghiari, for instance, he notes that in four hours of alleged combat only a single soldier was killed;[66] describing the even more farcical battle of Molinella, he adds that in the course of half a day's fighting there were no fatalities at all.[67] By focusing on these and similar cases, he builds up his evidence for saying that his fellow-countrymen were abjectly lacking in the kind of *virtù* needed to preserve their liberty.

If we turn to Machiavelli's sources, however, we find that they hardly support these conclusions at all. What they suggest is that a total of seventy soldiers were killed and six hundred wounded at Anghiari, while at Molinella there was fierce fighting and several hundred fatalities.[68]. If we turn, moreover, to later Renaissance discussions of the *Florentine History*, we find a number of commentators complaining about Machiavelli's deliberate fabrication of his evidence. Scipio Ammirato, for example, insists that Machiavelli gives no adequate grounds for his conclusions; he simply 'changes names and alters facts' in such a way as to make his authorities say what he already wants to believe.[69]

It is true that a sufficiently charitable historian could easily rescue Machiavelli at this point. Machiavelli fervently believed that the quality of *virtù* had been lost in the modern world. And he was not without strong grounds for this belief. He also believed that a willingness to behave courageously was one of the most obvious characteristics of a *virtuoso* people. But this means he could hardly fail to conclude that his fellow-countrymen were lacking in courage. Nor could he readily interpret their military conduct except in terms of their axiomatic lack of this *virtuoso* quality.

As his own contemporaries insisted, however Machiavelli was only able to maintain this particular article of faith at an extravagantly high cost. He was obliged to falsify the relevant authorities, and in consequence fell rather grievously short of the standards recognized by his own peers for the assessment of evidence and the justification of beliefs. As a number of them rightly observed, the outcome was a commitment which it was not appropriate for Machiavelli to uphold, or at least not in the unequivocal form in which he always upheld it. To put the point in the jargon I have been using, it was not a rational belief.

I have already emphasized why it matters to be able to make such judgements. As soon as we permit ourselves such an uncharitable conclusion, we confront a new set of questions about Machiavelli's beliefs, a set of questions we had no occasion to ask or even notice as long as we felt able to assume their rationality. Why is he so excessively insistent on the military incompetence of his fellow-countrymen? Is he nursing some private grievance? Or is he merely nostalgic for the bygone days of citizen militias? Or is he unduly influenced by the classical assumption that such forces are alone capable of displaying courage? These questions in turn suggest wider ones. Should we be looking for a strongly emotional component in others of Machiavelli's political beliefs? Should we think of him as habitually credulous in his response to the political writings of ancient Rome? Only by enquiring into the rationality of his beliefs can we hope to recognize the range of explanatory puzzles they actually pose.

II

The above argument in response to Taylor can in turn be expressed in the form of a set of maxims for historians concerned with the description and explanation of beliefs. The golden rule is that, however bizarre the beliefs we are studying may seem to be, we must try to make the agents who accepted them appear (in Hollis' phrase) to be as rational as possible.[70]

This golden rule in effect embodies three precepts. The first merely states a condition *sine qua non* of the whole enterprise. We need to assume what Lewis calls a convention of truthfulness among the people whose beliefs we are seeking to explain.[71] Our first task is obviously to identify what they believe. But our only evidence of their beliefs will normally be contained in whatever texts and other utterances they may happen to have left behind. It is of course likely that some of these may be pervasively marked by hidden codes such as irony. But we have no option but to assume that, in general, they can be treated as straightforward expressions of belief. Unless we can assume such a convention of truthfulness, we cannot hope to make any headway with the project of explaining what they believed.

The second and closely connected precept states that we must initially be prepared to take whatever is said, however bizarre it may seem, as far as possible at face value. If the people we are studying assert that there are witches in league with the devil, we must begin by assuming that this is exactly what they believe. This will not only serve to keep before us the precise character of our explanatory task; it will also enable us to steer clear of a familiar but condescending form of interpretative charity. It will prevent us from purportedly rescuing the rationality of the people we are studying by way of suggesting that, whenever they say something that strikes us as grossly absurd, it will be best to assume that the speech-act they were performing must have been something other than that of stating or affirming a belief.

There have been two widespread applications of this principle. One of them, essentially Durkheimian in inspiration, suggests that we ought rather to assume that such statements express in symbolic form a proposition about the structure of the speaker's society and his or her commitment to upholding it. This version was until recently popular with a certain school of social anthropologists, as the writings of Beattie, Leach and others attest.[72] The second, more Freudian in inspiration, suggests that we ought instead to assume that such statements express in a displaced or distorted form some deep and unacknowledged feelings, such as frustration or anxiety. It is this version of the principle we have already encountered in Ladurie's account of witchcraft.

The obvious difficulty with the principle in either form is that the only criterion we are offered for distinguishing those propositions we are to take literally from those we are to take symbolically is our own cognitive discomfort. If we find it too embarrassing to take what is said literally, we are in effect instructed to take it instead as a symbolic or displaced way of saying something else. To reject this approach is not of course to deny that beliefs may perform a crucial role in expressing a society's view of itself, its fears, its aspirations, its sense of solidarity. Nor is it to deny that the Freudian approach in particular may be able to furnish us with indispensable insights, unavailable to the agents themselves, into why they may have held (and held on to) their particular beliefs. It is only to assert that we shall be assuming what has to be established if we take it that we can move directly to such forms of causal explanation in advance of asking whether the agents in question may not in addition have had good reasons, by their lights, for holding what they believed to be true.

The third precept states the positive task to which we commit ourselves as historians by virtue of this approach. We must seek to surround the particular statement of belief in which we are interested with an intellectual context that serves to lend adequate support to it. As we have seen, this commits us to something more than trying to establish that the people we are studying may have had good practical reasons for saying what they said. It commits us to trying to establish that their utterances were not merely the outcome of a rational policy, but were also consistent with their sense of epistemic rationality. The primary task is therefore that of trying to recover a particular context of presuppositions and other beliefs, a context that serves to exhibit the utterance in which we are interested as one that it was rational for that particular agent, in those particular circumstances, to have held to be true.

We cannot know in advance what range of beliefs this may require us to investigate. So my proposal stands in contrast with one that has often been put forward in particular by historians of science. They have sometimes argued that, as Hesse puts it, we ought to concentrate on 'the received internal tradition' of scientific discovery, and hence on the established canon of major scientists, rather than trying to 'spell out in tedious detail every minor writing or trivial biography of forgotten figures'.[73]

In criticizing this approach I am not questioning the appropriateness of concentrating on the received tradition of discovery if that is what historians of science happen to find most interesting. Rather I take it that all forms of history are bound to be 'whiggish' in this sense. The problems on which historians feel it worth expending thier energies will be certain to reflect their own sense of intellectual priorities. It would be strange indeed if they were to conduct their researches according to a set of priorities they themselves felt to be mistaken.

I am only insisting that, once we recognize that an understanding even of a received canon of major figures requires us to surround them with whatever intellectual context makes best sense of them, we cannot afford to be too quick about dismissing any feature of that context as tedious or irrelevant. To an historian of science, the details of the Anglican Church hierarchy in Newton's time may very probably appear in that light. But it may well be that for Newton the isomorphism between such hierarchies and those he found in the heavens gave him good reason, by his lights, for believing in the truth of his celestial mechanics. To dismiss the first as a 'religious' belief, with no relevance for Newton's scientific studies, may well be to impose. such a deeply anachronistic sense of how to divide up the world, and of what can count as a reason for what, as to close off the possibility of understanding Newton's most obviously 'scientific' achievements. Any impatience with what we think of as irrelevance or triviality may cheat us of just the understanding we seek.[74]

Philosophers sympathetic to this approach, such as Rorty, are apt to insist that we can hope to state it a good deal more briskly than I have managed. What it amounts to, they assure us in Wittgensteinian style, is simply that we need to get into the swing of whatever exotic language-games are being played by the people whose beliefs we are trying to describe and explain.[75] This seems true but unhelpful. We surely need to ask about the most suitable strategy for breaking in upon such unfamiliar activities and forms of life.

As a first step, it will perhaps be best to recall that statements of belief rarely present themselves individually to the historian with evidence conveniently attached. As I have observed, the question of what it is rational to believe in part depends on what else we believe. Any particular belief in which an historian is interested will therefore be likely to present itself holistically as part of a network of beliefs, a network within which the various individual items supply each other with mutual support. As I have already implied, it follows that if an historian wishes, say, to discover whether it was rational for Bodin to believe in witches, the soundest course of action will be to begin by asking whether Bodin held any other beliefs in the light of which this admittedly bizarre conclusion might in some way have appeared to make good sense.[76]

Hollis objects that it will only be rational to hold such a belief if it was in turn rational to hold the core beliefs from which it is said to follow.[77] But this image of a rational bedrock strikes me as confused. What does it mean for a purportedly core belief to be rationally held? On the one hand, it can hardly mean that we are capable of giving good reasons for holding it. For in that case it would still be a derivative rather than a core belief. But on the other hand, I cannot see — as I have already conceded — what else it can mean to describe a belief as being held in a rational way.

I cannot see, in short, that Hollis' proposal can be deployed in such a way as to set limits to the kind of holism I am trying to expound. Even in the most primitive perceptual cases, even in the face of the clearest observational evidence, it will always be reckless to assert that there are any beliefs we are certain to form, any judgements we are bound to make, simply as a consequence of inspecting the allegedly brute facts. The beliefs we form, the judgements we make, will always by mediated by the concepts available to us for describing what we have observed.[78] And to employ a concept is always to appraise and classify our experience from a particular perspective and in a particular way. What we experience and report will accordingly be what is brought to our attention by the range of concepts we possess and the nature of the discriminations they enable us to make. We cannot hope to find any less winding a path from experience to belief, from observational evidence to any one determinate judgement.[79]

Hollis retorts that, at least in the case of 'simple everyday beliefs', the historian or ethnographer 'needs to discover' that the people he or she is studying have 'common perceptions, common ways of referring to things perceived and a common notion of empirical truth'.[80] If history and ethnography are to be possible, he maintains, there must be a firm bridgehead of shared experiences which are conceptualized in an invariant way. He infers that there must be some corresponding terms in any language for the expression of these bridgehead concepts, and he advises the historian or ethnographer to begin by finding and translating them.[81]

Quite apart from the fact that Hollis' principle still does not tell us exactly where to look, it strikes me as a serious misconception to suppose that we can ever hope, even in 'simple perceptual situations', to isolate and describe 'what a rational man cannot fail to believe'.[82] Even the simplest action or event can be fitted into a variety of more or less complex classificatory schemes, and can in consequence be labelled in an indefinite variety of ways. Consider, for example, a report of the simplest possible kind of 'perceptual situation': a report, say, to the effect that it is raining.[83] When Roman writers stated this belief, they used the word *imber*, this being the only term available in classical Latin to denote a fall or shower of rain. This means that, if an ancient Roman and a modern Briton were to confront this situation together, there might be many instances in which, faced with exactly the same evidence, they might arrive at conflicting statements of belief. If the Roman were to report that he was experiencing an *imber*, and if the Briton were to take this to mean a fall or shower of rain, the latter might actually dispute the judgement. The Briton might wish, for example, to insist that what he or she was experiencing was nothing more than a drizzle.

This is not of course to deny the obvious fact that in some sense the Roman and the Briton are experiencing and talking about the same thing. It is only to insist that, whenever we report our beliefs, we inevitably employ some particular classificatory scheme; and that, as Kuhn has especially emphasized, the fact that different schemes divide the world up in different ways means that none of them can ever be uncontentiously employed to report indisputable facts.[84] This is not to deny that there are facts to be reported. It is only to insist — *pace* Hollis' insistence that there must be 'a bridgehead of true assertions about a shared reality'[85] — that the concepts we employ to report the facts will always serve at the same time to help determine what are to count as facts.

In claiming that our concepts are not forced upon us by the world, but represent what we bring to the world in order to understand it, I may appear to be embracing a thesis of Idealism. But I do not mean to deny the existence of a mind-independent world that furnishes us with observational evidence as the basis of our empirical beliefs. I am only arguing that, as Putnam has put it, there can be no observational evidence which is not to some degree shaped by our concepts and thus by the vocabulary we use to express them.[86]

It is this consideration which, I must confess, seems to me somewhat crassly ignored by such critics of my work as Graham and Shapiro. The latter, for example, accuses me of failing to distinguish those concepts which mask from those which truly reveal 'what is actually going on' in the social world.[87] I can only repeat that it seems to me a gross oversimplification to conceive of our social world as containing unequivocal objects and states of affairs that an adequate system of signs can hope to pick out in such a way that no sensitive observer can fail to see what is actually going on. Any system of signs will serve to single out just those objects and states of affairs which it in turn enables us to denote, while other systems of signs will always be capable of performing that task in different and potentially conflicting ways.

One serious objection to this line of argument, however, has been that it runs the danger of rendering the task of the historian or ethnographer impossible. Keane insists in chapter 12 that I 'overlook' the fact that 'historical interpretation is possible only through the mutual participation of interpreter and interpreted in the medium of a common language' (12:210). Turner raises a similar doubt,[88] while Hollis examines the objection in considerable detail, not only in his criticisms of my own work but also in a number of his other articles.[89]

Hollis' main contention is that, if we cannot 'pair' the terms used by alien peoples with 'counterparts' in our own language, then we cannot embark on the task of translating their utterances.[90] But if we cannot be sure how to translate what they say, we can never hope to identify what they believe.[91] For Hollis, as for many other philosophers of social science, translatability is thus taken to be a condition of intelligibility, with the result that the main issue is held to be that of establishing how translation is possible.[92]

Sometimes this thesis has been stated in a form that makes it seem straightforwardly false. Gunnell, for example, contends that 'to learn a new language is only possible because one already knows a language'.[93] If this were true, no child would ever be able to master its own mother tongue. But even in the form in which Hollis and others have defended it − as a thesis about the need to be able to pair the basic terms of alien languages with equivalents in our own − the claim that intelligibility presupposes translatability strikes me as seriously overstated.

To see why this is so, consider again the primitive example of a Roman writer reporting the incidence of rain. Take, for instance, Tacitus' account in the *Histories* of Vespasian's *coup* against Vitellius. Describing the onset of fighting in Rome, Tacitus remarks that Vitellius' troops failed to keep a proper watch, especially after 'the sudden outbreak of a winter *imber* impeded their hearing and sight'.[94] How are we to translate *imber*? On the one hand, the tone of the passage is notably sardonic, even by Tacitus' standards. Is he suggesting that the Imperial troops allowed themselves to be hampered by nothing more than a shower of sleet? On the other hand, he admits that they found it difficult to hear. Is he conceding that their cause was jeopardized by what we should describe as a real downpour?

The answer is, I think, that there is no determinate way of translating the passage at all. But it does not follow that this renders it unintelligible. The fact that we cannot hope to pair *imber* with an equivalent English term forms no barrier to our learning the denotation of *imber* and the use Tacitus makes of it. It is true that, if we think in globally sceptical terms of trying to do so in the absence of any particular contexts of its occurrence, then perhaps we cannot hope to succeed. But this reason for concluding that we may be cut off from the users of alien languages, though sometimes urged in expositions of Quine's theory of indeterminacy,[95] is I think likely to strike a practising historian as a case of raising a false alarm. The term *imber* in fact appears with some frequency in classical Latin in a highly determinate range of contexts. Even if there were no Latin dictionaries, a sufficiently learned and patient historian could, I think, hope in the end to establish with some confidence how the term was generally used. Such an historian might eventually be able to discover, that is, that Roman writers employed it if and only if they wanted to refer to what a lexicographer would doubtless call the phenomenon of atmospheric vapour falling in a condensed form.

The assumption that intelligibility presupposes the capacity to pair words and sentences in different languages seems in short to be a mistake.

There will often be no prospect of translating terms in an alien language by means of anything approaching counterparts in our own. But this does not prevent us from learning alien terms, and in consequence finding out what discriminations they are used to make. If we can do this, we can eventually hope to understand the applications even of those terms which remain wholly resistant to translation. It is true that we can never hope to tell someone what those terms 'mean' by citing synonyms in our own language. The fact that translation is to this degree indeterminate seem to me inescapable. But the moral of this, as Quine long ago taught, is perhaps that we ought to give up the quest for 'meanings' in such an atomistic sense.[96]

It is perhaps needless to add that I am not pleading for historians to re-enact or re-create the experience of being a Roman historian, a Renaissance demonologist or any other such alien creature.[97] I am only pleading for the historical task to be conceived as that of trying so far as possible to think as they thought and to see things in their way. What this requires is that we should recover the concepts they possessed, the distinctions they drew and the chains of reasoning they followed in their attempts to make sense of their world. What I cannot see, however, is why it should also be thought to require us to to map their distinctions and the terms they used for expressing them on to the distinctions and expressions we happen to use ourselves. Historical understanding is a product of learning to follow what Hacking has called different styles of reasoning; it is not necessarily a matter of being able to translate those styles into less outlandish ones.[98]

Nothing in the above argument is intended to contradict Davidson's observation that the resources of a given language such as English seem adequate for dealing with even the most dramatic cases of purported incommensurability reported by writers like Whorf and Kuhn.[99] As I have emphasized in discussing the term *imber*, the fact that we cannot be sure of translating it satisfactorily does not mean that we cannot hope to describe its range of references by means of something approaching an adequate English periphrasis. The only sense, therefore, in which I am defending the thesis of incommensurability is an undramatic one. I am merely contending that it will always be a mistake for an historian to assume that the task of explicating an alien concept can be reduced to that of finding a counterpart in his or her own language for the term that expresses it.

This still strikes me, however, as a methodological precept of considerable importance. To illustrate why this is so, let me revert to the example I have already considered from Renaissance philosophy: that of the concept of *virtù* as employed by Machiavelli and his contemporaries. Seeking a translation for this term, historians have begun by observing that, even in Machiavelli, persons of courage and prudence are often described as *virtuosi*. This leads to the conclusion that Machiavelli 'sometimes uses *virtù* in a traditional Christian sense'.[100] But Machiavelli also describes a number of talented but wicked men as *virtuosi*. This leads to the suggestion that perhaps the term has in addition 'a different meaning', signifying *skill* or *ability* in political or military affairs.[101] As further anomalous usages are uncovered, however, commentators have generally come to the conclusion that the term appears to have no determinate meaning at all. Rather it bears 'a wide variety of meanings in the writings of Machiavelli', who uses it 'in a great variety of senses'.[102]

As the example indicates, such historians have taken the task of understanding the concept of *virtù* to be that of explicating its 'meanings' by discovering their English counterparts. But the examples also indicates, I hope, what is wrong with this approach. One outcome is that a different and far more promising line of enquiry is automatically closed off. The historian cannot consider the possibility that Machiavelli may have been using the term with perfect consistency to express a concept so alien to our own moral thought that we cannot hope nowadays to capture it except in the form of an extended and rather approximate periphrasis. Perhaps, for example, he used it if and only if he wished to refer to just those qualities, whether moral or otherwise, that he took to be most conducive to military and political success. (As far as I can see, this is in fact the case.) A further and consequential outcome is that a genuinely 'whig' fallacy is almost automatically embraced. Such historians begin with the assumption that, if Machiavelli's use of *virtù* refers to a clear concept, there must be some equivalent terms in English for expressing it. But they soon find themselves disappointed in their quest. As a result, it is all too easy to arrive at the completely unwarranted conclusion that Machiavelli must have been confused, since he appears (as one expert has put it) to be 'innocent of any systematic use of the word'.[103]

It would be easy to multiply examples. (Consider, for instance, the many 'confusions' that historians of philosophy have claimed to find in discussions about causation prior to Hume.) But I hope the general point needs no further emphasis. A term such as *virtù* gains its 'meaning' from its place within an extensive network of beliefs, the filiations of which must be fully traced if the place of any one element within the structure is to be properly understood.[104] Doubtless we can only hope to embark on such a task if there is some considerable overlap between our beliefs and the beliefs of those whom we are trying to investigate. But this overlap may nevertheless be far too exiguous to allow for anything approaching term-by-term translations of the concepts involved. To suppose otherwise is not merely a philosophical error, but one that leads to just the deleterious practical consequences I have tried to illustrate.

Having reached this position, it is possible to suggest an answer to a further and closely connected question that practising historians as well as philosophers of history have repeatedly raised.[105] As Taylor puts it in chapter 13, the question is whether we are ever justified in revising

the language of the people we are studying in such a way as to bring
our descriptions into conflict with those they offered themselves (13:221).

There is one way in which it will obviously be legitimate to go beyond,
even if not to contest, the stock of descriptions available to the people we
are studying. This will be if we wish not merely to identify what they
believed but to comment on the place of those beliefs within some larger
historical pattern or narrative. Among recent philosophers of history, Danto
in particular has emphasized the asymmetries that are bound to result.[106]
When Gibbon remarks, for example, that Boethius was the last Roman who
would have been recognizable as such by Cicero, he offers a comment on
Boethius' beliefs to which Boethius himself could not possibly have assented.
We may nevertheless wish to insist that what Gibbon says of Boethius'
beliefs is true; it would be absurd to reject the description as misleading
simply because Boethius himself was in no position to recognize its truth.

There is a further point at which it will often be legitimate not merely
to go beyond but to repudiate the descriptions offered by the people we are
studying. This will be when we are confident that we have identified what
they believe and wish to go on to explain why they believed it. It would
be a quixotic form of self-denying ordinance to insist that our language
of explanation must at this point match whatever language the people in
question applied or might have applied to themselves. If we wish to furnish
what we take to be the most powerful explanations available to us, we
are bound to employ what we believe to be the best available explanatory
theories and the concepts embodied in them. As a result, our vocabulary
of appraisal and explanation will be almost certain to include a number
of concepts that would have been incomprehensible to the people to whom
we apply them. These will certainly be cases in which – to comment on a
question raised by Taylor in one of his other articles – we shall want to
insist that, even if our resulting explanations conflict with those offered by
the people we are studying, ours must be regarded as the 'superior' ones.[107]
This is to say no more than that one of our beliefs is that our stock of social
explanations has become enriched over the course of recent centuries.

Some intellectual historians have wished to add a third type of case.
What matters, they have claimed, is not the terms in which people happen
to express their beliefs, but the nature of the distinctions they draw
by the use of those terms. This means that, as long as we preserve
their distinctions, it may be positively helpful to revise their terms. For
example, we may wish to say that, although Locke never uses the word
'image' in outlining his theory of ideas, we gain a clearer sense of what
he is talking about if we speak of 'images' where he speaks of 'ideas'.[108]

Although apparently unexceptionable, this proposal strikes me as tread-
ing on far more dangerous ground. The terms we substitute may well
perform the illuminating task of capturing more of the implications of

a theory than its own author may have recognized. But they will almost certainly serve at the same time to import a number of irrelevant and even anachronistic resonances. And as soon as this begins to happen, the intellectual historian will be failing in what I take to be his or her primary task: that of identifying and describing the beliefs to be explained.

I incline to the conclusion, therefore, that where an historian is trying to identify beliefs — as opposed to explaining or commenting on them — it will generally be fatal to revise the terms in which they are expressed. The beliefs in question will only be identifiable as having their precise subject matter by virtue of the particular terms in which the agents themselves express them. To revise those terms will in consequence be to talk about a different set of beliefs.

As an illustration of what I have in mind, let me end by reverting once more to the case of Machiavelli, and specifically to the political argument outlined in his *Discourses*. Historians have regularly discussed Machiavelli's theory in terms of its account of the relationship between the rights and interests of individual citizens and the powers of the state.[109] But Machiavelli himself never employs the terminology of rights (*diritti*) or interests (*interessi*) at any point. The effect of revising his vocabulary in this way has thus been to supply him with a range of alleged beliefs about a number of topics on which he never pronounced. It is of course possible that he possessed the concept of a right even though he never talked about rights. But as I began by stressing, historians have no option but to begin by assuming that what people actually talk about provides us with the most reliable guide to their beliefs. To begin by insisting that they must really be talking about something else is surely to run the highest possible risk of supplying them with beliefs instead of identifying what they believed.

III

The way we live now is such that anyone who defends the type of position I have outlined above is certain sooner or later to find themselves denounced (or commended) as a relativist. Sure enough, my critics have repeatedly thrown this piece of conceptual bric-à-brac at my head. Graham speaks of my 'conservative relativism',[110] Hollis speaks in the present volume even more disturbingly of 'a vicious relativism',[111] while King and Shapiro both suggest that I ought at least to explain more clearly why I think my position is not a relativist one.[112]

Here goes. I have certainly relativized the idea of 'holding true' a given belief. I have asserted that it may well have been rational for Bodin to hold it true that there are witches in league with the devil, even if such beliefs no longer strike us as rationally acceptable. But at no point have I endorsed the thesis of conceptual relativism. I have never asserted that it *was* true that at one time there were witches in league with the devil, even though such a belief would nowadays strike us as false. To put the point generally, I have merely observed that the question of what it may be rational to hold true can vary with the totality of one's beliefs. I have never put forward the reckless and completely different thesis that truth itself can vary in the same way.

I have certainly claimed that, when we say of a given belief that we hold it true, what we are saying is that we find it acceptable. But this is not to claim, as the conceptual relativist does, that there is nothing more to truth than acceptability. Unlike the relativist, I am not trying to offer a definition of truth at all. I am not in general talking about truth; I am talking about what people at different times may have had good reasons by their light for holding true, regardless of whether we ourselves believe that what they held true was in fact the truth.

I have not even suggested that the reasons people give for their beliefs have to be such that an historian who recovers them need find them so much as recognizable as reasons for holding true the beliefs concerned. Historians frequently study what Hollis calls ritual beliefs, cases in which the contents of the beliefs under investigation may remain unintelligible.[113] The most we can hope to do in such circumstances is to place the beliefs in question within an appropriate explanatory context of other beliefs.[114] We can certainly hope as a result to indicate why someone operating from within that context might have come to assent to the propositions we ourselves find unintelligible. But we cannot hope to do more. In such cases we discharge our task as interpreters if we can explain why, say, Aquinas believed that God is at once three persons and an indivisible Being.[115] We need not suppose that we have to be able in addition to perform what may be the impossible feat of explaining what exactly it was that Aquinas believed. To paraphrase Hollis, the aim of the historian is to produce as much understanding as possible, a task not to be confused with producing converts.[116]

I am convinced, in short, that the importance of truth for the kind of historical enquiries I am considering has been exaggerated. I take this to be a product of the fact that too much of the meta-historical discussion has hinged around the analysis of scientific beliefs. In such cases the question of truth may perhaps be of some interest. But in most of the cases investigated by historians of ideas, the suggestion that we need to consider the truth of the beliefs under examination is I think likely to strike an historian as strange. Take for example one of the cases I have already discussed: Machiavelli's fervently held belief that mercenary armies always jeopardize political liberty. Perhaps there is nothing to stop us from asking whether this is true. But the effect of doing so will be somewhat analogous to asking whether the king of France is bald. The best answer seems to be that the question does not really arise.

I am not of course adopting the position, sometimes ascribed to Wittgenstein, that we are *precluded* from asking about the truth of such beliefs on the ground that they can only be understood as part of a form of life that may be ultimately no less cognitively justifiable than our own.[117] On the contrary, that way of stating the thesis of conceptual relativism strikes me as self-refuting as it stands, embodying as it does the statement of a preferred point of view while denying that any such point of view can be attained.[118] I am merely insisting (to revert to my example) that our task as historians is to try to recover Machiavelli's point of view; and that, in order to discharge this task, what we need to employ is solely the concept of rational acceptability, not that of truth.

Some historians have admittedly sought to reintroduce the question of truth by arguing that their findings actually serve to underpin the thesis of conceptual relativism. Kuhn has been widely if mistakenly interpreted in this way, but the clearest positive statement of this claim has been put forward by Barnes and Bloor. As we have seen, they think they have established from their historical case-studies that all our beliefs have social causes, and that all such causes operate in such a way as to distort our capacity to get in touch with the objects of our beliefs. From this they have inferred in their latest theoretical pronouncement that the only possible judge of the truth of our beliefs must be whatever consensus over norms and standards may happen to prevail in what they call our local culture.[119]

I cannot see that the generalization extracted by Barnes and Bloor from their research bears on the thesis of conceptual relativism at all. Suppose it is true that the social causation of our beliefs is such as to mask their objects from us. The obvious inference is that we have no grounds for holding those beliefs to be true, not that we have satisfactory grounds for holding them to be true according to some relativized notion of truth.[120]

By contrast with Barnes and Bloor, it seems to me that if the practice of intellectual history serves to suggest any theoretical insights, these must be of an anti-relativist kind. I infer this from the fact that the truth of conceptual relativism and the practice of intellectual history appear to be incompatible.

The point I have in mind here is again an obvious and familiar one. If we are to use our ancestors' utterances as a guide to identifying their underlying beliefs, it is indispensable that we should hold in common with them a number of assumptions at least about the process of belief-formation itself.

The most basic of these assumptions – to which I have already alluded – is the one stressed above all by Quine.[121] We must be able to assume, in advance of our historical enquiries, that our ancestors shared at least some of our beliefs about the importance of consistency and coherence. We must be able, for example, to assume their acceptance of the principle that, if one affirms the truth of a given proposition, then one cannot at the same time affirm the truth of the denial of the proposition.[122] Beyond this, we also need to share with our ancestors some assumptions about the process of using our existing beliefs to arrive at others. Even if we can identify some of their individual beliefs, we may still find our efforts at understanding defeated unless we can make some fairly strong assumptions about the character of the reasoning they must have employed in fitting their beliefs together.[123]

It can easily be made to look like pure dogmatism to insist on such anti-relativist considerations in an *a priori* style. But the need to do so can I think be readily vindicated if we simply recall the nature of the historian's task. The primary aim is to use our ancestors' utterances as a guide to the identification of their beliefs. But if they display no concern for consistency, if they employ no recognizable modes of inference, then we shall have no means of marking off which of their utterances are to be classed as instances of the speech-acts of stating or affirming beliefs. If they are willing, for example, both to affirm and deny the truth of some particular proposition, then we can never hope to say what they believe about that proposition at all. As a number of philosophers have insisted, following in Quine's wake, the idea of holding rational beliefs and the idea of holding beliefs that are mainly true by our lights certainly come together at this point.[124]

This is not to assert that the idea of a 'pre-logical mentality' – an idea ritually cited by philosophers in this context – is necessarily an impossibility. (Although I confess that, for reasons emphasized by Davidson, I cannot see how such a people could in fact have any beliefs.) It is only to assert that, if an historian were really to encounter a people for whom it caused no discomfort to affirm and deny the same propositions, there would be no prospect of reporting what they believed. Nor am I denying that historians may well encounter abnormal forms of discourse in which the law of non-contradiction is deliberately flouted. I am only saying that such forms of discourse must be abnormal, and parasitic on recognizable forms, if we are to understand the linguistic community in which they take place. Nor am I even denying that agents engaged in normal discourse may turn out to have a number of beliefs about their beliefs which, strictly speaking, reveal inconsistencies.[125] I am only saying that an historian will be unable to grasp the content of any beliefs that turn out to be contradictory in and of themselves.

These conclusions can also be stated in the form of a further method-/ological precept. If as historians we come upon contradictory beliefs, we should start by assuming that we must in some way have misunderstood or mistranslated some of the propositions by which they are expressed.

As a simple instance of what I have in mind, consider yet a further example from Machiavelli's political works. In his *Discourses* Machiavelli affirms that liberty is possible only under a *repubblica*.[126] But he also affirms that Rome lived *in libertà* under her early kings.[127] What then does he believe? Does he or does he not think that liberty and monarchy are incompatible?

Historians have tended to reply that he seems to be confused: he accepts but also denies that liberty is only possible under a republic.[128] I am suggesting, however, that before we endorse such a conclusion we ought first to consider whether we may not in some way have misunderstood what he said. Sure enough, if we investigate the full range of contexts in which the term *repubblica* occurs, we discover that in Machiavelli the term is used to denote any form of government under which the laws may be said to foster the common good. It follows that for Machiavelli the question of whether a monarchy can be a *repubblica* is not an empty paradox, as it would be for us, but a deep question of statecraft. The question is whether kings can ever by relied upon to pass only such laws as will serve the common good. This gives us an alternative reading: Machiavelli is telling us that, under Romulus and his successors, the laws of Rome served the common good, so that the government, although monarchical in form, was an instance of a *repubblica*. Since this has the effect of resolving the contradiction, I am suggesting that this is also the interpretation we ought to prefer.

But what if the initial contradiction had refused to yield to any such re-interpretative efforts? I have already given my answer: at that point we have to admit that we cannot say what Machiavelli believed at all. It is true that some intellectual historians, especially followers of Leo Strauss, have taken this to be naive. They have instructed us instead to treat such apparent contradictions as clues to the presence of some esoteric doctrine still to be elicited. But I have already tried, in the article reprinted in this volume as chapter 2, to explain why this does not seem to me a very sensible way to proceed. Admittedly I can now see, re-reading my own argument, why it has struck certain admirers of Strauss, such as Tarcov, as less than completely decisive. But it hardly seems appropriate to restate my views at greater length, if only because this aspect of Strauss's writings has by now been so thoroughly discredited. I am content to end by reiterating the point of substance: that to treat all interpretations as failures unless they yield complete intelligibility is to adopt an unduly optimistic view of what we can hope to bring back with us from the foreign lands of the past.

ON MEANING AND SPEECH-ACTS

I should hate to find myself in agreement with the kind of critic who denies the poet supreme authority regarding his work – seeing nothing in his explanation of a poem, for example, but an attempt to limit its suggestiveness – and for this reason I should contend that if an author has read a passage fiercely, ironically, humorously, sadly,

then for ever after to read it softly, idealistically, seriously and gaily
will be a smart bit of wrong-headedness, like *Hamlet* in space dress.

Philip Larkin, *Required Writing*

I

Despite the scepticism voiced by a number of my critics, I persist in
believing that Austin's analysis of speech-acts provides us with a convenient
way of making a point of fundamental importance about the understanding
of utterances and hence the interpretation of texts. The theory reminds us
that, if we wish to understand any serious utterance, we need to be able
to grasp something over and above the sense and reference of the terms
used to express it. To cite Austin's own formula, we need in addition
to find a means of recovering what the agent may have been *doing* in
saying what was said, and hence of understanding what the agent may
have meant by issuing an utterance with just that sense and reference.[129]

The idea that speech is also action, that to say something is always and *eo
ipso* to do something, had of course been emphasized by many philosophers
of language before Austin. The central insight is most economically
conveyed by Wittgenstein's remark that 'words are also deeds'.[130] But the
abiding value of Austin's formulation lies in the fact that he furnished a
means of speaking precisely about the two separable dimensions of language
– for they are nothing less than that – which we need to consider if we wish
to understand serious utterances.[131] The interpreter must of course turn
first to the dimension on which I have so far concentrated, the dimension
conventionally described by speaking about the meanings of words and
sentences. But what the interpreter also needs to grasp, in Austin's
admirable formulation, is the particular *force* with which a given utterance
(with a given meaning) may have been issued on a particular occasion.[132]

Austin tried further to clarify his point by introducing a neologism
to distinguish the precise sense of 'the use of language' in which he was
principally interested. He stressed that, in speaking about the force of an
utterance, he was pointing to what an agent may have been doing *in* saying
what was said. He sought to distinguish this dimension from another whole
range of things we may be doing in using words. This further range incor-
porates the things we may succeed in bringing about (whether intentionally
or otherwise) as a result of speaking with a certain force. To separate the
question of what we may be doing *in* saying something from what we
may bring about *by* saying something, Austin proposed that we speak of
the illocutionary as opposed to the perlocutionary force of utterances.[133]

To illustrate the refinements Austin was thus able to introduce into
Wittgenstein's suggested analysis of 'meaning' in terms of 'the use of words',

consider the following dummy example. (I take it directly from my discussion in chapter 4, since I can think of no quicker way to make clear what is at stake.) A policeman sees a skater on a pond and says 'The ice over there is very thin'. The policeman says something and the words mean something. To understand the episode, we obviously need to know the meaning of the words. But we also need to know what the policeman was *doing in* saying what he (or she) said. For example, the policeman may have been *warning* the skater; the utterance may have been issued on the given occasion with the (illocutionary) force of warning. Finally, the policeman may at the same time have succeeded in bringing about some further (perlocutionary) consequences *by* saying what was said. For example, he may have succeeded in persuading or frightening or perhaps merely amusing the skater.

Austin's chief aim was to clarify the idea of 'the use of language' in communication. So he placed his main emphasis on the fact that speakers are able to exploit the dimension of illocutionary force in order – as the title of his lectures puts it – to do things with words. As a result, he had rather little to say about the nature of the relationship between the linguistic dimension of illocutionary force and the capacity of speakers to exploit that dimension in order to perform the range of speech-acts – and especially illocutionary acts – in the classification of which Austin was principally interested.

I take it, however, that the right way to think about this relationship is to focus on the fact that, as Austin always stressed, to speak with a certain illocutionary force is normally to perform an *act* of a certain kind, to engage in a piece of deliberate and voluntary behaviour. As this suggests, what serves to connect the illocutionary dimension of language with the performance of illocutionary acts must be – as with all voluntary acts – the intentions of the agent concerned.

Consider again the speech-act of warning someone. To perform that particular act, we must not only issue a particular utterance with the form and force of a warning. We must at the same time mean or intend the utterance as a warning and mean it to be taken as a warning by way of its being recognized as an instance of just that intentional act. As Austin put it with his customary exactitude, to recover the intended illocutionary force of a given utterance, and thus the nature of the illocutionary act performed by the agent in saying what was said, what we need to understand is the way in which the given utterance, on the given occasion, 'ought to have been taken'.[134]

It is true that Austin himself wavered on this point. When he first introduced the concept of an illocution, he certainly suggested that the question of whether someone has performed the act, say, of warning is essentially a question about how they meant their utterance to be understood.[135] But he assumed that the 'uptake' of illocutionary acts required the presence of such strong linguistic conventions that he later appeared to suggest that such conventions, rather than the intentions of speakers, must be definitive of illocutionary acts.[136]

Nevertheless, I still think it essentially correct to expand Austin's analysis in the direction subsequently taken by Strawson[137] and Searle,[138] and later by Schiffer and Holdcroft.[139] It seems to me, that is, that if we wish to furnish the definition of illocutionary acts which Austin failed to provide, we need to take seriously their status as acts and think about the kinds of intentions that have to go into their successful performance.[140] This is not of course to deny that the exact character of these complex and recursive intentions might become (as threatened to happen at one point) a subject of endless philosophical debate. It is only to assert that the right kind of analysis must be along those lines. So I see no reason to doubt the central claim I seek to defend in chapter 4 of the present volume: that to perform an illocutionary act will always be equivalent to speaking (or writing) with a certain intended illocutionary force.

Although my remarks so far have been expository, it is I think vital to add that we run a danger of missing their significance if we think of them as an exposition of something called 'the theory of speech-acts'. It seems to me seriously misleading to describe Wittgenstein or Austin as proposing a theory in the sense of putting forward an hypothesis about language. Their achievement is better described as that of finding a way of describing, and thereby of calling to our attention, a dimension and hence a resource of language that every speaker and writer exploits all the time, and which we need to identify whenever we wish to understand any serious utterance.

To express the point in this style is not just to insist on a preferred *façon de parler*. It is rather to insist that we shall miss the relevance of speech-act analysis if we think of it (as several contributors to this volume are content to do) as just another bit of fancy philosophical jargon we can brush aside if we happen not to like the sound of it. The terminology I have been describing points to a fact about language. We may of course wish to deny that it performs that task adequately. But we can hardly deny the fact itself – that anyone who issues a serious utterance will always be doing something as well as saying something, and doing it in virtue of saying what is said. That this is a fact is underlined by our language itself. It contains a wide range of verbs the precise function of which is to enable us to make explicit, in order to avoid misunderstanding, what exactly we see ourselves as doing in saying what we say. Thus we can subjoin comments like: I am warning you; I am ordering you (or else: I am not issuing orders, I am only only advising/suggesting/telling you something). The problem of interpretation arises in part because we do not generally trouble, even in such everyday cases, to make explicit exactly what we see ourselves as doing, still less in the case of such enormously complex acts of communication as those which normally attract the attention of literary critics and intellectual historians. It may indeed be impossible to recover more than a small fraction of the things that Plato, say, was doing in *The Republic*. My point is only that the extent to which we can hope to understand *The Republic* depends in part on the extent to which we can recover them.

II

I should now like to examine the bearing of these considerations upon the business of interpreting texts. Before I can do so, however, I first need to meet a serious objection raised by several of my critics. I cannot hope, they claim, to draw from the theory of linguistic action the implications I have proposed, since my proposals are based on a series of misunderstandings of the theory itself.

My account is held to be defective in two distinct ways. First of all, two contrasting errors have been detected in my exposition of the connections between the intentions of speakers and the force of their utterances. The first of these, Graham declares in chapter 8, stems from my assumption that intentions and illocutions are 'indissolubly linked'. This means, he argues, that I fail to recognize that illocutionary intentions may be present in the absence of the corresponding illocutionary act.[141]

Graham's criticism is ambiguously formulated. His initial complaint is that, by identifying what a speaker is doing 'with what he means or intends to be doing', I fail to acknowledge that such intentions may sometimes remain unrealized (8:151). Femia makes a similar point (9:157, 159). I may fail, for example, to execute my intention to warn you of something, simply because I may fail to perform the corresponding illocutionary act of bringing it about that you are warned.

It would certainly be absurd to deny that an agent can form the intention to speak with a certain force and then fail to perform the intended act. If I form the intention to warn you and drop dead before I can get the words out, then my intended act of warning will not be performed. But I have never denied this rather obvious fact. I have tried to make it clear, especially in the article reprinted as chapter 3, that I am not concerned at all with intentions in the sense of plans to act. I am solely concerned with intentions *in* acting, with intentional descriptions of action, and thus with the question of what an agent may have intended or meant by speaking or writing in a certain way.[142]

Femia seems to have missed the point; but Graham proceeds to reformulate the criticism in a more interesting way. He suggests that what I overlook is the fact that someone 'may issue an utterance meaning it as a warning but fail to warn' (9:152). Even if I speak or write with the intended force of a warning, I may still fail to perform the corresponding illocutionary act of bringing it about that you are warned.

This contention certainly seems true to Austin's original account, and even more clearly to Strawson's elaboration of it. Austin thought it essential to the successful performance of an act, say, of warning that the agent should secure 'uptake' of the act *as* an act of warning.[143] Austin makes it clear, moreover, and Strawson makes it even clearer, that this notion of 'uptake' depends upon a particular analysis of the descriptive element in the concept of action, an analysis that Graham's criticism in turn assumes to be correct.

This analysis itself is a standard one, originally Aristotelian in provenance. The basic idea is that any voluntary action must be capable of being represented by the formula 'bringing it about that p'. The value assigned to 'p' must in turn be such as to indicate the new state of affairs brought about as a result of the action.[144] To perform an action is thus to produce some discernibly new end-state, one that can be represented not merely as a consequence of, but as an indication of, the successful performance of the action. As Austin himself puts it, 'I cannot be said to have warned an audience unless it hears what I say and takes what I say in a certain sense'.[145] Something must be newly true of my audience for my act to have been performed; I must at least succeed in altering its state of understanding, even if I do not succeed in affecting its will.

It is this familiar analysis, however, which seems to me defective.[146] It is of course true that I cannot be said to warn you unless I bring it about that p (that you are warned). But this is only to put the description through a passive transformation; it remains to assign a value to 'p'. And here it seems to me (*pace* Austin as well as Graham) that there are very many locutions describing actions in which the only value we can hope to assign to 'p' – the state of affairs brought about by the action – is that it *is* the state of affairs brought about by the action. To put the point more elegantly, as Davidson has done, there are many cases in which 'p' merely designates an event, not a newly true state of affairs which can be represented as the consequence of the successful performance of the act.[147]

This certainly seems to apply to the case of warning. To warn someone is to point out or advert to the fact that they are in danger. To succeed in performing the illocutionary act of warning is thus to succeed in adverting to that fact. This being so, it makes no sense to suggest, as Graham does, that someone might succeed in speaking with the intended illocutionary force of a warning and yet fail to perform the corresponding illocutionary act of bringing it about that someone is warned. For to bring it about that someone is warned is simply to succeed in adverting to the fact that they are in danger.

I now turn to the contrasting mistake I am said to have made in analysing the relations between intentions and illocutionary acts. Graham argues that, just as there can be illocutionary intentions without corresponding acts, so 'I may perform an illocutionary act in the absence of an appropriate intention' (8:152). Shapiro and Boucher have both put forward a similar criticism. As Shapiro expresses it, my 'identification of illocutionary force with intention' leads me to overlook the class of what Graham calls 'unintentional illocutionary acts'.[148]

I cannot see that these critics have done anything to substantiate their point. Shapiro and Boucher merely follow Graham, while Graham merely offers a single example, the highly conventional one of 'redoubling' in the game of bridge (8:152). Even this, moreover, fails to support his conclusion that we have to recognize a class of unintentional illocutionary acts. The example does not indicate that, without having the intention of redoubling, I may nevertheless perform that illocutionary act. Rather it indicates something about the range of cases in which the illocutionary force of an utterance may be altogether determined by the meaning of the utterance and the context of its occurrence. It shows that there may be cases in which an utterance may properly be claimed to carry a certain illocutionary force, even if the corresponding illocutionary act of speaking with that intended force was not performed.

To insist on this point is by no means to fall into the absurdity of supposing, as Graham believes, that it is impossible to warn someone unintentionally. It is only to insist that, if I warn someone unintentionally, this will not be because I have performed the illocutionary act of warning, but unintentionally. To perform the illocutionary act of warning, as I have argued above, is always to speak with the form and intended force of a warning; the act is constituted as the act of warning by the complex intentions that go into its performance. The reason why it is nevertheless possible to warn someone unintentionally is that there may be circumstances in which the issuing of a certain utterance will inevitably be taken as a case of adverting to danger. In such circumstances the agent will be understood to have spoken, and will in fact have spoken, with the illocutionary force of a warning. This will remain the case even if the agent spoke without any intention of warning, and in consequence failed to perform the corresponding illocutionary act.

As this suggests, Graham's example underpins rather than undermines my contention that illocutionary acts must be identified in terms of the intentions of the agents who perform them. Graham claims that it may be possible to speak with the form and force of 'redoubling' in the absence of any such intention. But this is to say that, although the utterance may have carried that illocutionary force, the absence of the relevant kinds of intention on the part of the speaker meant that the corresponding illocutionary act was not performed. That this can happen is precisely my point.

Graham and Shapiro have failed to recognize what I take to be the distinction between illocutionary forces and illocutionary acts. The former term points to a resource of language; the latter to the capacity of agents to exploit it in communication. The illocutionary acts we perform are identified, like all voluntary acts, by our intentions; but the illocutionary forces carried by our utterances are mainly determined by their meaning and context. It is for these reasons that it can readily happen that, in performing an illocutionary act, my utterance may at the same time carry, though without my intending it, a much wider range of illocutionary force.[149] (For example, although I may intend only to warn you, my utterance may at the same time have the force of informing you of something.) But this is only to say that, due to the richness of our language, many and perhaps most of my utterances will carry some element of unintended illocutionary force.[150] It is not in the least to point to a class of unintentional illocutionary acts.

I now turn to the other main criticism levelled at my understanding of speech-act analysis. This relates to my argument in chapter 4 about the connections between illocutionary redescription and explanation. Suppose we come to understand (to continue with my example) that the policeman who says 'The ice over there is very thin' is warning the skater. This provides us with an illocutionary redescription of the policeman's utterance. But at the same time it supplies us with an understanding of the episode that we previously lacked. Graham quotes the inference I drew (8:150): not only do we understand what the policeman's utterance means, such that we can give an account of what he said; we also understand what the policeman meant or intended by what he said, such that we can give an account of why he said it.

When I originally put forward this argument, I was partly interested in its relevance to the debate then raging about the non-causal explanation of action. Some of Wittgenstein's disciples had argued that actions can be non-causally explained because motives, which explain actions, are not causes. Some of their opponents had retorted that motive-explanations are in fact causal, and had drawn the inference that there cannot be any non-causal explanations of action.[151] What the speech-act case suggested, I tried to argue, was that even if motives are causes, there can nevertheless be non-causal explanations of action.

Graham objects that such illocutionary redescriptions only provide us with additional information about what an agent may have been doing; they do not provide us with any additional information about why he or she may have been doing it (8:154). Hollis had earlier offered a similar criticism, as had Freundlieb. The point on which they all converge, to quote Graham's summary, is that 'what is unacceptable' is my suggestion that an illocutionary redescription 'answers any question "why?"' (8:154).

I now see that I misstated the point I was trying to make. As Freundlieb emphasizes in his analysis of my example, the illocutionary redescription of the policeman's utterance 'is not an explanation of the speaker's act at all but an explanation of why it publicly counts as a warning'.[152] What is explained, in short, is not the occurrence of the act but the character of the utterance. If we wish to explain the occurrence of the act, as Hollis correctly adds, we have no option but to go on to enquire into the agent's motives for performing it (7:139, 141, 146).

Nevertheless, my original thesis about the explanation of action stands. Suppose some bystanders were puzzled by the episode of the skater. One natural source of puzzlement might be the precise point or significance of the policeman's utterance. To inform them that it was meant as a warning would then be to remove their puzzlement. But to say that a sense of puzzlement (as opposed to a misconception) about a state of affairs has been removed is to say that an explanation has been provided. So there seems every reason to insist that illocutionary redescriptions function as explanations. On the other hand, such explanations are not causal. They are purely redescriptive, and cite no antecedents of the acts they explain. Hence my thesis stands: even if motives for action are causes of the actions they motivate, there can nevertheless be non-causal explanations of action.[153]

Nor is Graham justified in his further objection that such explanations leave us 'none the wiser about why anything occurred' (8:155). It is true that we still need to identify the policeman's motive for warning the skater. But the redescription of his utterance as an act of warning certainly leaves us considerably the wiser as to why he may have acted. For the motives he could in principle have had for issuing a warning are very different from the motives he could have had for issuing the same utterance with the intended force, say, of a criticism of the skater's recklessness. To recover an illocutionary description is always to trench upon, and thereby to circumscribe, the range of motives for the sake of which the agent may have acted. Their recovery may thus be said to constitute an indispensable step along the road to explaining why the act in question was performed.

Hollis wants me to go on to say whether I think motives are in fact the causes of the actions they motivate. Davidson and others have made it fashionable to suppose they are,[154] and I have generally been content to assume that they are right. It is true that I remain unclear about the nature of these alleged causes and their mode of operation, especially as it is evident that we cannot hope to identify them as constant conjunctions of their effects. Nor have I found my puzzlement much alleviated by the somewhat assertive manner in which Davidson and his followers have chosen to present their case. Fortunately, however, nothing in my own argument hinges upon the outcome of this long-standing debate. So it seems to me (although I shall disappoint Hollis by saying so) that the wisest course of action must be to leave it at that.

III

I now turn to those critics whose doubts have centred not on my understanding of speech-act analysis itself, but rather on my assumption that this type of analysis has something important to teach us about the interpretation of texts.

The criticisms they have advanced turn out to be based to a depressingly large extent on a failure to understand what I have said. It seems to me, for example, that Femia's discussion of my alleged views, in chapter 9, is almost entirely given over to attacking a series of positions I have never sought to defend. I should not have found it congenial to go over this ground again, so I am especially grateful to find that Jenssen's recent article about Pocock's and my work has rendered this task unnecessary.[155] Jenssen has generously rescued me from all the cruder misinterpretations to which my essays have given rise, and has in addition carried the argument forward into new areas with an enviable clarity and force.

I cannot hope, however, simply to bow out there. For I find that, even among the most careful and sympathetic contributors to the present volume, I have been misunderstood at a number of points. This must certainly be due to my own incapacities as an expositor. I am therefore very glad to have the chance to indicate where these misunderstandings have arisen, especially as this will enable me to restate my case in a somewhat different and I hope a less confusing way.

Minogue, for example, treats my approach as an instance of mere mystification. I speak of the 'decoding' of utterances, 'as if communication involved a special form of scrambling to prevent its meaning being known to outsiders' (10:188). Minogue is certainly justified in sneering at my jargon. But he misses the point when he complains that the meaning of an utterance like 'The ice over there is very thin' stands in no need of decoding. I have never suggested otherwise. When I speak about the need to decode the meaning of such episodes, I am referring to the need to decode what the speaker may have meant by saying what was said. Was the utterance (the meaning of which is certainly clear) meant as a warning, a criticism, a reproach, perhaps only a joke, or what? Even in such an oversimplified case, the answer will never be clear on the surface. And as soon as we turn to cases of any complexity, 'decoding' hardly seems such a bad term to describe the procedures which will become indispensable if we are to understand what was meant by what was said.

Behind Minogue's confusion there lurks, I discover to my consternation, a much wider and more radical misunderstanding of my argument. Within the present volume, it emerges most clearly in the contributions by Femia and Keane. Femia takes me to be saying that 'historicity demands that we focus on what an author consciously intended to say' (9:157). Keane adds that the sheer naiveté of this commitment prevents me from recognizing the force of 'the commonplace distinction between what authors intend to say and what their texts mean' (12:207). Several other critics have converged on the same point. Seidman construes my 'intentionalist thesis' as the claim that 'textual meaning' must be identified 'with the particular intentions of the author', so that 'to decode the meaning of the text the interpreter must recover the author's intention'.[156] Gunnell similarly believes that my aim is 'to develop hypotheses about what an author intended to say and therefore what a text means',[157] while LaCapra declares that I take the entire object of intellectual history to be 'the study of what authors meant to say'.[158]

I certainly wish to cleave to the figure of the author, and I certainly think it indispensable to the interpretation of texts to find out what their authors may have meant. But I have done my best – though I have clearly failed – to distinguish two separable questions that can be raised about authorial intentionality. Let me try again.

One is whether the understanding of the meaning of a text requires us to focus on what its author intended to say rather than on what the text itself may be said to mean. Some theorists, including Hirsch, Juhl and others, have of course defended this commitment. They have argued that, in Hirsch's formulation, to understand 'the meaning of a text' is to understand 'what the text says', which in turn requires us to recover 'the saying of the author'.[159] Their thesis, as Hirsch summarizes it, is thus that the 'verbal meaning' of a text 'requires the determining will' of an author, and that this is what the interpreter must concentrate on trying to recover.[160]

According to my critics, this is the thesis I endorse. As Jenssen has already pointed out, however, this is scarcely a thesis I engage with at all;[161] and in so far as I have considered it, I have largely endorsed the anti-intentionalist case.

I agree that, where a text says something other than what its author intended to say, we are bound to concede that this is nevertheless what the text *says*, and thus that it bears a meaning other than its author intended.[162] This is not perhaps a very subtle point on which to insist with as much vehemence as has recently become fashionable. But if the question is seen, in a sufficiently myopic style, as one about the understanding of texts, then of course the point must stand. It would certainly be amazing if all the meanings, implications, connotations and resonances that an ingenious interpreter might legitimately claim to find in a given text could in turn be shown to reflect its author's intentions at every point. And it would be a straightforward mistake to infer that, if we came upon some obviously unintended element, we should have to exclude it from our account of the meaning of the *text*.

As I vainly strove to make clear, however, in the essay reprinted here as chapter 3, I have only wished to say as much about this issue as will enable me to distinguish it from a second and different question we can raise about authorial intentionality. This is the question of what an author may have meant or intended by an utterance (whatever may be the meaning of the utterance itself). To put the point in the jargon I have been using, my principal concern has not been with meaning but rather with the performance of illocutionary acts.

As I have already argued, the question of what a speaker or writer may have meant by saying something arises in the case of all serious utterances. But it poses the most acute problems for interpretation in two main types of case. One is that of irony. Here it seems indisputable that our understanding depends on our capacity to recover what the author intended or meant by what was said. But at the risk of some repetition it is perhaps worth spelling out the way in which this is so. For it seems to me that the argument has been misstated by those, like Juhl, who have wished to uphold the thesis about authorial intentionality I have just considered and set aside.

Juhl and others have argued that the phenomenon of irony offers the clearest evidence in favour of their claim that we need to recover an author's intentions if we wish to understand 'the meaning of a work', the meaning of what was said.[163] But when someone speaks or writes ironically, it may well be that there is no difficulty at all about understanding the meaning of what was said. It may well be that everything was said in virtue of its ordinary meaning. Where there is a difficulty about the understanding of such utterances, it generally arises not because of any doubts about meaning, but rather because of some doubt as to whether (as we colloquially put it) the speaker really meant what was said.

The problem of detecting irony arises, in short, not as a problem about meaning but illocutionary acts. The ironic speaker issues an utterance with a certain meaning. At the same time, the speaker appears to perform an illocutionary act of a kind that falls within the range conventionally performed by such utterances. To take an immortal example, the form and apparent force of what Defoe says in 'The Shortest Way with the Dissenters' is that of suggesting, recommending or calling for a particular course of action. (That religious dissenters be suppressed and preferably executed.)

Reading Defoe's simple proposal, however, we begin to doubt whether the standard way in which the meaning of an utterance helps us to decode its intended illocutionary force applies in this particular case. We come to see that Defoe is making a comment about the very idea of issuing such an utterance with the intended force that a mere inspection of its meaning might tempt us to assign to it. The utterance has the undoubted form and apparent force of a recommendation, even of a demand. But Defoe is not performing the corresponding illocutionary act. On the contrary, his illocutionary intention is that of ridiculing the intolerance that would be embodied in performing it.

This, then, is one type of case in which it is I think indispensable to recover the intentions of authors if we wish to understand their utterances. But the reason for this is not, *pace* Juhl, that we shall otherwise fail to understand the meaning of what was said. The meaning of what Defoe said is perfectly clear. What he said was that religious dissent should be ranked among capital offences.[164] What this means is that religious dissent should be ranked among capital offences. The reason we need to recover Defoe's intentions is rather that we shall otherwise fail to understand what he was doing in issuing this utterance. The intentions we need to recover are the illocutionary intentions that went into his act of ridiculing and thereby questioning contemporary religious intolerance. They are the intentions we may be said to have recovered when we come to appreciate that this is how he meant his utterance (with its given meaning) to be understood.

There is another and vastly broader range of cases in which the recovery of this form of intentionality raises special difficulties. This is where the speaker or writer issues a serious utterance, but fails to make it clear how exactly the utterance is to be taken or understood. This may of course be because (as in the case of irony) the speaker lacks the standard motive we normally possess for making explicit the intended force of our utterances. But the most usual reason will rather be that the meaning of the utterance itself, together with the context of its occurrence, are such that the speaker feels no doubt about the capacity of the audience to secure 'uptake' of the intended illocutionary act.

Such confidence is generally well-founded in the case of ordinary and everyday communications. So we usually regard it as over-emphatic to employ what Austin called explicit performative formulae for making manifest how exactly we intend our utterances to be taken.[165] Even here, however, we may sometimes feel the need to reassure our intended audience. (This prompts us to say things like 'When I said that the ice over there is very thin, I wasn't criticizing you, I was only issuing a warning.') And as soon as we turn to more complex cases, especially historical utterances where we are no longer the intended audience, such problems of 'uptake' can readily become acute. In these instances it may be almost impossibly hard to recover what the writer was doing in saying what was said. But the point on which I have been insisting all along is that, unless we can somehow manage to do so, we shall remain cut off from an entire dimension of understanding.

To summarize: I have tried to distinguish two questions about the meaning and understanding of texts. One is the question of what the text means, the other the question of what its author may have meant. I have argued that, if we are to understand a text, both questions must be answered. It is true, however, that while these questions are separable, they are not in the end separate. If I am to understand what someone meant or intended by what they said, I must first of all be sure that the meaning of what they said was itself intended. For otherwise there will be nothing that they meant by it. As I have tried to insist, however, this must at all costs be distinguished from the thesis that the meaning of a text can be identified with what its author intended. Any text must include an intended meaning; and the recovery of that meaning certainly constitutes a precondition of understanding what its author may have meant. But any text of any complexity will always contain far more meaning – what Ricoeur has called surplus meaning[166] – than even the most vigilant and imaginative author could possibly have intended to put into it. So I am far from supposing that the meanings of texts are to be identified with the intentions of their authors; what must be identified with such intentions is only what their authors meant by them.

Several of my critics have continued to shake their heads over the sadly old-fashioned air of this commitment. Gunnell refers me to Gadamer's *Truth and Method*, with its claim that the yardstick of authorial intentionality is simply not available.[167] Seidman, as well as Keane in his contribution to the present volume (12:206), both remind me of Ricoeur's analogous point that in the case of historical texts new meanings will be continuously generated. I am held to have overlooked the implication that, with a text of any complexity, the position will soon be reached where the question of what its author may have intended to say and the question of what the text can legitimately be taken to mean will prove to have completely different answers. My critics agree with Ricoeur (although the conclusion hardly follows) that once this point is reached, what matters most will always be the 'public meaning' of the text.[168]

It has proved a short step from emphasizing the public character of meaning to abandoning any concern with authorial intentionality. One way of making the move has simply been to disavow any interest in what authors may have meant in favour of explaining what their texts mean to us. The study of texts thus becomes a purely consumer-orientated study of 'reader response'.[169] A yet more radical step has been to stress that authors merely follow 'discursive practices', and thus to call in question the very idea of an 'author': the object of historical analysis becomes 'the regularity of discursive practices' themselves.[170] This finally brings us to the point, interesting to connoisseurs of the more decadent forms of individualism, at which any concern with the determination of meaning is simply dismissed. The reason usually given is not so much that it cannot be determined; it is rather that any attempt to do so will interfere with what Derrida calls 'the joyous affirmation of the freeplay of the world'.[171]

There are two threads of argument here that need to be disentangled. Some of these theorists dismiss the study of intentions chiefly because they find them of no interest. They claim to have found something more important to investigate. But others claim that the attempt to recover intentions is actually misconceived. They first suggest that the idea of recovering what an author may have intended or meant to say provides us with an unattainable or at least an inappropriate guide to the meaning of what is said. And from this they infer that the recovery of authorial intentionality is irrelevant to the understanding of texts.[172]

I have no objection to the first of these commitments. I remain unrepentant in my belief that, if we are interested in recovering the historical identity of texts, we are bound to interest ourselves in what their authors meant. But if we are interested in something quite different – in the study of their impact upon us, or in the free play of signifiers – then there may indeed be no good reason to trouble about intentionality at all.

By contrast, the second argument strikes me as fallacious. As a result, I am far from agreeing with Gunnell and Keane that, had I paid more attention to it, I should have come to see that my emphasis on authorial intentionality is a mistake. On the contrary, it seems to me that the theory of speech-acts provides us with the best means of identifying the rather obvious non sequitur embodied in such statements of the anti-intentionalist case. As I have already stressed, I am perfectly willing to concede that the question of what an author may have intended to say cannot possibly be equated with the meaning of what is said. I am only objecting to the suggestion that it follows from this that the recovery of intentionality is irrelevant to the interpretation of texts. To draw this inference is simply to confuse all over again the two separable questions about authorial intentionality I have striven to keep separate.

IV

I must not over-emphasize the extent to which I feel misunderstood. Most of my critics seem to have followed without undue difficulty what I have tried to say about the recovery of intentions. Several of them, however, have gone on to raise a number of serious objections to my argument. And it is to those objections that I next want to devote myself.

The main criticism is one that Graham and, more recently, Boucher and Levine have especially stressed. Although Graham concedes that I may be right about the importance of decoding what he calls the 'actual illocutionary force' of utterances, he points out that I have failed to provide an adequate 'recipe' for doing so, an account of 'how it is that such decoding can take place'.[173]

I have in fact gestured at what I take to be the two main ingredients in any such attempt to analyse the concept of 'uptake'. The most obvious determinant of the intended illocutionary force of any utterance must be the meaning of the utterance itself. Consider only the most obvious fact: that meaning is affected by grammatical mood. When the policeman issues the utterance 'The ice over there is very thin', the intended illocutionary force of the utterance cannot, for example, be that of questioning the skater.[174] This is not to say – with Cohen, Schiffer and others – that the concept of illocutionary force simply describes an aspect of the meaning of utterances.[175] It has been my whole purpose to insist that it points to a separable dimension of language. But there can be no doubt that the meaning of utterances helps to limit the range of illocutionary forces they can bear, and thereby serves to exclude the possibility that certain illocutionary acts are being performed.

The other determinant I have tried to emphasize is the context and occasion of utterances. The notion of context, especially as Holdcroft has explicated it, is one of great complexity.[176] But we can readily single out the most crucial element in it. This is the fact that all serious utterances are characteristically intended as acts of communication. So they characteristically occur, as Austin always insisted, either as acts of a conventionally recognizable character, or else more broadly in the form of recognizable interventions in what Austin called a total speech-act situation.[177]

The point can be extended, and brought into line with my present concerns, by emphasizing that the types of utterance I am considering can never be viewed simply as strings of propositions; they must always be viewed at the same time as arguments. Now to argue is always to argue for or against a certain assumption or point of view or course of action. It follows that, if we wish to understand such utterances, we shall have to identify the precise nature of the intervention constituted by the act of uttering them.

As Tully observes in his Introduction, I take this to be the first step in any attempt to grasp what someone may have meant by saying something. If we fail to take it, as Wootton has excellently remarked, we shall find ourselves in a position comparable to that of someone listening to the prosecution or the defence in a criminal trial without having heard the other side's case. We shall find it impossible to understand 'why apparently promising lines of argument are never pursued, while at other times what seem to be trivial distinctions and secondary issues are subjected to lengthy examination'.[178]

To put it another way, there is a sense in which we need to understand why a certain proposition has been put forward if we wish to understand the proposition itself.[179] We need to see it not simply as a proposition, but also as a move in argument. So we need to grasp why it seemed worth making that precise move; to recapture the presuppositions and purposes that went into the making of it.

My first step is thus a generalization (as Wootton notes) of Collingwood's dictum to the effect that understanding any proposition requires us to identify the question to which the proposition may be regarded as an answer.[180] I am claiming, that is, that any act of communication always constitutes the taking up of some determinate position in relation to some pre-existing conversation or argument. It follows that, if we wish to understand what has been said, we shall have to be able to identify what exact position has been taken up. So far I have expressed this contention in terms of Austin's claim that we need to be able to understand what the speaker or writer may have been doing in saying what was said. But it is I think a fascinating though unnoticed feature of Austin's analysis that it can in turn be viewed as an exemplification of what Collingwood called the 'logic of question and answer'.[181]

One final observation about this notion of intervening in a context. There is no implication that the relevant context need be an immediate one.[182] As Pocock has especially emphasized, the questions and problems to which writers see themselves as responding may have been raised at a remote period, even in a wholly different culture.[183] The appropriate context for understanding the point of such writers' utterances will therefore be whatever context enables us to appreciate the nature of the intervention constituted by their utterances. To recover that context in any particular case, we may have to engage in extremely wide-ranging as well as extremely detailed historical research.

Graham, Lockyer and others among my critics have objected that this proposed method of identifying the intended illocutionary force of utterances 'can never start', since it involves 'an insuperable circularity'.[184] As I have just indicated, the process is undoubtedly circular; but there is surely no difficulty about seeing where to start. What I am claiming is that we should start by elucidating the meaning, and hence the subject matter, of the utterances in which we are interested. We should then turn to the context of their occurrence in order to determine how exactly they connect with, or relate to, other utterances concerned with the same subject matter. My suggestion is that, if we succeed in identifying this context with sufficient accuracy, we can eventually hope to read off what the speaker or writer in whom we are interested was doing in saying what he or she said.

By way of illustration, consider the most straightforward type of case, that of a simple declarative utterance. Let us again take Machiavelli's claim that mercenary armies always undermine liberty. There is little difficulty about understanding the meaning of the utterance itself. But we wish in addition to understand what Machiavelli may have meant by it. So we turn to the general context in which it occurred. Suppose we find that the sentiment expressed by the utterance was frequently expressed in the political literature of the time. Then we are already justified in saying that Machiavelli is repeating, upholding or agreeing with an accepted attitude or viewpoint. Looking more closely at the intervention constituted by his utterance, we may feel able to go further. We may feel justified in adding that he is endorsing, confirming or concurring with an accepted truth; alternatively, may find that he is only conceding, admitting or allowing it to be true.

On the other hand, we may find that he is saying something no longer generally accepted, even though it may at one time have been widely agreed. Then perhaps what he is doing is restating, reaffirming or recalling his audience to the truth of what he says. Perhaps, more specifically, he is at the same time emphasizing, underlining or insisting on its truth.

Or again, we may find that what he says is not generally accepted at all. Then perhaps what he is doing is denying and repudiating, or perhaps correcting and revising, a generally accepted belief. Or he may be enlarging, developing or adding to an established argument by drawing out its implications in an unexplored way. At the same time, he may be pressing or urging a recognition of this new viewpoint, or advising, recommending or even warning his audience of the need to adopt it.

A further range of possibilities comes into view as soon as we reflect on the point I seek to emphasize in chapter 6: that when we describe a situation or state of affairs, we often do so in such a way as to evaluate it at the same time. Thus we may find that Machiavelli is espousing, championing or commending a particular conclusion or course of action as well as describing it; alternatively, we may find that he is questioning, challenging or condemning it. More specifically, he may be applauding or celebrating it; or else visiting it with ridicule or scorn.

The upshot of employing this approach, it is perhaps worth underlining, is to challenge any categorical distinction between texts and contexts.[185] Keane maintains that I still adopt an 'author–subject' approach, thereby suggesting that I have yet to hear about the death of the author announced by Barthes and Foucault (12:205). It is true that these announcements. strike me as a trifle exaggerated. I cannot agree with Keane that authors are nothing more than 'prisoners of the discourse within whose boundaries they take pen in hand' (12:205). I agree of course (see chapter 5) that we are all limited by the concepts available to us if we wish to communicate. But it is no less true (see chapter 6) that language constitutes a resource as well as a constraint. This means that, if we wish to to do justice to those moments when a convention is challenged or a commonplace effectively subverted, we cannot simply dispense with the category of the author. A point that takes on added significance when we reflect that, to the extent that our social world is constituted by our concepts, any successful alteration in the use of a concept will at the same time constitute a change in our social world. The pen, as Tully puts it, can be a mighty sword.

Nevertheless, it ought to be obvious that the approach I am sketching leaves the traditional figure of the author in extremely poor health. Reiterating, defending, underpinning commonplace insights as they generally do, individual authors can readily – perhaps too readily – come to seem mere precipitates of their contexts. It is certainly an implication of my approach (as I pointed out in the first essay I ever wrote about these matters) that the idea of discourse, not individual authors, becomes the main focus of attention.[186] The historian primarily studies what Pocock calls 'languages' of discourse, and only secondarily the relationship between individual contributions to such languages and the range of discourse as a whole.[187]

A number of my critics have retorted that this is to fall rather obviously short of my stated aim of recovering what individual writers may have intended or meant. We may be able to say of a given contribution to a pre-existing discourse that it constituted an attack on one position, a defence of another, and so forth. We may be able, that is, to establish what its author was doing. But as Hollis observes, this is only to show that the cap fits, not that the author was wearing it (7:140). We arrive at a point, Tully similarly remarks, at which we may be able to show that a given argument served a given purpose. But this is not to show that the argument was designed or intended to serve that purpose (1:10) To express the objection – as Graham does – in the idiom I have been using, the recipe enables us to identify 'a range of possible illocutionary forces' but not the performance of any illocutionary acts.[188]

As I have already intimated, however, there are some cases in which the recipe will in fact enable us to identify what Graham calls the actual illocutionary force of certain utterances. These will be the cases, already examined, in which the meaning of the utterance and the context of its occurrence are already sufficient to fix its illocutionary force, regardless of whether the speaker issued the utterance with that intended force.

To put the point in Shapiro's jargon, the recipe is already sufficient to enable us to identify 'real acts'.[189] This is not to say that I find Shapiro's jargon acceptable. In fact it seems to me notably infelicitous, if only because the list of things I may properly be said to be doing may well include a number of items that cannot possibly be classified as acts. (For example, falling down stairs is undoubtedly an instance of doing something, but is not the description even of an unintentional act.) Still less do I agree with the point Shapiro employs his jargon to make. He claims that my approach 'takes no account' of real acts.[190] But in fact I begin by focusing on them, first singling out the range of things a speaker may be said to be doing in issuing a given utterance, and then asking whether the utterance in question may have been intended to carry just that illocutionary force.

Nor is it right to object, as Graham and Hollis have done, that this still leaves us without any means of moving from the first of these stages to the second.[191] Suppose that (to revert to my example) we already know the list of things that Machiavelli was undoubtedly doing in saying what he said about mercenaries. We also know that, if he was engaged in an intended act of communication, there must have been something he was intentionally doing in saying what he said. It seems to me that the best hypothesis to adopt at this stage will usually be to assume that he was doing what he was doing intentionally, and thus that we have in fact identified the range of intended illocutionary forces with which his utterance was produced.

Once this stage is reached, moreover, it becomes a matter of no great difficulty to close the gap still further by testing this hypothesis in various ways. I have already tried in chapter 3 to sketch how this can be done, and it hardly seems appropriate to rehearse those arguments here. Suffice it to underline the three most obvious points.

The first is that intentions depend on beliefs. We therefore need to make sure that Machiavelli possessed a set of beliefs appropriate to the formation of the kinds of intentions we are ascribing to him. As to how we can hope to recover such beliefs, and thereby avoid the dangers of anachronism that obviously loom at this point, I have already tried to give my answer in the section 'On describing and explaining beliefs', above.

The next point is that the intentions with which we act are closely connected with our motives. This provides a vital means of corroborating any hypothesis to the effect that a speaker or writer may have intended a certain utterance to bear a particular illocutionary force. For the suspicion that someone may have performed a certain action will always be greatly strengthened (as every reader of detective stories knows) by the discovery that they had a motive for performing it.

It is perhaps worth underlining this familiar point, if only because Hollis accuses me of paying too little attention to motives (7:136, 139). It is true that I have taken a special interest in the kind of redescriptive cases I have already discussed, where we are able to explain certain puzzles about actions without enquiring into the motives for performing them. But I certainly agree that, if we are trying to find out whether someone meant to perform an action they may appear to have performed, an investigation of their motives will always be an indispensable help.

Finally, ascriptions of intentionality can be further corroborated by examining the coherence of a speaker's or writer's beliefs. Suppose that, in issuing the utterance we have been considering, Machiavelli upheld one position in argument, rejected another, attacked one course of action, implicitly commended another, and so on. Assuming that he held minimally coherent beliefs, we can safely assume – in a sense we can predict – that he will also adopt a number of related attitudes. If he upholds position (a), we can expect him to reject the negation of (a); if he commends alternative (x), we can expect him to denounce the contrary of (x); and so on. If upon further investigation we find these expectations defeated, we shall begin to feel at a complete loss. But if we succeed in recovering just such a network of attitudes, we shall feel increasingly justified in our initial hypothesis: that, in issuing his utterance with the force of upholding and commending a certain position, he must have intended his utterance to bear exactly that force.

At this stage, however, I come to the most startling objection my critics have raised. Some have retorted that it is simply a misconception to suppose that, by these means or any other, we can ever hope genuinely to recover the intentions with which a given utterance was issued. Among contributors to the present volume, Keane in particular insists that we can never hope to 're-enact' intentionally produced utterances; the very idea embodies an old-fashioned, 'covertly positivist model' of interpretation, one 'long since abandoned within the most sophisticated circles' (12:209).

I am of course anxious not to be unfashionable, still less unsophisticated. So I have tried to follow with particular care the reasons Keane and others have given for supposing that the recovery of intentions is actually impossible. The main argument they have advanced is one they usually profess to derive from Gadamer. First it is claimed that the recovery of intentions presupposes the old hermeneutic ambition of trying (as Keane puts it) to understand other agents by 'empathetically looking them in the eye and stepping into their shoes' (12:209). It is then pointed out that the idea of taking up such a position inside other people's minds and thinking their thoughts after them is little short of absurd. From this it is said to follow that the project of trying to recover intentions is not just embarrassingly naive but obviously misconceived (12:209 – 10).

I find myself embarrassed in turn not just by the evident non sequitur embodied in this argument, but also by the old-fashioned positivism presupposed by it. I can only respond by trying to make clearer the logically behavourist, essentially Wittgensteinian argument on which I have been relying throughout, and which these critics appear altogether to have missed.

Of course we cannot hope to step into the shoes of past agents, still less into their minds. But it does not follow that we cannot hope to recover the intentions with which their utterances were issued, and hence what they meant by them. The reason is that the intentions with which anyone performs any successful act of communication must, *ex hypothesi*, be publicly legible. Suppose I come to understand that the man waving his arms in the next field is not trying to chase away a fly, but is warning me that the bull is about the charge.[192] To recognize that he is warning me is to understand the intentions with which he is acting. But to recover these intentions is not a matter of identifying the ideas inside his head at the moment when he first begins to wave his arms. It is merely a matter of grasping the fact that arm-waving can count as warning, and that this is the convention he is exploiting in this particular case. Nothing in the way of 'empathy' is required, since the meaning of the episode is entirely public and intersubjective.[193] As a result, the intentions with which the man is acting can be inferred from an understanding of the significance of the act itself.

I have been arguing that texts are acts. To understand them, we need to recover the intentions with which they are written. But I have also been arguing that this is not the mysterious empathetic process that old-fashioned hermeneutics may have led us to suppose. For acts are in turn analogues of texts: they embody intersubjective meanings which we can hope to read off.[194]

A number of my critics, however, raise a further objection at this point. To speak in this way about the recovery of intentions, Mulligan and others declare, is to concede that they are 'irrecoverable' after all. For this method of trying to recover them is such that I can never hope to 'demonstrate' any claims about intentionality with anything approaching certainty.[195]

This reason for abandoning all talk about intentionality is one that Derrida has also emphasized. Consider, for example, his much-discussed analysis in *Spurs* of the fragment, found among Nietzsche's manuscripts, which reads 'I have forgotten my umbrella'.[196] Derrida concedes that there is no difficulty about understanding the meaning of the sentence. 'Everyone knows what "I have forgotten my umbrella" means.'[197] His only objection to the despised figure whom he labels 'the hermeneut' is that such persons fail to recognize that this still leaves us without any 'infallible way' of recovering what Nietzsche may have meant.[198] 'We will never know *for sure* what Nietzsche wanted to say or do when he noted these words.'[199]

I have no wish to question such obvious truths. Some utterances are completely lacking in the sorts of context from which we can alone hope to infer the intentions with which they were uttered. We may well have to concede in such cases that we can never hope to arrive at even a plausible hypothesis about how the utterance in question should be understood. The example of the umbrella seems, indeed, to be just such a case. Even when an utterance can be assigned to a highly determinate context, moreover, the outcome of the hermeneutic enterprise can never be anything approaching the attainment of a final, self-evident and indubitable set of truths about the utterance concerned.

It scarcely follows from this, however, that we can never hope to construct and corroborate plausible hypotheses about the intentions with which a given utterance may have been issued. We can frequently do so in just the manner I have tried to set out. We can focus on the intersubjective meanings of illocutionary acts, and then seek further corroboration for such ascriptions of intentionality by enquiring into the motives and beliefs of the agent in question and in general the context of the utterance itself.

We can of course stipulate, if we like, that the result will not be a valid interpretation, since it will still fall far short of certitude. If we insist, as Derrida does, on such an equation between establishing that something is the case and being able to demonstrate it 'for sure', then admittedly it follows that we can never hope to establish the intentions with which a text may have been written. But equally it follows that we can never hope to establish that life is not a dream. The moral of this, however, is not that we have no reason to believe that life is not a dream. The moral is rather that the sceptic is insisting on far too stringent an account of what it means to have reasons for our beliefs. Haunted as Derrida seems to be by the ghost of Descartes, he has concentrated on attacking a position which no theorist of intentionality need defend.

This view of interpretation remains far too optimistic, some of my critics finally riposte; it forgets the special constraints under which an interpreter is obliged to operate. Here again Gadamer's name tends to be invoked. He is said to have established that, as Gunnell puts it, it is impossible 'to free one's self from the horizon of the present'.[200] The image of imprisonment is one that several others of my critics pick up. Hall assures me that, being 'trapped in time', I am 'incapable of neutrally reconstructing a past thinker's intentions'.[201] Keane similarly adjures me to recognize that I can never hope to 'jump freely over the boundaries' of my prejudices (p.210).

Keane finds it 'very surprising' that I have missed this point, but I find it surprising that he should have missed the emphasis I have tried to place on it. I have always insisted that, as I put it in chapter 2, we inevitably approach the past in the light of contemporary paradigms and presuppositions, the influence of which may easily serve to mislead us at every turn. I have also conceded that the enterprise of recovering the kinds of intentions in which I am interested requires a level of historical awareness and sheer erudition that few of us can aspire to reach. I have further conceded that, even when we feel confident about our ascriptions of intentionality, such ascriptions are of course nothing more than inferences from the best evidence available to us, and as such are defeasible at any time. My precepts, in short, are only claims about how best to proceed; they are not claims about how to guarantee success.

I protest only at the assumption that it follows from this that the kinds of intentions I have been discussing are, as Derrida claims, in all cases 'in principle inaccessible'.[202] If this were true, the effect would not only be to cut off the type of hermeneutics in which I am interested; it would also be to render meaningless a whole range of practices extending from the conducting of orchestras to the assessment of criminal responsibility. Such scepticism strikes me as unhelpfully hyperbolical, especially when we reflect that even animals are sometimes capable of recovering the intentions with which people act. Dogs often disclose by their responses that they are able to distinguish between an accidental and a deliberate kick. Derrida ought surely to be able to rise to at least the same interpretative heights.

V

Having restated my case, I am now in a position to clear up two undoubted confusions in my original presentation of my argument. One of the claims I put forward in the essay reprinted here as chapter 2 was that, because of the need to pay attention to the illocutionary dimension of utterances, there can never be any prospect of understanding a text simply by reading it over and over. But a number of my critics, especially Boucher and King, have objected that this was to set up a straw man: no one ever supposed that the meaning of a text can be recovered simply by studying 'the text in itself'.[203]

I cannot accept that I entirely missed the mark. Parekh and Berki have criticized me precisely on the grounds that I fail to appreciate that some texts have 'no specific context' and make 'eminent sense' when considered simply in themselves.[204] More recently, Mansfield has made it a leading principle of what he takes to be the right approach to studying Machiavelli's *Prince* and *Discourses* that they must be read 'each by itself without any reference whatever to anything outside them'.[205]

Nevertheless, I agree that I misstated my point. My objection is not so much to those who treat texts as self-sufficient objects of enquiry and understanding. My objection is rather to those who assume that the business of understanding a text is simply a matter of recovering, by whatever means, the meaning of the text itself. This is the assumption – at least as widespread as it was when I first wrote – that I still wish to reject in the name of the need to recover, at the same time, what the author of the text may have meant by it.

I can best summarize my dissatisfaction with those historians who fail to raise this further question by saying that they seem to me to suffer from what might be called insufficient puzzlement. Consider for example the exegetical literature on Descartes' *Meditations*. Descartes thinks it crucial to be able to vindicate the idea of indubitable knowledge. But why is this an issue for him at all? Traditional historians of philosophy have scarcely acknowledged the question; they have generally taken it for granted that, since Descartes is an epistemologist, and since the problem of certainty is one of the central problems of epistemology, there is no special puzzle here at all. They have thus been able to concentrate on what they take to be their basic interpretative task, that of critically examining what Descartes actually says about how we can come to know anything with certainty.[206]

My dissatisfaction with this approach stems from the fact that – to revert to Collingwood's idiom – it leaves us without any sense of the specific question to which Descartes may have intended his doctrine of certainty as a solution. In consequence it leaves us without any understanding of what he may have been doing in presenting his doctrine in the precise form in which he chose to present it. It has I think been one of the major advances in Descartes scholarship of recent years to establish that part of what he was doing was responding to Pyrrhonian scepticism. Not only was he addressing himself specifically to that challenge; it has also been shown that this helps to explain both the character of his own anti-sceptical arguments and the nature of the tactics he adopted in developing them.[207]

I made a further mistake in framing my criticism of such historians as a denial of the claim that there are any 'perennial problems' in philosophy. I wanted to get as far away as possible from the assumption that there is a canonical list of 'the problems of philosophy', that the list includes such ineliminable items as 'the problem of certainty', and that we only need to point to the list in order to explain the preoccupations of individual philosophers. But, as Boucher and others of my critics have observed, I went too far. My way of putting the point appeared to deny the obvious fact that western traditions of philosophy have contained long continuities, and that these have been reflected in the stable employment of a number of key concepts and modes of argument.[208]

I still feel that emphasizing such continuities is hardly the same as establishing their perennial status. So I still remain the sworn foe of those who wish to write the type of history in which – to take an example which has recently been discussed – the views of Plato, Augustine, Hobbes and Marx on 'the nature of the just state' are compared.[209] The reason for my nominalism, as I have tried to stress all along, is not so much that each of these thinkers appears to answer the question in his own way. It is rather that the terms employed in phrasing the question – 'nature', 'just' and 'state' – feature in their different theories, if at all, only in such divergent ways that it seems an obvious confusion to suppose that any stable concepts are being picked out. The mistake, in short, lies in supposing that there is any one question to which these various thinkers are all addressing themselves.

Nevertheless, it was an error to formulate this criticism as a doubt about 'perennial questions', especially as this in turn gave the impression[210] that my precepts and my own historical practice are out of line with each other. My objection is not of course to those who stress the long-standing character of many of our philosophical disputes. My objection is only to the practice of abstracting particular arguments from the context of their occurrence in order to relocate them as 'contributions' to such disputes. Even if we find that a given philosopher is merely reaffirming an established line of argument, we still need to be able to grasp what he or she was doing in reaffirming it if we wish to understand the argument itself.

I can best restate my objection by observing, in Wittgenstein's phrase, that concepts are tools.[211] To understand a concept, it is necessary to grasp not merely the meanings of the terms used to express it, but also the range of things that can be done with it. This is why, in spite of the long continuities that have undoubtedly marked our inherited patterns of thought, I remain unrepentant in my belief that there can be no histories of concepts as such; there can only be histories of their uses in argument.

VI

My friendliest critics have raised no objections to the general line of argument I have now tried to lay out. They have merely wondered whether it is of much importance. Seidman has declared in an Endnote to his critique of my approach that it has no 'legitimacy' beyond the narrow confines of the history of political philosophy.[212] Hough has added that, while we can undoubtedly hope to recover the intended force of utterances, the effect of doing so will merely be to supply us with meagre and generalized characterizations of the texts involved.[213]

I ought first to say that my emphasis on illocutionary acts is not primarily due to any belief in their special significance. I have never wished to suggest that the sole or even the principal business of the intellectual historian is that of recovering what authors may have meant.[214] I have placed my main emphasis on this dimension chiefly because it continues to be so readily and so frequently overlooked.

Nevertheless, these doubts about the scope and application of my arguments are, I think, misplaced. To see why this is so, consider some recent studies which have focused attention on the question of what particular authors may have meant. Take, for example, Donald Winch's study of Malthus. This establishes that the original *Essay on Population* was in part designed as a theodicy.[215] Or take Adkins's history of Greek moral values. This establishes that part of what Plato was doing in the *Republic* was trying to recover and assign a renewed prominence to the quieter virtues of social life.[216] Or take Butler's account of 'the war of ideas' in late eighteenth-century English literature. This establishes the precise way in which Jane Austen intended her novels to bear a message of a Christian and more specifically a socially conservative character.[217]

These are certainly brief characterizations of complex texts. But their implications are far from meagre. By claiming to indicate what each author was *doing*, they furnish us with a key to their texts and in consequence a means of explicating many of their detailed effects. Turning back to the texts with these characterizations in mind, we may find ourselves in a much better position to answer a wide range of questions about them. We may be able to explain why they are organized in a certain way, why certain arguments recur in them, why a particular normative vocabulary is employed, and in general why they possess a certain shape and identity.

Nor are such general characterizations all that this approach can hope to yield. I have perhaps encouraged this misconception by the way in which I have spoken, often in the singular, about the recovery of intended illocutionary force. But it ought to be obvious that an immense range of illocutionary acts will normally be embedded within the types of texts I have been discussing, and that even the smallest individual fragments of such texts may sometimes carry a heavy freight of intended illocutionary force.

As an example, consider the end of E. M. Forster's *A Passage to India*. The novel closes with the words: 'Weybridge, 1924'.[218] The meaning is clear enough: Forster is stating that he completed the book in a Surrey suburb in the year 1924. At the same time he is following a convention, more common at the time than nowadays, of informing his readers about the circumstances in which he wrote it. It may seem that there is nothing more to be said. Indeed, it may seem almost absurd to go on to ask the type of question in which I am interested – but what is Forster *doing* in stating such facts? Surely he is simply stating them.

But is this so clear? We may find ourselves reflecting that the convention of signing off novels in this way was sometimes used to draw attention to the romantically nomadic character of authorship. Joyce's *Ulysses*, for example, published only two years before, is signed 'Trieste–Zürich–Paris'.[219] By locating himself firmly in Weybridge – the classic instance of a prosaic English suburb – Forster introduces a definite note of mockery as well as self-ridicule. At the same time, we may find ourselves reflecting that the convention of signing-off was sometimes used in addition to underline the fact that literary labour can be an impressively protracted affair. The dates at the end of *Ulysses*, for example, read '1914–1921'. By confining himself to a single year, Forster allows himself a touch of hauteur, even of scorn, at the expense of those who preferred to emphasize their creative agonies. Once we see this much, we may well begin to suspect that Forster is satirizing the entire convention of signing-off fictional works by indicating the posturing to which the convention gave rise.

I end with this example as a way of underlining the fact that the proposal I am putting forward about the recovery of illocutionary acts is neither so jejune nor so restricted in scope as my critics have maintained. It is certainly a mistake to suppose that the recovery of this dimension will be of no interest except in the case of certain restricted genres of texts. The dimension is present in the case of all serious utterances, whether in verse or in prose, whether in philosophy or in literature. It is a further mistake to suppose that the recovery of this dimension will merely provide us with general characterizations of the works involved. Any text of any complexity will always contain a myriad of illocutionary acts, and any individual phrase in any such text – as I have just indicated – may even contain more acts than it contains words.

This is indeed one of the most obvious reasons why we can never expect our debates about interpretation to have a stop. As I have tried to indicate, the reason is not that there is nothing determinate to be said. It is rather that, in the case of a work of any complexity, there will always be room for legitimate and potentially endless debate about – to use Austin's phrase – how exactly the work may have been meant to be taken.

VII

I have now said as much as I want to say about the two central issues I promised to discuss at the outset. Before bringing this reply to a close, however, I should like to mention one final objection that a number of my critics have levelled against my entire argument. Among contributors to the present volume, Femia has expressed it most bluntly. He claims that I 'treat the ideas of our ancestors as purely historical phenomena' and thus regard them as 'completely without modern relevance' (9:159, 163). But if we take this approach seriously, he suggests, we shall rob the study of intellectual history of its point. The effect will be to 'reduce the history of thought to little more than a sterile celebration of intellectual pedigree' (9:158).

A number of my other critics have voiced similar anxieties. Tarlton wonders how the fruits of my approach could ever hope to be 'of any more than the dustiest antiquarian interest'.[220] Gunnell similarly complains that 'apart from scholarly antiquarianism, the purpose of the enterprise and its relationship to the wider endeavour of political inquiry is far from clear'.[221] And Warrender forthrightly concludes that, in the case of 'the classic texts in political philosophy', the outcome of adopting my approach would simply be 'to bury them'.[222]

There is much to be said about the depressingly philistine view of historical enquiry presupposed by this line of argument. But I shall not attempt a full consideration of that issue here. One reason is that I have already tried to explain why it seems to me needlessly blinkered to suppose that intellectual history can only be 'relevant' if it enables us to reflect our current beliefs and assumptions back at us.[223] A further reason is that Jenssen, in his recent article about my work, has admirably illustrated the falsity of the dichotomy between past-minded and present-minded approaches to the study of social and political thought, and has greatly extended and deepened the arguments I originally tried to lay out.[224]

Nevertheless, it is perhaps worth underlining two obvious points. The first might be labelled the anthropological justification for studying intellectual history. The investigation of alien systems of belief provides us with an irreplaceable means of standing back from our own prevailing assumptions and structures of thought, and of situating ourselves in relation to other and very different forms of life. To put the point in the way that Gadamer and Rorty have recently done, such investigations enable us to question the appropriateness of any strong distinction between matters of 'merely historical' and 'genuinely philosophical' interest, since they enable us to recognize that our own descriptions and conceptualizations are in no way uniquely privileged.[225]

But what, it is often asked, is the point of seeing ourselves in this way as simply one tribe among others? There are many cogent answers, although it is hard to avoid sounding sententious in mentioning them. We can hope to attain a certain kind of objectivity in appraising rival systems of thought. We can hope to attain a greater degree of understanding, and thereby a larger tolerance, for various elements of cultural diversity. And above all, we can hope to acquire a perspective from which to view our own form of life in a more self-critical way, enlarging our present horizons instead of fortifying local prejudices.[226]

This is not merely to say that our historical studies may help us to become less parochial in our attachment to inherited beliefs. We may also find, as a result of engaging in such studies, that some of what we currently believe about, say, our moral or political arrangements is actually false. We are prone, for example, to think that the concept of individual responsibility is indispensable to any satisfactory moral code. But Adkins' analysis of ancient Greek values casts considerable doubt on that article of faith.[227] We are prone to think that there can be no concept of the state in the absence of cen-tralized systems of power. But Geertz's study of classical Bali shows how the one is perfectly possible in the absence of the other.[228] We are prone to think that there can be no theory of individual liberty in the absence of a theory of rights. But my own studies of Roman and Renaissance moral thought simi-larly try to show that there is no necessary connection between the two.[229]

The alien character of these beliefs constitutes their 'relevance'. Reflecting on such alternative possibilities, we provide ourselves with one of the best means of preventing our current moral and political theories from degenerating into uncritically accepted ideologies.[230] At the same time, we equip ourselves with a new means of looking critically at our own beliefs in the light of the enlarged sense of possibility we acquire.

A resurgent conservatism tells us that this is merely another way of proclaiming the relativity of all values, and thus of leaving us bereft of any values at all.[231] This seems to me as far as possible from the truth. The kind of enquiries I am describing offer us an additional means of reflecting on what we believe, and thus of strengthening our present beliefs by way of testing them against alternative possibilities, or else of improving them if we come to recognize that the alternatives are both possible and desirable. As I have already stressed, a willingness to engage in this kind of reflection seems to me a distinguishing feature of all rational agents. To denounce such studies is not a defence of reason but an assault on the open society.

The other point I wish to make in justification of my approach is more specific to the discipline of intellectual history. Although the concepts we investigate as historians of western thought are often highly unfamiliar, our own concepts nevertheless evolved out of them.[232] This suggests that the 'purely historical' study of social and political thought may prove to have a further relevance. Suppose we have the patience to go back to the start of our own history and find out in detail how it developed. This will not only enable us to illuminate the changing applications of our key concepts; it will also enable us to uncover the points at which they may have become confused or misunderstood in a way that marked their subsequent history. And if we can do this — as Tuck, for example, has shown in the case of our theories about natural rights — we can hope not merely to illuminate but to dissolve some of our current philosophical perplexities.[233] Again, it is only by refusing the vulgar demand for relevance that we can hope to indicate the serious way in which the study of intellectual history is indeed relevant to the assessment of our present beliefs.

VIII

I cannot end without thanking my critics (bewilderingly vituperative though some of them have been). They have shown me a number of points where I have argued with insufficient clarity, and a number of points where I have either misstated or overstated my case. They have thereby prompted me to reconsider my whole argument, and to recast it in a more systematic and, I hope, a more lucid style. What they have not succeeded in showing me, however, is that my basic approach to textual interpretation is in any fundamental way misconceived. To end, as I began, with Thomas Hobbes, I am bound to say that 'as to the whole doctrine, I see not yet, but the principles of it are true and proper, and the ratiocination solid'.

Notes

CHAPTER 1   THE PEN IS A MIGHTY SWORD

1 His early work, 'History and ideology in the English revolution', *Historical Journal* (1965), contains all these elements.
2 For his adaptation of speech-act theory, see the second through ninth articles cited in the bibliography under the heading 'On early-modern intellectual history'.
3 For Jürgen Habermas, see 'What is Universal Pragmatics?', in *Communications and the Evolution of Society*, tr. Thomas McCarthy (Boston, Beacon Press, 1979).
4 See also *The Foundations of Modern Political Thought*, 2 vols (Cambridge University Press, Cambridge, 1978), vol. I, p. xii.
5 See *Machiavelli* (Oxford University Press, Oxford, 1981), rev. edn 1985, pp. 31–48; *Foundations*, vol. I, pp. 180–6.
6 See especially, 'Conventions and the understanding of speech-acts', *Philosophical Quarterly*, 20 (1970), pp. 118–38. (Let 'text' stand for any linguistic unit of analysis.)
7 *Foundations*, vol. I, p. xiii.
8 Ibid., p. xi.
9 Ibid., pp. 113–39.
10 Ibid., p. 9
11 This explicitly Weberian theme is analysed from the perspective of the legitimating agent in 'Some problems in the analysis of political thought and action', chap. 5, and from the perspective of the legitimating role of the language in 'Language and social change', chap. 6.
12 See 'The principles and practice of opposition: the case of Bolingbroke versus Walpole', in *Historical Perspectives: Essays in Honour of J.H. Plumb*, ed. N. McKendrick (Europa Publications, London, 1974), pp.93–128, for a case study.
13 *Foundations*, vol. I, pp. xii–xiii.

14 Ibid., vol. II, p. 64.

15 Ibid., pp. 20–113.

16 Ibid., vol. I, p. xi.

17 One exception is John Dunn who saw the challenge Skinner had launched at modern political theory. John Dunn, 'The cage of politics', *The Listener*, 15 March 1979.

18 *Foundations*, vol. I, p. ix. Not *precisely* our concept of the state, he carefully notes. His views on the formation of the concept of the state have changed significantly since 1978. See 'The modern state: acquisition of a concept', in *Political Innovations and Conceptual Change* (Cambridge, Cambridge University Press, 1987).

19 *Foundations*, vol. II, pp. 349, 358.

20 Ibid., vols I, II, back cover of paperback edition.

21 This conclusion of *Foundations* is taken up more recently in 'Machiavelli on the maintenance of liberty', *Politics*, 18 (1983), pp. 3–15 and 'The idea of negative liberty: philosophical and historical perspectives', in *Philosophy in History,* ed. Richard Rorty, J. Schneewind and Quentin Skinner (Cambridge, Cambridge University Press, 1984), pp. 193–221.

22 Michel Foucault, 'Lecture two: 14 January 1976', *Power/Knowledge,* ed. Colin Gordon (New York, Pantheon, 1980), pp. 92–108.

23 In 'Machiavelli on liberty', and 'The idea of negative liberty', Skinner pits the old republican humanist ideology against recent manipulations of the juridical ideology, including John Rawls' *A Theory of Justice* (Oxford, Oxford University Press, 1981).

24 *Foundations*, vol. II, p. 247.

25 This is summarized in four major steps in the Conclusion of *Foundations,* vol. II.

26 *Foundations*, vol. II, pp. 302–49; and see 'The origins of the Calvinist theory of revolution', in *After the Reformation*, ed. Barbara Malament (London, University of Pennsylvania Press, 1980), pp. 309–30.

27 *Foundations*, vol. I, pp. 86–89.

28 Ibid., pp. 69–112.

29 Ludwig Wittgenstein, *Philosophical Investigations* (Oxford, Basil Blackwell, 1984), p.10 and *On Certainty* (Oxford, Basil Blackwell, 1974), pp. 204–5.

30 Charles Taylor, 'Interpretation and the sciences of man', in *Understanding and Social Inquiry,* ed. F. R. Dallmayr and T. A. McCarthy (Notre Dame, University of Notre Dame Press, 1977), p. 117; Hans-Georg Gadamer, *Truth and Method*, tr. William Glen-Doepel (London, Sheed and Ward, 1979), pp.345–431.

31 Jürgen Habermas, 'A review of Gadamer's *Truth and Method'*, in *Understanding and Social Inquiry,* ed. Fred Dallmayr and Thomas McCarthy (Notre Dame, University of Notre Dame Press, 1977), pp. 335–63; and Richard Rorty, *Philosophy and the Mirror of Nature* (Princeton, Princeton University Press, 1979), pp. 343–56.

32 *Foundations*, vol. II, pp. 347–8. Cf., Foucault, 'Lecture Two', p. 103.

33 Carl von Clausewitz, *On War*, ed. A. Rapoport (Harmondsworth, Penguin, 1974), p. 402.

34 Michel Foucault, 'Truth and power', *Power/Knowledge*, p. 114. The similarity between the two thinkers should not be overstressed.

35 Michel Foucault, 'The subject and power', in Hubert L. Drefus and Paul Rabinow, *Michel Foucault. Beyond Structuralism and Hermeneutics* (Chicago, University of Chicago Press, 1982), pp. 208–26, 219–26.

36 The third thesis has been rewritten in the light of the helpful comments on it by Charles Taylor in his chapter, 'The hermeneutics of conflict'. His comments have aided me in clarifying a source of misunderstanding in the earlier version of the practical conflict thesis. 'Practical conflict' refers not only, and not primarily, to wars among states, but to any type of practical struggle in the early modern period that can be justifiably described in the language of war (tactics, strategy, campaigns, and so on): that is, strategic–instrumental action.

37 Skinner has analysed one aspect of the contemporary controversy over democracy in 'The Empirical theorists of democracy and their critics', *Political Theory*, 1 (1973), pp. 287–306.

CHAPTER 2   MEANING AND UNDERSTANDING IN THE HISTORY OF IDEAS

1 For an analysis of the now confusing variety of ways in which this inescapable phrase has been used, see Maurice Mandelbaum, 'The history of ideas, intellectual history, and the history of philosophy', in *The Historiography of the History of Philosophy, Beiheft 5, History and Theory* (Middleton, Conn., Wesleyan University Press, 1965), 33n. I use the term here consistently, but with deliberate vagueness, simply to refer to as wide as possible a variety of historical inquiries into intellectual problems.

2 I take these quotations from one of the many confrontations in the debate among literary critics between the 'scholars' and the 'critics'. The terms and issues of this debate seem to be repeated in an identical (though less conscious) manner in histories of philosophical ideas. It is from the latter disciplines, however, that I have mainly taken my examples. I have tried, moreover, in all cases to restrict my examples to works which are either classic or in current use. The fact that a majority of these are taken from the history of *political* ideas merely reflects my own specialism. The belief in 'contextual reading' being voiced here is by F. W. Bateson, 'The functions of criticism at the present time', *Essays in Criticism*, 3 (1953), p. 16. The contrary belief in the text itself as 'something determinate' is from F. R. Leavis, 'The responsible critic: or the functions of criticism at any time', *Scrutiny*, 19 (1953), p. 173.

3 Peter H. Merkl, *Political Continuity and Change* (New York, Harper and Row, 1967), p. 3. For the 'perennial configurations' of the classic texts and their 'perennial problems', cf. also Hans J. Morgenthau, *Dilemmas of Politics* (Chicago, University of Chicago Press, 1958), p.1, and Mulford Q. Sibley, 'The place of classical theory in the study of politics', in *Approaches to*

the Study of Politics, ed. Roland Yound (Chicago, University of Chicago Press, 1958), p.133 (a volume which includes many other similar claims).

4 William T. Bluhm, *Theories of the Political System* (Englewood Cliffs, New Jersey, 1965), p. 13.

5 G. E. G. Catlin, *A History of Political Philosophy* (London, 1950), p.x.

6 Andrew Hacker, '*Capital* and carbuncles: the "great books" reappraised', *American Political Science Review*, 48 (1954), p.783.

7 I employ this unlovely expression throughout, since it is habitually used by all historians of ideas, with an apparently clear reference to an accepted 'canon' of texts.

8 For the insistence that the study of 'classic texts' must 'find its major justification in relevancy', see R. G. McCloskey, 'American political thought and the study of politics', *American Political Science Review*, 51 (1957), p. 129. For the 'timeless questions and answers' see all the textbooks, and, for a more general precept, see Hacker's '*Capital* and Carbuncles', cited in n. 6, at p. 786.

9 For the need to concentrate on what each classic writer *says*, see for precept, K. Jaspers, *The Great Philosophers*, vol. I (London, Harcourt, Brace and World, 1962), Foreword; and Leonard Nelson, 'What is the history of philosophy?', *Ratio*, 4 (1962), pp. 32–3. For this assumption in practice, see for example N. R. Murphy, *The Interpretation of Plato's Republic* (Oxford, Clarendon Press, 1951), p. v, on 'what Plato said'; Alan Ryan, 'Locke and the dictatorship of the bourgeoisie', *Political Studies*, 13 (1965), p. 219, on 'what Locke said'; Leo Strauss, *On Tyranny* (New York, Political Science Classics, 1948), p. 7, on Xenophon and 'what he himself says'.

10 For 'fundamental concepts', see for example Charles R. N. McCoy, *The Structure of Political Thought* (New York, 1963), p. 7. For 'abiding questions' see for example the Preface to *History of Political Philosophy*, ed. Leo Strauss and J. Cropsey (Chicago, Rand McNally, 1963).

11 Bluhm, *Theories of the Political System*, p. v.

12 Alasdair MacIntyre, *A Short History of Ethics* (New York, Macmillan, 1966), p. 2. The remarks made in this Introduction, however, are extremely perceptive and relevant.

13 Sheldon S. Wolin, *Politics and Vision* (Boston, Little Brown, 1961), p. 27. The opening chapter gives a sensitive account of 'the vocabulary of political philosophy', esp. pp. 11–17.

14 Floyd H. Allport, *Theories of Perception and the Concept of Structure* (New York, Wiley, 1955) illustrates the way in which the concept of set 'ramifies into all phases of perceptual study' (p. 240), and recurs in otherwise contrasting theories.

15 Ibid., p.239.

16 That this must result in a history of philosophy conceived in terms of our own philosophical criteria and interests (whose else?) is fully brought out in John Dunn, 'The identity of the history of ideas', *Philosophy*, 43 (1968), pp. 97–8.

17 See esp. E. H. Gombrich, *Art and Illusion* (Princeton, Princeton University Press, 1961), from whom I adopt the vocabulary of 'paradigms'. Professor Gombrich has also coined the relevant epigram: only where there is a way can there be a will (p. 75).

18 See Thomas S. Kuhn, *The Structure of Scientific Revolutions* (Chicago, University of Chicago Press, 1962), esp. chap. 5, which takes over the notion of 'the priority of paradigms'. The conception is of course a familiar one, except to empiricists. Cf. the insistence that the thought of any period is organized according to 'constellations of absolute pre-suppositions', in R. G. Collingwood, *An Essay on Metaphysics* (Oxford, Clarendon Press, 1940), esp. chap. 7.

19 Marsilius of Padua, *The Defender of Peace*, 2 vols, tr. and ed. A. Gewirth (New York, Harper and Row, 1951–6), vol. 2, pp. 61–7, esp. p. 65.

20 As has been demonstrated in J. G. A. Pocock, 'Machiavelli, Harrington, and English political ideologies in the eighteenth century', *William and Mary Quarterly*, 22 (1965), pp. 549–83. Cf. also Bernard Bailyn, *The Ideological Origins of the American Revolution* (Cambridge, Mass., Harvard University Press, 1967).

21 Gewirth, *Defender*, vol. I, p. 232.

22 For a bibliography, see Gewirth, *Defender*, vol. I, p. 234 n. For a purely textual dismissal of the claim, see for example A. P. D'Entreves, *The Medieval Contribution to Political Thought* (Oxford, Oxford University Press, 1939), p. 58.

23 As has been demonstrated in J. G. A. Pocock, *The Ancient Constitution and the Feudal Law* (Cambridge, Cambridge University Press, 1957), esp. chap. 11.

24 W. B. Gwyn, *The Meaning of the Separation of Powers*, Tulane Studies in Political Science, vol. 9 (New Orleans, Tulane University Press 1965), p. 50 n.

25 Theodore F. T. Plucknett, 'Bonham's case and judicial review', *Harvard Law Review*, 40 (1926–7), p. 68. For the claim that it was actually Coke's 'own intention' to articulate the doctrine 'which American courts today exercise'; see also Edward S. Corwin, 'The "higher law" background of American constitutional law', *Harvard Law Review*, 42 (1928–9), p. 368. Cf. the same author's *Liberty against Government* (Baton Rouge, Louisiana, Louisiana State University Press, 1948), p. 42.

26 For a purely textual dismissal, see S. E. Thorne, 'Dr Bonham's Case', *Law Quarterly Review*, 54 (1938), pp. 543–52.

27 Christopher Morris, *Political Thought in England: Tyndale to Hooker* (Oxford, Oxford University Press, 1953), pp. 181–97.

28 J. W. Gough, *John Locke's Political Philosophy* (Oxford, Clarendon Press, 1950). On government by consent, chap. 3; on trusteeship, p. 145.

29 Gwyn, *Separation of Powers*, p. 52.

30 Arthur O. Lovejoy, *The Great Chain of Being* (Torchbook edn, New York, 1960), p. 15.

31 J. B. Bury, *The Idea of Progress* (London, Macmillan 1932), p. 7.

32 Corinne Comstock Weston, *English Constitutional Theory and the House of Lords* (London, Columbia University Press, 1965), p. 45.

33 Felix Raab, *The English Face of Machiavelli* (London, 1964), p.2.

34 Bury, *Idea of Progress*, p. 7.

35 R. V. Sampson, *Progress in the Age of Reason* (Cambridge Mass., Harvard University Press, 1956), p. 39.

36 M. J. C. Vile, *Constitutionalism and the Separation of Powers* (Oxford, Clarendon Press, 1967), p. 30.

37 Raab, *English Face of Machiavelli*, p. 2.

38 W. T. Jones, *Machiavelli to Bentham*, in *Masters of Political Thought*, 3 vols, ed. Edward M. Sait, (London, Houghton, Mifflin, 1947), p. 50.

39 Robert L. Armstrong, 'John Locke's "Doctrine of Signs": a new metaphysics', *Journal of the History of Ideas*, 26 (1965), p. 382.

40 R. H. Popkin, 'Joseph Glanvill: a precursor of David Hume', *Journal of the History of Ideas*, 14 (1953), p. 300.

41 Ernst Cassirer, *The Philosophy of the Enlightenment*, tr. Fritz C. A. Koelln and James P. Pettegrove (Beacon edn, Boston, 1955), p. 151. It sometimes seems in Cassirer's analysis as though the whole Enlightenment was striving to make Kant possible.

42 G. C. Morris, 'Montesquieu and the varieties of political experience', in *Political Ideas*, ed. David Thomson (London, Penguin, 1966), pp. 89–90.

43 Raab, *English Face of Machiavelli*, pp.1, 11. It is remarkable how far the methodological naiveté underlying this and many other such assumptions has gone unnoticed in the discussion of this greatly overpraised book. For another hostile but convincing appraisal, however, see Sydney Anglo, 'The reception of Machiavelli in Tudor England: a reassessment', *Il Politico*, 31 (1966), pp. 127–38.

44 Allan Bloom with Harry C. Jaffa, *Shakespeare's Politics* (New York, 1964), pp. 1–2, 4, 36.

45 Gwyn, *Separation of Powers*, p. 9.

46 Vile, *Constitutionalism*, p. 46.

47 J. W. Gough, *The Social Contract*, 2nd edn (Oxford, Clarendon Press, 1957), p. 59.

48 Leo Strauss, *What is Political Philosophy?* (Glencoe, Illinois, Free Press 1957), p. 12.

49 Bloom and Jaffa, *Shakespeare's Politics*, pp. 1–2. For a general critique of this belief in political philosophy as the articulation or recovery of certain 'final truths' of this kind, see Arnold S. Kaufman, 'The nature and function of political theory', *Journal of Philosophy*, 51 (1954), pp. 5–22. The belief has been (perhaps somewhat intemperately) defended by Joseph Cropsey, 'A reply to Rothman', *American Political Science Review*, 56 (1962), pp. 353–9, the reply being to a critique of Leo Strauss' approach published by Stanley Rothman in the same number of that journal.

50 See, on Hobbes, Leo Strauss, *Natural Right and History* (Chicago, University of Chicago Press 1953); on Machiavelli, Leo Strauss, *Thoughts on Machiavelli* (Glencoe, Illinois, Free Press, 1958).

51 See for example the attack on Ascham, and the defence of Clarendon, in these terms, in Irene Coltman, *Private Men and Public Causes*, (London, 1962).

52 Strauss, *Machiavelli*, pp. 11–12.

53 Ibid., 14.

54 Maurice Cranston, 'Aquinas', in *Western Political Philosophers*, ed. Maurice Cranston (London, Bodley Head 1964), pp. 34–5.

55 Marsilius, ed. Gewirth, *Defender*, vol. I, p. 312.

56 F. J. Shirley, *Richard Hooker and Contemporary Political Ideas* (London, S.P.C.K. 1949), 256.

57 T. D. Weldon, *States and Morals* (London, J. Murray 1946), pp. 26, 63, 64.

58 George H. Sabine, *A History of Political Theory*, 3rd edn (London, Holt, Rhinehart and Winston, 1951), p. 67.

59 Richard I. Aaron, *John Locke*, 2nd edn (Oxford, Oxford University Press, 1955), pp. 284–5.

60 C. J. Friedrich, 'On rereading Machiavelli and Althusius: reason, rationality and religion', in *Rational Decision*, ed. C. J. Friedrich, *Nomos* VII (New York, Atherton Press 1964), p. 178.

61 John Plamenatz, *Man and Society*, 2 vols (London, Longmans 1963), vol. I, p. 43, on Machiavelli's 'great omission'.

62 Bertrand Russell, *History of Western Philosophy* (New York, Simon and Schuster, 1946), p. 578, on Hobbes's failure to 'realize the importance of the clash between different classes'. It is a matter of scholarly dispute as to whether Hobbes lived in a society in which such an issue could have seemed of the least importance.

63 Andrew Hacker, *Political Theory: Philosophy, Ideology, Science* (New York, 1961), noting this 'great omission' in Machiavelli (p. 192) as well as in Locke (p. 285).

64 Max Lerner, 'Introduction' to Machiavelli, *The Prince* and *The Discourses* (New York, Random House, 1950), on Machiavelli's lack of 'any genuine insights into social organization as the basis of politics' (p. xxx).

65 E. T. Davies, *The Political Ideas of Richard Hooker* (London, 1964), p. 80.

66 Robert A. Dahl, *Modern Political Analysis* (Englewood Cliffs, New Jersey, Prentice Hall 1963), p. 113.

67 Richard H. Cox, *Locke on War and Peace* (Oxford, Oxford University Press, 1960), pp. xv, 189.

68 W. Stark, *Montesquieu: Pioneer of the Sociology of Knowledge* (London, 1960), pp. 144, 153.

69 A similar point about the problem of accommodating different 'levels of abstraction' has been made by J. G. A. Pocock, 'The history of political thought: a methodological enquiry', in *Philosophy, Politics and Society*, 2nd series, ed. Peter Laslett and W. G. Runciman (Oxford, Basil Blackwell 1962), pp. 183–202. This 'scripturalist tendency' is also mentioned by Peter Laslett *sub* 'Political philosophy, history of', in *The Encyclopedia of Philosophy*, 8 vols, ed. Paul Edwards et al. (New York, Macmillan and Free Press 1967), vol. VI, p. 371.

70 Arthur S. McGrade, 'The coherence of Hooker's polity: the books on power', *Journal of the History of Ideas*, 24 (1963), p. 163.

71 Howard Warrender, *The Political Philosophy of Hobbes* (Oxford, Clarendon Press 1957), p. vii.

72 John B. Stewart, *The Moral and Political Philosophy of David Hume* (New York, Columbia University Press, 1963), pp. v–vi.

73 F. M. Barnard, *Herder's Social and Political Thought* (Oxford, Clarendon Press, 1965), p. xix. Cf. also p. 139.

74 E.g., J. W. N. Watkins, *Hobbes's System of Ideas* (London, Hutchinson, 1965), p. 10.

75 Ernst Cassirer, *The Question of Jean Jacques Rousseau*, tr. and ed. Peter Gay (Bloomington, Indiana, Indiana University Press 1954), pp. 46, 62. As

Gay indicates in his Introduction, it may well have been salutary at the time when Cassirer was writing to have insisted on such an emphasis, but it remains questionable whether the somewhat *a priori* assumptions of the study are not misconceived.

76 F. C. Hood, *The Divine Politics of Thomas Hobbes* (Oxford, Clarendon Press, 1964), p. 28.

77 Charles Parkin, *The Moral Basis of Burke's Political Thought* (Cambridge, Cambridge University Press, 1956), pp. 2, 4.

78 Shlomo Avineri, *The Social and Political Thought of Karl Marx* (Cambridge, Cambridge University Press, 1968), p. 3.

79 See for example Sabine, *Political Theory*, p. 642.

80 F. J. C. Hearnshaw, 'Henry St John, Viscount Bolingbroke', in *The Social and Political Ideas of Some English Thinkers of the Augustan Age*, ed. F. J. C. Hearnshaw (London, G. G. Harrap, 1928), p. 243.

81 M.J. Adler, 'Foreword', in Otto A. Bird, *The Idea of Justice*, (New York, 1967), p. xi, and Bird p. 22. The Foreword includes the promise that the 'Institute for Philosophical Research' will continue to 'transform' (*sic*) the 'chaos of differing opinions' on other subjects 'into an orderly set of clearly defined points'. The subjects are to include progress, happiness, and love (pp. ix–xi).

82 For the full demonstration see the Introduction to John Locke, *Two Tracts on Government*, ed. Philip Abrams (Cambridge, Cambridge University Press, 1967).

83 See M. Seliger, *The Liberal Politics of John Locke* (New York, Praeger, 1969). These facts are alluded to only once (pp. 209–10), and only to be dismissed as not being his concern.

84 Thomas Hobbes, *Leviathan*, ed. M. Oakshott (Oxford, Basil Blackwell, 1946), pp. 466–7. This characterization has, of course, been much disputed, and is doubtless too baldly stated here. For a full defence, see my article 'Hobbes's *Leviathan*', *Historical Journal*, 7 (1964), pp. 321–33.

85 Hood, *Hobbes*, pp. 64, 116–117, 136–137.

86 W. Harrison, 'Texts in political theory', *Political Studies*, 3 (1955), pp. 28–44.

87 C. B. Macpherson, *The Political Theory of Possessive Individualism: Hobbes to Locke* (Oxford, Oxford University Press, 1962), p. viii.

88 Leo Strauss, *Persecution and the Art of Writing* (Glencoe, Ill., Free Press 1952), pp. 30–1.

89 For a survey of this approach amongst others, see Eric W. Cochrane, 'Machiavelli: 1940–1960', *Journal of Modern History*, 33 (1961), pp. 113–36. The assumption appears in Chabod's as well as (especially) in Meinecke's work. For a critical survey of such assumptions, based on important scholarly discoveries about the relations between *The Prince* and *Discourses*, see Hans Baron, 'Machiavelli the Republican Citizen and the Author of *The Prince*', *English Historical Review*, 76 (1961), pp. 217–53.

90 Avineri, *Marx*, p. 2.

91 Robert C. Tucker, *Philosophy and Myth in Karl Marx* (Cambridge, Cambridge University Press, 1961), pp. 7, 11, 21, and chap. II. This allows the useful conclusion, moreover, that the 'relevance' usually accorded to the classic texts decisively stops short at Marx (that notoriously irrelevant writer), for his religious obsession means that he 'has very little to say to us' about

capitalism (p. 233), and 'not only made no positive contribution but performed a very great disservice' in what he had to say about freedom (p. 243).

92 This is the theory outlined in Strauss, *Persecution*. Quotations from pp. 24–5 and 30, 32.

93 Ibid., p. 25

94 Ibid., p. 30

95 Ibid., p. 24, 32.

96 Arthur C. Danto, *Analytical Philosophy of History* (Cambridge, Cambridge University Press, 1965), p. 169.

97 K. R. Popper, *The Open Society and Its Enemies*, 4th edn, 2 vols (London, Routledge and Kegan Paul, 1962), vol. I, p. 169.

98 J. Bronowski and Bruce Mazlish, *The Western Intellectual Tradition* (London and New York, Harper and Row, 1960), p.303.

99 J. W. Chapman, *Rousseau – Totalitarian or Liberal?* (New York, 1956), p. vii. My italics. For the judgements there discussed, see for example Alfred Cobban, *The Crisis of Civilization* (London, 1941), p. 67. And especially, J. L. Talmon, *The Origins of Totalitarian Democracy* (London, Mercury Books, 1952), where it is actually claimed that Rousseau 'gave rise to totalitarian democracy' (p. 43).

100 Warren Winiarski, 'Niccolò Machiavelli', in *History of Political Philosophy*, ed. Strauss and Cropsey, p. 247.

101 Ernst Cassirer, *The Myth of the State* (New Haven, Yale University Press, 1946), 140.

102 Winiarski 'Niccolò Machiavelli', p. 273. My italics.

103 As is assumed in the works of Gough, Plamenatz, and Seliger (as well as others) already cited.

104 For a complete analysis of this confusion, and a corrective to it, see John Dunn, *The Political Thought of John Locke* (Cambridge, Cambridge University Press, 1969).

105 Otherwise it is hard to see how there can be any *understanding* at all. It is the force of this difficulty which seems to be ignored in the analysis by Peter Winch, 'Understanding a primitive society', *American Philosophical Quarterly*, I (1964), pp. 307–24. For a corrective, in anthropology, see Martin Hollis, 'Reason and ritual', *Philosophy*, 43 (1968), pp. 231–47.

106 Here I argue against myself, for it now seems to me that in my critique of the influence-model in my article, 'The limits of historical explanations', *Philosophy*, 41 (1966), pp. 199–215, I perhaps stressed too much the impossibility of making the model work, rather than its sheer elusiveness. I would still wish to insist, however, that it can very rarely be made to work, and that when it can be, there is scarcely ever any point in doing so.

107 Harvey C. Mansfield, Jr, *Statesmanship and Party Government* (Chicago, University of Chicago Press, 1965), p. 86. Cf. also pp. 41, 66, 80. For the corresponding claim that Bolingbroke 'anticipates' Burke, see Jeffrey P. Hart, *Viscount Bolingbroke, Tory Humanist* (London, Routledge and Kegan Paul, 1965), pp. 95, 149, etc.

108 Mansfield, *Statesmanship and Party Government*, p. 49, etc. Textbooks on eighteenth-century thought find 'the tradition of Locke' indispensable as a way of accounting for some of the most recurrent features of the period.

See for example Harold J. Laski, *Political Thought in England: Locke to Bentham* (Oxford, Oxford University Press, 1961), pp. 47–53, 131.

109 For this assumption see esp. Strauss, *Natural Right and History*, and Cox, *Locke on War and Peace*.

110 This is the theory in general circulation. E.g., even Wolin, *Politics and Vision*, for the insistence that 'a careful reader cannot fail to see' that Locke was refuting Hobbes (p. 26). The assumption figures in most textbooks of early modern political thought. See for example Kingsley Martin, *French Liberal Thought in the Eighteenth Century* (London, and New York, Harper and Row, 1962), p. 120.

111 See for example Strauss, *What is Political Philosophy?* for the claim that Hobbes 'accepted' (where?) 'Machiavelli's critique of traditional political philosophy' (p. 48).

112 See, as well as Raab's *English Face of Machiavelli*, the studies of Albert Cherel, *La Pensée de Machiavel en France* (Paris, 1935), and Guiseppe Prezzolini, *Machiavelli*, tr. G. Savini (London, 1968), esp. chap. 6.

113 This condition is mentioned by P. P. Wiener, 'Some problems and methods in the history of ideas', *Journal of the History of Ideas*, 22 (1961), pp. 531–48. The relevant (somewhat jaunty) paragraph is at p. 537. I have not elsewhere seen the problems raised by the use of the concept of 'influence' discussed. But cf. my own article, cited in n. 106 above.

114 For the large number and general drift of these, see for example Archibald S. Foord, *His Majesty's Opposition, 1714–1830* (Oxford, Oxford University Press, 1964), esp. chaps 3 and 4.

115 For the group of *de facto*-ists, and their relation to Hobbes, see my own article, 'The ideological context of Hobbes's political thought', *Historical Journal*, 9 (1966), pp. 286–317. For Locke's reading, see Peter Laslett, 'Introduction', to *The Library of John Locke* (Oxford Bibliographical Society Publications, 13), ed. John Harrison and Peter Laslett (Oxford, Oxford University Press, 1965).

116 I have tried to demonstrate this in detail for one recent case of this type of non-history. See my article, 'More's *Utopia*', *Past and Present*, 38 (1967), pp. 153–68, esp. pp. 163–5.

117 This is the paradigm applied even in the best recent scholarly study. See H. N. Brailsford, *The Levellers and the English Revolution*, ed. Christopher Hill (London, Cresset, 1961), p.118.

118 Ibid., pp. 118, 457, etc.

119 Ibid., p. 233.

120 That this was so was made clear by Petty at the Putney Debates. See A. S. P. Woodhouse, *Puritanism and Liberty* (London, J. M. Dent and Son, 1938), p. 83. The point has recently been emphasized by Macpherson in *Possessive Individualism*, chap. 3.

121 As for example Gough does in *John Locke's Political Philosophy*, chap. 3.

122 Presented by John Dunn, 'Consent in the political theory of John Locke', *Historical Journal*, 10 (1967), pp. 153–82.

123 For a superb statement of these themes, see Stuart Hampshire, *Thought and Action* (London, Chatto and Windus, 1959), esp. pp. 135–6, 153–5,

213–16. Some kindred issues are developed in part I of Charles Taylor, *The Explanation of Behaviour* (London, Routledge and Kegan Paul, 1964).

124 Armstrong, 'John Locke's "Doctrine of Signs"', p. 382.

125 For an elaboration of this point and of its implications for the suggestion that history is essentially to be defined as narrative, see Maurice Mandelbaum, 'A note on history as narrative', *History and Theory*, 6 (1967), pp. 413–19.

126 See P. F. Strawson, 'Social morality and individual ideal', *Philosophy*, 36 (1961), pp. 1–17, insisting on the tendency to underestimate this fact, as well as on the wide importance of its implications.

127 See the start of Dunn, 'Identity of the history of ideas', esp. pp. 87–8 on this point.

128 Cf. the title of Watkin's recent book, *Hobbes's System of Ideas*.

129 For Andrew Baxter on Berkeley, see *An Enquiry into the Nature of the Human Soul*, 3rd edn, 2 vols (London, 1745), vol. II, p. 280. For Thomas Reid, see *Essays on the Intellectual Powers of Man*, ed. A. D. Woozley (London, 1941), p.120. for the *Encyclopédie*, see vol. V, *sub* 'egoisme'.

130 On this issue generally, see Harry M. Bracken, *The Early Reception of Berkeley's Immaterialism, 1710–1733* (The Hague, Martinus Nijhoff, 1965), pp. 1–25, 59–81.

131 See Plamenatz, *Man and Society*, Introduction, I, p. x.

132 Hood, *Hobbes*, p. vii.

133 Frank Cioffi, 'Intention and interpretation in criticism', *Proceedings of the Aristotelian Society*, 64 (1963–4), p. 103.

134 A. E. Taylor, 'The ethical doctrine of Hobbes', *Philosophy*, 13 (1938), p. 418. The best recent analysis to take up a similar position is Warrender, *Hobbes*. A similar but more extreme statement is Hood, *Hobbes*.

135 The main work dedicated to this assumption is Elisabeth Labrousse, *Pierre Bayle*, Tome II: *Heterodoxie et rigorisme* (The Hague, Martinus Nijhoff, 1964). See esp. chap. 12 on 'The problem of evil', discussing Bayle's articles on David and on Manichaenism (pp. 346–86).

136 See P. Dibon, 'Redécouverte de Bayle', in *Pierre Bayle, le philosophe de Rotterdam: études et documents,* ed. P. Dibon (Amsterdam, Publications de l'Institut Français d'Amsterdam, 3, 1959), p. xv.

137 H. Dieckmann, 'Pierre Bayle: philosophe of Rotterdam', *Journal of the History of Ideas*, 22 (1961), p. 131. A review article of the work ed. Dibon, cited n. 136 above.

138 Hood, *Hobbes*, p. vii.

139 Labrousse, *Pierre Bayle*, p. x.

140 For Bayle's irony here, especially his emphasis on the ludicrous superstitions uncovered by news of the comet's appearance, see his adoption of the device of a series of questions allegedly put by a worried Catholic to a Doctor of the Sorbonne. Bayle's intentions here are discussed in Walter Rex, *Essays on Pierre Bayle and Religious Controversy* (The Hague, Martinus Nijhoff, 1965).

141 For a fuller account of the difficulties raised in the case of Hobbes, see my article 'The ideological context of Hobbes's political thought', cited in n. 115 above. For the case of Bayle there is a brief but useful sceptical review article on some of the recent work in D. P. Walker, 'Recent

studies of Pierre Bayle', *New York Review of Books*, 8 (5) (23 March 1967), pp. 20–3.

142 John Aubrey, *Brief Lives*, 2 vols, ed. Andrew Clark, (London, 1898), vol. 1, p. 339.

143 See, for Hobbes, S. I. Mintz, *The Hunting of Leviathan* (Cambridge, Cambridge University Press, 1962), and for Bayle, Howard Robinson, *Bayle the Sceptic* (New York, 1931).

144 Lovejoy, *Great Chain of Being*, pp. 15ff sets out the notion of 'unit ideas' as objects of study.

145 Sanford A. Lakoff, *Equality in Political Philosophy* (Cambridge, Mass., Harvard University Press, 1964), p.vii.

146 The phrase was coined by Peter Gay, *The Party of Humanity* (New York, Knopf, 1964), p. 191 in his discussion of Becker.

147 This is the argument of Carl Becker, *The Heavenly City of the Eighteenth Century Philosophers* (New Haven, Yale University Press, 1932), esp. pp. 8 and 30–1.

148 Gay, *Party of Humanity*, p. 193.

149 Sir Thomas Elyot, *The Book Named the Governor*, ed. S. E. Lehmberg (London, J. M. Dent and Sons, 1962), p. 104.

150 For example in the ambiguous discussion in Baldesar Castiglione, *The Book of the Courtier*, tr. and ed. Charles S. Singleton (New York, Anchor Books, 1959), pp. 28ff.

151 J. H. Hexter makes the point in 'The loom of language and the fabric of imperatives: the case of *Il Principe and Utopia*', *American Historical Review*, 69 (1964), pp. 945–68.

152 For this explicit statement of the assumption, see Bateson's 'Functions of criticism', cited in n. 2 above.

153 The implication that there are two senses of 'meaning' which have been confused by this approach could perhaps be demonstrated in a manner analogous to the way in which the confusions about meaning have been pointed out in the case of Russell's theory of descriptions. On this see Alan R. White, 'The "meaning" of Russell's theory of descriptions', *Analysis*, 20 (1959), pp. 7–8.

154 For the classic statement of this commitment, see Ludwig Wittgenstein, *Philosophical Investigations* (Oxford, Basil Blackwell, 1953), esp. para. 43; and for its application as a means of attacking the idea of fixed meanings, see esp. para. 79 *et seq*.

155 The need for the historian to distinguish in this way between sentences and statements is suggested in a rudimentary way in R. G. Collingwood, *An Autobiography* (Oxford, Oxford University Press, 1939), chap. 5, esp. pp. 34–5. The classic elaboration of the distinction between sentences, and statements as sentences used to refer, is owed to P. F. Strawson, 'On referring', *Mind*, 59 (1950), pp. 320–44. For applications, see also P. F. Strawson, *An Introduction to Logical Theory* (London, Methuen, 1952), esp. pp. 4, 9–12, 210–12. I am aware, of course, that the distinction has been criticized by W. V. Quine, 'Mr Strawson on logical theory', *Mind*, 62 (1953), pp. 433–51, on the grounds (amongst other things) that the 'statements' proposed here look like reified entities. I dare to hope that the historical examples themselves help to cast doubt on the validity

of such a criticism. But cf. also the more formal defence of Strawson's theory in J. Xenakis, 'Sentence and statement', *Analysis*, 16 (1955), pp. 91–4.

156 See Collingwood, *Autobiography*, chap. 5, 'Question and answer', esp. pp. 31ff.

157 For it is a crucial implication of Strawson's theory, of course, that truth and falsity are functions of statements, not sentences. It has been questioned whether these distinctions apply as well in logic as they do in ordinary discourse. See E. J. Lemmon, 'Sentences, statements and propositions', in *British Analytical Philosophy*, ed. Bernard Williams and Alan Montefiore (London, Routledge and Kegan Paul, 1966), pp. 87–107. Since my concern here, however, is obviously only with ordinary discourse, I am not concerned with the very complex issues thus raised, nor is my use of the distinctions affected by the possible validity of such criticisms.

158 D. Crabtree, 'Political theory', in *Political Science*, ed. H. Victor Wiseman (London, Routledge and Kegan Paul, 1967), p. 158. My italics.

159 J. Higham, 'Intellectual history and its neighbors', *Journal of the History of Ideas*, 15 (1954), p. 341. My italics.

160 Plamenatz, *Man and Society*, vol. I p. xxi.

161 Jaspers, *The Great Philosophers*, vol. I, p. viii.

162 Hacker, '*Capital* and carbuncles', p. 786.

163 The phrase is Bateson's summary of his recommended methodology in 'Functions of criticism', p. 19.

164 Even 'something of a shibboleth': see J. G. A. Pocock's remarks, *à propos* Raab's book, on this point in a review article in *Historical Studies: Australia and New Zealand*, 12 (1965), pp. 265–96. The approach there recommended is much more like the one I wish here to advocate (see esp. pp. 267–9).

165 Plamenatz, *Man and Society*, vol. I, p. ix.

166 Hacker, *Political Theory*, p. vii.

167 The classic study in English (based in part, it has been argued, on a misunderstanding of the nature of the connection Weber himself claimed to have established) is R. H. Tawney, *Religion and the Rise of Capitalism* (London, Murray, 1926).

168 Here the classic post-Weberian study is R. K. Merton, 'Science, technology and society in seventeenth-century England', *Osiris*, 4 (1938), pp. 360–632.

169 See the literature on Renaissance humanism, and especially on More (from Kautsky to Ames). For bibliographical references, see my article, 'More's *Utopia*', *Past and Present*, 38 (1967), esp. pp. 153–5.

170 For a bibliography for this judgement, as well as a challenge to it, see Keith Thomas, 'The social origins of Hobbes's political thought', *Hobbes Studies*, ed. K. C. Brown (London, Basil Blackwell, 1965), pp. 185–236, esp. nn. 185–6.

171 So called by Macpherson in *Possessive Individualism*, chap. 4.

172 H. R. Trevor-Roper, 'The gentry, 1540–1640', *Economic History Review Supplements*, vol. I, p. 50.

173 See Macpherson's chapter in *Possessive Individualism*.

174 Isaac Kramnick, *Bolingbroke and his Circle: The Politics of Nostalgia in the Age of Walpole* (Cambridge, Mass., Harvard University Press, 1968). See esp. chap. 3.

175 Joseph Cropsy, *Polity and Economy* (The Hague, Martinus Nijhoff, 1957).

176 The fact that to make a statement *is* to perform an action has been clearly emphasized by J. L. Austin in his discussion of how to *do* things in and by saying things. Cf. n. 193, below.

177 Cf. the parallel and immensely influential attempt by L. B. Namier to use the concept of a pre-existing political structure of interests both to explain political behaviour and to dismiss as of secondary significance in such an explanation the force of the ideas by which the actors might seem to have been moved. The ideas themselves ('flapdoodle') are treated as at best the reflections and attempted rationalizations of the given structure of power, and thus of no independent interest in the attempt to explain the pursuit of power itself. This classic interpretation, as applied to eighteenth-century England, has been much criticized on the grounds that the 'life of the mind' has been left out. But the precise nature of the conceptual error involved in the Namierite type of explanation has not I think so far received any proper *philosophical* attention. Recent critics have sought instead to raise the ghost of 'the influence of Bolingbroke', surely a ghost definitively laid by Namier himself. See Harvey C. Mansfield, Jr, 'Sir Lewis Namier considered', *Journal of British Studies*, 2 (1962), pp. 28–55.

178 See for example Crane Brinton, 'Introduction' to *English Political Thought in the Nineteenth Century* (Torchbook edn, New York, 1962), p. 3.

179 See Gay, *Party of Humanity*, p. xiii.

180 As L. B. Namier does in his essay 'Human nature in politics', in *Personalities and Powers* (London and New York, Harper Torchbooks, 1955), pp. 1–7.

181 For a parallel assertion concerning the relations between belief and action see Alasdair MacIntyre, 'A mistake about causality in social science', in *Philosophy, Politics and Society*, 2nd series, ed. Peter Laslett and W. G. Runciman (Oxford, Basil Blackwell, 1962), pp. 48–70. It will readily be seen how much I owe to this discussion. As will also be clear, however, I do not wholly agree with Professor MacIntyre's formulation, and still less with his re-formulation in 'The idea of a social science', *Proceedings of the Aristotelian Society*, supplementary vol. 41 (1967), pp. 95–114.

182 For this distinction between actions and performances (the latter as actions taking time) see Anthony Kenny, *Action, Emotion and Will* (London, Routledge and Kegan Paul, 1963), esp. chap. 8.

183 I am aware that this comes very close to raising one of the traditional difficulties about determinism. I am content, however, that it does not in fact raise the issue, and that I do not here need to do so.

184 Which seems very much to happen in such analyses as Raziel Abelson, 'Because I want to', *Mind*, 74 (1965), pp. 540–53, with its demand for 'expunging pseudo-mechanistic concepts from the purposive language of human affairs' (p. 541).

185 One of the best recent discussions is Donald Davidson, 'Actions, reasons, and causes', *Journal of Philosophy*, 60 (1963), pp. 685–700. See also A. J. Ayer, 'Man as a subject for science' in *Philosophy, Politics and Society*, 3rd

series, ed. Peter Laslett and W. G. Runciman (Oxford, Basil Blackwell 1967), pp. 6–24. And see Alasdair MacIntyre, who has changed his mind on this point, 'The antecedents of action' in *British Analytical Philosophy*, ed. Williams and Montefiore (London, Routledge and Kegan Paul, 1966), pp. 205–25. See generally the excellent bibliography on this topic now available in Alan R. White (ed.), *The Philosophy of Action* (Oxford, Oxford University Press, 1968).

186 See the sorts of examples in Ayer's essay cited in n. 185, e.g., at pp. 16–17.

187 An instance of a performance, according to Kenny's typology. See *Action, Emotion and Will*, p. 165.

188 See, for the use of this sort of example, MacIntyre, 'Antecedents of Action,' e.g., pp. 222–3.

189 For a skilful performance of this manoeuvre, see Ayer's essay cited n. 185.

190 For the use of the practical syllogism to elucidate intentionality, see the discussion, to which I am much indebted, in G. E. M. Anscombe, *Intention* (Oxford, Basil Blackwell, 1957).

191 See for example T. F. Daveney, 'Intentions and causes', *Analysis*, 27 (1966–7), pp. 23–8.

192 It might also be claimed, much more obviously as well as validly, that these remarks go very little way toward arguing a case against the assumption that the understanding of actions is essentially a matter of seeing the results of causes. It is true, of course, that the debate itself is marked by a high degree of assertion rather than argument. But I do hope shortly to complete a more systematic discussion of the subject. [See now chap. 4 of the present volume.]

193 See the reconstruction of Austin's William James Lectures for 1955 by J. O. Urmson, published as *How to do Things with Words* (Oxford, Oxford University Press, 1962).

194 I am aware, of course, that the claim that illocutionary force is co-ordinate with, rather than a part of, meaning, has been disputed. See L. J. Cohen, 'Do illocutionary forces exist?', *Philosophical Quarterly*, 14 (1964), pp. 118–37. I cannot accept this claim: (1) since again I dare to believe that examples – such as those I mentioned here – of any complexity must tell against it, and (2) since there seem to me to be more formal reasons for doubting the claim. These I have mentioned in a forthcoming article. [See now 'Conventions and the understanding of speech-acts', *Philosophical Quarterly*, 20 (1970), pp. 118–38.]

195 See, in favour of the first alternative, Allan H. Gilbert, *Machiavelli's 'Prince' and its Forerunners* (New York, Barnes and Noble, 1938), and, in favour of the second, Felix Gilbert, 'The humanist concept of the prince and *The Prince* of Machiavelli', *Journal of Modern History*, II (1939), pp. 449–83. The statement itself occurs in *The Prince*, chap. 15.

196 In my article cited in n. 194, above.

197 Here I merely assert this claim. Elsewhere I have attempted to substantiate it in detail. See my article, 'History and ideology in the English revolution', *Historical Journal*, 8 (1965), pp. 151–78.

198 See for example the introduction to Brinton, *English Political Thought in the Nineteenth Century*, on the 'fortunate' absence of any agreed methodology, p. 1.

199 A similar commitment is suggested (rather than fully *argued*, it seems to me) in John C. Greene, 'Objectives and methods in intellectual history', *Mississippi Valley Historical Review*, 44 (1957–8), p. 59.

200 That a development of such a rapport might be extremely fruitful has already been both suggested and demonstrated in L. Jonathan Cohen, *The Diversity of Meaning* (London, Methuen, 1962), esp. chap. 1.

201 Collingwood, *Autobiography*, p. 70.

202 John Passmore, 'The idea of a history of philosophy' in *The Historiography of the History of Philosophy, History and Theory, Bieheft 5* (Middleton, Conn., Wesleyan University Press, 1965), p. 12.

203 See for example the claims in Robert S. Brumbaugh, *Plato for the Modern Age* (New York, Collier Books 1962) to the effect that Plato 'offers a relevant contribution' to our problems (pp. 216 etc.).

204 For the explicit insistence that 'the central problems of politics are timeless', see for example Hacker, *Political Theory*, p. 20.

205 I am very grateful to the following for sending me their critical comments on earlier drafts of this paper, and for pointing out a number of mistakes: F. H. Hahn, M. Mandelbaum, J. G. A. Pocock, J. W. Burrow, M. H. Black, and J. A. Thompson. I owe a particular debt to John Dunn, and it will readily be seen that my own discussion owes a great deal to his article, 'The identity of the history of ideas', *Philosophy*, 43 (1968).

CHAPTER 3   MOTIVES, INTENTIONS AND THE INTERPRETATION
OF TEXTS

1 A revised and abbreviated version of an essay which was originally commissioned by *New Literary History* and first appeared as the discussion-article in their issue *On Interpretation* (vol. 3, no. 2, 1972). I have been much helped in revising it by the comments I received on the original article from Mr Michael Black.

2 H. D. Aiken, 'The aesthetic relevance of the artist's intentions', *Journal of Philosophy*, 52 (1955), p. 747.

3 E. D. Hirsch, 'Three dimensions in hermeneutics', *New Literary History*, 3 (1972), p. 246.

4 Morton W. Bloomfield, 'Allegory as interpretation', *New Literary History*, 3 (1972), p. 301.

5 The aim announced in Anthony Savile, 'The place of intention in the concept of art', *Proceedings of the Aristotelian Society*, 69 (1968–9), p. 101. (Italics added.)

6 See the valuable cautionary remarks in William Righter, 'Myth and interpretation', *New Literary History*, 3 (1972), pp. 319–44.

7 Richard Kuhns, 'Criticism and the problem of intention', *Journal of Philosophy*, 57 (1960), p. 7.

8 Hirsch, 'Three dimensions in hermeneutics', p. 248.

9 Wolfgang Iser, 'The reading process: a phenomenological approach', *New Literary History*, 3 (1972), p. 288.

10 Mario J. Valdes, 'Towards a structure of criticism', *New Literary History*, 3 (1972), pp. 263–5, 272–3.

11 Kuhns, 'Criticism and the problem of intention', p. 7.

12 Hirsch, 'Three dimensions in hermeneutics', p. 245.

13 David Lodge, 'The critical moment, 1964', *Critical Quarterly*, 6 (1964), p. 267.

14 Cleanth Brooks, *The Well Wrought Urn* (London, D. Dobson 1949), Preface.

15 F. R. Leavis, 'The responsible critic: or the function of criticism at any time', *Scrutiny*, 19 (1953), p. 163. For a contrasting position, however, see Leavis's *Lectures in America* (London, Chatto and Windus 1969), especially the chapter on Yeats, in which it is conceded that some texts can only be fully understood in relation to the author's life-experiences. See esp. pp. 80–1, where literary history is in consequence assigned a role in relation to literary criticism.

16 The discussion has usually focused on the alleged irrelevance of intentions, but this concept has been standardly used by literary theorists in an extended sense, which in effect covers both motives and intentions. This fact has been pointed out by H. Morris Jones, 'The relevance of the artist's intentions', *British Journal of Aesthetics*, 4 (1964), p. 143. For some examples, see Kuhns' discussion, which includes such motives as the desire 'to achieve fame' under the heading of intentions (p. 6), and John Kemp, 'The work of art and the artist's intentions', *British Journal of Aesthetics*, 4 (1964), pp. 147–8 which distinguishes 'immediate intentions' from 'ulterior intentions'. The latter class appears to be identical with the class of motives.

17 W. K. Wimsatt and M. C. Beardsley, 'The intentional fallacy', *Sewanee Review*, 54 (1946), pp. 477–8 and p. 484.

18 Iser, 'The reading process', p. 279.

19 Wimsatt and Beardsley, 'The intentional fallacy', p. 483.

20 Bloomfield, 'Allegory as interpretation', p. 309. Cf. also p. 301.

21 Hirsch, 'Three dimensions in hermeneutics', p. 249.

22 Morris Jones, 'Relevance of artist's intentions', p. 140. Cf. the comment in A. P. Ushenko, *The Dynamics of Art* (Bloomington, University of Indiana Press, 1953), p. 57 on the work 'speaking for itself'.

23 The connection between this claim and the anti-intentionalist position is noted (but not endorsed) by Aiken, 'Aesthetic relevance', p. 752.

24 Wimsatt and Beardsley, 'The intentional fallacy', p. 468.

25 R. Jack Smith, 'Intention in an organic theory of poetry', *Sewanee Review*, 56 (1948), p. 625.

26 T. M. Gang, 'Intention', *Essays in Criticism*, 7 (1957), p. 179.

27 Wimsatt and Beardsley, 'The intentional fallacy', p. 468.

28 Gang, 'Intention', p. 175. (Italics added.)

29 Smith, 'Organic theory of poetry', p. 625.

30 Wimsatt and Beardsley, 'The intentional fallacy', pp. 470, 477.

31 Ushenko, *Dynamics of Art*, p. 57.

32 Isabel C. Hungerland, 'The concept of intention in art criticism', *Journal of Philosophy*, 52 (1955), p. 733. For an account of the value and limitation

of this approach, see Michael Black, 'Reading a play', *The Human World*, I (1971), 12–33, esp. the discussion at pp. 13–18.

33 Wimsatt and Beardsley, 'The intentional fallacy', p. 470.

34 Smith, 'Organic theory of poetry', p. 631. Cf. Black, 'Reading a play' p. 12 noting the frequent citation of Coleridge's dictum to the effect that a successful work of art contains within itself the reasons why it is so and not otherwise.

35 Gang, 'Intention', p. 178.

36 Graham Hough, *An Essay on Criticism* (London, Duckworth 1966), p. 60.

37 This point is well brought out in Frank Cioffi, 'Intention and interpretation in criticism', *Proceedings of the Aristotelian Society*, 64 (1963–4), esp. pp. 104–6.

38 Ibid., p. 88.

39 For a valuable general analysis of the concept of intention, which distinguishes it from the concept of a motive, see G. E. M. Anscombe, *Intention* (Oxford, Basil Blackwell, 1957) I am much indebted to this account and to Anthony Kenny, *Action, Emotion and Will* (London, Routledge and Kegan Paul, 1964), pp. 76–126. My own account of intentions in relation to interpretation has recently been given a partial endorsement (in a discussion which I find generally congenial in its conclusions) by Michael Hancher, 'Three kinds of intention', *Modern Language Notes*, 87 (1972), pp. 827–51. See esp. pp. 836 n. and 842–3 n. It has also been deployed (in what seems to me an interesting practical application) by A. J. Close 'Don *Quixote* and the "intentionalist fallacy"', *British Journal of Aesthetics*, 12 (1972), pp. 19–39. See esp. p. 39.

40 I have tried to give an analysis of the relations between discerning the intention in, and the *point* of, an action, in the second part of my article, 'On performing and explaining linguistic actions', *Philosophical Quarterly*, 21 (1971), pp. 1–21.

41 See esp. the account posthumously published as *How to do Things with Words*, ed. J. O. Urmson (Oxford, Oxford University Press, 1962).

42 I have tried to given a fuller account of this point in my article 'Conventions and the understanding of speech-acts', *Philosophical Quarterly*, 20 (1970), pp. 118–38.

43 For this notion see Austin, *How to do Things*, pp. 101–31. For a deployment of the distinction, relevant to my present argument, see J. O. Urmson, *The Emotive Theory of Ethics* (London, Hutchinson 1968), pp. 27–9.

44 This is the example given in Gang, 'Intention', p. 177 of 'the intention to produce a certain emotional effect'. One influential source for this way of talking about intentions appears to have been I. A. Richards, *Practical Criticism* (London, Routledge and Kegan Paul, 1929), pp. 180–3.

45 For a general account of this issue, see P. F. Strawson, 'Meaning and truth', *Logico-Linguistic Papers* (London, Methuen, 1971).

46 Note that the sense of 'meaning' with which I have been concerned is such that my claims apply potentially to other than literary works of art. This point is brought out by Kuhns, 'Criticism and the problem of intention', p. 7.

47 F. W. Bateson, 'The function of criticism at the present time', *Essays in Criticism*, 3 (1953), p. 16. Hirsch ('Three dimensions in hermeneutics', p. 247) has discussed the traditional claim (the view, for example, of Schleirmacher) that the aim of exegesis must always be to get as close as possible to the 'original meaning'. For recent accounts of the debate between the

'historical' and 'critical' schools, see (for an account inclining to the former side) Lionel Trilling, *The Liberal Imagination* (London and New York, Doubleday, 1951), esp. pp. 185ff, and (for an account inclining to the latter side) Black, 'Reading a play', esp. pp. 12ff.

48 Here I retract an overstatement which I made in my essay, 'Meaning and understanding in the history of ideas', *History and Theory*;(2) above.

49 This point is well brought out both in Cioffi, 'Intention and interpretation', in discussing Edmund Wilson's interpretation of James's *Turn of the Screw*, and in Morris Jones, 'Relevance of artist's intentions', p. 141. It seems to me, however, that Morris Jones draws the wrong moral from his story.

50 For a discussion of this example, see my article 'Meaning and understanding in the history of ideas'; (2) above, p. 33.

51 C. B. Macpherson, *The Political Theory of Possessive Individualism: Hobbes to Locke* (Oxford, Oxford University Press, 1962), chap. 5, esp. pp. 206–9.

52 I derive the whole of this example from John Dunn, *The Political Thought of John Locke* (Cambridge, Cambridge University Press, 1969), esp. pp. 208–13, 214–20. It is true that Dunn's objections might be partly countered by the suggestion that Locke may have held the belief that his society was likely to become concerned with unlimited capital accumulation, and would thus come to need a justification which he decided immediately to supply. I do not see, however, that this would adequately counter Dunn's third point.

CHAPTER 4 'SOCIAL MEANING' AND THE EXPLANATION OF SOCIAL ACTION

I am particularly indebted to Dr John Burrow, Mr John Dunn, and Mr Geoffrey Hawthorn for comments on earlier drafts of this paper.

1 Here and throughout I adopt the terminology suggested by Sidney Morgenbesser, 'Is it a science?', *Social Research*, 33 (1966), p. 255.

2 H. P. Rickman, *Understanding and the Human Studies* (London, Allen and Unwin 1967), p. 23.

3 Alfred Schutz, 'The social world and the theory of social action', *Social Research*, 27 (1960), p. 203.

4 Peter Winch, *The Idea of a Social Science* (London, Routledge and Kegan Paul, 1958), p. 45.

5 Quentin Gibson, *The Logic of Social Enquiry* (London, Routledge and Kegan Paul, 1960), p. 52.

6 A. J. Ayer, 'Man as a subject for science' in *Philosophy, Politics and Society*, ed. P. Laslett and W. G. Runciman series III (Oxford, Basil Blackwell, 1967), p. 23.

7 May Brodbeck, 'Meaning and action', *Philosophy of Science*, 30 (1963), p. 309.

8 A. I. Melden, *Free Action* (London, Routledge and Kegan Paul, 1961), pp. 87–8, 102, 104, 184.

9 R. G. Collingwood, *The Idea of History* (Oxford, Oxford University Press, 1946), pp. 214–15.

10 Max Weber, *Economy and Society*, 2 vols, ed. G. Roth and C. Wittich (Berkeley, University of California Press, 1978), p. 8.

11 Schutz, 'Social world', pp. 206, 211, 214.

12 Winch, *Idea of a social science*, pp. 45, 72.

13 Donald Davidson, 'Actions, reasons and causes', *Journal of Philosophy*, 60 (1963), pp. 685–700.

14 Ayer, 'Man as a subject', pp. 16, 17, 21, 22–3.

15 C. Hempel, 'The function of general laws in history', *Journal of Philosophy* (1942), pp. 44–5.

16 E. Durkheim, *The Rules of Sociological Method*, tr. Solovay and Mueller (New York, Free Press, 1964), p. 110.

17 A. MacIntyre, 'A mistake about causality in social science', in *Philosophy, Politics and Society*, 2nd series, ed. P. Laslett and G. Runciman (Oxford, Basil Blackwell, 1969), pp. 48–70, esp. pp. 56–7.

18 Ayer, 'Man as a subject', pp. 21–3.

19 See my article 'On performing and explaining linguistic actions', *Philosophical Quarterly*, 21 (1971), pp. 1–21. I make use of this material here by permission of the editor.

20 Here I adopt an example from P. F. Strawson, 'Intention and convention in speech-acts'. I also follow the argument of this article (1) in extending (and in this sense rejecting) Austin's concept of a convention, and (2) in relating Grice's theory of meaning to Austin's theory of illocutionary force. I have tried to defend both these commitments in 'Conventions and the understanding of speech-acts', *Philosophical Quarterly*, 20 (1970), pp. 118–38.

21 See H. P. Grice, 'Meaning', *Philosophical Review*, 66 (1957), pp. 377–88 and his revisions in 'Utterer's meaning and intentions', *Philosophical Review*, 78 (1969), pp. 147–77.

22 J. L. Austin, *How To Do Things with Words*, ed. J. O. Urmson (Oxford, Oxford University Press, 1962), p. 118.

23 Grice, 'Meaning', p. 388.

24 Martin Hollis, 'Reason and ritual', *Philosophy*, 43 (1968), p. 231.

25 R. D. Laing and A. Esterton, *Sanity, Madness, and the Family*, 2nd edn (London, Tavistock, 1970), p. 46.

26 Ibid., p. 35.

27 Ibid., p. 34.

28 Felix Gilbert, 'The humanist concept of the prince and *The Prince* of Machiavelli', *Journal of Modern History*, 11 (1939), pp. 449–83, 477.

29 Ibid., p. 480.

30 Melden, *Free Action*, pp. 83–9; Rickman, *Understanding and the Human Sciences*, p. 69; Winch, *Idea of a Social Science*, pp. 45–51.

31 Ayer, 'Man as a subject', p. 9; Davidson, 'Actions, reasons and causes', p. 699; Alasdair MacIntyre, *Against the Self-Images of the Age* (London, Duckworth, 1971), p. 226.

32 Ayer, 'Man as a subject', pp. 9–10.

33 See for example Peter Winch, 'Mr Louch's idea of a social science', *Inquiry*, 7 (1964), p.203.

34 For example, I. C. Jarvie and Joseph Agassi speak of 'a general criticism' in current social anthropology of 'the entire assumption that people's actions can be explained by their beliefs' in *Rationality* ed. Bryan R. Wilson (London, Basil

Blackwell, 1970), p. 179. (But this is denied by J. H. M. Beattie in ibid., p. 246.)

35 Hollis, 'Reason and ritual', pp. 235–6 criticizes this type of explanation.

36 Gibson, *Logic of Social Enquiry*, p. 156.

37 Wilson, *Rationality*, p. 173.

38 MacIntyre, 'Mistake about causality', p. 247.

39 This is the position taken up in Peter Winch, 'Understanding a primitive society', *American Philosophical Quarterly*, 1 (1964), p. 316.

40 They seem, for example, to be conflated in Steven Lukes, 'Some problems about rationality', *European Journal of Sociology*, 8 (1967), p. 262.

41 This is the commitment of the methodological introduction to J. P. Plamenatz, *Man and Society*, 2 vols (London, Longmans, 1964), vol. I, p. x.

42 For these claims see respectively A. R. Louch, *Explanation and Human Action* (Oxford, Blackwell, 1966), p. 238; Melden, *Free Action*, p. 184; Raziel Abelson, 'Because I want to', *Mind*, 74 (1965), p. 541.

43 Ayer, 'Man as a subject', p. 24.

CHAPTER 5 SOME PROBLEMS IN THE ANALYSIS OF POLITICAL THOUGHT AND ACTION

1 I am very grateful to Stefan Collini and John Thompson for reading the draft of this article. I owe a special debt to John Dunn for numerous discussions about the issues I have considered in it. (This article appeared in a symposium in *Political Theory*, 2 (3) (August 1974), to which Professors Weiner and Schochet contributed articles.)

2 Keith Thomas, 'The social origins of Hobbes's political thought', in *Hobbes Studies* ed. K. C. Brown (Oxford, Basil Blackwell, 1965).

3 M. Leslie, 'In defense of anachronism', *Political Studies*, 18 (1970), pp. 433–47; P. Mew, 'Conventions on thin ice', *Philosophical Quarterly*, 21 (1971), pp. 352–6; B. Parekh and R. N. Berki, 'The history of political ideas: a critique of Q. Skinner's methodology', *Journal of the History of Ideas*, 34 (1973), pp. 163–84; C. D. Tarlton, 'Historicity, meaning and revisionism in the study of political thought', *History and Theory*, 12 (1973), pp. 307–28; Gordon Schochet, 'Quentin Skinner's method', *Political Theory*, 2 (3) (1974), pp. 261–76. Professor Tarlton's critique is also concerned with the methodological writings of John Dunn and J. G. A. Pocock. I have confined my remarks about his article exclusively to those sections which are concerned with my work.

4 Tarlton, 'Historicity, meaning and revisionism', p. 311. Q. Skinner, 'The limits of historical explanations', *Philosophy*, 41 (1966), pp. 199–215, and 'On two traditions of English political thought', *Historical Journal*, 9 (1966), pp. 136–9.

5 Parekh and Berki, 'History of political ideas', p. 183.

6 Howard Warrender, *The Political Philosophy of Hobbes* (Oxford, Clarendon Press, 1957); F. C. Hood, *The Divine Politics of Thomas Hobbes* (Oxford,

Oxford University Press, 1964); Leo Strauss, *Natural Right and History* (Chicago, Chicago University Press, 1953); C. B. Macpherson, *The Political Theory of Possessive Individualism: Hobbes to Locke* (Oxford, 1962).

7 Tarlton, 'Historicity, meaning and revisionism', p. 312.

8 M. Levin, 'What makes a classic in political theory?', *Political Science Quarterly*, 88 (1973), pp. 462–76.

9 Macpherson, *Possessive Individualism*.

10 H. Parris, 'The nineteenth-century revolution in government: a reappraisal reappraised', *Historical Journal*, 3 (1960), pp. 17–37; J. Hart, 'Nineteenth-century social reform: a Tory interpretation of history', *Past and Present*, 31 (1965), pp. 39–61.

11 See, for example, J. G. A. Pocock, *Politics, Language and Time* (New York, Atheneum, 1971), pp. 3–41.

12 See, for example, P. M. Rattansi, 'The intellectual origins of the Royal Society', *Notes and Records of the Royal Society*, 23 (1971), pp. 129–43.

13 See M. Hesse, 'Reasons and evaluations in the history of science', in *Changing Perspectives in the History of Science* ed. M. Teich and R. Young (London, Heinemann, 1973).

14 H. Butterfield, *The Whig Interpretation of History* (Harmondsworth, Penguin, 1973), p. 28.

15 Leslie, 'Defense of anachronism', p. 433.

16 Tarlton, 'Historicity, meaning and revisionism', p. 314.

17 Ibid., p. 314 n.

18 See A. MacIntyre, *A Short History of Ethics* (New York, Macmillan, 1966) and *Against the Self-Images of the Age* (London, Duckworth, 1971).

19 See, for example, W. H. Greenleaf, 'Theory and the study of politics', *British Journal of Political Science*, 2 (1970), pp. 467–77; L. Kreiger, 'The autonomy of intellectual history', *Journal of the History of Ideas*, 34 (1973), pp. 499–516.

20 Parekh and Berki, 'History of political ideas', p. 169.

21 Ibid., P. 170; Tarlton, 'Historicity, meaning and revisionism', p. 321.

22 Parekh and Berki, 'History of political ideas', p. 175.

23 J. W. Burrow, *Evolution and Society* (Cambridge, Cambridge University Press, 1970), pp. xxii–xxiv.

24 See, for example, C. Olsen, 'Knowledge of one's own intentional actions', *Philosophical Quarterly*, 19 (1969), pp. 324–36, and the references in W. Alston, 'Varieties of privileged access', *American Philosophical Quarterly*, 8 (1971), pp. 223–41.

25 See, also, Q. Skinner, 'Conventions and the understanding of speech-acts', *Philosophical Quarterly*, 20 (1970), pp. 118–38, and 'On performing and explaining linguistic actions', *Philosophical Quarterly*, 21 (1971), pp. 1–21.

26 Mew, 'Conventions on thin ice'.

27 See A. J. Close, 'Don Quixote and the intentionalist fallacy', *British Journal of Aesthetics*, 12 (1972), pp. 19–39; M. Hancher, 'Three kinds of intention', *Modern Language Notes*, 87 (1972), pp. 827–51.

28 For two recent and impressive contributions, see S. R. Schiffer, *Meaning* (Oxford, Clarendon Press, 1972); and especially see D. K. Lewis, *Convention: A Philosophical Study* (Cambridge, Mass., Harvard University Press, 1969).

29 Parekh and Berki, 'History of political ideas', pp. 174, 170, 173.
30 Ibid., p. 172.
31 J. Plamenatz, *Man and Society*, 2 vols (London, Longmans, 1964), vol. I, p. x.
32 Parekh and Berki, 'History of political ideas', p. 168.
33 Tarlton, 'Historicity, meaning and revisionism', p. 325.
34 Parekh and Berki, 'History of political ideas', p. 184.
35 Ibid., p. 180.
36 See Jeffrey Hart, *Viscount Bolingbroke: Tory Humanist* (London, Routledge and Kegan Paul, 1965), Pocock, *Politics, Language and Time*, p. 134; and see, similarly, C. Robbins, *The Eighteenth-century Commonwealthman* (Cambridge, Mass., Harvard University Press, 1959).
37 See Q. Skinner, 'The principles and practice of opposition: the case of Bolingbroke versus Walpole', in *Historical Perspectives: Essays in Honour of J. H. Plumb*, ed. N. McKendrick (London, Europa Publications, 1974), pp. 93–128.
38 Parekh and Berki, 'History of political ideas', p. 176.
39 Tarlton, 'Historicity, meaning and revisionism', p. 313, see also pp. 321–2.
40 G. Holmes, *British Politics in the Age of Anne* (London, Macmillan, 1967).
41 I. Kramnick, *Bolingbroke and his Circle: The Politics of Nostalgia in the Age of Walpole* (Cambridge, Mass., Harvard University Press, 1968).
42 L. B. Namier, *England in the Age of the American Revolution* (London, Macmillan, 1930), p. 147.
43 L. B. Namier, *The Structure of Politics at the Accession of George III* (London, Macmillan, 1957), p. vii.
44 Butterfield, *Whig Interpretation of History*, p. 209.
45 J. Brooke, 'Namier and Namierism', *History and Theory*, 3 (1963), p. 341.
46 While there is I think no doubt about the existence of such a group of terms, the category is, of course, a diverse one. The spectrum includes a number of cases where the criteria for the application of the given term are relatively fixed, while their evaluative direction is less so; a number of cases where the opposite applies; and a number of cases where both criteria and the evaluative uses of the term are subjects of ideological debate. (For further examples and discussion, see P. Foot, 'Moral arguments', *Mind*, 67 (1958), pp. 502–13).
47 See J. Searle, 'Meaning and speech-acts', *Philosophical Review*, 71 (1962), pp. 423–32.
48 See C. L. Stevenson, *Facts and Values* (New Haven, Yale University Press, 1963).
49 J. L. Austin, *How to do things with Words*, ed. J. O. Urmson (Oxford, Oxford University Press, 1962), pp. 99–105.
50 Parekh and Berki, 'History of political ideas', p. 168.
51 H. R. Trevor-Roper, 'Religion, the Reformation and social change', in G. A. Hayes-McCoy (ed.) *Historical Studies*, 4 (1963), p. 29.

CHAPTER 6   LANGUAGE AND SOCIAL CHANGE

1 First published in 1976, issued in a revised and expanded form in 1983. My

critique of the book originally appeared (under the title 'The idea of a cultural lexicon') in *Essays in Criticism*, July 1979. For help with that version I remain greatly indebted to John Dunn, Susan James, Jonathan Lear, Christopher Ricks and Richard Rorty. The present essay is a revision and extension of the (slightly altered) reprint of the 1979 article which appeared in L. Michaels and C. Ricks (eds), *The State of the Language* (Berkeley, University of California Press, 1980), pp. 562–78. Most of the claims in Williams 1976 which I criticized in 1979 and 1980 have been revised or deleted in Williams 1983. I have therefore given page-references to both editions of his book.

2 Williams 1976, p. 21: 1983, p. 24.

3 Williams 1976, pp. 20–1; 1983, pp. 23–4.

4 Williams 1976, p. 13; 1983, p. 15.

5 Williams 1976, pp. 12–13; 1983, p. 15.

6 Or she, of course. But in what follows, as in earlier chapters, I shall allow myself the convenience of treating 'he', 'his' etc., as abbreviations, where appropriate, for 'he or she', 'his or her', etc.

7 Williams 1976, pp. 84, 189. But in Williams 1983, pp. 95, 224 these claims are deleted, and in the new Introduction Williams explicitly acknowledges (1983, p. 21) 'the difficult relations between words and concepts'.

8 Williams 1976, p. 9; 1983, pp. 11–12.

9 Williams 1976, pp. 13, 19–20, 1983, pp. 15, 22–3.

10 Williams 1976, pp. 12, 15, 1983, pp. 14,17.

11 Among moral philosophers I am most indebted to P. Foot, 'Moral arguments', *Mind* 67 (1958), pp. 502, 13; I. Murdoch, *The Sovereignty of Good* (London, Routledge and Kegan Paul, 1970) and the very illuminating comments in S. Hampshire, *Thought and Action* (London, Chatto and Windus, 1959), esp. pp. 195–222. Among philosophers of language, my approach owes most to J. Austin, *How to Do Things with Words*, ed. J. Urmson and M. Sbisa, 2nd edn, (Oxford, Oxford University Press, 1975); L. Wittgenstein, *Philosophical Investigations* (Oxford, Basil Blackwell, 1959); and the analysis of Frege's views presented in M. Dummett, *Frege: Philosophy of Language* (London, Duckworth, 1973), esp. pp. 81–109.

12 Williams 1976, p. 272; 1983, p. 322.

13 For an attack on this line of thought see H. Putnam, *Mind, Language and Reality* (Cambridge, Cambridge University Press, 1975), pp. 117–31.

14 Even Putnam's examples are unconvincing. Putnam, *Mind, Language and Reality*, pp. 127–8 takes the case of *gold* and argues that the meaning of the word would not be affected even if we found gold rusting, and were thus obliged to change our beliefs about the substance. This seems dogmatic. Would we really go on saying things like 'as good as gold'? If not, might we not have to concede that the meaning of *gold* had changed?

15 Williams 1983, pp. 22–3, slightly revised from Williams 1976, p. 20. Williams 1983, p. 23 protests at the kind of reader who, in criticizing this approach, is 'content to reassert the facts of connection and interaction from which this whole inquiry began'. Williams' new Introduction is thus explicit about the problems posed by a holistic (and in that sense a sceptical) approach to 'meanings'. But I cannot see that the implications of this

scepticism have been accommodated even in the revised version of his text.

16 Otherwise it is hard to see how the disputants could be *arguing*.

17 On this point see M. Dummett, 'The justification of induction', *Proceedings of the British Academy*, 59 (1973), pp. 201–32.

18 Hampshire, *Thought and Action*, p. 197.

19 Ibid., p. 196.

20 Ibid., p. 197.

21 Williams 1976, p. 99, 109, 143; 1983, pp. 115, 131, 171.

22 Here I offer what I take to be a corrected account of an example originally mentioned in 5 above, p. 116.

23 For a fuller discussion for this example see my article, 'The principles and practice of opposition: the case of Bolingbroke versus Walpole', in *Historical Perspectives: Essays in Honour of J. H. Plumb*, ed. N. McKenrick (London, Europa Publications, 1974),, pp. 93–128.

24 Williams 1976, pp. 50, 80; 1983, pp. 59, 91.

25 Williams 1976, pp. 176–8; 1983, pp. 210–12.

26 Williams 1976, p. 117; 1983, p. 211.

27 Here I draw on the classic account in J. Searle, 'Meaning and speech-acts', *Philosophical Review*, 71 (1962), 423–32. However, Searle does not I think succeed in showing that meaning and speech-acts are wholly separate. All he shows is that sense and reference are capable of remaining stable while speech-act potential is undergoing a change. Depending on one's view of meaning, one might still want to insist that speech-act potential is part of meaning, even if it is distinct from both sense and reference.

28 Note, however, that Williams 1983, p. 22 now counters this criticism.

29 Williams 1976, p. 43. But in Williams 1983 this claim is deleted.

30 Williams 1976, p. 53; 1983, p. 62.

31 Williams 1976, pp. 13–14. But in Williams 1983, p. 16 this claim is modified.

32 Here I draw heavily on the Introduction to my book, *The Foundations of Modern Political Thought*, 2 vols. (Cambridge, Cambridge University Press, 1978), vol. I, pp. xi–xiii.

33 C. Taylor, 'Interpretation and the sciences of man', *Review of Metaphysics*, 24 (1971), p. 24.

CHAPTER 7   SAY IT WITH FLOWERS

1 This paper owes a great debt to Skinner's many articles, especially to 'The ideological context of Hobbes' political thought', *Historical Journal*, 9 (1966), pp. 286–317; 'Meaning and understanding in the history of ideas', above, 2; '"Social meaning" and the explanation of social action', above, 4; 'The principles and practices of opposition': the case of Bolingbroke versus Walpole', in *Historical Perspectives: Essays in Honour of J. H. Plumb*, ed. N. McKendrick (London, Europa Publications, 1974), pp. 93–128; and 'Some problems in the analysis of political thought and action', above, 5. I should like to thank him for many previous discussions and help

which would no doubt have included the present paper, had we not tried to preserve a shadow of the Joint Session's jousting tradition.

CHAPTER 8   HOW DO ILLOCUTIONARY DESCRIPTIONS EXPLAIN?

For helpful comments I am grateful to Alison Assiter, G. A. Cohen, Trevor Pateman, the participants in the Bristol Philosophy of Mind Workshop 1978 and the editor of *Ratio*.

1 In the 1955 William James Lectures, published posthumously as *How To Do Things With Words*, ed. J. O. Urmson, in 1962. Page references are to the 2nd edn, 1975.

2 For recognition and acknowledgement of his influence, compare M. R. Ayers, 'Analytical Philosophy and the History of Philosophy' in *Philosophy and Its Past*, ed. J. Ree et. al. (Brighton, Harvester, 1978), p. 42; John Dunn, 'Practising history and social science on "realist" assumptions', in *Action and Interpretation*, ed. C. Hookway and P. Pettit (Cambridge, Cambridge University Press, 1977), p. 154 n.; Martin Hollis, *Models of Man* (Cambridge, Cambridge University Press, 1977), pp. vii, 74–5, n. 4; Martin Hollis, 'Say it with flowers', 7 above; Gordon Schochet, 'Quentin Skinner's method', *Political Theory* 2 (1974).

3 I treat as equivalent the ideas of the illocutionary *force* of an utterance and the idea of the illocutionary *act* performed in uttering it. Strawson (in 'Intention and convention in speech-acts', *Philosophical Review*, 73, reprinted in *Symposium on J. L. Austin*, ed. K. T. Fann (London, Routledge and Kegan Paul, 1964), p. 381), distinguishes between the two on the grounds that an utterance may have the force of, say, a warning but if it is not understood as such by its audience no act of warning will have been performed. Such a distinction is faithful to Austin's own insistence (*How To Do Things*, p. 117) that the performance of an illocutionary act involves the securing of uptake. However, in the case of a number of the examples Austin gives of illocutionary acts it is not easy to see why he did insist on this (cf. L. J. Cohen, 'Speech-acts', in *Current Trends in Linguistics*, vol. 12, ed. T. A. Sebeok (1974), pp. 178–9). I believe that the making of audience's uptake into a necessary condition for the performance of an illocutionary act is in any case dubiously consistent with other claims Austin wants to make and is better dropped. But to pursue the point here would take me too far from my present concerns. See further n. 14.

4 Austin, *How To Do Things*, pp. 99–101.

5 Compare, Keith Graham, *J. L. Austin: A Critique of Ordinary Language Philosophy*, (Brighton, Harvester, 1977), pp. 87–108.

6 Strawson, 'Intention and convention', and J. R. Searle, 'What is a speech-act?', in *Philosophy in America*, ed. Max Black (London, Allen and Unwin, 1965).

7 Compare, Q. Skinner, 'Hermeneutics and the role of history', *New Literary History*, 7 (1975–6), p. 212.

8 Q. Skinner, *The Foundations of Modern Political Thought*, 2 vols (Cambridge, Cambridge University Press, 1978), vol. I, p. xiii, italics in original.

9 For a discussion of this part of Skinner's account, see Keith Graham, 'The recovery of illocutionary force', *Philosophical Quarterly* 30 (1980).

10 Compare, Q. Skinner, 'On performing and explaining linguistic actions', *Philosophical Quarterly*, 21 (1971), p. 13.

11 Compare ibid., p. 13.

12 Compare ibid., p. 16.

13 For an apposite discussion see Hollis, *Models of Man*, pp. 115–22.

14 I should be happy to say all, but it is not clear that Austin would. There is some suggestion that he would exclude parasitical uses of language, as in play-acting or soliloquy (*How To Do Things*, p. 22) and exclamations (p. 133). Presumably his doubts about the latter stem from his view (not shared by Skinner) that there can be no illocutionary act where there is no locutionary act (p. 114) coupled with a doubt whether, e.g., 'Ouch' or 'Damn' is a locutionary act. Certainly there is no *propositional* content in such cases but they do involve language and it makes a difference *what* word is spoken ('Damn' rather than 'Flour'). Unlike Austin I should see nothing wrong with regarding them as cases of the illocutionary act of swearing (p. 105). In the same vein I should be prepared to regard, e.g., play-acting as itself a kind of illocutionary act.

15 Acts of non-verbal communication share the features of straightforward utterances but present us with the reverse problem. That is, when someone issues a straightforward utterance we shall know (at least in an ordinary synchronic, monolingual case) what message it carries and our problem will be to work out what act(s) it also constituted; whereas we standardly know what is *done* in an act of non-verbal communication and our problems concern precisely what message it carries.

16 Skinner there cites Ayer, 'Man as a subject', pp. 21–23 as a place where this assumption is made. I see nothing in Ayer's argument to justify such an attribution, but do doubt the assumption is worth discussing on its merits in any case.

17 As Hollis points out, *Models of Man*, pp. 115–22.

18 This at least will apply to the cases where the initial datum is an utterance. It may be felt that my modification cannot possibly apply to those cases where it is a voluntary action. Many problems are raised by Skinner's extension of Austin's original theory to cover voluntary actions, and indeed by the more general tendency to use the idea of a 'text' to refer 'not just to speech but to any act whose author intends others to understand something by it' (Hollis, *Models of Man*, p. 44). I wish to avoid those problems in the present context, and the shortest way of doing so is explicitly to confine my claim to the original cases of utterances proper, a strategy I also employ in Graham, 'The recovery of illocutionary force'.

19 I here skate over many problems. For a discussion of some of them, see J. Kim, 'Events and their descriptions', in *Essays in Honor of Carl G. Hempel*, ed. N. Rescher (Dordrecht, D. Reidel, 1969).

20 D. Davidson, 'Psychology as philosophy' in *Philosophy of Psychology*, ed. S. C. Brown (London, 1974), pp. 42–3.

21 This has remained as a constant in the course of the development of his theory, from 2:61 to *Foundations*, pp. xii–xiv.

22 Some (though not all) of these cases could be discounted as counter-examples to Skinner's thesis on the grounds that the utterer does warn, though his audience fails to understand his utterance as a warning. This would necessitate abandoning Austin's own view that the execution of an illocutionary act requires the audience's *uptake* (*How To Do Things* pp. 116–17) and that what we have here are, precisely, only unsuccessful *attempts* to warn. It is not clear whether Skinner shares Austin's view. He certainly favours an analysis which is congenial with it but he never actually says that illocutionary force requires uptake – only that uptake requires understanding of speaker's intentions. If Skinner does share Austin's view my argument works *ad hominem*; if he does not, I rely on the remaining cases where intentions are unfulfilled for reasons other than failure of uptake. (Of course, it may be that in all of my cases *there is* failure of uptake. But in some, at least, failure of uptake will be a consequence of failure to perform the illocutionary act rather than vice versa.)

   It is doubtful whether Austin's view can be retained in unmodified form. Strawson qualifies it to read 'the aim, if not the achievement, of securing uptake is essentially a *standard, if not an invariable*, element in the performance of the illocutionary act' (Strawson, 'Intention and convention', p. 389; italics in original). For more radical criticism cf. Cohen, 'Speech-acts', p. 179.

23 Hollis, 'Say it with flowers', 7:136.

24 Quentin Skinner, 'Action and context', Supplementary Proceedings of the Aristotelian Society, 52 (1978), pp. 57–69, p. 58.

25 Graham, 'The recovery of illocutionary force'.

26 Graham, *J. L. Austin*, pp. 75–7.

27 Strawson, 'Intention and convention', p. 397.

28 Cohen, 'Speech-acts', pp. 184–5.

29 Compare, E. Gellner, 'The new Idealism', in *Problems in the Philosophy of Science*, ed. I. Lakatos and A. Musgrave (Amsterdam, North Holland Publishing Co., 1968), pp. 377–8.

30 Someone might object that I have no business to suppose that what I describe here are genuine possibilities at all, and that in doing so I am begging a number of questions in the philosophy of social action. But this, in a way, makes my point for me. To rule out these possibilities is *also* to make assumptions. Constructing a theory of illocutionary force which is neutral with regard to such issues is not possible. I attempt to argue these points more systematically in my 'Illocution and ideology' in *Issues in Marxist Philosophy*, ed. D. H. Ruben and J. Mepham, vol. 4, (Brighton, Harvester Press, 1984).

31 Davidson, 'Psychology as philosophy', p. 41.

32 Davidson's thesis is in any case questionable. It is plausible to suppose that there are absent-minded actions which are not intentional under *any* description. Compare Davidson, 'Agency', in *Agent, Action and Reason*, ed. R. Binkley, R. Bronaugh and A. Marras (Oxford, Oxford University Press, 1971), p. 7, and J. Cornman, 'Reply' to Davidson, in *Agent, Action and Reason*, p. 31. For further complications see Graham, 'The recovery of illocutionary force', pp. 228–33.

33 Compare G. A. Cohen *Karl Marx's Theory of History*, (Oxford, Oxford University Press, 1978), pp. 251–3.

CHAPTER 9   AN HISTORICIST CRITIQUE OF 'REVISIONIST' METHODS
FOR STUDYING THE HISTORY OF IDEAS

1 J. G. A. Pocock, 'Languages and their implications: the transformation of the study of political thought', *Politics, Language and Time: Essays on Political Thought and History* (London, Methuen, 1972), p 11.

2 A Gramsci, *I1 materialismo storico e la filosofia di Benedetto Croce* (henceforth *MS*), vol. II, *Collected Works* (Turin, 1948), p. 159. All quotations from Gramsci in this paper are taken from his *Prison Notebooks (Quanderni del Carcere)*, published in six volumes by Einaudi.

3 See 'On performing and explaining linguistic actions', *Philosophical Quarterly*, 21 (1971), pp. 1–21 'Motives, intentions and the interpretation of texts', 3, '"Social meaning" and the explanation of social action', 4, 'Conventions and the understanding of speech-acts', *Philosophical Quarterly*, 20 (1970), pp. 118–38, 'Some problems in the analysis of political thought and action', 5, and 'Hermeneutics and the role of history', *New Literary History*, 7 (1975–6) pp. 209–32.

4 At the very least, he has never repudiated the basic points that interest me in this paper.

5 H. A. Hodges, *Wilhelm Dilthey: An Introduction* (London, K. Paul, Trench, Trubner and Co., 1944), p. 155.

6 Clearly, our definition of historicism bears no relation to that of Karl Popper, who (idiosyncratically) gives this name to 'an approach to the social sciences which assumes that *historical prediction* is their principal aim, and which assumes that this aim is attainable by discovering the "rhythms" or the "patterns", the "laws" or the "trends" that underlie the evolution of history' *The Poverty of Historicism* (London, Routledge and Kegan Paul, 1974), p. 3.

7 J. Dunn, 'The identity of the history of ideas', *Philosophy* 43 (1968), pp. 98–9.

8 Pocock, while stressing authorial intention, also declares that it is historically legitimate to search for 'a set of assumptions and paradigms, situated just below the normal level of critical consciousness'. We can reasonably claim knowledge 'about an author's paradigm-situation and his response to it of which he was not himself conscious'. Historical reconstruction, in other words, often requires 'rendering explicit what may have been implicit before'. See 'Languages and their implications', pp. 29, 33, 34. (Pocock, it might be added, is talking about paradigms of political language, similar in form and function to the scientific paradigms isolated by Kuhn.)

9 C. B. Macpherson, *The Political Theory of Possessive Individualism* (Oxford, Oxford University Press, 1964).

10 Skinner does, on occasion, betray a certain uneasiness about his elevation of subjective designs or aims: 'This special authority of an agent over his intentions does not exclude, of course, the possibility that an observer might be in a position to give a fuller or more convincing account of the agent's

behaviour than he could give himself. (Psychoanalysis is indeed founded on this possibility.)' (2:48). It is difficult, however, to see how this statement fits in with a methodology which frowns upon all attempts to 'read in' ideas a given writer in fact has no intention to convey, and which recoils with horror from the 'astonishing' assumption that it may be quite proper 'to discount the statements of intention which the author himself may have made about what he was doing' (2:40). From this last point, though, Skinner has since retreated. Authors may, after all, prevaricate, fail to remember their previous mental states, or simply be incompetent at relating their positions. Thus, it is legitimate (in certain 'very unusual' circumstances) to deny the veracity of a writer's own explicit declarations about what he was trying to achieve in a given work; but in so doing we must not impute to him intentions which are inconsistent with his 'mental world', his consciously held beliefs. If, says Skinner in the course of an attack on Macpherson, a critic wishes to depict Locke's intention in *Two Treatises of Government* as one of defending the rationality of unlimited capital accumulation, then he must show that Locke adhered to *at least* the following beliefs: 'first, that his society was in fact becoming devoted to unlimited capital accumulation; second, that this was an activity crucially in need of ideological justification; third, that it was appropriate for him to devote himself to accomplishing precisely this task'. The author's overt purposes and preoccupations therefore remain paramount (3:73 – 6).

11 Skinner's detailed exposure of 'historical absurdity' is explicitly endorsed, for example, by Pocock in 'Languages and their implications', pp. 5–6.

12 Pocock, 'Languages and their implications', p. 6.

13 Dunn, 'The identity of the history of ideas', pp. 87–8.

14 Yet again, the historicist connection needs to be underlined. Note this passage from Vico: 'It is another property of the human mind that whenever men can form no idea of distant and unknown things, they judge them by what is familiar and at hand. This axiom points to the inexhaustible source of all the errors about the principles of humanity', *The New Science of Giambattista Vico* (1744) tr. T. G. Bergin and M. H. Fisch (Ithaca, Cornell University Press, 1961), paras 122–3.

15 2:37–9. See also page 34, where Skinner states: 'For it cannot (logically) be a correct appraisal of any agent's action to say that he failed to do something unless it is first clear that he did have, and even could have had, the intention to try to perform *that* action.' This is a bizarre statement – to put it mildly. If it is correct, then we cannot (logically) denounce the Chilean junta for failing to uphold basic human rights, because they never had any intention of doing so in the first place. Either Skinner has invented his own logic or he is working with an arbitrarily narrow definition of the verb 'to fail'.

16 *MS*, p. 233.

17 Ibid., p. 4. For other expression – in Gramsci – of the 'historicity' of philosophy, see ibid., p. 93 and *Passato e presente* (henceforth *PP*), vol. VII, *Collected Works* (Turin, Einaudi, 1951), pp. 62–3.

18 *MS*, p. 95.

19 B. Croce, *Logic as the Science of the Pure Concept*, tr. D. Ainslie (London, 1971), pp. 310–11. It is not my intention to conflate Gramsci's historicism with

that of Croce. Whereas Gramsci was a Marxist, for whom ideas belonged to the complex pattern of human life woven around the fundamental human relationships of the mode of production, Croce was basically an idealist, tending to minimize the impact of concrete socio-economic activity. For this he was roundly criticized in the prison notebooks. While I am inclined to endorse Gramsci's position on this issue, my argument, I am satisfied, does no require me to defend the materialist conception of history.

20 Bergin and Fisch, *The New Science*, paras. 144–5, 333, 347.

21 His writings, it must be stressed, remain unfinished and fragmentary. The *Quanderni* constitute but a rough draft of what was meant to be a major contribution to Marxist thought. His intellectual labours were aborted by his premature death (at the age of forty-six) just after his release from a fascist jail.

22 *MS*, p. 234.

23 *PP*, p. 63.

24 *MS*, p. 234.

25 Ibid., p. 151.

26 *PP*, p. 63.

27 What he seems to have in mind here is some sort of dialectical supersession, or *dépassement*, of an Hegelian kind.

28 *MS*, p. 149.

29 Ibid., p. 239, my emphasis.

30 Ibid., p. 94.

31 Ibid., p. 149.

32 Pocock, 'Languages and their implications', pp. 6–7.

33 *W. Dilthey: Selected Writings*, tr. and ed. H. P. Rickman (Cambridge, Cambridge University Press, 1976), p. 203.

34 B. Croce, *History: Its Theory and Practice*, tr. D. Ainslie (New York, Russell and Russell, 1960), pp. 12, 15.

35 Ibid., p. 110.

36 *MS*, pp. 217–18.

37 A. Gramsci, *I1 Risorgimento* (henceforth *R*), vol. IV, *Collected Works* (Turin, Einaudi, 1949), p. 62.

38 Ibid., p. 63.

39 *MS*, p. 156.

40 *R*, p. 62–3.

41 *PP*, pp. 57–9, 62–3.

42 *Note sul Machiavelli, sulla politica e sullo stato moderno* (henceforth *Mach.*), *vol. V, Collected Works* (Turin, Einaudi, 1949), pp. 3–17.

43 M. Leslie, 'In defense of anachronism', *Political Studies* 18 (1970), p. 437.

44 *Mach.*, p. 14.

45 Ibid., 13. Gramsci was indeed anxious to show how an historicist approach could prevent exegetical mistakes. For instance, he urged 'a more historicist estimation of the so-called anti-Machiavellians'. Taking account of the cultures and epochs in which they lived, we discover them to be 'not really anti-Machiavellians but politicians who express the needs of their time or of conditions different from those which affected Machiavelli; the polemical form is nothing but a contingent literary device'. To take one example, Bodin

found it necessary to be 'polemically anti-Machiavellian' only because the Florentine's thought was – in the circumstances of contemporary France – at the service of his (Bodin's) enemies – the French reactionaries, ibid., pp. 15–16.

46 Dunn, 'The identity of the history of ideas', pp. 87–8.

47 Rickman, *Dilthey: Selected Writings*, p. 226.

48 *Dilthey: Selected Writings*, pp. 235–6.

49 I do not wish to suggest that Dilthey's usage of 'meaning' is either uniform or devoid of obscurity. For helpful discussions, see Hodges, *Wilhelm Dilthey*, pp. 19–21; and H. P. Rickman, *Meaning in History: W. Dilthey's Thoughts on History and Society* (London, Allen and Unwin, 1961), pp. 37–50.

50 *Mach.*, p. 14.

51 *MS*, p. 6.

52 Ibid., p. 4.

53 A Labriola, *Essays on the Materialist Conception of History*, tr. H. Kerr (Chicago, 1908), p. 161.

CHAPTER 10   METHOD IN INTELLECTUAL HISTORY:
QUENTIN SKINNER'S *FOUNDATIONS*

1 Q. Skinner, *The Foundations of Modern Political Thought*, 2 vols (Cambridge, Cambridge University Press), vol. I, p. x.

2 Q. Skinner, 'Actions and context', *Proceedings of the Aristotelian Society*, supplementary vol. 52 (1978), pp. 57–69.

3 Skinner, *Foundations*, vol. I, Preface, p. xi.

4 At its most extreme, the claim plays round with the notion that the correct method is not only necessary but also sufficient. 'Some problems in the analysis of political thought and action' (5:99).

5 Skinner, *Foundations*, vol. I, p. xiv.

6 Ibid., p. xv.

7 See, for example, Howard Warrender, 'Political theory and historiography: a reply to Mr Skinner on Hobbes', paper presented to the 1979 Political Studies Association Conference held at Sheffield.

8 J. Plamenatz, *Man and Society: A Critical Examination of Some Important Social and Political Theories from Machiavelli to Marx*, 2 vols (London, Longmans, 1963), p. ix.

9 An enthusiasm later 'mildly regretted': Skinner, 'Some problems' (5:99).

10 Referring to Robert A. Dahl, *Modern Political Analysis* (Englewood Cliffs, New Jersey, Prentice Hall, 1970), p. 113.

11 Referring to 'Locke's "Doctrine of Signs"', *Journal of the History of Ideas*, 26 (1965), p. 382.

12 I refer to such works as Sheldon Wolin, *Politics and Vision* (London, Allen and Unwin, 1961); Leo Strauss, *Natural Right and History* (Chicago, University of Chicago Press, 1943) and Hannah Arendt, *The Human Condition* (Chicago, University of Chicago Press, 1958). There are, of course many other such works.

13 See the review by Harro Hopfl in *Philosophical Books*, 21 (January 1980).

14 Q. Skinner, 'Conquest and consent: Thomas Hobbes and the engagement controversy', in *The Interregnum: The Quest for Settlement*, ed. G. E. Aylmer (London, Macmillan, 1972), pp. 79–98.

16 Thomas Hobbes, *De Cive*, The Preface to the Reader, ed. Sterling Lamprecht (New York, Appleton Century, 1949), pp. 16–17: 'monarchy is the most commodious government (which one thing alone I confess in this whole book not to be demonstrated, but only probably stated) . . .'

17 Herbert Butterfield, *The Whig Interpretations of History* (London, G. Bell and Sons, 1931), p. 28.

18 On p.000 of 'Some problems' (5) where we learn that 'the key to excluding unhistorical meanings must lie in limiting our range of descriptions of any given text to those which the author himself might in principle have avowed, and that the key to understanding the actual historical meaning of a text must lie in recovering the complex intentions of the author who wrote it'. This goes further than Butterfield, but is essentially the same point.

19 Plamenatz, *Man and Society*, p. x.

20 The thing about Locke's *Second Treatise* is that it won't keep still. Once thought to be written in 1689, it was transferred by Peter Laslett to 1679. More recently, however, it has been argued that the work really belongs to 1683 and the milieu of the Rye House Plot, in which this abstract style of argument was much more common. See Richard Ashcraft in *Political Theory*, November 1980.

21 P. L. Strawson, 'Intention and convention in speech-acts', *Philosophical Review* (October 1964), p. 439. Strawson's remark that 'It would equally be a mistake . . . to generalize the account of illocutionary force derived from Grice's analysis; for this would involve holding, falsely, that the complex overt intention manifested in any illocutionary act always includes the intention to secure a certain definite response or reaction in an audience over and above that which is necessarily secured if the illocutionary force of the utterance is understood' (p. 459) is a useful warning of how too much conceptualization might tempt the historian, if he gets it wrong, into searching for intentions to secure responses that don't exist.

22 Skinner, 'Action and context', p. 69.

23 J. W. Allen, *Political Thought in the Sixteenth Century* (London, Allen and Unwin, 1928).

24 Ibid., p. 456.

25 Skinner, *Foundations*, vol. I, Preface, p. ix.

26 Ibid., vol. II, p. 349 (italics supplied).

27 Even more vulnerable to criticism along these lines would be such a judgement as that Jean Bodin's *Colloquium of the Seven* was 'perhaps the most *emancipated* discussion of religious liberty produced in France in the course of the religious wars', Skinner, *Foundations* vol. II, p. 246 (italics supplied).

28 See, for example, A. O. Lovejoy, 'The historiography of ideas', in *Essays in the History of Ideas* (Baltimore, Johns Hopkins Press, 1948).

29 See A. O. Lovejoy, *The Great Chain of Being: A Study of the History of an Idea* (New York, Harper and Row, 1936).

30 See J. Pocock, *Politics, Language and Time* (London, Methuen, 1972).

31 K. Popper, 'On the theory of objective mind', in *Objective Knowledge* (London, Routledge and Kegan Paul, 1972), p. 178. It is interesting to observe that, for at least some cases, Popper's analysis in terms of three worlds (the material, psychological and intellectual) corresponds precisely to Austin's analysis of the perlocutionary, illocutionary and locutionary acts involved in speech.

32 See Ellen Meiskins Wood and Neal Wood, *Class Ideology and Ancient Political Theory: Socrates, Plato and Aristotle in Social Context* (Oxford, Basil Blackwell, 1978).

33 C. B. Macpherson, *The Political Theory of Possessive Individualism* (Oxford, Oxford University Press, 1962).

34 Skinner, *Foundations*, vol. II, p. 114.

35 Ibid., p. 89.

36 Ibid., p. 253.

37 Q. Skinner 'Hermeneutics and the role of history', *New Literary History*, 7 (1975–6), p. 210.

38 Ibid., p. 211.

39 Ibid., p. 211.

40 John Dunn 'The cage of politics', *The Listener* (15 March 1979).

41 Q. Skinner, 'Action and context', p. 43.

42 Skinner, *Foundations*, vol. I p. xiii.

43 Perhaps Professor Skinner has identified with Peachum, the hero of Peter de Vries's recent novel *Consenting Adults, or the Duchess will be Furious*: 'When they brought the news to me that another bunch at Oxford had scrapped Causality, I stretched out with an iceberg on my head. Then it was all random. Certainty was a gone goose, and the soul with it . . .'

CHAPTER 11   QUENTIN SKINNER'S METHOD AND MACHIAVELLI'S
PRINCE

1 For a fuller discussion of Skinner's methodological writings, see 'Quentin Skinner's method and Machiavelli's *Prince*', *Ethics*, 92 (July 1982), pp. 692–709, pp. 692–701.

2 Unless otherwise indicated, page numbers in parentheses in this section are to volume I of Q. Skinner's *The Foundations of Modern Political Thought*, 2 vols (Cambridge, Cambridge University Press, 1978).

3 Skinner is much more successful in fulfilling this aim in his second volume. Cf. my 'Political thought in early modern Europe II: *The Age of Reformation*', *Journal of Modern History*, 54 (1982), pp. 555–65.

4 Notes to Machiavelli are to chapters in *The Prince* and books and chapters in the *Discourses*; translations are my own from Niccolò Machiavelli, *Il Principe e Discorse*, ed. Sergio Bertelli (Milan: Feltrinelli, 1968) except those within quotations from Skinner, which are from Niccolò Machiavelli, *The Prince*, tr. George Bull (Harmondsworth, Penguin, 1975).

5 Leo Strauss, *Thoughts on Machiavelli*, (Seattle and London, Free Press, 1969), p. 9.

6 Compare Leo Strauss, *Persecution, and the Art of Writing*, (Glencoe, Ill., Free Press, 1952), p. 78.

7 Strauss, *Thoughts*, pp. 10, 13.

8 Strauss, *Persecution*, p. 30; cf. his *What is Political Philosophy?* (Glencoe, Ill., Free Press, 1959), pp. 230–31.

CHAPTER 12 MORE THESES ON THE PHILOSOPHY OF HISTORY

1 J. G. A. Pocock, *Virtue, Commerce and History, Essays on Political Thought and History, Chiefly in the Eighteenth Century* (Cambridge, Cambridge University Press, 1985), p. 3.

2 Michel Foucault, 'What is an author?' *Screen*, 20 (spring, 1979), pp. 13–33 (with replies by Lucien Goldmann and Jacques Lacan); Roland Barthes, 'The death of the author', *Image, Music, Text*, tr. Stephen Heath, (Glasgow, Fontana Collins, 1977), pp. 142–8.

3 F. R. Leavis, 'The responsible critic or the functions of criticism at any time', in *A Selection from Scrutiny*, ed. F. R. Leavis (Cambridge, Cambridge University Press, 1968): cf. the classic argument of W. K. Wimsatt and Monroe C. Beardsley, 'The intentional fallacy', *Sewanee Review*, 54 (1946).

4 Eric D. Hirsch, Jr, *Validity in Interpretation* (New Haven and London, Yale University Press, 1967), pp. 51–7; Anthony Giddens, *Central Problems in Social Theory* (London, Polity Press, 1979), pp. 56–9.

5 Sigmund Freud, *The Interpretation of Dreams* (New York, 1965).

6 Paul Ricoeur, *Interpretation Theory: Discourse and the Surplus of Meaning* (Fort Worth, Texas Christian University Press, 1976), chap. 3. This point is admitted in J. G. A. Pocock's recent survey of the achievements of the new history: 'Skinner's method ... has impelled us toward the recovery of an author's language no less than of his [sic] intentions, toward treating him as inhabiting a universe of *langues* that give meaning to the *paroles* he performs in them', *Virtue, Commerce and History*, p. 5.

7 Q. Skinner, Cf. 'Conventions and the understanding of speech-acts', *Philosophical Quarterly*, 20 (1970), pp. 118–38; 'Hermeneutics and the role of history', *New Literary History* 7 (1975–6), pp. 221, 227–8.

8 B. Parekh and R. N. Berki, 'The history of political ideas: a critique of Q. Skinner's methodology', *Journal of the History of Ideas*, 34 (1973), pp. 167ff.

9 John Plamenatz, *Man and Society*, 2 vols, (London, Longmans, 1964), vol. I, p. x.

10 Cf. Q. Skinner, 'Conquest and consent: Thomas Hobbes and the engagement controversy', in *The Interregnum: The Quest for Settlement*, ed. G. E. Aylmer (London, Macmillan, 1972), pp. 79–98; and 'History and ideology in the English Revolution', *Historical Journal*, 8 (1965), pp. 151–78.

11 Q. Skinner, *The Foundations of Modern Political Thought*, 2 vols (Cambridge, Cambridge University Press), vol. I, p. xi.

12 Q. Skinner, *Machiavelli* (Oxford, Oxford University Press, 1981), p. 88.

13 R. G. Collingwood, *The Idea of History* (Oxford, Clarendon Press, 1956), pp. 282–302.

14 Cf. Skinner's sympathetic discussion of certain anti-positivist trends in historical research in an early essay, 'The limits of historical explanations', *Philosophy*, 41 (1966), pp. 199–215.

15 Skinner, 'Hermeneutics and the role of history', p. 228.

16 5:000. Here Skinner explicitly exposes the objectivist claims of H. Butterfield, *The Whig Interpretation of History* (Harmondsworth, Penguin, 1973).

17 This point resembles Collingwood's thesis (*The Idea of History*, pp. 29–45) that historians' attempts to find out what actually happened in the past is facilitated by their 'constructive imagination'. Neither Collingwood nor Skinner grasps the subversive implications of this thesis for their copy model of historical explanation. They assume that the 'constructive imagination' is a *neutral* medium in the process of composing historical narratives. Thereby, they overlook the essential point, argued below, that this constructive imagination always and inescapably conditions both the form and content of historians' pictures of the past, which therefore cannot be understood as stories of 'what really happened' in a given time and place.

18 Ricoeur, *Interpretation Theory*, pp. 43–4, 89–95; Hans-Georg Gadamer, *Truth and Method* ed. G. Barden (New York, Seabury Press, 1975), pp. 273ff, 337ff, 358; cf. Manfred Frank's recent criticisms of the hermeneutic approach in *Was ist Neostrukturalismus?* (Frankfurt am Main, 1984) and *Die Unhintergehbarkeit von Individualität: Reflexionen über Subjekt, Person und Individuum aus Anlass ihrer postmodernen Toterklärung* (Frankfurt am Main, 1986).

19 J. Habermas, *Zur Logik der Sozialwissenschaften* (Frankfurt am Main, 1973), p. 273.

20 C. D. Tarlton, 'Historicity, meaning and revisionism in the study of political thought', *History and Theory*, 12 (1973), pp. 307–28; M. Leslie, 'In defense of anachronism', *Political Studies*, 18 (1970), pp. 433–47.

21 Karl Mannheim, *Ideology and Utopia: An Introduction to the Sociology of Knowledge* (New York, Harcourt, Brace and World, 1946), pp. 180–2, 206–15, and 'Conservative thought', in *Essays in Sociology and Social Psychology*, ed. Paul Kecskemeti (New York, 1953), pp. 74–164.

22 For example, see H. von Wright, *Explanation and Understanding* (London, Routledge and Kegan Paul, 1971), and Charles Taylor, 'Explaining action', *Inquiry*, 13 (1973), pp. 54–89.

23 This approach is elaborated in my 'The modern democratic revolution: reflections on Jean-Francois Lyotard's '*La condition post-moderne*', *The Chicago Review* vol. 35, no. 4, 1987, pp. 4–19.

24 This conclusion is almost reached by Hayden White's insightful discussion of contemporary historiography in *Tropics of Discourse: Essays in Cultural Criticism* (Baltimore and London, Johns Hopkins University Press, 1978), esp. chaps 1–4. Arguing at length that all historiography entails the telling of many and often different kinds of stories, White draws back from the pluralist implications of his thesis. He argues, tentatively, that different types of narration, explanation and normative commitment in different 'schools' of historiography consist in the projection of a limited number of identifiable tropes – metaphor, metonymy, synecdoche and irony – which prefigure the historian's fields of perception of historical events.

Stimulated by Kenneth Burke's *A Grammar of Motives* (Berkeley and Los Angeles, University of California Press, 1969), White's attempt to ground and explain different modes of interpretation in a tropological theory of poetic language prompts *tu quoque* questions – which remain unanswered – about the exhaustiveness and validity of this generalizing theory itself.

25 The idea that democracy requires a plurality of memories can be inferred from two quite different, if extreme, possible situations. At one extreme, it is possible to imagine a former society – such as Palestine – whose members' historical senses have been interrupted, uprooted violently against their will, and scattered to the winds. Lacking shared memories, the citizens of this former society without history find themselves virtually powerless in a world that seems to them impermanent, empty and threatening. A quite different, and equally extreme possibility is that of a political order – such as contemporary Czechoslovakia – which permits only *one* view of history among its subjects. This gives rise to a strange feeling of a-historicity among the subjects of this political order. Time appears to stand still. Even though individuals continue being born, growing up, falling in love, having children and dying, everything around them becomes motionless, petrified and repetitious. Under these circumstances, any attempt, however limited, to preserve past memories represents an act of citizens' self-defence, a resistance against the oblivion of non-time, while the struggle of memory against the officially-enforced forgetting, as Kundera says, is also a struggle against authoritarian power.

26 Walter Benjamin, 'Theses on the philosophy of history', in *Illuminations*, ed. Hannah Arendt (London, New Left Books, 1973), pp. 257–8.

27 Friedrich Nietzsche, 'The use and abuse of history', in *The Complete Works of Friedrich Nietzsche*, ed. O. Levy (London, 1921), vol. 5, pp. 1–100.

28 This type of future-oriented memory guides my recent attempts to develop a political theory of civil society. See *Democracy and Civil Society* (London and New York, 1988) and John Keane (ed.), *Civil Society and the State. New European Perspectives* (London and New York, 1988). For their comments on an earlier draft of this essay, I should like to thank Peter Uwe Hohendahl, Quentin Skinner, and Patrick Wright.

CHAPTER 13   THE HERMENEUTICS OF CONFLICT

1 James Tully, 'The pen is a mighty sword: Quentin Skinner's analysis of politics', *British Journal of Political Science*, 13 (1983), pp. 489–509. [Because the introductory article in this collection is a considerably revised version of this article, I, James Tully, have retained the references to the original article and added references to the revised version above as well. Also, see note 36 to chapter 1.]

2 Ibid., p. 491, and above, 1: 8 – 9.

3 Ibid.

4 Tully quotes from Skinner, 'It is essentially by manipulating this set of terms [sc. those which help constitute the character of our political practices] that any society succeeds in establishing or altering its moral identity'. 'The pen', p. 495, and above, 1:13.

5 Weber's thesis, in spite of its superficial similarity to positivism, in fact had, I believe, very different philosophical roots, which had more to do with Nietzsche than Hume. I will recur to a Nietzschean approach below.

6 Tully, 'The pen', p. 502, and above, 1: 20.

7 Ibid., p. 500, and above, 1:18.

8 Ibid., p. 504, and above, 1:21.

9 Ibid., p. 506, and above, 1:24.

10 Ibid.

11 I have tried to make an assessment of Foucault's enterprise in my 'Foucault on freedom and truth', *Political Theory* 12, 2 (May 1984), pp. 152–83, reprinted in Charles Taylor, *Philosophical Papers*, vol. 2, *Philosophy and the Human Sciences* (Cambridge, Cambridge University Press, 1985), pp. 152–84.

12 Clifford Geertz, *Negara* (Princeton, Princeton University Press, 1982).

13 Tully, 'The pen', p. 505, and above, 1:23.

CHAPTER 14   A REPLY TO MY CRITICS

For reading and commenting on earlier drafts of this reply I am deeply grateful to Anthony Giddens, Susan James, Jonathan Lear, John Thompson and James Tully.

Onl my alleged Idealism, see for example Ian Shapiro, 'Realism in the study of the history of ideas', *History of Political Thought*, 3 (1982), pp. 535–78, esp. pp. 550, 578, and for a discussion of this charge cf. Mark Goldie, 'Obligations, utopias and their historical context', *Historical Journal*, 26 (1983), pp. 727–46, esp. at pp. 728–9. On materialism, see Philip Corrigan, 'Curiouser and curiouser', *British Journal of Sociology*, 31 (1980), pp. 292–7, at p. 292 and note. On positivism, see B. Parekh and R. N. Berki, 'The history of political ideas: a critique of Q. Skinner's methodology', *Journal of the History of Ideas*, 34 (1973), pp. 163–84, at p. 175. On relativism, see the references below, nn. 110 to 112. On antiquarianism, see the references below, nn. 216 to 218. On historicism, see Femia, above, 9:157.

2 John G. Gunnell, *Political Theory: Tradition and Interpretation* (Cambridge, Mass., 1979), pp. 103, 119–20, and cf. John G. Gunnell, 'Interpretation and the history of political theory: apology and epistemology', *American Political Science Review*, 76 (1982), pp. 317–27, at p. 319. Gunnell does not succeed in characterizing my views at all accurately. But cf. the surprisingly respectful discussion of his work in J. G. A. Pocock, 'Political theory, history and myth: a salute to John Gunnell', in *Annals of Scholarship*, 1 (1980), pp. 3–25.

3 Charles D. Tarlton, 'Historicity, meaning and revisionism in the study of political thought', *History and Theory*, 12 (1973), pp. 307–28, at p. 321; Joseph M. Levine, 'Method in the history of ideas: More, Machiavelli and Quentin Skinner', *Annals of Scholarship*, 3, 4 (1986), pp. 37–60, at pp. 38–9.

4 For a general sceptical statement along these lines, see Thomas Baldwin, 'Moore's Rejection of Idealism', in *Philosophy in History*, ed. Richard Rorty,

J. B. Schneewind and Quentin Skinner (Cambridge, Cambridge University Press, 1984), pp. 357–74, at pp. 358–9.

5 See John Dunn, 'The identity of the history of ideas' in *Political Obligation in its Historical Context* (Cambridge, Cambridge University Press, 1980), pp. 13–28.

6 This is also the burden of Levine's article cited above, n. 3. See also the prefatory methodological remarks in Stefan Collini, Donald Winch and John Burrow, *That Noble Science of Politics* (Cambridge, Cambridge University Press, 1983), esp. pp. 5–6.

7 See Gunnell, 'Interpretation', claiming (p. 319) that I 'confuse' methodological with epistemological issues.

8 See Levine, 'Method', esp. pp. 37–9, 55–6.

9 See ibid., esp. pp. 39–41. David Wootton, 'Preface' to *Divine Right and Democracy* (Harmondsworth, Penguin, 1986), esp. pp. 11–12, rightly observes that the 'new history of political theory' amounts to little more than an overdue application to the history of ideas of the ordinary methods and values of professional historians. But for the long pre-history of a comparable approach in the history of hermeneutics, see Donald R. Kelley, 'Horizons of intellectual history: retrospect, circumspect, prospect', *Journal of the History of Ideas*, 48 (1987), pp. 143–69.

10 I am conscious of owing a particular debt to the account of the different 'levels of abstraction' of political theory given in J. G. A. Pocock, 'The history of political thought: a methodological enquiry', in *Philosophy, Politics and Society*, 2nd series, ed. Peter Laslett and W. G. Runciman (Oxford, Basil Blackwell 1962), pp. 183–202.

11 It was I think entirely due to discussions with John Dunn, and to reading the article cited in n. 5 above, that I came to understand the way in which speech-act theory might be relevant to the interpretation of texts. See especially the invocation of J. L. Austin in Dunn's article, 'Identity of the history of ideas', p. 22.

12 I am conscious of being especially indebted to Peter Laslett's Introduction to his edition of John Locke, *Two Treatises of Government* (Cambridge, Cambridge University Press, 1960) in at least two ways. First for his insistence that Locke was basically replying to Filmer, a claim that served to highlight the question of what Locke was *doing* in the *Two Treatises*. Second, for his consequential emphasis on the specific and local character of Locke's arguments, and on the need to undertake a detailed study of their intellectual context in order to explain their distinctive emphases and shape.

13 This initially led me to write sceptically about the use of the concept of 'influence' in the history of ideas. See 'The limits of historical explanations', *Philosophy*, 41 (1966), pp. 199–215. I think this argument was in part inspired by Laslett's scepticism, in his analysis of Locke's political theory, about the capacity of Hobbes's alleged influence to explain any features of Locke's *Two Treatises*.

14 See R. G. Collingwood, *An Autobiography* (Oxford, Oxford University Press, 1939), p. 62. But I was helped to recognize the centrality of this insight by Pocock's discussion of 'levels' of thought in his article cited in n. 10 above, and by Alasdair MacIntyre's splendid opening chapter, 'The philosophical point of the history of ethics', in *A Short History of Ethics*

(London, Macmillan, 1966), pp. 1–4. For a discussion of Collingwood's views about these issues, see Andrew Lockyer, '"Traditions" as context in the history of political theory', *Political Studies*, 27 (1979), pp. 201–17, esp. at pp. 212–4.

15 Some of the names involved are so eminent that I hesitate to associate them with my efforts. But I cannot fail to mention how much I learnt from the discussions I was able to hold, while at Princeton between 1974 and 1979, with Clifford Geertz, Raymond Geuss, Thomas S. Kuhn and Richard Rorty, and how much help I have received, since returning to Cambridge, from John Dunn, Jonathan Lear and Susan James.

16 Levine, 'Method', p. 39.

17 Compare Conal Condren, *The Status and Appraisal of Classic Texts* (Princeton, Princeton University Press, 1985), p. 26 on the inevitably intermittent significance of discussions about method.

18 David Boucher, *Texts in Context: Revisionist Methods for Studying the History of Ideas* (Dordrecht, D. Reidel, 1985), p. 200.

19 Shapiro, 'Realism', p. 537 and note.

20 Jean Bodin, *La Demonomanie des Sorciers* (Paris, 1595), p. 49. For a sympathetic view of how Bodin might have arrived at this belief, see E. William Monter, 'Inflation and Witchcraft: the case of Jean Bodin', in *Action and Conviction in Early Modern Europe*, ed. Theodore K. Rabb and Jerrold Seigel (Princeton, Princeton University Press, 1969), pp. 371–89. But for a strong attack cf. Sydney Anglo, 'Melancholia and witchcraft: the debate between Wier, Bodin and Scot' in *Folie et déraison à la Renaissance* (Brussels, 1973), pp. 209–22.

21 For this formulation of Aristotle's belief, see Thomas S. Kuhn, *The Essential Tension* (Chicago, University of Chicago Press, 1977), p. xii.

22 This point is excellently made in Kuhn, *Essential Tension*, pp. xi–xii.

23 For the suggestion that the moral of this is that we should adopt a pragmatic concern with solidarity at the expense of our traditional quest for objectivity, see Richard Rorty, 'Solidarity or objectivity', in *Post-Analytic Philosophy*, ed. John Rajchman and Cornel West (New York, Columbia University Press, 1985), pp. 3–19.

24 See Donald Davidson, 'A coherence theory of truth and knowledge', in *Truth and Interpretation*, ed. Ernest LePore (Oxford, 1986), pp. 307–19. But it might be argued that Davidson's recursive characterization of truth amounts to an inductive definition.

25 See I. C. Jarvie, 'Understanding and explanation in sociology and social anthropology', in *Explanation in the Behavioural Sciences*, ed. Robert Borger and Frank Cioffi (Cambridge, Cambridge University Press, 1970), pp. 231–48, esp. at pp. 245–7; Steven Lukes, 'On the social determination of truth', in *Modes of Thought*, ed. Robin Horton and Ruth Finnegan (London, 1973), esp. p. 247; Alasdair MacIntyre, 'A mistake about causality in social science', in *Philosophy, Politics and Society*, 2nd series, ed. Laslett and Runciman, pp. 48–70, at p. 62, a passage cited with approval in Martin Hollis, 'Witchcraft and winchcraft', *Philosophy of the Social Sciences*, 2 (1972), pp. 89–103, at p. 101; W. H. Newton-Smith, *The Rationality of Science* (London, Routledge and Kegan Paul, 1981), esp. p. 252–7; Graham MacDonald and Philip Pettit, *Semantics and Social Science*, (London, 1981), esp. pp. 33–4.

26 For Graham's views, closely followed by Shapiro, see especially Keith Graham, 'Illocution and ideology', in *Issues in Marxist Philosophy*, ed. John Mepham and D. H. Ruben (Brighton, Harvester Press, 1981), vol. IV, pp. 153–94, esp at pp. 173, 177. Cf. the implications of the assumptions stated by Shapiro, 'Realism', at pp. 556, 577.

27 MacDonald and Pettit, *Semantics*, p. 186–7, give a valuable list of the articles by Davidson on which they rely. For their application of Davidson's theory, see esp. pp. 18–29.

28 Donald Davidson, 'On the very idea of a conceptual scheme', in *Inquiries into Truth and Interpretation* (Oxford, Clarendon Press 1984), p. 197.

29 Cf. Colin McGinn, 'Charity, interpretation, and belief', *Journal of Philosophy*, 74 (1977), pp. 521–35. See also Ian Hacking, 'Language, truth and reason', in *Rationality and Relativism*, ed. Martin Hollis and Steven Lukes (London, Basil Blackwell, 1982), pp. 48–66, esp. p. 60.

30 See Graham, 'Illocutions', p. 177.

31 Lukes, 'Social determination', p. 242.

32 MacDonald and Pettit, *Semantics*, p. 34.

33 Ibid., pp. 9, 34, 42.

34 For an explicit statement to this effect, see Steven Lukes, *Essays in Social Theory* (London, Macmillan, 1977), pp. 121, 132, 135.

35 My attempt to construe the concept in an informal way is deeply indebted to Hilary Putnam, *Reason, Truth and History* (Cambridge, Cambridge University Press, 1981), esp. pp. 150–200.

36 To speak of rationality, as several recent commentators have done, simply in terms of having good reasons for one's beliefs is to run the danger of eliding this distinction between epistemic and practical rationality. See for example Larry Laudan, *Progress and its Problems* (Berkeley, University of California Press, 1977), p. 123 and cf. Jeffrey Stout, *The Flight from Authority* (Notre Dame, University of Notre Dame Press 1981), pp. 165–6. It is of course true that the distinction is one that pragmatists bid us elide. See for example Richard Rorty, *Philosophy and the Mirror of Nature* (Princeton, Princeton University Press, 1979), pp. 328–9. As I shall emphasize below, however, I do not see how historians can hope to operate satisfactorily without it. For an excellent analysis of the distinction itself, see G. W. Mortimore and J. B. Maund, 'Rationality in belief', in *Rationality and the Social Sciences*, ed. S. I. Benn and G. W. Mortimore (London, Routledge and Kegan Paul, 1976), pp. 11–33.

37 David Lewis, 'Radical interpretation', *Synthese*, 27 (1974), pp. 331–44, at p. 336.

38 This is the class of what Putnam calls 'directive' beliefs; see *Reason, Truth and History*, pp. 38–40. But in spite of what some commentators have implied – for example, Macdonald and Pettit, *Semantics*, pp. 26–8 – this class seems to me of almost vanishingly small significance from the point of view of intellectual historians.

39 See Putnam, *Reason, Truth and History*, esp. pp. 54–6, 155–68 and cf. the discussion of Putnam's views in C. Behan McCullagh, 'The intelligibility of cognitive relativism', *Monist*, 67 (1984), pp. 327–40.

40 Cf. on these points, Putnam, *Reason, Truth and History*, esp. pp. 105–13; Mortimore and Maund, 'Rationality in belief', esp. pp. 14–20.

41 This point is vehemently pressed in D. C. Stove, *Popper and After* (Oxford, Pergamon Press, 1982). A little too vehemently? If a certain proposition would be easily falsifiable if false, then a failure to falsify it would surely give us *some* grounds for supposing it to be true.

42 This point has often been made in relation to both Freud's and Darwin's theories. For a valuable discussion see Putnam, *Reason, Truth and History*, esp. pp. 196–200. But for a spirited attempt to restate a version of the falsifiability criterion, see Imre Lakatos, *The Methodology of Scientific Research Programmes: Philosophical Papers*, vol. I, ed. John Worrall and Gregory Currie (Cambridge, Cambridge University Press, 1978), esp. pp. 8–101.

43 I urge this objection against Hollis in my article 'Action and context', *Proceedings of the Aristotelian Society*, supplementary vol. 52 (1978), pp. 57–69, at pp. 61–3. Cf. also the discussion in Jon Elster, 'Belief, bias and ideology', in *Rationality and Relativism*, ed. Hollis and Lukes, pp. 123–48.

44 See Alasdair MacIntyre, *Against the Self-Images of the Age* (London, 1971), p. 255 and the discussion at pp. 246–7. Cf. Hollis' discussion in chap. 7 of the present volume, esp. at pp. 140, 144–5, and his strong distinction between 'rational' and 'structural' explanations of belief in 'The social destruction of reality', in *Rationality and Relativism*, ed. Hollis and Lukes, esp. pp. 80, 85.

45 David Bloor, *Knowledge and Social Imagery* (London, Routledge and Kegan Paul, 1976), p. 5. Cf. Barry Barnes, *Scientific Knowledge and Sociological Theory* (London, Routledge and Kegan Paul, 1974), p. 43; Barry Barnes and David Bloor, 'Relativism, rationalism and the sociology of knowledge', in *Rationality and Relativism*, ed. Hollis and Lukes, pp. 21–47, at p. 23.

46 See for example Barnes and Bloor, 'Relativism' p. 25.

47 Cf. the discussions in Laudan, *Progress and its Problems*, pp. 188–9; Stout, *Flight from Authority*, pp. 170–1; Newton-Smith, *Rationality of Science*, pp. 253–7.

48 Bloor, *Knowledge and Social Imagery*, p. 5.

49 Barnes, *Scientific Knowledge and Sociological Theory*, pp. 43, 128–30.

50 For the suggestion that the study of witchcraft beliefs offers a good illustration of the place played by rationality postulates in historical study, I am indebted to MacIntyre, *Against the Self-Images of the Age*, chap. 21, pp. 244–59.

51 E. Le Roy Ladurie, *The Peasants of Languedoc*, tr. John Day (London, University of Illinois Press, 1974), pp. 203–5. For a full discussion of this example and its implications, see Susan James, *The Content of Social Explanation* (Cambridge, Cambridge University Press, 1984), pp. 166–71.

52 Ladurie, *Peasants*, p. 210.

53 Ibid., p. 208.

54 Ibid., pp. 203–4, 206–7. Cf. also the Postscript to Norman Cohn, *Europe's Inner Demons* (London, Basic Books, 1976), esp. p. 258 for the assumption that witchcraft beliefs constituted nothing more than a 'collective fantasy'.

55 Ladurie, *Peasants*, p. 207.

56 Ibid., p. 203.

57 See respectively Deuteronomy 13.10–12 and Gal., 5.20; and Exod., 22.18.

58 Newton-Smith, 'Relativism', p. 110 nevertheless assures us that if we find ourselves saying – to follow the schema he lays out – that R (in the present case, the indubitability of the Bible) is a reason for holding that p is true (that witches exist) for u (the sixteenth-century peasants of Languedoc) while R is not a reason for holding that p is true for o (for Newton-Smith), then we have fallen into an elementary error of a kind that tends to lead to the Kingdom of Darkness. So the task of intellectual history becomes that of showing, on pain of becoming a public danger, that only what Newton-Smith regards as a reason for a given belief can count as a reason for that belief.

59 Barnes, *Scientific Knowledge and Sociological Theory*, pp. 69–70, 130. For Winch's own argument, see Peter Winch, 'Understanding a primitive society', in *Rationality* ed. Bryan R. Wilson (Oxford, Basil Blackwell, 1970), pp. 78–110. But Wittgenstein's argument cannot in fact be assimilated to that of the sceptical relativist. This is fully established in Jonathan Lear, 'Leaving the world alone', *Journal of Philosophy*, 79 (1982), pp. 382–403.

60 Barnes and Bloor, 'Relativism', p. 27 and Barnes, *Scientific Knowledge and Sociological Theory*, p. 41.

61 See Hollis's contribution to the present volume, chap. 7, pp. 141–2 and his discussion of 'objectively rational' beliefs in his essay 'The social destruction of reality', in *Rationality and Relativism*, ed. Hollis and Lukes, esp. p. 72. For a similar assumption, see Laudan, *Progress and its Problems* and the discussion of his position in Newton-Smith, *Rationality of Science*, esp. pp. 245–7, 270–73.

62 Rorty, *Philosophy and the Mirror of Nature*, p. 331.

63 See Rorty, *Philosophy and the Mirror of Nature*, esp. p. 174 and cf. his 'Postmodernist bourgeois liberalism', *Journal of Philosophy*, 80 (1983), pp. 583–9, esp. at pp. 585–6.

64 See for example Stuart Clark, 'Inversion, misrule and the meaning of witchcraft', *Past and Present*, 87 (1980), pp. 98–127, esp. at p. 100.

65 W. H. Greenleaf, 'Hobbes: the problem of interpretation' in *Hobbes and Rousseau*, ed. Maurice Cranston and Richard S. Peters (New York, Anchor Books, 1972), pp. 5–36, at p. 28. See also W. H. Greenleaf, 'Hume, Burke and the General Will', *Political Studies*, 20 (1972), pp. 131–40, at p. 140.

66 Niccolò Machiavelli, *The History of Florence*, in *The Chief Works and Others*, 3 vols, tr. Allan Gilbert, (Durham, North Carolina, Duke University Press, 1965), vol. III, pp. 1029–435, at V.33, p. 1280.

67 Machiavelli, *History of Florence* in *Chief Works*, vol. III, at VII.3, p. 1363.

68 For these details, and for a discussion of contemporary sources (especially Biondo, Capponi and Poggio), see Pasquale Villari, *The Life and Times of Niccolò Machiavelli*, new edn, 2 vols, tr. Linda Villari (London, Unwin, 1892), vol. II, pp. 452, 458–9.

69 Scipio Ammirato, *Istorie Fiorentine*, 6. vols, ed. F. Ranalli, (Florence, 1846–49), book 23, chap. 5, p. 169. Cf. also the discussion in Sydney Anglo, *Machiavelli: A Dissection* (London, Gollancz 1969), pp. 185, 258.

70 See Martin Hollis, 'The limits of irrationality', in *Rationality*, ed. Wilson, pp. 214–20, at p. 219. Cf. the discussion of this 'slogan' in John Skorupski, 'The meaning of another culture's beliefs' in *Action and Interpretation*, ed.

Christopher Hookway and Philip Pettit (Cambridge, Cambridge University Press, 1978), pp. 83–106, at pp. 88 –9.

71 See the discussion of the need for this convention within any system of signalling in David Lewis, *Convention* (Cambridge, Mass., Harvard University Press, 1969), pp. 148–52.

72 Of late, however, this assumption has been extensively criticized. See Martin Hollis, 'Reason and ritual', in *Rationality* ed. Wilson, pp. 221–339, esp. p. 226; John Skorupski, 'Meaning' in *Action and Interpretation*, ed. Hookway and Pettit, pp. 85–6; Macdonald and Pettit, *Semantics*, p. 15 and note. Cf also the excellent general discussion, to which I am much indebted, in David Papineau, *For Science in the Social Sciences* (London, Macmillan, 1978), chap. 6, pp. 132–58.

73 Mary Hesse, 'Hermeticism and historiography: an apology for the internal history of science', in *Minnesota Studies in the Philosophy of Science*, vol. V, ed. Roger H. Stuewer (Minneapolis, University of Minnesota Press, 1970, pp. 134–60, at p. 149. Cf. also Mary Hesse, 'Reasons and evaluations in the history of science' in *Changing Perspectives in the History of Science*, ed. M. Teich and Robert Young (London, Heinemann, 1973), pp. 127–47.

74 See, on this issue, Margaret C. Jacob, *The Newtonians and the English Revolution, 1689–1720* (Ithaca, Cornell University Press, 1976), and James R. Jacob and Margaret C. Jacob, 'The Anglican origins of modern science: the metaphysical foundations of the Whig constitution', *Isis*, 7 (1980), pp. 251–67. My only doubt about this line of argument is that those who have embraced it have not always distinguished sufficiently clearly between two possibilities. One is that a figure such as Newton may have held some of what we should describe as his scientific beliefs in part because of his social interests. The other is that some of what we might be tempted, anachronistically, to regard as a mere expression of his social interest may have amounted to a good reason, in his circumstances, for supposing the beliefs in question to be true.

75 See Rorty, *Philosophy and the Mirror of Nature*, p. 267.

76 The classic statement of this kind of holism remains the concluding sections of W. V. O. Quine, 'Two dogmas of empiricism' in *From a Logical Point of View*, rev. edn (Cambridge, Mass., Harvard University Press, 1961), esp. pp. 37–46. But even Quine seems to me too inclined, while his admirers (such as Hollis in the essays I discuss below) seem far too inclined, to employ the metaphor of core and periphery.

77 Hollis, 'Social destruction', pp. 67–86, at pp. 75, 83–4.

78 For the claim that any disposition to think of a world of neutral materials awaiting conceptualizations amounts to a third dogma of empiricism, and for the suggestion that this is a world well lost, see Richard Rorty, 'The world well lost', *Journal of Philosophy*, 69 (1972), pp. 649–65.

79 For an influential source of this line of argument, see Mary Hesse, 'Is there an independent observation language?', in *The Nature and Function of Scientific Theories*, ed. R. G. Colodny (Pittsburgh, University of Pittsburgh Press, 1970), pp. 35–77 and Mary Hesse, *The Structure of Scientific Inference* (London, University of California Press, 1974), esp. pp. 9–73. Hesse's arguments are invoked and developed in Barnes, *Scientific Knowledge and Sociological*

Theory, esp. p. 16, in Barnes and Bloor, 'Relativism', pp. 37–39, and in Papineau, *For Science*, esp. pp. 134–8.

80 Hollis, 'Reason and ritual, pp. 228, 230–31.

81 Hollis defends this commitment in both the articles reprinted in *Rationality*, ed. Wilson. See 'The limits of irrationality', esp. p. 216 and 'Reason and ritual', p. 229.

82 Hollis, 'Social destruction', in *Rationality and Relativism*, ed. Hollis and Lukes, p. 74.

83 My example is adapted from the excellent discussion in Papineau, *For Science*, pp. 135–6.

84 See Thomas S. Kuhn, *The Structure of Scientific Revolutions*, 2nd edn (Chicago, University of Chicago Press, 1970), esp. chap. 5, pp. 43–51 and chap. 10, pp. 111–35.

85 See Hollis, 'The limits of irrationality', p. 216 and cf. the even stronger stress on 'the independence of facts' in 'an independent and objective natural world' in Hollis, 'Social destruction', p. 83.

86 Putnam, *Reason, Truth and History*, p. 54.

87 Shapiro, 'Realism', p. 556.

88 Stephen Turner, '"Contextualism" and the interpretation of the classical sociological texts', *Knowledge and Society*, 4 (1983), pp. 273–91, esp. pp. 283–4. But for a sympathetic appraisal of my approach by a sociologist, see Robert A. Jones, 'Review essay: on Quentin Skinner', *American Journal of Sociology*, 87 (1981), pp. 435–67 and cf. Robert A. Jones 'On understanding a sociological classic', *American Journal of Sociology*, 83 (1977), pp. 279–319.

89 In both the articles reprinted in *Rationality*, ed. Wilson, Hollis insists on the very strong claim that, on pain of employing his approach, ethnography will actually be rendered impossible. See 'The limits of irrationality', p. 216 and 'Reason and ritual', p. 222.

90 Hollis, 'The limits of irrationality', p. 215.

91 This is the assumption underlying both the articles by Hollis reprinted in *Rationality*. Hollis reaffirms the same assumption in 'Social destruction', p. 74.

92 On this assumption see also John Dunn, 'Practising history and social science on "realist" assumptions', in *Political Obligation*, pp. 81–111, esp. at p. 96; Geoffrey Hawthorn, 'Characterizing the history of social theory', *Sociology*, 13 (1979), pp. 475–82, esp. at p. 477; Macdonald and Pettit, *Semantics*, esp. p. 45.

93 Gunnell, *Political Theory*, p. 111.

94 See Tacitus, *Historiae*, III.69: 'hibernus imber repente fusus oculos aurisque impediebat'.

95 Most recently in Robert Kirk, *Translation Determined* (Oxford, Oxford University Press, 1986)), esp. pp. 34–5.

96 Cf. W. V. O. Quine, *Word and Object* (New York, Massachusetts Institute of Technology Press, 1960), esp. pp. 206–9.

97 For an excellent account of why the aspiration to produce such empathetic re-creations is beside the point, see Clifford Geertz, '"From the native's point of view": on the nature of anthropological understanding', in *Local*

Knowledge (New York, Basic Books, 1983), pp. 55–70. Cf. also Dunn, 'Practising social science', pp. 102–3.

98 See the very valuable remarks in Ian Hacking, 'Language, truth and reason', in *Rationality and Relativism*, ed. Hollis and Lukes, pp. 48–66, esp. at pp. 59–61 and in Geertz, *Local Knowledge*, esp. pp. 58, 68–70.

99 For Davidson's attempted deflation see *Inquiries into Truth and Interpretation*, pp. 183–98. It is arguable, however, that Davidson employs an unduly strict test in applying a verification principle to rule out the idea of an alternative conceptual scheme. For an exploration of this doubt see Simon Blackburn, *Spreading the Word* (Oxford, Oxford University Press, 1984), pp. 60–2.

100 Russell Price, 'The senses of *virtù* in Machiavelli', *European Studies Review* 3 (1973), pp. 315–45, at pp. 316–17.

101 Price, 'The senses of *virtù*', p. 319.

102 Ibid, pp. 315, 344.

103 J. H. Whitfield, *Machiavelli* (Oxford, Oxford University Press, 1947), p. 105.

104 As Nelson Goodman remarks in *Ways of Worldmaking* (Hassocks, Harvester Press, 1978), p. 93, 'meanings vanish in favour of certain relationships among terms'.

105 See for example J. G. A. Pocock, *Virtue, Commerce, and History*, (Cambridge, Cambridge University Press, 1985), p. 13.

106 See Arthur C. Danto, *Analytical Philosophy of History* (Cambridge, Cambridge University Press, 1965), pp. 149–81, and cf. the discussion of Danto's point in Dunn, 'Practising social science' pp. 104–5.

107 Charles Taylor, 'Understanding and explanation in the *Geisteswissenschaften*', in *Wittgenstein: To follow a Rule*, ed. Steven Holtzman and Christopher Leich (London, Routledge and Kegan Paul, 1981), pp. 191–210, esp. at pp. 208–9. Cf. also Taylor's stress on the cognitive superiority of the theories generated by our modern scientific conception of rational acceptability in his essay on 'Rationality', pp. 87–105.

108 For a sceptical view of this proposal, see John W. Yolton, 'Textual vs conceptual analysis in the history of philosophy', *Journal of the History of Philosophy*, 13 (1975), pp. 505–12, at pp. 507–8.

109 For the claim that Machiavelli was articulating a theory about the relationship between individuals and the state, see for example Ernst Cassirer, *The Myth of the State* (New Haven, Yale University Press, 1946), esp. pp. 133–41. For the claim that he can be credited with a theory of individual rights see Marcia Colish, 'The idea of liberty in Machiavelli', *Journal of the History of Ideas* 32 (1971), pp. 323–50, at pp. 345–6.

110 Graham, 'Illocutions', p. 173.

111 See above, 7:146.

112 Preston King, 'The theory of context and the case of Hobbes', in *The History of Ideas*, ed. Preston King (London, 1983), pp. 285–315, at p. 297; Shapiro, 'Realism', p. 537.

113 See Hollis, 'Reason and ritual', pp. 221, 235–37. For a contrasting viewpoint, see Papineau, *For Science*, p. 150.

114 On this point see the very valuable discussion in John Skorupski, 'Meaning', in *Action and Interpretation*, ed. Hookway and Pettit, at pp. 98–102, and the

Appendix to John Skorupski, *Symbol and Theory* (Cambridge, Cambridge University Press, 1976), pp. 225–43.

115 For an excellent account of how we can hope to do this much, see Stout, *Flight from Authority*, pp. 38–9, 106–9, 173–4 and references there.

116 Hollis, 'Reason and ritual', p. 237.

117 For an excellent discussion of this issue in relation to the exegesis of Wittgenstein's *Philosophical Investigations*, see Jonathan Lear, 'Ethics, mathematics and relativism', *Mind*, 92 (1983), pp. 38–60, esp. at pp. 44–6.

118 For this objection, see Putnam, *Reason, Truth and History*, pp. 119-20 and cf. also Lear, 'Relativism', esp. p. 55.

119 See Barnes and Bloor, 'Relativism', esp. pp. 22–29.

120 This point is excellently made by Hollis in 'Social destruction', pp. 82–3. It is taken up in John Skorupski, 'The consensus and beyond', *Times Literary Supplement*, April 15 1983, p. 385.

121 See Quine, *Word and Object*, esp. p. 59.

122 Following Quine, a large number of philosophers have stressed this point. See for example Steven Lukes, 'Some problems about rationality', in *Essays*, pp. 133–5; Hollis, 'Reason and ritual', pp. 231–2.

123 This further point is excellently brought out in Lear, 'Leaving the world alone', esp. pp. 389–90.

124 In addition to the discussions cited in n. 122 above, see MacIntyre, *Self-Images*, pp. 250, 256; Papineau, *For Science*, p. 138; Macdonald and Pettit, *Semantics*, pp. 30–31.

125 See Jon Elster, *Logic and Society* (New York, Wiley, 1978), esp. p. 88 on this point.

126 Machiavelli, *Discourses* in *Chief Works*, vol. I, pp. 175–529, at II.2 p. 329.

127 Machiavelli, *Discourses*, vol. I, pp. 175–529, at III.5, p. 427.

128 See for example Colish, *Journal of the History of Ideas*, p. 330 for Machiavelli's alleged 'lack of univocity' on this point.

129 See J. L. Austin, *How To Do Things With Words*, 2nd edn, corrected, ed. J. O. Urmson and Marina Sbisà (Oxford, Oxford University Press, 1980), pp. 94, 98.

130 Ludwig Wittgenstein, *Philosophical Investigations*, 2nd edn, tr. G. E. M. Anscombe (Oxford, Basil Blackwell, 1958), para. 546, p. 146.

131 On the force of utterances as an abstractable dimension of language, see David Holdcroft, *Words and Deeds* (Oxford, Clarendon Press, 1978), pp. 143–55. I am greatly indebted to Professor Holdcroft for correspondence on this point.

132 Austin, *How To Do Things*, p. 99.

133 Ibid., chap. 9, pp. 109–20.

134 Ibid., p. 99.

135 Ibid., p. 98.

136 Ibid., p. 128.

137 Strawson's expansion took the form of questioning the prominence Austin had assigned to conventions (as opposed to speaker's intentions) in his analysis of 'uptake'. See P. F. Strawson, 'Intention and convention in speech-acts', in *Logico-Linguistic Papers*, (London, Methuen, 1971), pp. 149–69.

138 For the place of reflexive intentions in Searle's analysis of illocutionary acts, see John R. Searle, *Speech Acts* (Cambridge, Cambridge University Press, 1969), esp. pp. 60–1.

139 Schiffer deploys a version of Grice's intentionalist theory of meaning to analyse the relationship between meaning and speech-acts. See Stephen R. Schiffer, *Meaning* (Oxford, Oxford University Press, 1972), esp. pp. 88–117. Holdcroft offers an extended criticism of Schiffer's analysis in *Words and Deeds*, pp. 131–43. Cf. also the centrality assigned to the recognition of communicative intentions in Kent Bach and Robert M. Harnish, *Linguistic Communication and Speech Acts* (Cambridge, Mass., Harvard University Press, 1979).

140 As I originally argued in my article 'Conventions and the understanding of speech-acts', *Philosophical Quarterly*, 20 (1970), pp. 118–38.

141 See Graham, above, 8:151. See also Graham, 'Illocutions', pp. 162–3.

142 As Boucher rightly emphasizes, *Texts in Context*, p.201.

143 Austin, *How To Do Things*, p. 116.

144 For a full elaboration of this proposal, see Anthony Kenny, *Action, Emotion and Will* (London, Routledge and Kegan Paul, 1963), chap. 8, pp. 171–86.

145 Austin, *How To Do Things*, p. 116.

146 As I originally tried to show in my article 'On performing and explaining linguistic actions', *Philosophical Quarterly*, 21 (1971), pp. 1–21, esp. pp. 3–12.

147 Donald Davidson, 'The logical form of action sentences', in *The Logic of Decision and Action*, ed. Nicholas Rescher (Pittsburgh, University of Pittsburgh Press, 1966), p. 86.

148 See Shapiro, 'Realism', p. 563 and Boucher, *Texts in Contexts*, pp. 220, 230. For Graham on 'unintended illocutionary acts' see above, 8:153 and on 'illocutions', p. 163.

149 On this point see Holdcroft, *Words and Deeds*, pp. 149–50, 154.

150 As Holdcroft notes, it is not clear that this is recognized in Schiffer's account. Cf. Also the 'generative' account of illocutionary forces given in Charles Travis, *Saying and Understanding* (Oxford, Basil Blackwell, 1975), which operates without the distinction between the illocutionary force of utterances and the intended illocutionary force with which speakers may issue them, and concludes (p. 49) that, in general, 'each utterance will have exactly one illocutionary force'.

151 For references to this debate, see my discussion above, 4:79–96, esp. 80–2.

152 Dieter Freundlieb, 'Identification, interpretation, and explanation: some problems in the philosophy of literary studies', *Poetics*, 9 (1980), pp. 423–40, at p. 436.

153 Nor is it undermined by the claim that illocutionary redescriptions cannot be explanatory, since only the recovery of causes can yield explanations. It is precisely that stipulation which my thesis challenges. For the stipulation itself, see for example Lotte Mulligan, Judith Richards and John Graham, 'Intentions and conventions: A critique of Quentin Skinner's method for the study of the history of ideas', *Political Studies*, 27 (1979), pp. 84–98, at p. 97.

154 For the classic statement of the argument, see Donald Davidson, 'Actions, reasons and causes', in *Essays on Actions and Events* (Oxford, Oxford University Press, 1980), pp. 3–19.

155 Peter L. Janssen, 'Political thought as traditionary action: the critical response to Skinner and Pocock', *History and Theory*, 24 (1985), pp. 115–46. For other sympathetic, mainly exegetical discussions, cf. Wilhelm Vossenkuhl, 'Rationalität und historisches Verstehen. Quentin Skinner's Rekonstruktion der politischen theorie', *Conceptus*, 16 (1982), pp. 27–43; and Maurizio Viroli, '"Revisionisti" e "ortodossi" nella storia delle idee politiche', *Rivista di filosofia*, 78 (1987), pp. 121–36.

156 Steven Seidman, 'Beyond presentism and historicism: understanding the history of social science', *Sociological Inquiry*, 53 (1983), pp. 79–94, at pp. 83, 88.

157 Gunnell, 'Interpretation', p. 318. Cf. also Deborah Baumgold, 'Political commentary on the history of political theory', *American Political Science Review*, 75 (1981), pp. 928–40, at p. 935.

158 Dominick LaCapra, 'Rethinking intellectual history and reading texts', *History and Theory*, 19 (1980), pp. 245–76, at p. 254.

159 E. D. Hirsch, Jr, *Validity in Interpretation* (New Haven, Yale University Press, 1967), pp. 12, 13. See also P. D. Juhl, 'Can the meaning of a literary work change?', in *The Uses of Criticism*, ed. A. P. Foulkes (Frankfurt, Herbert Lang, 1976), pp. 133–56.

160 Hirsch, *Validity*, p. 27. For Juhl's comments on Hirsch, see P. D. Juhl, *Interpretation* (Princeton, Princeton University Press, 1980), chap. 2, pp. 16–44.

161 Jenssen, 'Political Thought', pp. 130–33.

162 A point excellently made in Dunn, 'Practising social science', p. 84.

163 Juhl, *Interpretation*, pp. 62, 64. See also Laurent Stern, 'On interpreting', *Journal of Aesthetics and Art Criticism*, 39 (1980), pp. 119–29, who appears to assume (pp. 122–4) that, in claiming that the recovery of intentionality is indispensable to the understanding of works of irony, what is being claimed is that such intentions are indispensable to understanding the text, the meaning what is said.

164 Daniel Defoe, 'The shortest-way with the dissenters', in *Daniel Defoe*, ed. James T. Boulton (London, Batsford, 1965), pp. 88–99, at p. 96. Stern, 'On interpreting', p. 124 mentions this example, but in my view draws the wrong moral from it.

165 See Austin, *How To Do Things*, pp. 56ff and cf. p. 116, note.

166 For the centrality of this theme in Ricoeur's hermeneutics, see T. M. van Leeuwen, *The Surplus of Meaning* (Amsterdam, 1981).

167 Compare Gunnell, *Political Theory*, pp. 96–103 with pp. 104–5, 110–16. It is worth observing, however, that what Gadamer is actually talking about, in some of the passages cited by Gunnell, is the criterion of intentionality in relation to the evaluation of works of art. Compare Gunnell, *Political Theory*, p. 113 with Hans-Georg Gadamer, *Truth and Method*, pp. 148–9.

168 For Seidman citing Ricoeur to this effect, see 'Beyond presentism', p. 84. For a similar claim about the value of studying 'word sequences' as opposed to intended meanings, see Jack W. Meiland, 'The meanings of a text', *British Journal of Aesthetics*, 21 (1981), pp. 195–203, at p. 203.

169 See for example the essays collected in Stanley Fish, *Is There a Text in this Class?* (Cambridge, Mass., Harvard University Press, 1980), especially Fish's opening insistence (p. vii) on the allegedly overriding impact upon the act of interpretation of 'the perspective of whatever interpretive assumptions happen to be in force'.

170 Such, according to Foucault, is the outcome of his 'archaeological' approach. See Michel Foucault, *The Archaeology of Knowledge*, tr. A. M. Sheridan Smith (London, Tavistock 1972), pp. 144–5. Cf. also pp. 75–6, 93–4, 172–3. For 'the death of the author' see Roland Barthes, 'From work to text', and Michel Foucault, 'What is an author?', in *Textual Strategies*, ed. Josué V. Harari (Ithaca, Cornell University Press, 1979), pp. 73–81 and 141–60.

171 See Jacques Derrida, 'Structure, sign and play in the discourse of the human sciences', in *The Languages of Criticism and the Sciences of Man*, ed. Richard Macksey and Eugenio Donato (Baltimore, Johns Hopkins Press, 1970), pp. 247–65, at p. 264. For an interesting critique of this standpoint, invoking Gadamer to stop the anti-historical rot, see Iain Wright, 'History, hermeneutics, deconstruction', in *Criticism and Critical Theory*, ed. Jeremy Hawthorn (London, Edward Arnold 1984), pp. 83–96. But Derrida also argues for the irrelevance of intentionality to communicable meanings, a conclusion he takes to follow from the 'iterability' of linguistic forms. See Jacques Derrida, 'Signature event context', *Glyph*, 1 (1977), pp. 172–97, esp. at pp. 179–85.

172 For this fallacious line of reasoning, see Gadamer, *Truth and Method*, p. 262–4, and cf. Gunnell, *Political Theory*, pp. 113–14.

173 Keith Graham, 'The recovery of illocutionary force', *Philosophical Quarterly*, 30 (1980), pp. 141–48, at pp. 147–8. Shapiro, 'Realism', p. 548 repeats the criticism. See also Boucher, *Texts in Context*, p. 212 and Levine, 'Method', pp. 38, 44–5.

174 On interrogatives and performatives cf. Holdcroft, *Words and Deeds*, chap. 5, pp. 102–6.

175 I have already tried to rebut Cohen's scepticism in my article 'Conventions', pp. 120–1, 128–9. Cf also the helpful discussion in Keith Graham, *J. L. Austin: A Critique of Ordinary Language Philosophy* (Brighton, Harvester Press, 1977), pp. 87–101.

176 See Holdcroft, *Words and Deeds*, esp. pp. 151–70.

177 See Austin, *How To Do Things*, pp. 116–20.

178 Wootton, 'Preface' to *Divine Right and Democracy*, p. 10.

179 For this formulation see Michael Ayers, 'Analytical philosophy and the history of philosophy', in *Philosophy and its Past*, ed. Jonathan Rée (Brighton, Harvester Press, 1978), pp. 41–66, at p. 44 and Peter Hylton, 'The nature of the proposition and the revolt against idealism', in *Philosophy in History*, ed. Rorty, Schneewind and Skinner, pp. 375–97, at p. 392.

180 See Wootton, 'Preface' to *Divine Right and Democracy*, pp. 12–13.

181 See especially Collingwood, *Autobiography*, chap. 5, pp. 29–43. On the pragmatics of explanation see also Alan Garfinkel, *Forms of Explanation* (New Haven, Yale University Press, 1981), esp. pp. 7–14.

182 Turner, 'Contextualism', pp. 283–6 rightly observes that I have not sufficiently acknowledged this point.

183 See J. G. A. Pocock, 'Political ideas as historical events', in *Political Theory and Political Education*, ed. Melvin Richter (Princeton, Princeton University Press, 1980), esp. pp. 147–8, and 'Verbalizing a political act: towards a politics of speech', *Political Theory*, 1 (1973), pp. 27–45.

184 See Graham, 'Recovery', pp. 146–7; Lockyer, 'Traditions', p. 206.

185 Jenssen, 'Political Thought', p. 129 valuably emphasizes this point. On genres and the expectations they arouse, see also Hans Robert Jauss, 'Literary history as a challenge to literary theory', *New Literary History* 2 (1970), pp. 7–37, esp. at pp. 11–14.

186 See 'Hobbes's *Leviathan*', *Historical Journal*, 7 (1964), pp. 321–33, at p. 330. For Foucault's conception of 'discourse', and for an excellent discussion, cf. David A. Hollinger, 'Historians and the discourse of intellectuals', in *In the American Province* (Bloomington, Indiana University Press, 1985), pp. 130–51.

187 See Pocock, *Virtue, Commerce, and History*, pp. 7–8, 23.

188 Graham, 'Recovery', 1980, pp. 144–5.

189 Shapiro, 'Realism', pp. 554, 556, 562.

190 Ibid., p. 562.

191 See Graham, 'Recovery', pp. 144–5 and Hollis above, 7:140.

192 I have adapted the example from A. R. Louch, *Explanation and Human Action* (Oxford, Basil Blackwell, 1966), pp. 107–8.

193 For an eloquent elaboration of this point, see Clifford Geertz, *Negara* (Princeton, Princeton University Press, 1980) pp. 134–6.

194 On social actions as texts, see Paul Ricoeur, 'The model of the text: meaningful action considered as a text', *New Literary History*, 5 (1973), pp. 91–117, and Geertz, *Local Knowledge*, esp. pp. 30–3.

195 See Mulligan, Richards and Graham, 'Intentions and Conventions', p. 87.

196 Jacques Derrida, *Spurs: Nietzsche's Styles*, tr. Barbara Harlow (Chicago, University of Chicago Press, 1979), p. 123.

197 Ibid., p. 129.

198 See ibid., p. 123 on the lack of any 'infallible way of knowing' and cf. ibid., p. 125 on the 'inaccessibility' of 'what Nietzsche meant to say'. Cf. also pp. 127 and 131 for the assumption that the 'hermeneutic' claim has to be one about certainty. See also the interesting observations in Alexander Nehamas, *Nietzsche: Life as Literature* (Cambridge, Mass., Harvard University Press, 1985), esp. pp. 17, 240 on the lack of any defence by Derrida of 'his assumption that infallibility and certainty are necessary if interpretation is to be possible'.

199 Derrida, *Spurs*, p. 123. Italics in original.

200 Gunnell, *Political Theory*, p. 111 See also Seidman, 'Beyond presentism', p. 85. For Gadamer's own discussion of 'horizons', see *Truth and Method*, esp. pp. 269–74.

201 John Hall, 'Illiberal liberalism?', *British Journal of Sociology*, 31 (1980), pp. 297–99, at p. 299.

202 Derrida, *Spurs*, p. 125. Cf. also p. 133 for a generalization of the claim.

203 On my overstatements, see David Boucher, 'New histories of political thought for old?', *Political Studies*, 31 (1983), pp. 112–21, at pp. 112–13 and especially (a strong but justified criticism) King, 'Theory of context', pp. 290–5.

204 As I note above, 5:104 where I quote them to this effect.

205 Harvey C. Mansfield, Jr, 'Strauss's Machiavelli', *Political Theory*, 3 (1975), pp. 327–84, at p. 378.

206 For a recent history of philosophy which self-consciously makes this distinction between genuinely philosophical and purely historical questions,

see Roger Scruton, *From Descartes to Wittgenstein* (London, Routledge and Kegan Paul, 1981), chap. 1, pp. 3–12.

207 See, for example, Richard Popkin, 'The sceptical origins of the modern problem of knowledge', in *Perception and Personal Identity*, ed. Norman S. Care and Robert H. Grimm (Cleveland, Press of Case Western Reserve University, 1969), pp. 3–24, and especially Richard Popkin, *The History of Scepticism from Erasmus to Spinoza* (Berkeley, University of California Press, 1979). See also E. M. Curley, *Descartes Against the Skeptics* (Oxford, Basil Blackwell, 1978).

208 Boucher, *Texts in Context*, p. 238. See also Michael Freeman, *Edmund Burke and the Critique of Political Radicalism* (Chicago, University of Chicago Press, 1980).

209 See Lockyer, 'Traditions', pp. 216–17. The same example is discussed in Collingwood, *Autobiography*, pp. 61–3. Cf. also MacIntyre, *Short History*, pp. 1–2.

210 See for example Boucher, *Texts in Context*, p. 238, and Joyce Appleby, 'Ideology and the history of political thought', *Newsletter: Intellectual History Group*, 2 (1980), pp. 10–18, at pp. 12–13.

211 Wittgenstein, *Philosophical Investigations*, esp. para. 11, p. 6 and para. 23, pp. 11–12. For a discussion see Putnam, *Reason, Truth and History*, pp. 19–21.

212 Seidman, 'Beyond presentism', p. 91.

213 Graham Hough, 'An eighth type of ambiguity', in *On Literary Intention*, ed. David Newton-De Molina (Edinburgh, Edinburgh University Press, 1976), pp. 222–41, esp. at p. 227.

214 See above, 5:102 and references there.

215 See Donald Winch, *Malthus* (Oxford, 1987), esp. pp. 18–19, 32–5. Cf. also Winch's stress (p. 94) on the importance of asking what Malthus was 'trying to *do* in his various writings on population and political economy'.

216 Arthur W. H. Adkins, *Merit and Responsibility* (Oxford, Oxford University Press, 1960), esp. pp. 283–93.

217 Marilyn Butler, *Jane Austen and the War of Ideas* (Oxford, Clarendon Press, 1975), esp. the Introduction, pp. 1–4 and chap. 6, pp. 161–7. John Dunn originally drew my attention to this fascinating book.

218 E. M. Forster, *A Passage to India* (London, Edward Arnold, 1924), p. 325. It seems a pity that the signing-off has been omitted, without explanation, from the Abinger Edition of *A Passage to India*, ed. Oliver Stallybrass (London, Edward Arnold, 1978).

219 James Joyce, *Ulysses*, Penguin Modern Classics edn (Harmondsworth, Penguin 1969), p. 704.

220 Tarlton, 'Revisionism', p. 314.

221 Gunnell, 'Interpretation', p. 327.

222 Howard Warrender, 'Political theory and historiography', *Historical Journal* 22 (1979), pp. 931–40, at p. 939. Cf. also Margaret Leslie, 'In defence of anachronism', *Political Studies* 18 (1970), pp. 433–47.

223 See above, 2: esp. 64–7 and my further remarks in 'The idea of negative liberty: philosophical and historical perspectives', in *Philosophy in History*, ed. Rorty, Schneewind and Skinner, pp. 193–221, esp. at pp. 198–202.

224 Jenssen, 'Political thought', pp. 117–25.

225 See Rorty, *Philosophy and the Mirror of Nature*, pp. 362–5, 371 and references to Gadamer there.

226 For these and other considerations about the value of diversity, see the Introduction to Clifford Geertz, *Local Knowledge* (New York, Basic Books 1983), pp. 3–16 and cf. also Clifford Geertz, 'The uses of diversity', in *The Tanner Lectures on Human Values*, vol. VII, ed. S. McMurrin (Utah, University of Utah Press, 1986), pp. 253–75.

227 See Adkins, *Merit and Responsibility*, *passim* and esp. the conclusions at pp. 348–51.

228 See Geertz, *Negara*, and esp. the conclusions at pp. 121–36. Cf. my own attempted appraisal of the significance of Geertz's finding in 'The world as a stage', *New York Review of Books*, vol. 28 (16 April 1981), pp. 35–7.

229 See my article cited above, n. 223 and cf. also my lectures 'The paradoxes of political liberty', in *The Tanner Lectures*, vol. VII, ed. McMurrin, pp. 225–50.

230 This point is excellently made in MacIntyre, *Self-Images*, Introduction, esp. pp. viii–ix.

231 See for example the arguments cited and criticized in Clifford Geertz, 'Anti anti-relativism', *American Anthropologist* 86 (1984), pp. 263–78.

232 Collingwood stresses this point in his *Autobiography*, esp. pp. 61–3. For a helpful pursuit of the implications, see Lockyer, 'Traditions'.

233 See Richard Tuck, *Natural Rights Theories: Their Origin and Development* (Cambridge, Cambridge University Press, 1979), pp. 1, 7, 13ff and the discussion in James Tully, 'Current thinking about sixteenth and seventeenth-century political theory', *Historical Journal* 24 (1981), pp. 475–84, esp. at pp. 475–7.

Bibliography

QUENTIN SKINNER: PRINCIPAL PUBLICATIONS

BOOKS AND MONOGRAPHS

The Foundations of Modern Political Thought, vol. I: *The Renaissance* (Cambridge, Cambridge University Press, 1978)
The Foundations of Modern Political Thought, vol. II: *The Age of Reformation* (Cambridge, Cambridge University Press, 1978)
Machiavelli (Oxford, Oxford University Press, 1981; rev. edn, 1985)
Ambrogio Lorenzetti: The Artist as Political Philosopher (London, The British Academy, 1987)

BOOKS EDITED

Philosophy, Politics and Society, series IV, (Basil Blackwell, Oxford, 1972) as co-editor and contributor
Philosophy in History, (Cambridge, Cambridge University Press, 1984) as co-editor and contributor
The Return of Grand Theory in the Human Sciences (Cambridge, Cambridge University Press, 1985) as editor and contributor
The Cambridge History of Renaissance Philosophy (Cambridge, Cambridge University Press, 1988) as co-editor and contributor

PRINCIPAL ARTICLES

In social theory and the philosophy of the social sciences

'The limits of historical explanations', *Philosophy*, 41 (1966), pp. 199–215
'Meaning and understanding in the history of ideas', *History and Theory*, 8 (1969), pp. 3–53
'Conventions and the understanding of speech-acts', *Philosophical Quarterly*, 20 (1970), pp. 118–38

'On performing and explaining linguistic actions', *Philosophical Quarterly*, 21 (1971), pp. 1–21

'"Social meaning" and the explanation of social action', in *Philosophy, Politics and Society*, series IV, ed. Peter Laslett, W. G. Runciman and Quentin Skinner (Oxford, Basil Blackwell, 1972), pp. 136–57

'Motives, intentions and the interpretation of texts', *New Literary History*, 3 (1972), pp. 393–408

'The empirical theorists of democracy and their critics', *Political Theory*, 1 (1973), pp. 287–306

'Some problems in the analysis of political thought and action' (in *Symposium on Quentin Skinner*), *Political Theory*, 2 (1974), pp. 227–303

'Hermeneutics and the role of history', *New Literary History*, 7 (1975–6), pp. 209–32

'Action and context', *Proceedings of the Aristotelian Society*, supplementary vol. 52 (1978), pp. 57–69

'The idea of cultural lexicon', *Essays in Criticism*, 29 (1979), pp. 205–24

'The return of grand theory' in *The Return of Grand Theory in the Human Sciences*, ed. Quentin Skinner (Cambridge, Cambridge University Press, 1985), pp. 1–21

'The paradoxes of political liberty', in *The Tanner Lectures of Human Values*, vol. 7, ed. S. McMurrin (Utah, University of Utah Press, 1986), pp. 225–50

On early modern intellectual history

'Hobbes's *Leviathan*', *Historical Journal*, 7 (1964), pp. 321–33

'Hobbes on sovereignty: an unknown discussion', *Political Studies*, 13 (1965), pp. 213–8

'History and ideology in the English revolution', *Historical Journal*, 8 (1965), pp. 151–78

'Thomas Hobbes and his disciples in France and England', *Comparative Studies in Society and History*, 8 (1965), pp. 153–67

'The ideological context of Hobbes's political thought', *Historical Journal*, 9 (1966), pp. 286–317

'More's *Utopia*', *Past and Present*, 38 (1967), 153–68

'Thomas Hobbes and the nature of the early Royal Society', *Historical Journal*, 12 (1969), pp. 217–39

'Conquest and consent: Thomas Hobbes and the engagement controversy', in *The Interregnum: The Quest for Settlement*, ed. G. E. Alymer, (London, Macmillan, 1974), pp. 79–98

'Thomas Hobbes et la defense du pouvoir "de facto"', *Revue philosophique*, 98 (1973), pp. 131–54

'The principles and practice of opposition: the case of Bolingbroke versus Walpole', in *Historical Perspectives: Essays in Honour of J. H. Plumb*, ed. N. McKendrick (London, Europa Publications, 1974), pp. 93–128

'The origins of the Calvinist theory of revolution', in *After the Reformation*, ed. Barbara Malament (London, University of Pennsylvania Press, 1980), pp. 309–30

'Machiavelli on the maintenance of liberty', *Politics*, 18 (1983), pp. 3–15

'The idea of negative liberty: philosophical and historical perspectives', in *Philosophy in History*, ed. Richard Rorty, J. Schneewind and Quentin Skinner (Cambridge, Cambridge University Press, 1984), pp. 193–221

'Political philosophy', in *The Cambridge History of Renaissance Philosophy*, ed. Charles Schmitt, Eckhart Kessler and Quentin Skinner (Cambridge, Cambridge University Press, 1987), pp. 389–452.

'More's *Utopia* and the language of Renaissance humanism', in *The Languages of Political Theory in Early-Modern Europe*, ed. Anthony Pagden (Cambridge, Cambridge University Press, 1986), pp. 123–57

'The State', in *Political Innovation and Conceptual Change* (Cambridge, Cambridge University Press, 1987) pp. 90–131.

'L'idée anglaise de la liberté', *Esprit*, 1987.

'Introduction' to Niccolò Machiavelli, *The Prince*, tr. Russell Price, ed. Quentin Skinner (Cambridge, Cambridge University Press, 1988), pp. ix–xxiv.

Index